BETWEEN MARS AND MAMMON

INTERNATIONAL LIBRARY OF HISTORICAL STUDIES

BETWEEN MARS AND MAMMON
Colonial Armies and the Garrison State in India 1819-1835

Douglas M. Peers

Tauris Academic Studies
I.B. Tauris Publishers
LONDON • NEW YORK

Published in 1995 by
Tauris Academic Studies
An imprint of I.B.Tauris & Co Ltd
45 Bloomsbury Square
London WC1A 2HY

175 Fifth Avenue
New York
NY 10010

In the United States of America
and Canada distributed by
St Martin's Press
175 Fifth Avenue
New York
NY 10010

A full CIP record for this book is available from the British Library

A full CIP record for this book is available from the Library of Congress

ISBN 1 85043 954 0

Library of Congress catalog card number: 95 - 060218

Typesetting by Cliff Kadatz
Printed and bound in Great Britain by
WBC Ltd, Bridgend, Mid Glamorgan

Contents

List of Maps
and Appendices

Acknowledgements

I gratefully acknowledge the assistance rendered by the following institutions: the Controller of Her Majesty's Stationery Office for the use of Crown Copyright material in the Oriental and India Office Collections (British Library) and the Public Record Office, the Trustees of the British Library, the National Army Museum, the National Library of Scotland, the Earl of Dalhousie for permission to use and quote from the Dalhousie muniments in the Scottish Record Office, the Chester City Record Office, the National Library of Wales, the University of Southampton Archives, the University of Nottingham Archives, the Somerset Record Office, the Scottish United Service Institution, and the North Yorkshire Record Office. The cartoon on page xiv is reproduced courtesy of the Trustees of the British Museum and is taken from collection DG 14786.

Portions of this study have previously appeared in print. Elements in my discussion of military finance in chapters five and seven first came out in 'War and Public Finance in Early Nineteenth-Century British India: the First Burma War,' *International History Review*, 11(1989): 628-47. British appreciations of North Indian military culture have been partly addressed in The Habitual Nobility of Being; British Officers and the Social Construction of the Bengal Army in the Early Nineteenth Century,' *Modern Asian Studies*, 25(1991): 545-69.

This book would not have been possible without generous financial assistance. A scholarship from the Imperial Order of the Daughters started me on the path, and my initial research was assisted by a grant from the University of London's Irwin Fund. Further research was made possible by travel grants from the University of Calgary and the Social Sciences and Humanities Research Council of Canada. Publication has been made possible, in part, by grants from the Endowment Fund of the University of Calgary and from the Isobel Thornley Bequest Fund of the University of London.

Preface

One problem that confronts those who wish to plumb the origins and evolution of the colonial state in India is how to treat the state in its entirety. This colonial regime comprised numerous departments and branches, all of which were interlocked in an extremely complex matrix. The prevailing approach to this problem has been to encourage the production of a series of detailed studies of particular branches of the administration, or sectors of its operations, such as revenue policies, judicial proceedings, financial strategies and so on. Eventually, a composite picture should emerge. This study has taken a different tack. It began when I was confronted by the paradox that India was ruled by a commercial Company, yet in its exercise of territorial responsibilities it was not acting in ways that I thought a commercial organization would. In pursuing this contradiction, I was impressed by the overwhelming centrality accorded to the army within the Anglo-Indian body-politic. The emphasis placed by the colonial state on monopolizing the means of coercion in India and ensuring the stability and security of British rule, which made the army the focus of its attention, has suggested that the military dynamics of British rule would make a valuable point of entry into the inner workings of the colonial state. By making the army the core of this study, and tracing its lineaments and influences through other aspects of colonial rule — in peacetime as well as in wartime, during a time of expansion as well as one of retrenchment — we can begin to see not only how the state conducted its business, but why it thought it had to act in the ways it did. From that perspective, this study is more than an analysis of the army of the early British Raj. It is a foray into the inner workings of colonial rule and one that I hope will encourage further work on this important topic. In particular, there is a need for a more 'history from below' approach, looking at the army from the perspective of the people it recruited as well as from the vantage point of those it coerced. The current work is unabashedly a top-down study, taking as its point of departure the colonial state. Much could be gained by a complementary study that begins with the sepoy and the peasant and moves upwards.

Writing a book has often been compared to a long journey and, like most travellers, I could neither have embarked or completed it without the assistance and temptations of others. Friends, family and fellow scholars and students have consistently popped up at opportune times, to set me on course, to provide the victuals, to remind me of why I started it in the first place and why it was important to complete the voyage, and to distract me by revealing that there is life beyond the archive. First and foremost of the debts I owe is to Peter Marshall who piloted my dissertation through the University of London. I can only hope that it matches to some degree the high standards that he sets by his own example. My external examiners, C.A. Bayly and Sir C.H. Philips, gave the thesis a thorough going over and from them I learned much, and hopefully the lessons have been properly incorporated here. Edward Ingram has criticized my work over the years with a persistence and an incisiveness that are truly remarkable. Perhaps he will be pleasantly surprised to see how much I have benefited, though a complete truce is likely (and thankfully) years away. Portions of this work have been presented to conferences over the years and, while it would be insidious to single out all those whose comments and questions helped me along, the regulars at the Imperial History Seminar at the Institute of Historical Research have collectively made their presence felt. Time will tell whether I sold them on Anglo-Indian militarism but I certainly enjoyed trying. Refitting the manuscript was eased by the trenchant criticisms made by anonymous readers. Others who have lent their support over the years include Michael Fisher, David Omissi, Philippa Levine and Javed Majeed. I have also been extremely fortunate in having such supportive colleagues at the University of Calgary; Holger Herwig, Chris Archer, John Ferris, Francine Michaud, and Louis Knafla have in particular been generous with their time and forthcoming with their help. My editor at Tauris Academic Press, Dr. Lester Crook, has patiently put up with all the questions of a novice and has helped me navigate through tricky waters at times. Cliff Kadatz worked his wizardry on the layout and prepared the copy for printing.

I would like to thank the staff of the following libraries and archives for not only making this study possible, but also making the research such a pleasant experience. The India Office Library and Records (now the Oriental and India Office Collections — British Library) have always gone the extra mile to help their readers, and regulars such as myself will always be indebted to them. Richard Bingle, Martin Moir, Tim Thomas and Andrew Cook were especially helpful at critical stages. Elsewhere, generous assistance and expert advice were unfailingly provided at the National Army Museum, the British Library, the Public Record Office, the National Library of Wales, the National Library of Scotland, the Scottish Record Office, the Somerset Record Office, the North Yorkshire Record Office, the Chester City Record Office, the University of Southampton Archives and the University of Nottingham Archives. At Calgary, the staff in Interlibrary Loans are unsung heroes; they resigned themselves to seemingly endless searches for obscure nineteenth-century printed works on India. To my pleasant surprise, and perhaps to theirs, they had a success rate that nearly hit one hundred per cent — it might have been perfect had I been more careful in proofreading my requests. And I especially thank the anonymous staff member at the Scottish United Service Institution who kindly lent me her desk while the library was being renovated — the oak-lined office, leather chair and the view out the window convinced me at a critical juncture that in choosing history over law or accountancy, I had made the right choice.

This book would never have reached this stage had it not been for the help and support of my family on both sides of the Atlantic. They have lived with it as long as I have and while they may have wondered at the madness I sometimes displayed, they humoured and cajoled me and were always there when I needed them. I can only hope that the final product will justify their faith. Sandra and Winston, who often saw less of me than has my computer, managed to keep me sane and motivated through their help, encouragement and most importantly, their distractions. And to Jennifer and Robyn, who were fortunate to arrive near its completion and thereby escape many of the trials and tribulations, this book is dedicated together with their mother.

Notes
on Spelling and Usage

Any writer on an Indian topic is confronted with the difficulty of settling on what spellings are to be used for Indian places, persons or terms. There are numerous possibilities. In the absence of any consensus on this issue, I have tried to use those modernized spellings that are regularly to be found in English-language writings on India. Diacriticals have been avoided and where there is any chance of a mistaken identity I have tried to list alternative spellings. The major exception to this rule is when I have quoted from a contemporary writer in which case the original spelling has been left intact. To avoid unnecessary semantic contortions the term 'native' has occasionally been used in this study. Although this term has rightly been criticized in many quarters on account of its derogatory undertones, when dealing with the military forces of the British in India, the continued use of 'native' has been reluctantly decided upon, but only as a means of distinguishing between European and indigenous troops. The alternative expressions 'Indian army' or 'Indian officer' are too confusing as these terms are often used to distinguish between the men and officers of the Company army and those serving in the British regular army. I have also chosen to use the term Anglo–Indian to refer to the British community in India and thereby distinguish them from metropolitan society. In neither case do I mean to imply anything further.

I have also employed contemporary nomenclature when dealing with currencies. When listing Indian revenues and expenditures, large amounts are given in their Indian form, namely *lakhs* written as 1,00,000 and *crores* written as 1,00,00,000. Unless otherwise noted, rupee (or Rs.) refers to the *sicca* rupee, the most common coin in Bengal. In the 1820s, the average rate of exchange was 1 rupee for 2 shillings.

Politics

Affairs of India, or how to astonish the Natives

"The Native rebel troops refusing to lay down their arms, a signal was made, the artillery opened in their rear with such effect that they were immediately thrown into confusion, 480 it is said, were left dead on the field, 30 or 100 taken prisoners, some which were hung in chains, and the rest sent to work on the roads in chains, for fourteen years" — Calcutta Gazette.

1. THE ARMIES OF INDIA AND THE DYNAMICS OF IMPERIAL RULE

> Our government of that country is essentially military, and our means of preserving and improving our possessions through the operation of our civil institutions depend on our wise and politic exercise of that military power on which the whole fabric rests.[1]

The statement above sets out what had become for many British in India a self-evident truth. John Malcolm has clearly articulated the pre-eminence accorded the army: it took precedence over the other colonial institutions in the establishment and maintenance of British rule. The conjunction of strategic and fiscal imperatives, together with the search for an understanding of India and the means to control its peoples, forged a colonial superstructure bolstered in the first instance by the army. Consequently, a system of colonial rule was created which would last, albeit with modifications, until Indian independence in 1947. Curzon's fights with Kitchener at the beginning of the twentieth century, the appointment of Lord Wavell as Viceroy during World War II, the preferential treatment meted out to the Punjab on account of it being the nursery of the Indian army, all indicate the persistent military influences on colonial rule. The British in India saw themselves as a beleaguered garrison, and despite the differences that emerged between individuals or between London and India, a consensus took shape setting out the configurations of a garrison state. Even John Shore's evangelical leanings became muted following his accession to the governor-generalship: the saving of heathen souls would have to await the construction of a stable and secure imperial edifice.[2]

The significance of the army in the conquest of India is undeniable and has often been discussed. Possible enemies were never lacking; imaginative or enterprising officers could always detect a potential threat tucked away somewhere in the interior of the subcontinent; failing that, one could always be found mobilizing along one of the far-flung frontiers of the British sphere of influence. However, most discussions of the army treat only the operational aspects of warfare and seek to establish the right combination of factors which gave the British the edge over their Indian adversaries. Explanations resting upon technological factors have to a large extent been successfully put to rest by several studies which indicate that the British possessed no decided advantage, at least until the mid-nineteenth century by which time most of the major conquests had been secured.[3] Alternative explanations, focusing for the most part on allegedly inherent traits of the British character (obedience, courage, loyalty and organization) have proven equally popular and particularly persistent and are often drawn from contemporary prejudices.[4] The chauvinism of these comments and the racist implications concerning peoples of India destroy their academic credibility. However, as the fixation on character is one which figured strongly in nineteenth-century colonial discussions, the historical roots of these theories deserve consideration, for in them we can detect some of the crucial assumptions shaping British policy in India.

We need note that this association of warfare and India was not confined to the British domiciled in India. British imaginations in the nineteenth century situated India in an atmosphere in which war was viewed as a constant. Violence was considered to be deeply impregnated into Indian society. India became stereotyped, transformed in domestic eyes to a land not only of exoticism but also of persistent war. Public attention was directed to British feats of arms in India, not only because it was patriotic, but also because of the innate fascination with warfare being conducted in distant and exotic lands. From the time of the Third Mysore War (1789-92), the British press began to treat news from India with greater enthusiasm: India was no longer treated as marginal to national life.[5] The nineteenth-century passion for melodrama and spectacle was readily met by news from India; as one observer noted, 'The Indian Army forms, perhaps, the most extraordinary spectacle on which the eyes of the philosopher has ever rested.'[6] The popularity of this image of India is further attested to in the following quote.

> We are too much inclined, in these western latitudes, to regard India
> simply as a great camp. The very name has recently suggested little
> but gigantic visions of tented fields, and armed legions...[7]

Despite such warnings of over-exaggeration and simplification, popular literature made much of this image of India; William Makepeace Thackeray capitalized on popular sentiments in 1838-39 by serializing the 'The Tremendous Adventures of Major Gahagan' in the *New Monthly Magazine*.[8]

Though Gahagan's adventures were clearly a satire aimed at the exaggerated exploits of army officers, it clearly linked India with military adventures and adventurers. Children's novels also drew upon India for inspiration. For example, Frederick Marryat, one of the major early nineteenth-century writers of this genre, employed his experiences in the Burma War to develop an Asian backdrop against which his archetype of English character could be portrayed. Even ostensibly domestic novels responded to the growing fascination with conquest and conflict in India: Elizabeth Gaskell's hero in *Cranford* was a recently returned veteran from the Burma War.[9] This fascination with India was also evident in early nineteenth-century theatre. Melodramatic spectacles were staged in London with colonial conquest figuring as a central theme: at Astley's Amphitheatre in 1826, a very elaborate production, entitled *The Burmese War: a Grand Naval and Military Melo-Drama in Three Acts*, was produced, complete with elephants and mock naval battles. By responding to the interest generated by the recent war with Burma, and using it in turn for its setting, this melodrama could claim to be accurate and historical.[10] Satirists and engravers also found a market for prints and commentaries on developments in India. Cruikshank's engraving used to advertise the spectacle noted above made an explicit connection between the army and empire: a large number of British redcoats are set against a backdrop which includes elephants and temples. Significantly, only two 'natives' are featured in this engraving and they both appear in the capacity of servants. British nonfiction in the nineteenth century also played up the heroic and militarized character of British rule. Writers such as G.R. Gleig and J.W. Kaye predated the later writers of the *Rulers of India* series by serving up sanitized histories of British exploits that drew heavily upon colonial military operations.[11] These allegedly real accounts of British rule reinforced contemporary ideas not only of India, but also of the characteristics necessary to administer an empire. Foremost among these traits were military valour, skill and preparation.

It was between 1820 and 1830 that the army assumed its dominant position within the dynamics of colonial rule, for these years signalled the establishment of British authority over most of India. Through an examination of the Anglo-Indian state in this period, years marked by wars with the Burmese, and the small states of Kittur, Bharatpur and Coorg, the nature and evolution of what can aptly be termed a garrison state will become more obvious. Despite their efforts to demilitarize Indian society, significant pockets of resistance persisted that made the maintenance of a large standing army a colonial imperative. In early nineteenth-century India, there were no clear-cut distinctions between peace and war, frontiers were not clearly delineated, and zones of contact and consolidation overlapped with zones of conflict. In 1824–25, Reginald Heber, the newly arrived Bishop of Calcutta, went on a tour of northern India and commented upon the underlying violence which he noted everywhere, in one instance observing that, 'the nation is still one of lawless and violent habits...'.[12] Charged with the responsibilities of ruling a vast and variegated land, and faced with such apparent restlessness, the British saw themselves as beleaguered and with war, or the possibility of war, uppermost in their reckoning, they set about establishing their political and economic infrastructures with the army firmly in mind. Having made the initial concession that preparation for war was their first priority, the subsequent policies, assumptions and ideologies of the British in India bore the imprint of military calculations. Britain's changing strategic position in India was complemented by its shifting economic relationship with India. The changes to the Company's charter in 1813 and 1833 that opened up India to free traders meant that territorial revenues soon began to eclipse trade as the financial underpinning of Company activities in India. A symbiotic relationship was struck between the army and territorial revenues — a condition which I have termed 'military fiscalism'.[13] While territorial revenues were increasingly dedicated to paying for the military's upkeep, the army was crucial in creating the stability required for efficient revenue collection.

The army's infiltration of the body politic in India was further encouraged by developments in domestic British society where the collective experience of the French, Industrial and Haitian revolutions had made a significant impact. Broadly speaking, the period 1790 to 1815 witnessed the emergence of new mentalities and institutions that came about following an alliance between traditional landed interests, the monarchy and the church, and the increasingly powerful commercial and financial interests.[14] These institutions confidently pursued an aggressive policy of national aggrandizement and domestic reforms that was intended to shore up Britain's international position while perpetuating the political domination of Britain's traditional ruling classes. As Linda Colley has recently indicated, one of the consequences of this was the militarization of Britain's ruling elite with upwards of twenty per cent of MPs having commissions in the regular army, and many more having served in the militia or volunteers.[15] Hence, domestic changes reinforced the militarized values of Anglo–Indian society.

Yet this preeminent position accorded to the army has passed largely unnoticed in the discussions of several generations of historians. Some scholars have evaluated the two decades following the end of the Napoleonic

Wars in terms of the corporate activities of the 'Cheesemongers of Leadenhall Street', examining in minute detail the Company's trading operations and using these studies to illuminate the clash between mercantile and free trade ideologies. Contrasted to these studies were those historians who shifted their attentions to the periphery, and found the driving force for British imperialism in India to be located at those points where the British came in contact with Indians. Colonial rule did not merely supplant or subordinate existing political, military and economic elites in India; instead, colonial rule often co-opted them, though the resulting alliances were often very unstable. Such examinations have revealed the limitations of imperial rule and stressed the extent to which developments in India were the consequences of initiatives taken by Indians as well as the structural and cultural constraints in the subcontinent. This theme has tended to dominate the recent volumes in the New Cambridge History of India.[16]

Recently, however, the peripheralists have come under attack from a reinvigorated metropolitan approach to imperial dynamics vigorously set forth by P.J. Cain and A.G. Hopkins.[17] Inspired in part by the earlier works of Thorstein Veblen, Joseph Schumpeter and J.A. Hobson, their theory of 'gentlemanly capitalism' not only calls into question existing explanations for the expansion and consolidation of colonial rule, but also is intended to revise our understanding of the modern British economy. Put simply, 'gentlemanly capitalism' was the political, social and economic hegemony that the landed, commercial, financial and some service and professional elites in Britain obtained at home and pursued abroad. The economic and political conditions that followed on from the Revolution of 1688 resulted in Britain's traditional landed elite striking up a partnership with emerging financial and commercial interests. The result was an alliance that in pursuing the political and economic advantages of a world trading system dominated by British financial and commercial services created the values and made available the opportunities that quickly ushered in significant numbers of the service and professional classes in Britain. It was an alliance that was based upon the diffusion of the benefits of financial capitalism and held together on a cultural plane by the values and codes of the 'English gentleman'. In the authors' words, it was the 'economic and political dominance of a reconstructed and commercially progressive aristocracy.'[18] Deliberately omitted from this group were the industrialists whose power and influence Cain and Hopkins argue has been exaggerated and whose values and behaviour were not easily assimilated to that of the gentleman. From their power base around London, this nexus of business and political elites spread their influence throughout the empire. In India, which the authors describe as a 'particularly apposite example of our argument',[19] the van-guard of 'gentlemanly capitalism' comprised the military and civil servants of the Company and Crown, who acted as the local agents for the metro-politan interests of London's commercial, financial and political elite.

Space does not permit a thorough engagement with this theory and its consequences for Britain's empire in India, though those aspects which bear directly on India will be considered later in the text. Generally speak-ing, in its emphasis on the ties that bound together the periphery and the core, particularly those of a social and economic nature, this approach has much to recommend it. Parallels can be drawn between the codes of con-duct and styles of rule that were advocated in India and those to which the 'gentlemanly capitalists' were attached. In that sense, there is some truth to the comment that 'the imperial mission was the export version of the gen-tlemanly order',[20] and the contemporary definition of what constituted a gentleman, and in particular its emphasis on character, was to prove to be a cornerstone of Anglo-Indian militarism. Yet the pre-eminence accorded to metropolitan control and the assumption of a high degree of unanimity amongst such a potentially disparate group as financiers, commercial agents, the gentry, the aristocracy, and the military and other emerging professions can be called into question. Gentlemanly capitalists embraces such a po-tentially large group, neglecting none but the lowest orders and the manu-facturers, that fractures are bound to present themselves. In the case of India the service elites associated with the Company often had diametri-cally opposed objectives to those employed by the Crown — this is very apparent when relations between the Company's army and the King's army are considered. Moreover, though it can be argued that when viewed from London, proximity and shared social spaces could encourage the conver-gence of these elites, the same does not necessarily hold when the British were transplanted to the colonies. On the frontiers of the empire such uni-fying forces would have to contend with the pressure of local circumstances and the difficulties in maintaining reliable and regular social networks. In part the problem rests in the way Cain and Hopkins have developed their chronology. Their book is strongest and most detailed on the period after 1850 when developments in transportation and communications and a more systematic form of colonial administration could encourage a coalescing of attitudes and impressions. Prior to 1850 vested interests and the degree to which the periphery was cut off from London made consensus and coordi-nation that much more haphazard.

Elsewhere, scholarly discourse has been directed at sketching out the conflict between the rival dogmas of 'orientalism' and 'utilitarianism'. And while such attentions to the ideological debates are of obvious importance, too often it is assumed that ideology was constructed and re-constructed in an atmosphere where questions of security were not admitted. The crucial role played by the army and its central position in the make-up of the evolving colonial state have been downplayed and relegated to the point where the army appears merely to be the agent of other forces, whether these are presented as grasping capitalists or zealous humanitarians. In effect, we are presented with a picture of two decades in which the driving forces are variously seen as reforming, free trade liberalism, utilitarian, secularizing or modernizing.[21] Such a reconstruction favours London-based explanations over Calcutta and, more fundamentally, posits an unchanging East against a progressive West.

A closer examination of contemporary debates reveals that while there were many differences of opinion, not only were such differences often mere rhetorical devices, but even when such differences were substantial, they were mitigated by the presence of certain underlying assumptions, of which the pressing need to guarantee security was foremost. British behaviour in India can be defined as a particular variant of militarism — a form designed to meet Anglo–Indian conditions of rule and perceptions of security. Unlike many other styles of militarism which pitted civilians against the army, the Anglo–Indian variant bound together army officers and civilian employees of the East India Company, as well as king's officers serving in India, for ultimately they shared the same ideas of how Indian society was configured and consequently what constituted the gravest threat to their position in India. Hence, divisions between the allegedly different schools of thought and practice in India often disappeared in the face of pragmatic demands. Though ideological differences may persist in the memos and memoirs of colonial officials, practical demands drew divergent interests together as they all sought to shore up British rule in the face of what they thought were immediate and violent challenges to colonial domination.

There have been some allusions to the debates between civilians and military personnel. John Malcolm and Thomas Munro are often portrayed as the standard bearers of a conservative, cautionary and at times romantic movement which sought to construct linkages between the British conquerors and the pre-modern institutions of India — deliberately and vigorously fighting off all attempts to impose western values and institutions upon Indian society.[22] Conversely, many scholars have employed the policies and deliberations of Holt Mackenzie to attest to the spread of utilitarian dogma in India; some have even gone so far as to depict him as the ultimate representative of that school of thought in India. The debates between 'orientalists' and 'utilitarians', while vigorous, sustained, and drawing in a considerable swath of contemporary observers and officials, were in themselves dependent upon a remarkable degree of consensus over how best to secure stability of British rule. Holt Mackenzie argued that in the last resort, utilitarian schemes of improvement and administration must yield to the pressing security concerns of the British in India.[23] Even the so-called era of reform ushered in by William Bentinck from 1828 did not really alter the nature of the colonial state: a single governor-general, normally appointed for five years and often destitute of any Indian experience or information (though this was obviously not the case with Bentinck) can hardly be expected to institute profound and revolutionary changes even if that was his intention. Furthermore, careful scrutiny of Bentinck's actions and writings suggest that even such a widely-acclaimed liberal as Bentinck — some have gone so far as to label him a utilitarian — became equally fixed upon military concerns once he became established in India. Bentinck did not challenge the pre-eminence of military concerns for he was as alive as others to Britain's exposed position. Where he did differ was over the identification of the primary threat and how the army should be set up to meet it. Consequently, his reforms were sweeping and the effects on the army considerable, but the ultimate necessity of the army to prop up British rule was never queried.

This quest for stability prompted a colonial ideology in which three interrelated themes commanded attention. Security, financial solvency, and political legitimacy were the three imperatives of colonial rule; the satisfaction of all three was deemed essential for continued British rule. Common strategies were pursued in which a monopoly over the instruments of coercion was to be reinforced by gaining sufficient knowledge of and command over financial resources to allow the army to be deployed when and where needed. Colonial rule was to be further consolidated by the weaving together of a network of allegiances that would knit key sections of Indian society into the fabric of the colonial state. The army lay at the heart of all these objectives and consequently it was given first call on Indian resources and was given first priority in financial planning, thereby creating the preconditions for military fiscalism. As the British were never in a position to subdue completely all potential threats, alliances were crucial and here again the army played a major role. Key sections of Indian society could be coopted by selective recruitment into the Indian army. These alliances were further bolstered by the British practice of seeking out Indian capitalists and princes as subscribers to their loans.

But the importance of the army goes beyond simple pragmatic calculations; it was also crucial to how the British understood legitimacy in India.
Convinced that their predecessors had ruled by the sword, colonial officials
insisted that they too must maintain a visible military presence if they were
to have any credibility. If naked military power was insufficient to sustain
colonial domination, then a solution was sought in the impression that such
power conveyed to the Indian people. The theory of an 'empire of opinion'
emerged which argued that British domination rested not upon actual military prowess, but upon the conviction that the Indian people had of British
omnipotence. One contemporary wrestled with defining this 'empire of
opinion' and concluded that 'it is difficult to attach a definite meaning,
unless it be the opinion of our ability to crush all attempts at insurrec-
tion.'[24] A very similar definition was reached by David Ochterlony who
argued in his political testament that he understood 'empire of opinion' to
mean 'a belief in the governed, that the Wisdom, Resources, but above all,
the Military strength of the Rulers, remains unexhausted and invincible.'[25]
Hence, a great deal of attention was directed at promoting an image of British superiority to reinforce those conclusions the British had convinced
themselves that the Indians had reached about British strength and character. In effect a cyclical discourse emerged in which the army provided the
central theme. Thomas Munro noted presciently in 1826 that 'It is one of
the great evils attending employment in India that we are never sure we can
get away, for either our neighbours are restless, or they make us so restless.'[26]

   To explain their success the British looked to their military victories and
in explaining these victories came not only to emphasize the army, but to
interpret the structures and characteristics of Indian society in military
terms. Indian society was viewed as inherently violent and consequently
such notions as individual liberty or rule by consensus were seen as inap-
propriate in a land where political authority had always been maintained by
the sword. A sharp contrast was drawn between English society and Indian
society: 'We are now, indeed, in a country where, till very lately, a fort was
as necessary to the husbandman as a barn in England.'[27] Ironically, though
the British did embark upon a 'general offensive against Oriental governments', they simultaneously adopted what they considered to be the characteristics of those governments — specifically the premium placed upon
the military — in constructing their own systems of rule.[28] Directly and
indirectly the army was seen as the chief instrument in the monopolization
of coercion; its own military capacity used to defeat would-be challengers,
while the demilitarization of Indian society was to be achieved in part by

the army acting as a sponge, drawing into its ranks those communities deemed to be inherently warlike or most opposed to colonial rule.

Anglo–Indian militarism performed another and more limited objective. The continued emphasis on the British being beleaguered by enemies from within and without served the self-interests of army personnel. Quickened promotion, lucrative transfers into civil positions — particularly diplomatic postings to Indian courts— and prize money all helped sustain the war-footing of the East India Company. While there is some truth to the observation that 'the Indian army was organized by its officers, not to make it an efficient fighting force ... but to provide an equal chance for everybody to make his own fortune', this impression should not be pushed too far.[29] In part, important seams of sub-imperialism in India account for this scare-mongering. The lesser presidencies of Madras and Bombay, whose strategic importance had diminished following the shifting of the military frontier to the northwest, took advantage of real and invented threats in their respective neighbourhoods to bolster their position in the imperial arena. Narrow interest groups abounded in India and certainly their priorities were read into official planning, but they could only do so because the system was already receptive to their demands.

The commonplace idea that the army was to have first demands on the Company treasury ensured that military considerations were a constant factor in economic planning. That 'the British system in India has always been to keep the troops in a constant state of preparation for war' ensured that the army had the first claim on the public purse.[30] One contemporary summed up the situation in stark terms: 'the good or bad government of India is mainly a question of money and, therefore, a question of War or Peace.'[31] Charles Metcalfe took the reasoning one step further, arguing that financial planning must yield to military imperatives as it was 'necessary to make views of economy and retrenchment secondary to those of safety and power'.[32] Similarly, John Malcolm wrote wistfully to Charles Metcalfe that, 'I recognize in all your letters the unaltered Charles Metcalfe with whom I used to pace the tent at Muttra and build castles; our expenditure on which was neither subject to the laws of estimate nor the rules of audit.'[33] The resulting military fiscalism was to shape profoundly the institutions and character of British rule. The economic role of the army was further consolidated through its important revenue collection functions. Confronted with widespread peasant resistance to British revenue demands, the army was the means through which peasant resistance could be checked, either through direct punitive actions, or more frequently by displays of force designed to impress upon rural society the omnipotence of colonial rule.

The army's role as a gendarmerie of last resort is attested to by the geographical distribution of troops and garrison. As indicated in maps 1 and 2, troops were not concentrated along India's vulnerable frontier. Instead they were scattered across India in small garrisons, where they were in a position to monitor local society and if need be stamp out any signs of resistance.

One aspect of military fiscalism which has attracted considerable attention is the cost of expansionary policies.[34] Direct connections are drawn between the East India Company's financial difficulties, seen most clearly in its burgeoning debt, and the monies spent on military operations and preparation. While expansion was undoubtedly expensive and the army was the single largest consumer of Indian revenues, to attach financial embarrassment solely to the army reveals only part of the story. Military charges were not the only costs attendant upon expansion; as will be shown later, increases in civil costs often outpaced those incurred by the army and civil costs often proved to be more intractable in the face of retrenchments. One can also see that the cash demands of armies in the field acted as powerful incentives to local contractors and bankers while credit links between major banking centres were spurred on by the movement of armies.[35] Many contemporaries argued that these financial operations were ultimately beneficial to British rule as cash flows operated to bind Indian monied classes more closely to the British juggernaut. C.A. Bayly's study of urban growth in North India argues persuasively that 'the presence of the Bengal army was second only to cotton servicing as an influence on town growth during this period.'[36] Furthermore, arguments were made by contemporaries that the Company's debt was in some instances strategically advantageous. The willingness of Indian rulers and capitalists to invest in Company loans not only acted as a barometer of public confidence, but spun together a net which effectively integrated Indian and British sources of capital and the individuals who possessed them.[37]

Despite the widespread acceptance in India of the army's prominent position in the policies and actions of the colonial state, dispatches and instructions from London illustrate that the East India Company (and to a lesser extent the Cabinet) were far less susceptible to military propoganda. Despite such symbolic gestures as the votes of thanks given to successful armies and their commanders by both the Company and the British Parliament, metropolitan authorities were far less enthusiastic about the army and more prone to view militarized mentalités sceptically. Company directors were moved more by the annual dividends and their extensive patronage network, as well as resisting parliamentary inroads into Indian affairs, and the army was suspected as undermining these goals. The British Government, acting through the Board of Control, considered Indian affairs within a much broader context and concerned themselves with how India impinged upon Britain's global interests as well as anticipating India's ramifications upon domestic politics. Neither group was willing to accord the same importance to threats of rebellion or invasion that authorities in India were, and frequently berated officials in India for their lavish military expenditure and susceptibility to alarm. Increasingly, the army was viewed suspiciously owing to its growing influence and credibility in Indian official circles. Both the Court and the Board grew worried at what they correctly interpreted as signs of militarism in India which ultimately threatened to overturn the established chain of command and undermine metropolitan objectives. This disjunction between what was advocated in India and what was feared in Britain was to cause a great deal of friction between the two as observers in India complained that, 'Whatever delusions prevail in England respecting the security to be derived from the affections of our Indian subjects ... it will probably be admitted in India, that our power depends solely on our military superiority'.[38] London's scepticism was to play an important role in obstructing military influences, and though its ability to impose its will on Calcutta was never complete nor consistent, the Court and the Board were nevertheless able to contain some of the more rampant militarists in India. Ultimately, however, the consequence of these checks was that warfare did not become less likely, it became more inefficient.

Moving beyond the army's obvious strategic and financial importance we need also to consider the military's contributions to the ideological props upon which the imperial polity was ultimately founded. While the military roles of army officers are self-evident, what is often overlooked are their important contributions to the collection, analysis and dissemination of knowledge. The establishment of an impression of legitimacy demanded not only the expropriation of symbols and the building of alliances with Indian elites, but the more problematical issue of identifying exactly who these elites were and what were the symbols then in use. Here again the army was in the forefront for military officers were often best placed to observe local society; the impressions they received and the interpretations which they assigned to them became imbedded in the growing body of knowledge which both facilitated colonial rule and legitimated it. As one gazette compiler noted in 1820 his primary objective was 'to reduce the Geography of Hindostan to a more systematic form ... and to present a description of the vast internal economy ...'[39] Military officers occupied key positions in India, both within the army and as political residents. This gave many of them the opportunity to observe, categorize and evaluate Indian society, conquering India not simply by force but also through knowledge. Moreover, service in the field with sepoy corps provided a context in which officers believed they could observe Indian society better than civilians shut up in the presidency capitals. While obviously life in a cantonment or on the march cannot be considered as the equivalent of everyday life in India, for the British this was often the closest they came to Indian society. The intellectual conquest of India was a crucial step in the establishment of British hegemony as Indian society became strait-jacketed into fixed categories. The essences that were used to explain India, and were presented in such works as James Mill's *History of British India* were in part the product of army officers.[40] Army officers participated in significant numbers in the various scientific and literary societies that flourished in the major enclaves of Bengal, Madras and Bombay. As these societies increasingly moved away from abstract debates over religion and antiquities and towards detailed studies of contemporary institutions and structures, military officers were in the forefront of this analytic turn.[41] Two such officers, John Malcolm and Thomas Munro, developed elaborate theories of Indian society which contributed to colonial thought; James Tod explored in great detail the intricacies of Rajput society; others such as John Briggs and William Henry Sleeman documented extensively the *brinjaras* [itinerant grain dealers] and the *thags* [gangs of purported ritual murderers and thieves] respectively. Other officers, such as Henry Lawrence, Philip Meadows Taylor and J.W. Kaye, were among the most frequent contributors to the literary journals and newspapers of the day. Their enquiries were not simply prompted by academic curiosity; Indian institutions such as caste figured greatly in military organization. Caste was for many British officers the key to their man-management problems. By the early nineteenth century, 'caste' had come to be appreciated by the British as the fundamental building block of Indian society, and it was assumed that each caste had its own characteristics and aptitudes. If Indian society could be broken into its constituent elements, and if each of these elements could have its characteristics indexed (especially which 'castes' were inherently more martial), then the identification of the most suitable recruits would be simplified. Although there were considerable discrepancies in their accounts of these institutions and continual disagreements between officers as to their salient characteristics, the military pursued these questions vigorously. Ultimately, their efforts would come to fruition in the second half of the nineteenth century when systematic caste handbooks intended for British officers became widely available.[42]

The culmination of this pursuit and organization of knowledge was to reinforce the emphasis on the army as the arbiter of imperial rule. A firm impression was created that India was best administered through authoritarian policies mediated through strict hierarchies of rule. The obvious features of subordination and domination, and the emphasis on the maintenance of this unequal relationship — which not coincidentally echoed the values and institutions of military life — encouraged the authoritarian and conservative tendencies in individuals hitherto thought of as liberal. The Marquess of Hastings, who through his close relationships with the Prince Regent was thought of as a Whig, underwent a transformation when he arrived in India. In effect, he was a Whig to the west of the Cape of Good Hope and a Tory to the east. Almost exactly one hundred years later, another recent arrival in India, Edward Lutyens, was prompted to remark, 'India, like Africa, makes one very Tory and pre-Tory Feudal'.[43]

[1] John Malcolm, *The Political History of India from 1784 to 1823*. London: John Murray, 1823. II, 245

[2] Penelope Carson, 'An Imperial Dilemma: the Propagation of Christianity in Early Colonial India,' *Journal of Imperial and Commonwealth History*, 18(1990): 173

[3] P.J. Marshall, 'Western Arms in Maritime Asia in the Early Phases of Expansion,' *Modern Asian Studies* 14(1980): 13-28; Bruce Lenman, 'The Transition to European Military Ascendancy in India, 1600-1800,' *Tools of War: Instruments, Ideas and Institutions of Warfare, 1445-1871*. John Lynn, ed. Bloomington: University of Indiana Press, 1990. Both of these authors conclude that in dealing with technological superiority before the mid-19th century, the only obvious and sustained imbalance was in maritime technology. On land, technological differentials were far less apparent, and even when they did exist, they were rarely sustained as one side learned from the other.

[4] Philip Mason, *A Matter of Honour; an Account of the Indian Army, its Officers and Men*. London: Cape, 1974; J.W. Fortescue, *A History of the British Army*. 13 volumes, London: Macmillan, 1899-1930. For India, see volume 11 (1815-1838) in particular.

[5] P.J. Marshall, 'Cornwallis Triumphant': War in India and the British Public in the late Eighteenth Century,' *War, Strategy and International Politics; Essays in Honour of Sir Michael Howard*. Lawrence Freedman, Paul Hayes and Robert O'Neill, eds. Oxford: Clarendon, 1992. 57-74

[6] [anon], 'The Indian Army,' *United Services Journal*. 19(1835): 311

[7] [anon], 'Society in India,' *Bentley's Miscellany*. 31(1852): 242

[8] reprinted in William Makepeace Thackeray, *Yellowplush Papers and Early Miscellanies*. George Saintsbury, ed. London: Oxford University Press, nd

[9] Elizabeth Gaskell, *Cranford*. London: Penguin, 1976. Frederick Marryat recounted portions of his Burma War experience in *Olla Podrida*. 3 vols. London: Longman, Orme and Brown, 1840. See also Patrick Brantlinger, *Rule of Darkness; British Literature and Imperialism, 1830-1914*. Ithaca: Cornell University Press,

1988 for a stimulating discussion of the connections between literature and imperialism in the Victorian era.

[10] J.H. Amherst, *The Burmese War: a Grand Naval and Military Melo-Drama in Three Acts*. London, nd. There does not appear to be any connection between the author, J.H. Amherst, and the then governor-general of India, William Amherst. A brief discussion of this play can be found in Heidi J. Holder, 'Melodrama, Realism and Empire on the British Stage,' *Acts of Supremacy: the British Empire and the Stage, 1790-1930*. J.S. Bratton et al. Manchester: Manchester University Press, 1991, pp.129-132

[11] A good overview of the 19th century nonfictional accounts of India is presented in Eric Stokes, 'The Administrators and Historical Writing on India,' *Historians of India, Pakistan and Ceylon*. London: Oxford University Press, 1961. Surprisingly, there has been remarkably little interest in Gleig and Kaye who produced between them many biographies of pre-rebellion British administrators.

[12] Reginald Heber, Bishop of Calcutta, 30 Sept 1824, *Narrative of a Journey through the Upper Provinces of India*. London: John Murray, 1846, I, 193

[13] The military fiscalism discussed here bears some similarities to what John Brewer has identified as the 'fiscal-military state' of eighteenth century Britain in that both regimes sought to maximize their revenue collections in such a way as to support the activities of their armed forces. John Brewer, *The Sinews of Power: War, Money and the English State, 1688-1783*, London: Unwin Hyman, 1989, xvii

[14] For imperial developments, see C.A. Bayly, *Imperial Meridian; the British Empire and the World*. London: Longman, 1989. Changes in British society are mapped out in Linda Colley, *Britons: Forging the Nation, 1707-1837*. New Haven: Yale University Press, 1992. For Britain's ruling classes, see Peter Jupp, 'The Landed Elite and Political Authority in Britain, ca. 1760-1850,' *Journal of British Studies*. 29(1990): 53-79.

[15] Linda Colley, *Britons*, 184-5

[16] See for example C.A. Bayly, *Indian Society and the Making of the British Empire*. Cambridge: Cambridge University Press, 1988. In this book, Bayly convincingly shows the extent to which the course and nature of Britain's empire in India was dictated by developments in Indian society and the Indian economy, developments that were often well beyond British control. More recently, his *Imperial Meridian; the British Empire and the World*, Harlow: Longman, 1989 has situated Indian developments within a broader global context, thus balancing periphery against the metropole.

[17] P.J. Cain and A.G. Hopkins, *British Imperialism: Innovation and Expansion, 1688-1914*, Harlow: Longman, 1993. Not surprisingly, such an ambitious and provocative reassessment has begun to produce criticisms. Two of the more telling critiques are those by Andrew Porter and M.J. Daunton who look respectively at the imperial and economic aspects of the theory. Andrew Porter, "Gentlemanly Capitalism' and Empire: the British Experience since 1750?' *Journal of Imperial and Commonwealth History*, 18(1990): 265-95. M.J. Daunton, 'Gentlemanly Capitalism' and British Industry, 1820-1914,' *Past and Present*, 122(1989): 119-58. Another criticism that has been made is that Cain and Hopkins have been perhaps a little too hasty in writing industrialists out of the equation. See J.R. Ward, 'The Industrial Revolution and British Imperialism, 1750-1850,' *Economic History Review*, 47(1994): 44-65.

[18] Cain and Hopkins, *British Imperialism*, 58

[19] Cain and Hopkins, *British Imperialism*, 319

[20] Cain and Hopkins, *British Imperialism*, 34

[21] Many texts contain symbolic representations of this perspective. For example, the chapter on the 1820s and 1830s entitled 'The Utilitarian Deluge' in Ravinder Kumar, *Western India in the Nineteenth Century*. London: Routledge, 1968

[22] See for example. G.D. Bearce, *British Attitudes towards India, 1784-1858*. Oxford: Oxford University Press, 1961 and Thomas H. Beaglehole, *Thomas Munro and the Development of Administrative Policy in Madras, 1792-1818*. Cambridge: Cambridge University Press, 1960. A much revised perspective of Thomas Munro, which moves us beyond the simple labels previously used, figures in Burton Stein, *Thomas Munro: the Origins of the Colonial State and his Vision of Empire*. Delhi: Oxford University Press, 1989.

[23] Eric Stokes, *The English Utilitarians and India*. Oxford: Oxford University Press, 1959, 95. Percival Spear, 'Holt Mackenzie - Forgotten Man of Bengal,' *Bengal Past and Present*. 86(1967): 24-38. For a very different impression, see Holt Mackenzie's evidence, S.C. on the East India Company, PP, 13(1831/32): 167-68

[24] [W.W.], 'Consideration on the Native Army and General Defence of India,' *United Services Journal*. 7(1831): 1

[25] Ochterlony to Court, 1825, David Ochterlony, *Selections from the Ochterlony Papers (1818-1825) in the National Archives of India*, Calcutta: University of Calcutta, 1964, 435

[26] National Library of Scotland [NLS], Munro to Lady Liston, 12 March 1826, Liston Papers, NLS 5676, f.34

[27] Heber, 22 Jan 1825, *Journey*, 2, 23

[28] C.A. Bayly, *Indian Society and the Making of the British Empire. II.1 The New Cambridge History of India*. Cambridge: Cambridge University Press, 1988, 5

[29] Edward Ingram, *In Defence of British India*. London: Cass, 1984. p.51

[30] Walter Hamilton, *A Geographical, Statistical and Historical Description of Hindostan and the Adjacent Countries*. London: John Murray, 1820, I, xxxix

[31] J.W. Kaye, *The Administration of the East India Company: a History of Indian Progress*. 2nd ed. London: Bentley, 1853, 161

[32] Memo by Charles Metcalfe, 1816, in J.W. Kaye, *The Life and Correspondence of Lord Metcalfe*. London: Smith, Elder and Co., 1858, 1, 443-44

[33] Malcolm to Metcalfe, nd, Kaye, *Metcalfe*, 1, 483

[34] This exploration is best explored in Amales Tripathi, *Trade and Finance in the Bengal Presidency, 1793-1833*. 2nd ed. Calcutta: Oxford University Press, 1979

[35] Lakshmi Subramanian, 'Banias and the British: the Role of Indigenous Credit in the Process of Imperial Expansion in Western India in the Second Half of the Eighteenth Century,' *Modern Asian Studies*. 21(1987): 489-90

[36] C.A. Bayly, 'Town Building in North India, 1790-1830,' *Modern Asian Studies*. 9(1975): 496

[37] J.R. Ward, 'The Industrial Revolution and British Imperialism', has argued that the Company was primarily dependent on English capital for its activities. As will be shown in chapter 7, this was not the case in the late 1820s when Indian capital featured more prominently in the Company's ledgers.

[38] Metcalfe to Hastings, Nov 1814, Kaye, *Metcalfe*, 1, 388

[39] Hamilton, *Description of Hindostan*, 1, v

[40] Ronald Inden, *Imagining India*. Oxford: Blackwell, 1990. In identifying what he labels as hegemonic texts, those that informed British actions and thoughts about India, Inden lists Mill's *History of British India*, and Tod's studies of Rajput polities. James Mill, *History of British India*. 6 vols, London: 1818; James Tod, *Annals and Antiquities of Rajasthan or the Central and Western Rajput States of India*. 3 vols. 1812-1823. Reprint. Delhi: Banarsidass, 1971. Omitted from his list, however, are such widely-read experts as John Malcolm, Mountstuart Elphinstone and G.R. Gleig's life of Thomas Munro. Elphinstone's *History of India* had gone through seven editions by 1889. These three texts were written by individuals who not only had served in India, but had risen to senior positions from which their views could influence policies in a very direct way. John Malcolm, *The Political History of India*. op cit; John Malcolm, *A Memoir of Central India including Malwa and Adjoining Provinces*. 2 vols. 1823. Reprint. New Delhi: Sagar Publications, 1973; John Malcolm, *The Government of India*. London: John Murray, 1833; Mountstuart Elphinstone, *The History of India*. London: 1841; G.R. Gleig, *The Life of Major General Sir Thomas Munro*. 3 vols. London: Colburn and Bentley, 1830. An alternative and persuasive reading of James Mill is offered in Javed Majeed, *Ungoverned Imaginings*, Oxford: Oxford University Press, 1990

[41] Gyan Prakash, 'Writing Post-Orientalist Histories of the Third World: Perspectives from Indian Historiography,' *Comparative Studies in Society and History*. 32(1990): 383-409

[42] For the latter 19th century, the relationship between ethnography and recruiting is addressed by David Omissi, *The Sepoy and the Raj*, London: Macmillan, 1994

[43] Thomas Metcalfe, *An Imperial Vision: India's Architecture and Britain's Raj*. Berkeley: University of California Press, 1989. p.234. David Washbrook has made the stimulating observation that by drawing such militarized and authoritarian values out of England, the colonial state in India effectively safeguarded Britain from 'feudal-military' reactions. David Washbrook, 'South Asia, the World System and World Capitalism,' *Journal of Asian Studies*. 49(1990): 480

2. THE STRUCTURES AND IDEOLOGIES OF COMPANY RULE

> A Company which carries a sword in one hand, and a ledger in the other, which maintains armies and retails tea, is a contradiction, and if it traded with success, would be a prodigy.[1]

The rapid extension of British hegemony over India, particularly in the first quarter of the nineteenth century, forced considerable adjustments upon the East India Company and its employees as they sought to shift from a largely mercantile focus to one which emphasized the Company's sovereign responsibilities. The transition was not, however, particularly smooth, nor was it uniform, for the Company had to make considerable adjustments to its institutional makeup as well as its ideological underpinning. Tensions ensued, both within Indian administrative circles, and in the relations between metropolitan authorities and their representatives in India, as officials tried to come to grips with their dual mandate of securing the East India Company's commercial prosperity and the stability of British political control over India. Such tensions operated against the emergence of anything as uniform or monolithic as 'gentlemanly capitalism' for these tensions could not be easily resolved, pitting London against India, and Company against Crown, and even within the Company there were serious divergences. New institutions and policies were created to assist in managing these demands, though as frequently noted by contemporaries the processes by which forms and ideas of rule developed were never systematically pursued. Instead the administration of India fell into the hands of a bureaucracy that was largely the byproduct of *ad hoc* responses to mounting responsibilities. Peter Auber, secretary to the Company's Court of Directors — the chief executive body of the East India Company — commented that, 'Our Indian legislation has advanced by springs and jerks ... slow without deliberation, sudden without vigour.'[2] It is in the nature and processes of the institutional development of British hegemony that the first seeds of militarized rule were implanted, for the army was able to insert its people and its assumptions into the body-politic as a direct consequence of the tensions and uncertainties characteristic of the first stages of colonial domination.

One of the most pressing questions besetting policy-makers in India and Britain was what was to be the precise nature of the relationship between metropolitan authorities and their subordinates in India. The eighteenth-century fear of Indian money and Indian attitudes corrupting British society, although somewhat abated, pushed parliament towards intervention; yet, on the other hand, parliament was pulled away by the fear of treading on the sanctity of a chartered corporation, a fear that was given added immediacy by the potential political power of Indian interests in the House of Commons.[3] Set against this potential was the generally low level of parliamentary interest in Indian affairs. For most of the first half of the nineteenth century India did not figure in domestic political agendas. Rather, those who did express a commitment to Indian affairs were frequently angered by public and parliamentary apathy. G.R. Gleig, author of Thomas Munro's biography and confidant of the Duke of Wellington, sarcastically commented on this state of affairs in 1827. 'We know, too, that the very mention of British India in the generality of mixed companies, is met by the most unequivocal manifestation of nausea, and that men shrink back from the conversation of an Indian statesman as if a scorpion had crossed their path.'[4] Even in 1831, with the East India Company's charter coming up for renewal and a parliamentary enquiry undertaking an extremely searching enquiry into Indian affairs, public and parliamentary lethargy was hardly disrupted, prompting one observer to write that 'the concerns of India have at no time been a welcome subject in English society, or before an English Parliament.'[5]

While Indian affairs never ranked that high on domestic agendas, governments still had to proceed cautiously when considering actions that might affect India. There was at least in theory a considerable number of MPs in the House of Commons who could claim some interest in India. Between 1790 and 1820 there were upwards of one hundred MPs with East India Company stock.[6] Added to this were the several military officers who had seen service in India. Taken together this amounts to a not insubstantial proportion of MPs out of the 657 members of the unreformed parliament. Yet there is no indication that they viewed themselves as a votebank; their behaviour suggests no significant degree of cooperation among them. In 1825 the seventy-seven MPs with identifiable Indian interests did not band together.[7] Thirty-seven were generally in the government's camp, twenty-six tended to side with the opposition, while the remaining fourteen were non-aligned. Furthermore, these seventy-seven individuals included ten of the twenty-four directors of the East India Company. Once again, we find that there was no apparent political unity amongst them — five were pro-government, four were non-aligned and one sided with the opposition — and this despite the Directors having a much more direct interest in Indian affairs.[8] Four years earlier we find a similar split in those Directors with seats in parliament; of the twelve, six were viewed as government supporters, five were with the opposition, and one fluctuated between them.[9] For the administration the Indian interest was not viewed as requiring constant attention, unlike for example the West Indian Plantocracy. As one political commentator of the period noted with respect to the Indian interest, 'its express advocates there be not very able, nor yet exceedingly powerful'.[10] Consequently decisions made in London regarding India could generally be taken without any significant level of parliamentary scrutiny or public interest. At the same time, however, the Indian interest could not be completely ignored. The substantial numbers of MPs with Indian interests were in themselves worthy of attention and it was their potential, rather than their efficacy, which governments had to consider. In the absence of strict party discipline administrations needed to ensure that this powerful lobby group was at least neutralized if not actually enlisted. Such was the case with the government of Lord Liverpool which by the 1820s was encountering considerable opposition. With dwindling support in the House of Commons, and the endless fights within the cabinet between factions following such leaders as George Canning, the Duke of Buckingham, and the Duke of Wellington, Liverpool had to take care not to provoke the East India Company into lending its support to any of his opponents.

The absence of sustained parliamentary interest in India also arose because there were few political figures of the time who held Indian affairs in any high regard. With the exception of the Duke of Wellington, none of the prime ministers during this period demonstrated any commitment or interest in Indian affairs. Lord Liverpool (prime minister 1812-1827) was apathetic as far as India was concerned: the two volumes of his correspondence which deal with India reveal that India only received his attention when it offered patronage opportunities or when a crisis made it unavoidable.[11] He pressed his venal cousins, the Rickett family, upon Indian administrators, intervened when Indian events shook his government, but was otherwise content to leave India to the Board and the Court. Robinson, Grey, Melbourne, and Peel likewise avoided India as far as possible.

If the potential of the Indian interest in parliament was sufficient to discourage the government from introducing Indian affairs into the House of Commons, the same degree of circumspection marked the Company's relations with parliament. Given the increasingly vocal displays of the free trade lobby inside and outside of the House of Commons, the East India Company wisely chose not to pursue their interests in parliament. Even when such powerful directors as G.A. Robinson or William Wigram secured seats in parliament, the Indian interest still failed to make much of an impression as Robinson and Wigram were notably lax in their attendance and rarely addressed parliament.

It was within this narrow band of interested parties that the basic infrastructure of Company rule evolved. The Court of Directors viewed India from a corporate perspective and used their power and influence to try and secure policies and institutions that would preserve their extensive commercial and patronage interests in India. On the other hand, the British government, acting through the Board of Control which had been established in 1784 as the parliamentary watchdog on Indian affairs, tried to harness India to Britain's domestic and global needs. The Board of Control's original mandate gave it the authority and responsibility of intervening in Indian affairs when they impinged upon national interests. The Board was expected to 'superintend, direct and control all acts, operations and concerns which in any wise relate to or concern the civil or military government or revenues.'[12] These sweeping powers were only subject to one major exception: the Company's commercial operations were outside the competency of Parliament. However, with the diminished importance of commercial activities to the Company, following the loss of the Indian trade monopoly in 1813 and subsequent opening up of the China trade in 1833, the Board of Control, on paper at least, was clearly in a commanding position as far as executive powers were concerned. There were some caveats on the Board's power; they were not allowed to send their own instructions direct to India, but they could in matters of war and foreign policy command the Court to draft and send despatches to India. However, the Board was clearly loath to use such extensive powers; only forty-nine of the more than eight thousand despatches sent to India between 1813 and 1830 were prepared on the Board's express instructions.[13]

Despite the Board of Control's apparent responsibility for Indian affairs, its actual exercise of authority throughout the years covered in this study was less than might be deduced from its commanding position. The emphasis was on control rather than initiation; the British government was often reluctant to intervene because of the possible political ramifications arising from any perceived attacks on the rights of a chartered corporation, and because of the lack of an institutional framework within the government which could deal effectively with Indian questions. Membership on the Board consisted in theory of the chancellor of the exchequer, one secretary of state and at least four members of the privy council. Had this ideal been met in practice the British government would have been able to command greater influence in Indian affairs. Instead this membership list was completely nominal. Parliament control over India was vested in the hands of a President who may or may not have a seat in the cabinet, assisted by a small cadre of salaried clerks who divided Indian affairs into five fields: revenue, military, political, judicial and public. Commanding influence within this tiny cohort rested in the hands of the Secretary to the Board, held between 1812 and 1828 by Thomas Courtenay.[14] The lengthy duration of Courtenay's tenure, which lasted through several changes in the Presidency of the Board of Control, provided the Board with a measure of constancy and consistency it might otherwise have lacked. Following his retirement in 1828, the secretariat passed through a rapid succession of hands, five in the space of three years, which in effect denied the Board the expertise and respect it had hitherto built up.[15] A considerable degree of influence was also exercised by James Cumming (Head of the Revenue and Judicial Department, 1807-1823), widely respected for his expertise in Indian revenue matters, but like Courtenay suspected of being too inclined towards *ryatwari* [a revenue settlement made directly with the principal cultivator] rather than the *zamindari* system [revenue settlement made with the holder of superior proprietary land rights] that had been entrenched in Bengal by Cornwallis's Permanent Settlement of 1793. Advocates of *zamindari* emphasized that it ensured that local authority remained in the hands of the traditional elites who would then be encouraged to become improving landlords on British lines. Proponents of *ryatwari* stressed instead the benefits to be gained by dealing more directly with the actual workers of the land. Despite these few outstanding examples of expertise within the Board, its deliberations were greatly circumscribed by its small office establishment. Staffing had not kept pace with the growth in Indian business; there were simply not enough clerks to give despatches received from India the necessary scrutiny that would have provided the Board with an authoritative voice in Indian affairs.[16]

Ultimately, however, the Board's ability to intervene was undermined by its relatively weak voice within the cabinet. In the words of Lord Ellenborough, who was the President between 1828 and 1830, and returned to it in 1834-35 and again in 1841, it was 'an incognito office'.[17]

Appointments were generally made to serve domestic political agendas rather than because the appointee possessed any particular skills or aptitude for the office. One contemporary suggested that the Board of Control should be renamed the 'Board of Connivance' on account of the blatant use to which it was put in the dispensation of patronage.[18] Presidents were rarely found within the cabinet's inner circle. There were of course exceptions — Henry Dundas (1784-1801) whose relations with Pitt gave him considerable influence, or George Canning (1816-1821). In Canning's case, while he was arguably one of the more powerful and capable members of cabinet, this did not mean that he tackled Indian affairs with energy or determination. One of his subordinates complained that Canning left Indian affairs to the permanent staff in the Board of Control and instead passed his time in pursuit of those issues that seemed more important, domestic politics and foreign affairs.[19] Ironically, it was Canning's offhand ways that endeared him to the Court of Directors — better a powerful President with little commitment than a meddler working from the cabinet sidelines. As long as Canning was President the Court was generally able to retain a tight grip on Indian business. These were, however, the exceptions for most of the time the Board of Control was in the hands of second-string politicians. Gilbert Eliot, Lord Minto, (president in 1806) did not even have a seat in cabinet. The occupant between 1822 and 1827, Charles Watkin Williams Wynn, only secured his appointment as dowry for an alliance in 1821 between the government and the Grenville faction in parliament with which he was associated. Wynn was placed on the Board of Control for this was the cabinet position which possessed the least influence, a fact which caused considerable offence to the Duke of Buckingham, the clan leader.[20] It was an unhappy alliance all around; the government disliked Wynn who Canning mockingly referred to as 'Squeaker' on account of his thin reedy voice; Buckingham was angry at his limited influence, while Wynn would have preferred the speaker's chair and only reluctantly accepted the presidency when his cousin, 'that huge hill of flesh', pressured him to do so.[21] When first appointed, Wynn knew very little about India and cared even less. This did change over time as Wynn's interests in India grew, partly because of his close ties with Reginald Heber whose appointment as Bishop of Calcutta Wynn was instrumental in obtaining. From Heber's letters and his dealings with the Court of Directors, Wynn drew unfavourable conclusions as to the consequences of Company rule and came out, though not strongly, in favour of Crown rule for India.[22]

Even Lord Ellenborough's tenure at the Board of Control reflected his political marginalization. He desperately wanted the Foreign Office from which he could give full reign to his Russophobia, but Wellington took care to isolate this combustible aristocrat in an office where he could do little harm. In setting up his administration, Wellington heeded Peel's advice that while Ellenborough would be useful in giving the government greater strength in the House of Lords, he was not competent enough to be entrusted with the Foreign Office, nor was he important enough for either the Admiralty or the Board of Trade. By default he was given the Board of Control.[23] This denigration of the office of President was repeated in 1841 when Peel recommended that Lord Fitzgerald be appointed President on the sole ground that the government needed Irish representation.[24] The alternatives, some of whom were much better qualified, were discounted because they represented interest groups already well provided for in the cabinet.

In light of the Board's relative weakness within the cabinet, we find not surprisingly that other members of the administration could intervene in Indian affairs if they so desired. Horse Guards in particular often flouted the established conventions which governed communications with India and corresponded directly with officers in India. With twenty-thousand or more men and officers of the Royal army serving in India, commanders-in-chief frequently insisted that they had the right of intervening when Indian affairs affected the king's forces. Patronage opportunities also dictated that the Board's position might often be overruled; when a successor to Mountstuart Elphinstone in Bombay became necessary, Wynn found that his recommendations were sabotaged by George Canning who saw an opportunity to place a friend in the position as well as to take another gratuitous jab at Wynn.[25]

The Duke of Wellington largely filled the vacuum that resulted from the low priority accorded to the Board of Control.[26] His fame as the 'sepoy general', earned during his service in India at the turn of the century, when combined with his political and economic pre-eminence following the successful conclusion of the Napoleonic Wars, created a ready audience for his opinions. Wellington became the *de facto* minister for India, particularly but not necessarily in those governments in which he was a member. Wellington's reputation and a belief in his ability to isolate Indian affairs from domestic politics led the cabinet, the King and even the East India Company to look to him for advice. Wellington was especially popular with the East India Company for he not only provided advice when asked, he defended their prerogatives. Wellington brought his own particular understanding of India to bear on policy-making in Britain. While serving as a warrior cum diplomat cum civil servant under his brother, Richard Wellesley (governor-general 1798-1805), Wellington was thoroughly convinced that Indian policy had to be carefully designed so as not to upset local societies and possibly trigger rebellion. Security and order were his lifelong concerns, not surprising given his military background and exposure to contemporary events in France and Ireland. India had been taken by military force, and given what Wellington saw as the lack of any deep-seated attachment to British rule on the part of India's population, it would likely need to be maintained by military force — if not by actual coercion then at least by the impressions made by a vigilant and efficient army. Wellington lobbied on behalf of the Indian army whenever it appeared that financial reductions threatened their efficiency.[27]

The considerable weight which Wellington's opinions carried was used by him not only to impose his visions of colonial rule, but also to ensure the appointment of like-minded officials to senior positions in India. A network emerged which provided Wellington with on-site observers from whom he could glean the latest intelligence. While Wellington tended to downplay his influence on appointments, in one instance reminding John Malcolm that his power was largely negative and extended at best to preventing bad appointments, evidence suggests otherwise.[28] In choosing individuals for governorships or major military commands in India, Wellington was invariably called upon. In 1824, when the then commander-in-chief, Edward Paget, whose earlier appointment had been brokered by Wellington, announced his intention of resigning, it was Wellington who provided a shortlist of possible successors. After private and unofficial talks with the two officers who headed his list Wellington eventually settled on his third choice, Stapleton Cotton, Lord Combermere, who was duly appointed to the command of the Indian army.[29] Wellington's influence on the military staffing and policies of India was a lasting one. As commander-in-chief in the 1840s it was his recommendation that sent Henry Hardinge to India and once in India Hardinge looked to Wellington for advice.[30]

Within the East India Company the most influential body was the Court of Directors, consisting of twenty-four holders of East India Company stock elected annually by the Court of Proprietors, the stockholder's assembly. The powers of the Court of Proprietors, which had been considerable in the mid-eighteenth century, had since grown quite limited. By the nineteenth century they were expressly prohibited from directly interfering in Indian affairs. However much their direct powers had waned, the Court of Proprietors could not be completely written off as there was nothing to prevent them from informally discussing Indian affairs, and after taking into account that many were also engaged in other commercial and political activities, their weight was not inconsiderable. The fact that many held seats in parliament, such as Joseph Hume and Charles Forbes, convinced Company directors that there was always a possibility that they could become an unwelcome nuisance should they drag Indian affairs into Parliament.[31]

The Court of Directors' guiding philosophy was firmly anchored in London. Despite the onset of territorial responsibilities, especially marked after 1800, the Court persisted in viewing India from a corporate perspective, though not necessarily a united one. While this corporate nature did provide for an efficient and by contemporary standards a very professional bureaucracy, it also led them to apply 'the maxims of factories to the government of a mighty empire.'[32] Drawing on their memories of the eighteenth-century crises which they had weathered, the Court's greatest fear was financial embarrassment and its likely political consequences. War and rising administrative costs undermined their solvency and opened up the possibility of public enquiry; hence, there was a persistent emphasis on a pacific and economical administration of India. As one director claimed 'the policy of the Court of Directors has always been pacific and for obvious reasons — wars are inevitably attended with a large expenditure of money, and are generally followed by financial embarrassment.'[33]

In practice there was a remarkable degree of permanence on the Court. The only limitation on the Court was that directors had to stand down for one year in every four; this meant in practice a yearly rotation of one quarter of the directors. Vacancies on the Court were only created by the death or retirement of a sitting member. The Court was presided over by a Chairman and a Deputy Chairman, the only paid members of the Court of Directors. The rest were reimbursed in patronage for they controlled most of the appointments to the Company's civil and military service.[34] The directors themselves represented, in varying ratios, the four dominant interests in Indian affairs: shipping, City finance and commerce, private traders, and the returned civil and military servants from India, the latter often referred to as the 'Indian interest'. While one might expect the Indian interest to be the most qualified to make decisions regarding India, members of the 'Indian interest' were frequently blocked from serving on any of the more important committees. Instead, the Court of Directors continued to be dominated by directors representing shipping, private trade or financial interests. This domination represented a legacy from times when it was commercial activities that were uppermost in Company concerns; it also reflected the workings of the Court's seniority system which, by rewarding longevity at the expense of expertise, ensured that returned officials from India would have to spend at least twelve years on the Company's junior committees before they could hope to rise to one of the committees which deliberated on Indian political, military or revenue affairs, that is provided they were initially elected to be directors by the Court of Proprietors.[35] Even getting elected to the Court of Directors was not easy; a prospective candidate had to reside in Britain for at least two years before one could try (a qualification which reflected the eighteenth-century fear of returned nabobs and their corrupting influences) and then election would require considerable lobbying which in itself was so expensive that many suitable candidates were dissuaded from trying.[36] The absence of hands-on experience was most noticeable in the offices of the chairman and deputy chairman; Wynn while president of the Board of Control complained to Parliament that one of his biggest handicaps was that of the seven chairman with which he worked only one had actually been to India.[37] Frederick John Shore, an East India Company official in Bengal and son of John Shore, Lord Teignmouth (governor-general 1793-1798), argued that at any given time only three or four of the twenty-four directors had any first-hand knowledge of India.[38]

In the absence of a powerful Indian block in the higher echelons of the Court of Directors we find instead that financial, shipping and commercial magnates from the City dominated. Between 1815 and 1835 eighteen per cent of the directors were primarily associated with private trade, twenty-three per cent with shipping, seventeen per cent with the financial sector, and forty-two per cent were listed as 'Indians'.[39] While these figures would tend to indicate that the 'Indians' were well-represented on the Court, when we look at who were elected to be the chairs, the 'Indians' do not fare so well. They might have had forty-two per cent of the director's seats, but 'Indians' were chairs only twenty-five per cent of the time. In contrast, shipping and city interests together occupied the chairs' seats sixty-five per cent of the time. And even here the figures are somewhat misleading. If we deduct the first five years of the period, a time when returned 'Indians' served five times as chair or deputy chair, we find that metropolitan interests are even more clearly in the ascendant. Power remained firmly in the hands of these city and shipping interests ('gentlemanly capitalists'); two lobbies that for the most part cooperated quite well with each other. Yet there were still cleavages such as the time when duties on East Indian sugar split the shipping interest from the city interest; the former favoured lowering duties while the latter, with their financial connections to the West Indian plantocracy, agreed to the maintenance of prohibitory duties against Indian production.[40] And as we shall see later the fact that there appears to be a convergence in London around what can be termed 'gentlemanly capitalism' did not mean that the Company as a whole adhered to the same beliefs and codes of conduct.

The Court transacted its business through a series of committees with the committee of correspondence being the most important as far as territorial administration was concerned. A Secret Committee also existed, comprising the chair, deputy chair and most senior director, but it had by the nineteenth century been reduced to a cipher, passing on the Board's secret instructions to India.[41] Compared with the Board of Control the Directors could count upon a well-staffed and well-informed bureaucracy. A secretary and a chief examiner of Indian correspondence watched over four assistant examiners and a military secretary and their respective assistants. There was a remarkable degree of permanence in the higher echelons of the Company's bureaucracy; good salaries and working conditions encouraged long tenures on Leadenhall Street.

The Court made its decisions after deliberating on the vast number of despatches received from India. These despatches would first be opened by the secretary and then presented to the Court by the chairman, or the deputy chairman acting in his place, at their weekly meetings. This procedure gave the chairman great powers, for it limited the Court's deliberations to those topics which the chair wished to pursue. More detailed scrutiny of incoming mail, and the drafting of suitable replies fell into the hands of the relevant committee, assisted by the Company's permanent bureaucracy. The draft reply would first be approved by the Court, and then relayed to the Board for their reaction. Although the Board could challenge a draft despatch this possibility was considerably lessened by the informal practice of providing the Board with unofficial drafts prior to the drafting of the 'official' draft despatch. These 'previous communications' gave the Board the opportunity to register their dissent or demand amendments before the draft became official. On the surface at least an outward appearance of unity on Indian affairs was preserved.[42] Previous communications served a further function: when the Board was presided over by a particularly dynamic President, and or one who commanded the attention of his cabinet colleagues, it allowed the President to participate in the early stages of policy formulation. Such was the case with Lord Ellenborough who used previous communications to push his own agenda with effect.

The most obvious flaw in this administration was the absence of carefully defined responsibilities. A dual government such as this prevented a coherent sense of direction from emerging; authorities in India could never be certain whether it was the Board or the Court who was responsible for the initiative over a particular issue. It was noted scathingly by one observer that, 'The Court of Directors and the Board of Control have been long bandying the name of responsibility while in reality no party has been responsible to the public.'[43] While it would be incorrect to portray these two parties as locked in perpetual conflict with one another, there were none the less enough outstanding issues dividing them that a coherent unified policy from London was largely absent throughout this period. Frederick Shore offered a damning indictment of the consequent paralysis. '[The public] had for its object the opening of the China trade: the other [the Court of Directors], to secure the regular payment of the dividends; while the ministry have been tacking and trimming before them, willing to do anything that should please both, and gain a little popularity.'[44]

The absence of consensus in London prevented constructive and positive directions from being sent to India; instead, most of their directives were prohibitory injunctions that only revealed what could not or should not be done, and even then these instructions usually arrived after a decision had already been taken in India. Officials in London prided themselves on their efforts to constrain local officials; the Court of Directors boasted that, 'Was the Indian government as it is presently constituted to be characterized by a single word, it might with no impropriety be denominated a government of checks.'[45] This frequently meant that British officials in India were forced to muddle their way through the periodic crises which beset their administrations. Furthermore, officials in India had to bear in mind that they were expected to serve two masters — the Court of Directors and the Board of Control. This split loyalty was to cause no end of difficulty for officials who, when confronted with contradictory signals from London, were forced to decide between the Company and the Crown.

The various parliamentary bills of the eighteenth century which had attempted to systematize British relations with India contained within them a framework for political authority in India.[46] The governor-general in India stood at the apex, possessing an immediate executive authority over the presidency of Bengal, and supervisory powers, albeit vaguely defined, over the lesser presidencies of Madras and Bombay. By 1800 it had become customary to appoint members of the British aristocracy to Indian governorships. Political alliances could be purchased, embarrassing colleagues disposed of, and loyal allies rewarded through controlling Indian appointments. The offices of governor-general and governor in India and elsewhere in the empire were becoming increasingly important to the British government as a solution to their man-management problems. These problems had become particularly acute with the ending of the Napoleonic Wars when so many high-ranking officers and ambassadors had been thrown out of work. Particularly noticeable were the great numbers of officers who had been associated with Wellington's peninsular campaigns. These veterans would dominate many of the imperial postings until the mid-nineteenth century. If an overabundance of underemployed aristocrats provided the supply, demand was offered by the high salaries paid to such officials. The office of governor-general of India was undoubtedly the most lucrative position within the British Empire. Although its salary of £25,000 was in absolute terms less than that of Ireland (£30,000), Indian office holders had far fewer expenses to meet out of their salary. Those who took up the duties of governor-general frequently indicated that the financial perquisites were uppermost in their reckonings, with the prospect of an elevation in the peerage being an added bonus.[47]

The decisions and deliberations of the governor-general, and likewise the governors of Madras and Bombay, were expected to be undertaken with the active involvement of their respective councils. These councils included in addition to the governor-general (or governor) the local commander-in-chief, and two civilians. Councils were designed in part to restrain proconsular autocracy: they were also intended to provide the governor with a local perspective. Expert advice was thought to be crucial with so many of the individuals chosen to be governor-general or governor lacking any previous experience of or exposure to India. In 1841, Peel reassured the Queen that despite his rash temperament, Ellenborough would be quite safe in India for Peel expected that Ellenborough 'would be checked by the experience and mature judgment of Indian advisors on the spot.'[48]

The governor-general's authority was considerably strengthened by his control over much of the available patronage in India. The great volume of requests sent to governor-generals seeking appointments for the writer's relatives or protégés attests to the importance of this responsibility. *The Cadet's Guide to India* strongly emphasized the need for candidates to arrive in India equipped with letters of reference from important persons in Britain if they wished their careers to prosper.[49] During Amherst's term in India the only letters he received from Robert Peel were requests of support for Peel's candidates.[50] Beyond what powers they possessed by virtue of the depth of support underlying their appointment, there were the all-important connections which most governor-generals had with Britain's patrician classes. Despite the requirement that the governor-general pass all his official communications through the Court of Directors, the contacts which most had with members of the government ensured that a secondary line of communication was opened. These demi-official forms of communication persisted because governor-generals could exploit divisions between the government and the Company so as to secure their own position, or ensure the survival of their policies. Furthermore, such communications also attested to the tacit recognition that appointments to the office of governor-general were really in the hands of the government.

The actual qualification or suitability of prospective governor-generals for the office was not a high priority. One contemporary claimed that 'however great their abilities, they were more indebted to their Whig or Tory friends than to the former, no matter how splendid.'[51] The case of Charles Metcalfe demonstrates this. The Court had settled on him as Bentinck's successor in 1835, but the government had other ideas. Despite Metcalfe's long exposure to India, and experience as acting governor-general, he was passed over in favour of Lord Auckland who had never served in India before.[52] Earlier, when Mountstuart Elphinstone, recognized by many as one of the most experienced Indian officials, tried to cap his political career with promotion to governor-general, he was told that 'when the highways are broke up and the waters are out you may be sought for but when all is smooth and clear any muffer who can collect the tolls will serve.'[53] Lord Amherst was certainly one such muffer: he had no obvious qualification for the office and in the words of Curzon, left 'the most inconspicuous and impalpable of impressions'.[54] The intricate manoeuvres which led to Amherst's appointment indicate quite clearly just how far domestic politics and the search for stable domestic alliances impinged upon Indian affairs. Unlike either his predecessors or his successors, whose claims to high office were derived from their political affiliations, in Amherst's case, it was his very anonymity which secured his appointment.

When discussions began in 1821 to find a successor to Hastings the individual most frequently mentioned was George Canning who was himself receptive to the opportunity, largely because of the monies involved. The Court of Directors were favourable for Canning had proven to be tractable when president of the Board of Control; moreover, the government who ultimately had the power of confirming the nomination were also interested as this was an ideal way of dealing with an indispensable yet troublesome ally. Castlereagh's suicide ended these negotiations as Canning was sent to replace him at the Foreign Office. The search for a successor proved to be very difficult as the Court and the Board found each other's nominations unacceptable for a variety of reasons. *The Times* ridiculed the situation, noting that 'one journal has at different times announced seven different personages, and each with equal confidence.'[55] In fact there were nine names in circulation. With the entry of Canning into the cabinet the Liverpool administration had to restructure itself so as to make room for Canning's allies, particularly Huskisson.[56] The Court's role in these deliberations was distinctly a subordinate one once their favourite, William Bentinck, had been rejected. Bentinck was unappointable because of his whiggish political leanings and because his appointment did nothing to assist in the restructuring of the cabinet.[57] The Court were not totally excluded from deliberations; they were successful in blocking two possible candidates and more importantly their insistence that Hastings' successor must be a civilian was conceded. The latter qualification was pushed with particular vigour for the Court wished to avoid the expense of and responsibility for a policy of aggressive expansion to which military figures like Hastings were considered to be inclined. When they failed to use the vacancy to restructure the cabinet, the government's choice then fell on an individual who was loosely identified with them. Lord William Pitt Amherst, a classmate of Canning's at Oxford, was presented as the most acceptable alternative. Schooled at Westminster and later Christ Church Oxford and the nephew and ward of Jeffrey Amherst, one time commander-in-chief in Britain, Amherst made a remarkably faint impression upon those who knew him. Robert Southey, a classmate of Amherst, described him as a 'mild inoffensive boy, who interfered with no one … liked and respected by everybody.'[58] At the time of his appointment to India's highest office, Amherst lacked any significant administrative or political experience. Politically he was identified with the Canningites, but by his own admission his attendance at the House of Lords was at best sporadic and he was an infrequent and weak speaker.[59] Actual political service was limited to a brief stint in 1810 as ambassador to the Court of the Two Sicilies and a later unsuccessful embassy to China in 1816. While the government saw him as having 'good political principles' as well as being 'a government man without implication', the Court of Directors were far from enthusiastic in their response.[60] There was even some concern in the cabinet that the Court might reject Amherst, but apprehensions of getting an even more undesirable man persuaded fourteen of the twenty-two directors in attendance to vote for him.[61] In Canning's opinion, the 'appointment which takes place today is not a very strong one.'[62] This would become blatantly obvious in the following years.

While the appointment process certainly demonstrates that patronage played the key role, and that 'old corruption' was alive and well in Britain, it should not be overlooked that one principle was always adhered to when making an appointment — the man chosen was always from the aristocracy. An aristocratic pedigree was considered crucial for contemporary understandings of authority placed a great premium on force of character as a means of commanding respect. This was particularly crucial in a land such as India where British claims to legitimacy were tenuous. Birthright as a qualification for rule was thought particularly appropriate in a land where lineage was believed to have always constituted the prime requirement for a ruler. The reports produced by Elphinstone, Malcolm and Tod on the allegedly ancient lineages of central India led many to conclude that India could be best ruled if the British ensured that their supreme representatives were of equally noble birth. The concern which British officials expressed over the issue of maintaining the noble status of their representatives in India often reached extremes. In one instance Peel wrote to Queen Victoria of his great concern that Lord Hardinge's uniform was decorated by a Prussian riband. He requested that the Queen invest Hardinge with the Garter, for 'the ribbon born in India by the governor-general on state occasions in the presence of the natives should be the ribbon of an English and not of a Foreign Order.'[63] An aristocratic character was also calculated to be better suited to keep the lower orders in a state of awe, and not only the Indian lower orders. By the early nineteenth century there was concern that the small but vociferous European community in India was growing disorderly.[64] In 1818 the Court of Directors expressed its concerns over the European lower classes in a letter to the Board of Control. They noted that 'the English, especially those of the lower orders, are addicted to excesses disgusting to the natives, and which frequently lead to acts of violence and outrage.'[65] Yet the use of stricter laws and more rigorous punishments to keep them in order was quickly dismissed as these would only tend to diminish what the Company thought was the esteem that Europeans were held in by Indians.

In theory the governor-general's authority was very extensive. If he so chose he could act independent of his council for there were no positive injunctions which required him to defer to their opinions. The greatest check to the governor-general's authority lay in the feelings of London towards him. The latter stages of Hastings' tenure were marked by his increasing anxiety at what he perceived to be a hardening attitude towards him on the part of the Court. Amherst's political situation was even more precarious: his appointment had not been greeted with any enthusiasm, and even Canning began to intrigue against Amherst. Two of the chairmen with whom Amherst had to deal, namely William Astell and Campbell Marjoribanks, were among the eight who had held out against his nomination.[66] Even the King was personally hostile to Amherst for Amherst had spoken out in favour of Catholic Emancipation as well as supporting the claims made by Queen Caroline.[67] Amherst's successor, Lord William Bentinck, encountered similar problems in his relations with London. While his initial appointment went through with little difficulty, largely because of the support he received from George Canning (prime minister in 1827), Bentinck arrived in India to find that Canning's death had led to the creation of a ministry under the Duke of Wellington. Wellington's dislike of Bentinck reached as far back as 1809 when Bentinck had served in Sicily, and Wellington's animosity was echoed by Ellenborough, president of the Board of Control in the Wellington government.[68] As far as Wellington was concerned, Bentinck was 'a wrong-headed man, and if he went wrong, he would continue in the wrong line.'[69] Nor could Bentinck call upon the Court's support as easily as he might have in 1822 when they had favoured his appointment. The new members of the Court were not as favourably inclined towards him. As shall be seen both Amherst and Bentinck had to face up to the possibility that they might be recalled. The possibility was very real and both were kept well informed by their London contacts of just how precarious their positions were.

In theory a council composed of a governor-general who could call upon his aristocratic status and domestic political connections, a respected military figure as commander-in-chief, and two civilians each of whom possessed lengthy exposure to India should have produced an executive which struck the right balance of expertise and influence. The council was expected to guide the governor-general, offering expert knowledge, and if need be registering their dissent. For the most part, however, the council failed to live up to these expectations. In part the council's effectiveness had been limited by regulation. Memories of the obstructionist tactics of Philip Francis and the other councillors during Warren Hastings' administration (1774–1785) had persuaded authorities in London to give the governor-general the right to overrule his council. This meant that the council did not really possess any executive powers; instead they were left with what was largely a consultative function though they did retain the capacity to hinder discussion. Wellesley's dislike of working through his council was frequently made evident: on one occasion he referred to them as a 'useless, if not a dangerous expense', and in the entire period of his tenure, he never attended more than one-half of their meetings.[70] The council's lack of weight would persist throughout the period under review here. Elphinstone decided against following up his governorship in Bombay with an appointment to the Supreme Council when he thought of the 'insignificance and perhaps the depression of a Councillor's life'.[71] Council's nadir was almost certainly reached in the mid-1820s when the two councillors, John Fendall and John Harington, were almost universally described in very unflattering terms. The *Oriental Herald* described the latter as 'thinking of nothing but singing anthems [and] attending charity school meetings', while Fendall was dismissed as 'gouty and stupid'.[72] Colleagues were equally disparaging in their dismissal of these two; John Adam summarized Harington as 'the most intolerable old bore.'[73] The requirement that councillors needed ten years of Indian service was by itself a poor guarantee of broad experience. Appointments were made on the basis of seniority and frequently they fell on those officials exhausted after years of service in a single branch of the Company's administration. In the words of one secretary, life on council was notable for its 'somnolent bewilderment', with councillors 'idly dreaming of a prodigious army of state affairs flitting obscurely before [them].'[74]

The fourth member of the Council, the commander-in-chief, was equally limited as to his effective contribution. His appointment was designed to assist the executive with expert military advice as well as provide a bridge between the government and the army. Much like the governor-general the commander-in-chief was normally appointed on the basis of his social and political standing in domestic society and in many cases lacked prior Indian experience. The commander-in-chief's effectiveness was further compromised by his having to wear two different hats and perform two different functions. He held a joint appointment; a commission from the Company authorized his command over the Company's military forces while a second commission from the Crown gave him executive powers over king's forces in India. The latter commission, coming as it did direct from the Crown, gave him an independent source of authority. This separate commission frequently led to collisions between the commander-in-chief and the governor-general. The commander-in-chief was also torn between his military duties and those associated with his seat on council. As a councillor the commander-in-chief was expected to attend Council meetings in Calcutta; yet as commander-in-chief he was often called away on tours of inspection. For some, such as Edward Paget, military tours provided a ready excuse for avoiding council duties. In the whole of his term of office Paget attended less than one-third of council's meetings, even avoiding those that dealt explicitly with military affairs.[75]

It was the secretaries who filled the breach left by council's failure to provide the governor-general with expertise. The secretariat, the highest ranking administrative body in India, was staffed by six secretaries who controlled the implementation of the council's decisions and provided council with the expert information they needed for their deliberations. One secretary oversaw the secret and political activities of the Company, another dealt with judicial policies, a third took charge of territorial (revenue) business, a fourth handled military correspondence, the public secretary was charged with miscellaneous business such as education or public works, while the Persian secretary was responsible for translations and negotiations with Indian princes. These secretaries were not cyphers: their control over the flow of information to and from council give them considerable influence and they often joined in policy deliberations. Ever since the Marquess of Wellesley had discovered how useful an expert but subordinate secretariat was compared to an inefficient and possibly hostile council, governor-generals had tended to depend upon the secretariat for the implementation of their plans.[76] In contrast to what had been intended as a limited role, secretaries by the 1820s had become full participants in council deliberations though neither their names nor their comments were recorded. A hand-written note by Lord Amherst indicates quite clearly that in many instances, secretaries were taking precedence over councillors in the discussion of business.[77]

Set against the authority of the governor-general and the supreme council in Bengal were the local governments of Madras and Bombay. Bengal's authority over these subordinates was never clearly articulated and certainly it was greater in theory than in practice. Each of the three presidencies had their own well-entrenched political cultures and traditions and took great care to protect them. The separate paths of development followed by Bombay and Madras created strong local identities that often conflicted with the aims and aspirations of Calcutta. For much of the 1820s these imperial sub-cultures were boosted by the reputations of their governors. With Thomas Munro in Madras (1820-1827), and Mountstuart Elphinstone (1819-1827) and later John Malcolm (1827-1830) in Bombay, these presidencies were governed by individuals who could call upon a wide range of supporters in Britain as well as in India. Their administrative reputations were enhanced by their production of several studies which became standard readings for those interested in India. Elphinstone's *An Account of the Kingdom of Cabul* (1815) and *History of India* (1841) and Malcolm's *Political History of India from 1784 to 1823* (1826) and *Memoir of Central India* (1823) allowed for the dissemination of their ideas and perspectives to a wide audience. Thomas Munro never wrote anything explicitly for publication, but the extent to which his views were accepted by later generations was made evident in 1857 when, with the outbreak of the great rebellion, a minute he wrote in 1822 on the subject of the press in India was reprinted to show the dangers of complacency when ruling India.[78] As well, a two volume biography and collection of Munro's correspondence was published shortly after his death.[79] Wellington held these Anglo-Indian worthies in particular respect, listing their works as required readings for his sons.[80]

The aura which surrounded them not only assisted in perpetuating their local independence, it also encouraged them to go further and try to extend their authority and influence.

The one area in which the sub-imperialisms of Madras and Bombay most notably collided with Calcutta was over the respective distribution of military resources. Attempts to reduce military expenditure in India fell principally upon Madras and Bombay. While strategic arguments were advanced to support this, namely that both presidencies were located far from the sites of any future conflicts, officials in Madras and Bombay interpreted these decisions as merely the opening moves in an attack that was intended to culminate in their complete subordination, if not extinction. With the eclipse of the Maratha threat in 1819 Bombay and Madras were forced to invent new strategic roles for themselves. From Madras Munro argued with some success that the battle-tested record of the Madras army, together with its proven willingness to serve anywhere, proved that it was still an essential reservoir of troops for imperial service.[81] Bombay officials were equally alive to the need to convince authorities in London that they were strategically vital, and used conditions along their frontier with Sind to justify their need for a large army.

Confronted with such an awkward and often unresponsive political superstructure, decision-making in India often relied upon the informal networks which connected officials in ways either obscured or in theory prevented by the official system. Communication lags further reinforced these unofficial ways of conducting business as distance isolated the various nodes from each other. In many instances a reply from London to a decision taken in India could be as much as a year away, and hence the man on the spot could claim the necessity of reaching an immediate decision as justification for his arbitrary acts. When coupled to the titanic egos of many Indian officials conditions were ideal for the exercise of sweeping plans for aggrandizement. Forceful and determined individuals could often lubricate the wheels of Indian bureaucracy and direct it along paths of their own devising, especially if they could draw upon the active support, or even passive acquiescence, of fellow officials. The capacity for individual initiative in India was great and because British officials demonstrated a remarkable consensus over how British rule should be consolidated, it often pointed to a very aggressive policy of expansion and consolidation. It would be wrong to attribute the evolution of colonial rule solely to the actions of dynamic individuals; the drive of a Wellesley or a Hastings are by themselves unsatisfactory in accounting for British expansion. Instead their insatiable egos and persistent quests for glory struck sympathetic chords in India where they in effect legitimated a long-standing commitment to a militarized empire.

One network stood out amongst the rest in this period for its ability to impose its vision of Indian rule upon authorities in India as well as in Britain. Collectively known though somewhat misleadingly as the Wellesley Kindergarten on account of all having served under the Marquess Wellesley, this group had achieved very prominent positions in the colonial body-politic. With Munro at Madras, Elphinstone and later Malcolm at Bombay, John Adam and Charles Metcalfe serving the central government in Calcutta in a variety of roles, and Wellington in London pushing their ideas and claims upon the government, this pressure group was ideally positioned to shape the unfolding colonial state. Wellington was the linchpin of this alliance: his stature in London when coupled with his frequent communications gave this group both the position and the communications network necessary for the successful dissemination of their views. They shared broadly similar views and through frequent communications, they advised each other, provided detailed précis of events within their jurisdictions, and cooperated to bring about decisions which had received their collective sanction. Of crucial importance were their deliberate and usually successful efforts to inculcate into newly-arrived governor-generals a 'local' perspective in place of what they saw as the misleading instructions of London. Their experience, stature, and powerful allies in Britain and India guaranteed to them a persuasiveness and permanence which was denied to others. Of Elphinstone it was noted that 'even in his retirement ... he became the Nestor of Indian politicians, consulted by the Indian government at home and by its servants abroad in all cases of importance and difficulty.'[82] Moreover, by the 1820s they had secured a very useful entry point into the supreme government. Very close ties had been established with the secretariat, largely through John Adam, and with this their influence over incoming governor-generals grew even more considerable. As John Adam explained: 'I would most certainly prefer inducing a governor-general to adopt a measure as his own, or that of the collective government, rather than propose it myself officially in council ... I may perhaps have sometimes carried this principal too far.'[83] Even during the vigorous leadership of the Marquess of Hastings the combined forces of the kindergarten and the secretariat were sufficiently powerful to sway Hastings' decisions. By appealing to Hastings' vanity, the secretaries were able to impose their views simply by persuading the governor-general that their views could easily become his own.[84] With Hastings' successor, Lord Amherst, different techniques of influence and control were used though with broadly similar results. Amherst's attention was secured not through his vanity, but rather through his misgivings about his own competence. In an astonishing admission Amherst confided to Lord Morley that, 'I would not have you suppose that I deem myself a man of sufficient calibre to govern India in difficult times'.[85] Amherst was very willing to defer to those he viewed as more expert. The secretariat's influence was, however, partly blunted by Amherst's successor. William Bentinck made a concerted effort to escape from what he dismissively referred to as Amherst's 'government of secretaries'.[86]

The administrative system of British India was a curious amalgamation of legislative provisions, elaborate checks and balances, informal networks and *ad hoc* experiments, shot through with inconsistencies and handicapped by its multi-faced personality. There is no single dominant decision-making power with respect to Indian policies, nor was there a single over-arching set of assumptions to bind the metropole and periphery together. Negative injunctions from London were in themselves insufficient to bring local officials under control, nor could they give much in the way of future policy, especially as the Board and the Court frequently failed to speak with the same voice. Metropolitan demands, however, could not be completely ignored and they did make their mark upon Indian events. Given the often tortured relations between the governor-general and his superiors in London governor-generals were often restrained from acting too hastily. Within India decision-making was conducted through a very complicated system of official and unofficial channels. Given their general lack of prior exposure to India and their worries over the state of their following in London, governor-generals and governors were careful to ensure that they worked closely with other senior officials. Watchdog bodies like the presidency councils were employed to maintain the fiction of collective responsibility though the real collective decision-making was taken by the undefined network of secretaries, governors and residents which tied Indian policy-making together. This should not be viewed as collective responsibility; distance and the hierarchies of political structures precluded such a form of government from emerging. Instead it might properly be described as a form of collective authority in which likemindedness as well as apprehensions about annoying London brought officials into a form of consensus politics. By working together they could better deflect incoming criticisms from London as well as strive to impose their collective vision of how and for whom India should be ruled.

[1] J.R. McCulloch, 'Indian Revenues,' *Edinburgh Review*. 45(1827): 365
[2] Peter Auber, *Supplement to an Analysis of the Constitution of the East India Company*. London: Parbury and Allen, 1828, 11

[3] For a fuller discussion of the eighteenth century background, see H.V. Bowen, *Revenue and Reform; the Indian Problem in British Politics, 1757-1773*. Cambridge: Cambridge University Press, 1991. A broader survey of the East India Company is offered by Philip Lawson, *The East India Company; a History*, Harlow: Longman, 1993

[4] G.R. Gleig, 'The Indian Army,' *Blackwood's Magazine*. 21(1827): 563

[5] R.D. Mangles, 'The Government of India,' *Edinburgh Review*. 53(1831): 439

[6] R.G. Thorne, ed., *The House of Commons, 1790-1820*. London, 1986, I, 322. C.H. Philips in his monumental study has a slighter lower figure for the 1820s; he argues for a total of 84 MPs with Indian interests. C.H. Philips, *The East India Company, 1784-1834*. Manchester: Manchester University Press, 1961, 327-29

[7] Data taken from the *The Session of Parliament for 1825*. London, 1825

[8] Ibid

[9] 'Analysis of the British House of Commons, 1822 and 1823,' *Pamphleteer*. 12(1823): 452-74

[10] *The Session of Parliament for 1825*. London, 1825, 43

[11] British Library [BL], Add MS 38411-38412

[12] Sec 9, 33 Geo III, c.52 [1784]

[13] Select Committee of the House of Commons on the Affairs of the East India Company [hereafter S.C. on the East India Company], Parliamentary Papers [hereafter PP], 1831/32, ix, p.v

[14] BL, Liverpool to Bathurst, 29 Dec 1820, Add MS 38288, f.386

[15] George Bankes [May 1829-Feb 1830], J.S. Wortley [Feb 1830-Dec 1830], Lord Sandon Dudley [Dec 1830-May 1831], Thomas Hyde Villiers [May 1831-Dec 1832], Thomas B. Macauley [Dec 1832-1834] C.H. Philips, *The East India Company, 1784-1834*. Manchester: Manchester University Press, 1961, 339

[16] Edward Law, Lord Ellenborough, 19 Sept 1828, *Political Diary*. London: R. Bentley and Son, 1881, II, 391

[17] Ellenborough, 5 Sept 1828, *Diary*, I, 208

[18] [anon], 'Constitution and Government of India,' *Westminster Review*. 17(1832): 102

[19] Oriental and India Office Collections [OIOC], Cumming to Munro, 9 May 1823, MSS Eur F151/73

[20] C. Arbuthnot, *The Journal of Mrs. C. Arbuthnot, 1820-1832*. London: [ ], 1950, I, 100. See also University of Southampton Archives [hereafter Southampton], Buckingham to Wellington, 16 Sept 1823, WP1/771/8

[21] Tierney to Bagot, 1 May 1827, *The Formation of Canning's Ministry*. A.A. Aspinall, ed. Camden 3rd Ser. 59(1937): 206

[22] OIOC, Cumming to Munro, 3 May 1823, MSS Eur F151/72.

[23] Peel to Wellington, 18 Aug 1828, Arthur Wellesley, Duke of Wellington, *Letters, Correspondence and Memoranda of the Duke of Wellington*. 2nd series, London: John Murray, 1871, iv, 632

[24] BL, Peel to Victoria, 9 Oct 1841, Add MS 40432

[25] Wynn to Buckingham, 7 Sept 1824, Richard Plantagenet Temple Nugent Bridges Grenville, 2nd Duke of Buckingham and Chandos, *Memoirs of the Court of George IV, 1820-1830*. London: Hurst and Blackett, 1859, 1, 120

[26] See Douglas M Peers, 'The Duke of Wellington and British India during the Liverpool Administration, 1819-1827,' *Journal of Imperial and Commonwealth*

History. 17(1988): 5-25

[27] See for example: Southampton, Wellington to Wynn, 3 Nov 1825, WP1/832/5 and Public Record Office [hereafter PRO], Wellington to Ellenborough, 14 Oct 1829, PRO 30/9/4/1

[28] Southampton, Wellington to Malcolm, 8 Feb 1827, WP1/884/8

[29] Southampton, Wellington to Combermere, 13 March 1824, WP1/789/7; Beresford to Wellington, 21 Dec 1824, WP1/807/18; Wynn to Wellington, 24 Dec 1824, WP1/807/22

[30] Peers, 'Duke of Wellington,' 21

[31] Southampton, Wynn to Wellington, 27 Oct 1825, WP1/829/16

[32] Auber, *Supplement*, 19

[33] Henry St. George Tucker, *Memorials of Indian Government*, J.W. Kaye, ed. London: Bentley, 1853, 228-29

[34] John Malcolm, *A Political History of India from 1784 to 1823*. London: John Murray, 1824, II, 120. For a fuller discussion, see J.M Bourne, 'The Civil and Military Patronage of the East India Company, 1784-1858.' (Ph.D. diss., University of Leicester, 1977)

[35] Henry St. George Tucker, *A Review of the Financial Situation of the East India Company in 1824*. London: np, 1825, 24-5

[36] John Malcolm, *The Government of India*. London: John Murray, 1833, 231. [Henry Ellis], 'Review of John Malcolm's *Political History of India*,' *Quarterly Review*. 35(1827): 38. The legislation that required a two year residency is found in Sec 2, 13 Geo III, c.63

[37] Charles Wynn, Speech to the House of Commons, 13 June 1832, *Hansard*. 3rd series, 18, 743

[38] F.J. Shore, *Notes on Indian Affairs*. London, 1837, i, 345

[39] Date for tables taken from Philips, *The East India Company*, 327-29 and *Session of Parliament*.

[40] This episode is recounted by Henry St. George Tucker. See *The Life and Correspondence of Henry St. George Tucker*. J.W. Kaye, ed. London: Bentley, 1854, 341

[41] C.H. Philips, 'The Secret Committee of the East India Company,' *Bulletin of the School of Oriental and African Studies*. 10(1939-42): 299-315, 695-716

[42] OIOC, Wynn to Chairs, 17 Aug 1827, F/2/7

[43] [anon], 'Constitution and Government of India,' *Westminster Review*. 17(1832): 99

[44] Shore, *Notes on Indian Affairs*, I, 389

[45] OIOC, Court to Ellenborough, 27 Aug 1829, MSS Eur E/424/2

[46] See C.H. Philips, *East India Company* for the political context and administrative consequences of these pieces of legislation.

[47] Amherst's decision to go to India was based almost completely on the salary. BL, Amherst to Morley, 15 Sept 1822, Add MS 48225 ff 69-70. The peerage was also on his mind; before he left for India, Amherst left a list of possible titles should he be granted an earldom. OIOC, Morley to Amherst, 16 Nov 1826, MSS Eur F140/111(a)

[48] BL, Peel to Victoria, 9 Oct 1841, Add MS 40432

[49] [Bengal Lieutenant], *Cadet's Guide to India*, Calcutta: 1834, 29

[50] OIOC, Amherst papers, MSS Eur F140

[51] C.R.M. Martin, *The Political, Commercial and Financial Conditions of the Anglo-Eastern Empire in 1832*. London: np, 1832, 83–4

[52] Yet ironically Metcalfe was sent to Canada as governor-general. J.W. Kaye, 'Mr. Thornton's Last Volume,' *Calcutta Review*, 5(1846): 147-9

[53] OIOC, Strachey to Elphinstone, 13 Nov 1823, MSS Eur F88/7/D3

[54] George Curzon, *British Government in India*. London, 1925, II, 172

[55] *The Times*, 16 Oct 1822

[56] OIOC, Ravenshaw to Munro, 18 Sept 1822, MSS Eur F151/77

[57] BL, Canning to Huskisson, 22 Oct 1822, Add MS 38743; Nottingham, Liverpool to Bentinck, 22 Oct 1822, PwJe 469

[58] C.C. Southey, ed. *The Life and Correspondence of Robert Southey*. London, 1849-50, III, 137

[59] BL, Amherst to Morley, 15 July 1820, Add MS 48225, f.51

[60] BL, Canning to Huskisson, 23 Oct 1822, Add MS 38743

[61] OIOC, Ravenshaw to Munro, 10 Oct 1822, MSS Eur, F151/77; OIOC, Court Minutes, 23 Oct 1822, B/175, pp. 579-80

[62] BL, Canning to Huskisson, 23 Oct 1822, Add MS 38743

[63] BL, Peel to Victoria, 24 May 1844, Add MS 40438

[64] P.J. Marshall, 'British Immigration into India in the Nineteenth Century,' *European Expansion and Migration*. P.C. Emmer and M. Mörner, eds. Leiden: Brill, 1992, 179-196; D. Arnold, 'White Colonisation and Labour in Nineteenth Century India,' *Journal of Imperial and Commonwealth History*. 11(1983)

[65] Court to Board, 27 Feb 1818, S.C. on the East India Company, PP, 8(1831/32): 257

[66] BL, Canning to Morley, 11 Nov 1826, Add MS 48221; Wynn to Buckingham, 3 Sept 1825, Buckingham, *Memoirs*, II, 274

[67] BL, George IV to Liverpool, 9 Oct 1822, Add MS 38190

[68] John Rosselli, *Lord William Bentinck; the Making of a Liberal Imperialist, 1774-1839*. New Delhi: Thomson Press, 1974

[69] Ellenborough, *Political Diary*, II, 56

[70] Wellesley to Dundas, 25 Jan 1800, *Two Views of British India: the Private Correspondence of Mr. Dundas and Lord Wellesley, 1798-1801*. Edward Ingram, ed. Bath: Adams and Dart, 1970, 215; B.B. Misra, *The Central Administration of the East India Company, 1773-1834*. Manchester: Manchester University Press, 1959, 86

[71] OIOC, Elphinstone's diary entry, 4 March 1823, MSS Eur F88/14/J/5

[72] *Oriental Herald*, 8(1826): 559

[73] OIOC, Adam to Elphinstone, 5 Mar 1823, MSS Eur F88/9/F/27

[74] Tucker, *Life and Correspondence*. II, 162

[75] OIOC, Nicolls' Diary, 6 Oct 1825, MSS Eur F175/31

[76] B.B. Misra, *The Central Administration of the East India Company*. Manchester: Manchester University Press, 1959. p.82

[77] OIOC, Note by Amherst, nd, MSS Eur F/140/116. Lorenzo Crowell's work on the Madras army during this period has revealed that secretaries at that presidency were also participating in council discussions. Lorenzo Crowell, 'Logistics in the Madras Army circa 1830,' *War & Society*, 10(1992): 5

[78] Thomas Munro, *Liberty of the Press in India*. (London: np, 1857)

[79] G.R. Gleig, *The Life of Major-General Sir Thomas Munro*. 2nd ed., 2 vols,

London: Colburn and Bentley, 1831

[80] Peers, *Wellington*, passim

[81] OIOC, Munro to Bathurst, 28 Sept 1821, MSS Eur F151/92. OIOC, Ravenshaw to Munro, 25 April 1823, MSS Eur F151/79

[82] John Wilson, 'Short Memorial of the Honorable Mountstuart Elphinstone, and of his Contributions to Oriental Geography and History,' *Journal of the Bombay Branch of the Royal Asiatic Society*. 6(1862): 109

[83] Charles Lushington, *A Short Notice of the Official Career and Private Character of the Late John Adam*. Calcutta: privately printed, 1825, 12

[84] Richard Bingle, 'The Governor-Generalship of the Marquess of Hastings, 1813-1823,' D.Phil. diss., Oxford University, 1964, pp.2-3, 174-76

[85] BL, Amherst to Morley, 23 Aug 1825, Add MS 48225, f.120

[86] Nottingham, Bentinck to Auber, 6 May 1830, PwJf 198

3. IDEOLOGIES OF THE GARRISON STATE

It is difficult to make this Court understand that their territorial possessions here are not precisely like an estate in Yorkshire, or that they are not to expect as blind a compliance with their orders in the one case as they might in the other.[1]

In contrast to London, policy-making in India was largely determined with reference to actual conditions in the sub-continent as interpreted by those on the spot. Security became the paramount concern, especially in the wake of the Marquess of Hastings' wars with the Pindaris and the Marathas which had resulted in the extension of British authority over much of the interior of India. The East India Company's annual dividend, or the state of its China trade, were matters of secondary importance to officials more concerned with squaring the territorial revenues of India with government expenditure, or dealing with what they thought were endemic challenges to their authority. Home charges, domestic machinations, and the broad issues of imperial defence and corporate stability were all secondary to the principle imperatives of security and stability. Policy in India was conceived in the first instance with reference to the army and the financial resources necessary to sustain it. Hence, officials in India would assert that 'the British System in India has always been to keep the troops in a constant state of preparation for war.'[2] This set of priorities was guaranteed to collide with metropolitan interests.[3] Officials in India continually bemoaned what they saw as the shortsighted vision of their superiors in London. Equally disparaging comments were made of those Calcutta officials who insisted on working within the Company's mental framework: 'I do not think that there is a human being, certainly no nabob, half as mad as an able Calcutta civilian, whose travels are limited to two or three hundred miles ... the Regulations in his right hand, the Company's charter in his left, and a quire of wire-wove foolscap before him.'[4]

44

An image of how Britain should rule India, and one which had its genesis in the grouping of officials around the Marquess of Wellesley during his tenure as governor-general, stressed the need for a militocracy to rule India. Perhaps the most complete articulation of this school of thought can be extracted from John Malcolm's *Political History of British India*. There it was stated quite bluntly that, 'The only safe view that Britain can take of her empire in India is to consider it, as it really is, always in a state of danger.'[5] The widespread acceptance of Malcolm's line of thought can be seen in a journal article from 1845 when it was said, 'No man ... better understood the habits and feelings of our subjects in that part of the world than Sir John Malcolm.'[6] Malcolm's conclusion that, 'Our government of that country is essentially military', was one that many officials in India would have agreed with.[7] Thomas Munro remarked that, 'in this country we always are, and always ought to be prepared for war.'[8] These sentiments were further echoed by Charles Metcalfe who proclaimed that 'the main object of all the Acts of our Government [is] to have the most efficient army that we can possibly maintain.'[9]

The highly militarized interpretation of rule set out here must be understood as a form of militarism unique to India, for it stemmed from a particular interpretation of the relationship between Indian polities and politics and the mechanisms through which the British could maintain control. Anglo-Indian militarism founded itself upon a reading of Indian political and social culture, and the means by which the British could work within these cultural parameters. Therefore, Anglo-Indian militarism can be said to have been partly informed by orientalist thought. Adherents to this militarized ideology of rule worked from the assumption that Indian society was inherently militarized and that the only sound basis for authority in India must continue to rest on the ability to monopolize the means of coercion.

Anglo-Indian militarism was an ideology entered equally into by the civilians and the military. The army was an equal if not senior partner in empire. Nearly all concerned accepted the army's unique identification with the national interest; there was no premeditated destruction or subversion of civilian institutions. This penetration by military values was made easier by the blurring of the boundary between civil and military spheres of authority, seen most clearly in the use of military officers in many civilian posts. Militarism became even further entrenched when it was discovered that it offered an acceptable face to mask over private interests. Personal glory, promotion, and private gain were just some of the advantages of campaigning.[10] A later governor-general confided to his stepson that 'I care little for Indian [i.e. Anglo-Indian] opinions because they are to a certain degree influenced by personal considerations — that is, a certain desire to annex territory and increase officers.'[11]

The hierarchy of military authority in India was constructed on lines similar to that of its political machinery, namely an emphasis on providing as many checks and balances as possible. In both cases, the most pronounced feature was the dual government, the sharing of authority between the East India Company and the British government. In the case of the military forces in India this dual government stood in even sharper relief due to the presence of Crown troops and officers in India. The stationing of these troops in India introduced a third level into the political matrix of Indian rule: the commander-in-chief and his staff at Horse Guards. So long as what was essentially a British force remained outside their control Horse Guards strove to bring the Indian army to heel. It was not simply the Company army that exasperated the Duke of York and his staff; British regular troops in India were in effect leased out to the Company and so largely passed out of Horse Guards' administrative and operational control. In 1813, when the Company's charter was coming up for renewal, the Duke of York had tried to make renewal conditional on the transfer of the Company's army to the Crown.[12] Despite his failure at this time the Duke of York would continue to intrigue to expand his influence over military affairs in India, particularly through the very extensive unofficial communications that he kept up with officers in India. Officers such as Jasper Nicolls were encouraged to send him regular and confidential reports on the state of the army in India.[13]

The Company's charter renewal of 1793 had laid down that the Board of Control was to have ultimate powers over decisions of war and peace.[14] The Company was obliged to present the Board with copies of all correspondence that related to military matters. Furthermore, the Board was entitled to alter any despatches to India on military or strategic affairs without seeking the Company's approval.[15] Even the internal affairs of the Company's army came partially under the British government's scrutiny for the Mutiny Act which governed the internal order of Company regiments was voted in by the British parliament.[16] The influence of the Board of Control, and through it the Horse Guards, was made clear in Thomas Courtenay's evidence before a parliamentary enquiry. He claimed that, 'a very great part of the arrangements concerning the Indian army, its formation, and the allowances to the officers and men, have been the work of the Board.'[17]

The Board not only had to deal with the East India Company when considering military affairs, it had to contend with Horse Guards' persistent poaching on Indian positions and revenues. Charles Wynn reluctantly found himself defending many of the Company's military prerogatives. While he personally would have favoured a unified army under parliamentary control, just as he would have preferred direct British rule, he none the less was highly suspicious of Horse Guards' motives, particularly as he feared that their inroads would lead to intolerable burdens on Indian finances.[18] At a time of reductions to Britain's military establishment, Horse Guards tried to foist more troops onto India as these would then be paid out of Indian revenues. As well, the reductions in the British army following the ending of the Napoleonic Wars had produced a large number of half-pay officers; Horse Guards looked to Indian positions as a means of reducing the intense competition among officers for full-time employment. Of special interest to the king's officers were the very lucrative staff positions on the armies of the Company's Indian allies. These positions were carefully reserved for Company officers and not even Horse Guards' offer of brevet rank for Company officers could induce the Board and the Company to open up such positions to king's officers.[19]

For its part the East India Company strove to preserve as much control over its army as possible. Two objectives dominated its thinking: keeping as many of the military appointments in its hands as possible and the need to keep military costs under control. The former lay at the heart of the Company's lucrative patronage network while the latter was essential to maintaining the Company's fiscal solvency. Given the nature of early nineteenth-century British political culture, the openings offered in India for military cadets, and to a lesser extent civil appointments, should not be underestimated. Though it was illegal to sell these appointments there were some instances of appointments actually being sold with one cadetship fetching £600.[20] Each director could normally expect to have thirteen nominations per year, the chair, deputy chair and president would each have twenty-six.[21] Approximately seventy-five per cent of the appointments were for the army. The president of the Board of Control's nominations, though originally intended as a personal gift, came to be coveted by the rest of the administration. Within days of being made president, Wynn was complaining of the avalanche of requests he had received, particularly from, 'Lady C[onyngham] and the rest of the vermin that haunt the palace.'[22]

A further impediment to the Company's development of a comprehensive military policy was the absence of military experience within the directorate. The only exception to this in the 1820s was George Robinson who had served as military auditor general under Cornwallis and Wellesley. The Court of Director's decidedly civilian and metropolitan outlook conflicted with the more parochial and militarized attitudes that prevailed in India, though they did work together to frustrate attempts by the King's army to poach on their preserve. The Court of Directors also ran afoul of the Board's occasionally more aggressive policies that stemmed from the British government's efforts to harness India's military capacity to British global objectives. To some, however, the Court's lack of military expertise was a blessing. Malcolm was secretly quite pleased at their ignorance as it prevented them from successfully interfering with the operational control of the Indian army.[23]

In seeking to preserve their control of military events in India the Company was assisted by the Duke of Wellington to whom they frequently looked for advice and support. Even the post of military examiner at the Company's training establishment at Addiscombe was filled on Wellington's recommendation.[24] Not only did Wellington provide the Company with recommendations for the senior positions in India, he also obstructed the efforts by Horse Guards to gain greater influence over Indian military matters; 'indeed, the Duke of Wellington paralyzes all HRH's endeavours ... and prevails so far in the cabinet that his [the Duke of York] considerations seem altogether suspended.'[25] Wellington reasoned that the king's troops in India were simply an 'auxiliary force' and were therefore not entitled to any treatment not already agreed upon; even more importantly, Wellington did not see any immediate benefit in the transfer of the Company's troops to Horse Guards' control.[26] King's officers in India already had seniority over Company officers of the same rank as well as a widely recognized social superiority over them.

The day to day supervision of the army in India was vested in the office of the commander-in-chief. Owing to the vast territory administered by the British in India, as well as the perpetuation of the semi-autonomous presidencies of Madras and Bombay, each of the lesser presidencies had their own commander-in-chief who was nominally subject to the higher authority of the commander-in-chief stationed in Calcutta. Their situation was analogous to the relationship between the governor-general and the governors of Madras and Bombay: Company charters had set out the governor-general and commander-in-chief at Fort William as supreme, but had not provided any efficient mechanisms to produce strict subordination. In fact the only explicit provisions for the Bengal commander-in-chief's authority over the Madras and Bombay commanders-in-chief was when he was physically present at their presidencies.[27] Otherwise there was no stipulation for any regular contact and supervision.

The position of commander-in-chief at any of the three presidencies was normally filled by a king's officer though there were some exceptions at Madras and Bombay. In Calcutta the office holder was nearly always a king's officer. In a few instances, where death or incapacity made an interim appointment necessary, a Company officer could hold the post, but in these cases, the officer was not given the accompanying seat on the Supreme Council.[28] Given that the commander-in-chief possessed a great deal of authority over king's troops in India, the British government was extremely reluctant to accept any Company officer for this post. Therefore, although the office was nominally filled by the Court of Directors, subject only to the approval of the British government, the Court of Directors only submitted their nomination after extensive prior discussions with the government. The office itself was much sought after for those who held it were paid very well and received generous allowances. Pay and allowances together totalled nearly £20,000, considerably more than what was paid in Ireland (£3,400), the next best paying command in the British Empire.[29] And like the governor-general, the commander-in-chief also stood to benefit from the patronage opportunities that went with the office, though these were principally confined to field commands for staff positions remained under the governor-general's care. In his two years as commander-in-chief, Lord Dalhousie listed over five hundred requests for his patronage.[30]

The authority of the commander-in-chief was derived from three sources: his commission as commander-in-chief East Indies came from the East India Company, his commission as commander-in-chief of the king's forces in India was a Royal prerogative, and lastly his commission as a member of the supreme council in Bengal. He was answerable to both the Company and the Crown and as these two bodies were often in disagreement the commander-in-chief was left to balance precariously between them. The consequences of the very ambiguous structuring of military authority were widely felt in India. It was noted in Madras that orders issued to the army could come from four distinct authorities: general orders of the governor-in-council to king's and Company troops, general orders of the Bengal commander-in-chief to king's regiments only, general orders from the local commander-in-chief to king's troops in Madras, and general orders from the local commander-in-chief to all troops in the Madras presidency. As one officer described it, this 'creates confusion as to require no mean ability to enable one officer to comprehend which applies to himself' and in many cases, before these orders are straightened out and reach their destination, 'the subject is forgotten, or the object of it is no longer of any moment.'[31]

While the commander-in-chief's authority over the internal management of the army was largely unquestioned, there were significant questions, principally of an operational nature, in which his role was greatly circumscribed. Broad questions of deployment, including the plum appointments to command troops attached to the Company's Indian allies, force strength, and strategic planning were subject to the governor-general's controlling authority. It was recognized that in times of peace all of the commander-in-chief's decisions regarding troop deployments and appointments were subject to the governor-general's approval.[32] This system of checks and balances was obviously conducive to friction and the history of the Indian army provides many examples of disputes between governor-generals (and governors) and commanders-in-chief over each other's respective authority. However, in those instances when the governor-general or governor and the local commander-in-chief established congenial working relations, as was the case between Amherst and Paget and between Munro and Campbell, the resulting harmony could obviate much of the dissension.

The commander-in-chief's effectiveness was further limited by his short term in office. Normally appointed for five years, though sometimes serving for less and often never having been exposed to India before, an incoming commander-in-chief had to depend heavily on the advice and guidance of senior king's and Company officers already in India. This situation proved to be very fertile for the growth of factions and the dissemination of rumours as various groups of officers tried to establish their influence over the commander-in-chief. In particular the adjutant generals of the Company forces and the king's forces, and the Supreme Council's military secretary found themselves to be in very influential positions. Throughout this period the military secretary to the government occupied a powerful position owing to his proximity to the governor-general. This office had been established in 1796, partly to provide the government with advice independently of the army on military matters and partly to supervise the army's budget. For the latter reason, those departments of the army which were most heavily involved in expenditure (commissariat, paymaster and ordnance) were placed under the military secretary's control. By transferring these departments away from the army's direct control and under the Supreme Council, the governor-general gained access to a very large number of appointments. This enhancement of the governor-general's military patronage further strengthened his control over the army.

During the 1820s, the military secretary was Colonel Casement, a Bengal army officer well versed in the intricacies of presidency politics. John Malcolm described him as 'quite competent to the duties of his station', but 'not a man of remarkable talent, and reputed and I believe with justice, to be very prejudiced ... his principal and almost avowed object ... is to advance the interests of the Bengal army.'[33] This opinion seemed to be widely shared, particularly among king's officers who noted that his 'spirit of malice, revenge and persecution' was largely directed at themselves and the commander-in-chief.[34] According to one commander-in-chief, General Barnes, Casement was the principal cause of the breach between the government and the commander-in-chief, and justified his own reluctance to tour outlying garrisons on the grounds that in his absence from the presidency capital, Casement's intrigues against the commander-in-chief's authority would go unchecked.[35]

The two commanders-in-chief who served the longest during this period were Edward Paget (1823-25) and Stapleton Cotton, Lord Combermere (1825-29). Paget was the younger brother of the first Marquess of Anglesey and had earned Wellington's praise for his service at Corunna. After the Napoleonic Wars, Paget had hoped for the command in Ireland, but was beaten to it by a more senior officer. He was then made governor of Ceylon and later accepted the command in India when the Company offered it to him after Wellington's recommendation. His decision to accept with alacrity seems to have been largely financial in inspiration. As commander-in-chief, Paget exhibited a particular dislike of Council activities and for the most part even avoided the army. He actively loathed India and the Indian army: 'My aversion to this country, and to all its concerns so daily increases in growth that I am in a state of constant terror ... of any intention to condemn me to another year's purgatory here.'[36] Consequently, Paget's relations with the Council and the army were for the most part very negative, though he seems to have got on well with Lord Amherst. His own adjutant general described his influence on the army as 'absolutely nil' and control over the army was transferred by default into the hands of the government's military secretary.[37] The army's morale suffered from Paget's antipathy to his duties. One contemporary officer explained that, 'No confidence exists between Sir Edward and the Army ... He is spoken of without any good will by the military ... for he has secluded himself for many months.'[38]

Paget's replacement in 1825, Lord Combermere, initially restored the army's morale and also took a more active role in Council deliberations. Bishop Heber singled out for praise Combermere's tactful handling of the European and Indian officers and men of the Company army who had been shunned by Paget.[39] A cavalry officer of some skill and one who had seen some earlier service in India (1796-1800), there had been some doubts about whether Combermere had the ability to master the political and administrative responsibilities of the office. While Combermere had been recommended by Wellington for the office he had not been Wellington's first choice. Wellington noted of Combermere, 'I do not know where we should find an officer that would command our cavalry as well as he does [but] this is not exactly the person I should select to command the army.'[40] Combermere's principle flaws were his vanity — 'he never goes into battle but in the richest of dresses and puts himself at the head of everything' — and his greed. It was the hopes of financial gain that led him to lobby Wellington incessantly for the Indian appointment for his father's careless habits and his own self-indulgences had reduced the family fortunes by more than £200,000.[41] Initially Combermere did manage to profit from India, particularly from the £60,000 in prize money he was awarded after the capture of Bharatpur, but most of it was lost in the Agency House crashes of the late 1820s. It was also said of him that he enjoyed the company of Indian rulers too much and 'liked to visit those in high stations which is always attributed to a desire to secure presents from them.[42]

In India the difficulties imposed upon the army by its organizational handicaps were accompanied by an even more fundamental conflict, one which originated in disputes over what the army's role was to be. The army in India not only served several different masters, it also served several different and frequently incompatible functions. For ministers of the Crown the Indian army was increasingly regarded as an imperial task force to be deployed throughout the eastern hemisphere in support of British interests. The accelerating penetration of Asia and Africa by British political and commercial interests required a military reservoir that India seemed destined to provide. Beginning with Draper's expedition to Manila (1762) Indian sepoys had been employed in several Asian campaigns. They had served on expeditions to Egypt (1798), Ceylon (1805), Macao (1808), Mauritius (1810), and Java (1810). For the directors of the East India Company the army was a costly drain on Indian finances, in need of urgent retrenchments but providing abundant patronage opportunities in compensation.

The British government also looked to India as a means of subsidizing its military establishment. This calls into question recent studies of the costs of empire that argue that in terms of defence expenditure, the empire cost the British taxpayer more than it paid back.[43] While Britain provided military establishments at little or no cost to colonies such as Canada or Australia, Indian revenues and Indian manpower were diverted to Britain's service. Legislation was in place that obliged the East India Company to garrison India with up to twenty thousand king's troops; the total cost of these troops, including a prorated calculation of their pensions, was to be paid out of Indian revenues.[44] In 1824 the twenty-thousand king's troops in

India amounted to one-quarter of the entire British army. Any troops sent to India beyond this ceiling were only to be paid for by the Company if they had explicitly requested them. Pressure on the Company to take more king's troops grew after the Napoleonic Wars when postwar economies compelled the government to reduce its forces. India offered a solution to this dead-lock; instead of breaking up regiments, they could be sent to India where they would be removed from parliamentary scrutiny and treasury respon-sibility. King's troops stationed in India were not listed in the army esti-mates submitted to parliament and were thus unlikely to raise the ire of the House of Commons. In 1824 the British government considered the need to increase their military establishment by 15,338 men to cover their over-seas commitments; however, the cabinet knew that the House of Commons would not accept such a large increase. The suggested solution was to try and persuade the East India Company to take four extra regiments (5500 men) which would leave only 9,828 men to be approved of by parliament.[45] The outbreak of the Burma War at that time was a fortunate break for the government as it forced the Company to request more troops. The financial advantage of shipping king's troops off to India was even greater than the number of regiments alone would indicate. Regiments sent to India went out with larger establishments than king's regiments serving elsewhere in the empire. A king's regiment in India had a nominal strength of one thou-sand rank and file compared to only 740 in Britain and just over five hun-dred in other colonies.[46] King's regiments in India also had a dispropor-tionately greater number of officers attached to them, between eight and ten extra subalterns and an extra lieutenant colonel.[47] Horse Guards tried to defend this excess by pointing to the mortality rates in India, but they conveniently overlooked conditions elsewhere in the empire. Casualty rates were just as high if not higher in Ceylon, the West Indies and Sierra Leone.[48]

In contrast to the varied ideas held in London of the Indian army's role, soldiers and administrators in India advocated a much more simple and all-encompassing responsibility for the army. By asserting that 'it is an empire of conquest and the hearts of the people are not with us', the argument was put forward and strenuously defended that it was the army and only the army that could ultimately safeguard British India.[49] Soon after his arrival in India William Bentinck was forcibly reminded that 'we deceive ourselves if we ascribe the stability of our power in India to our popularity, and not to our strength.'[50] Malcolm and Munro put the situation just as bluntly; the former argued that the 'army was the only means by which we can preserve India' while Munro insisted that 'Our government rests almost entirely upon the single point of military power.'[51] Fundamental to their calculations was an appreciation of the precariousness of British rule which does seem somewhat out of place given the apparently unstoppable progress of British rule across the subcontinent. The most pessimistic of contemporary officials, Charles Metcalfe, put Britain's position in a stark light: 'There is perhaps no other power on earth, judging from the superficial nature of our tenure, between whose highest elevation and utter annihilation the interval would be so short.'[52]

Working together, John Malcolm, Mountstuart Elphinstone, Thomas Munro and Charles Metcalfe, as well as their fellow travellers John Adam, T.C. Robertson and W.B. Bayley, bombarded officials in London and Calcutta with dire warnings about the tenuous nature of British authority and the urgent need to maintain a strong military presence. Munro and Elphinstone presented their views calmly and persuasively and certainly won the respect of George Canning, the Duke of Wellington and Charles Wynn. Wellington did not need much convincing; his earlier experience in India had convinced him that, 'in that part of the world there is no power excepting that of the sword.'[53] They also made very strong impressions on the Marquess of Hastings and Lord Amherst. Malcolm took his self-appointed role as the school's publicist to extremes and wrote long-winded and frequently unrequested reports. Wynn referred to Malcolm as 'my indefatigable and unsilenceable friend.'[54] Malcolm's incessant efforts to gain an audience were the cause of some mirth and exasperation as well as downright hostility. Jasper Nicolls, like some others around him, was aggravated by Malcolm's vanity and bombastic ways, such as Malcolm's boast that Metcalfe 'belongs to the same school as myself ... of which I have lived to be the acknowledged father'.[55] Nevertheless, Malcolm's publications retained their credibility. According to Malcolm's biographer, 'There was no one to whom the Duke of Wellington wrote more unreservedly than to Sir John Malcolm.'[56] Metcalfe was certainly the most alarmist of the group; his reports on India's security situation were always tinged with a depressing note on how fragile British control was.

The strength of Anglo–Indian militarism was largely derived from the cohesiveness and insularity of the Anglo-Indian community of which the military were the most numerous. One estimate of the European population of India in 1830 lists 36,409 officers and soldiers, 3,550 civilian employees of the East India Company, and 2,149 Europeans not formally attached to the East India Company or to the military.[57] Support for the military and their opinions was very pronounced in the Anglo–Indian press as the army provided not only the bulk of the readership, but in many instances army officers were their principle financial backers. The *Mofussilite* was set up after officers stationed at Meerut, Agra and Delhi put up the required capital.[58] Regarding James Silk Buckingham's *Calcutta Journal*, Nicolls claimed that 'the military are really his supporters, they subscribe largely and they fill his columns with a variety of communications.'[59] According to Hardinge the Anglo-Indian press 'hates peace' for they are 'paid by the army.'[60]

In a political culture such as that of British India it was quite easy for the army to dominate colonial discourse for the army could not only point out the obvious threats to Britain's position in India, but it could also draw upon its own internal cohesiveness and strength. The army in India, like most military institutions, could present an imposing external unity on account of its regimented and hierarchical internal organization. Moreover, the frontier between civilian and soldier was not clearly defined. Many governors and governor-generals had prior military experience, military officers often served in political or administrative positions, civilians manned key positions in the army's administration, and civilians and military officers alike were acutely conscious of their isolation from Indian society. Civilians took pride in mimicking soldiers; many took to wearing military-style clothes.[61] Telling proof of the acceptance of military attitudes by civilians is witnessed in John Adam's obituary. Despite having never served in the army Adam was described by an admiring biographer as being 'as excellent a general as he was a statesman'.[62] Some contemporaries pushed for an even greater assimilation of the two services; one respondent to a parliamentary enquiry suggested that all officials in India, civilian and military, should be placed in a common pool and that after having served ten years in the Indian army, they could then be distributed to civil or military positions depending upon their skills and aptitudes.[63]

Despite the apparent ease with which India had been conquered, officials in Calcutta, Madras, Bombay or any one of the numerous outstations of colonial rule were convinced of the fragility of their rule. This fixation on security shaped local decisions respecting political arrangements and financial policy to a degree beyond either the tolerance or comprehension of the Court of Directors or the Board of Control. The Indian perspective, as set out persuasively by Thomas Munro, was that London's terms of reference had been conceived too narrowly within European standards and did not accord sufficient weight to the nature of Indian political culture. He warned that 'we should not be led away by fanciful theories founded on European models.'[64] Munro particularly indicted attempts by London authorities to conceive of Indian political relations in terms of a balance of power, for in India 'there is no such thing as a Balance of Power amongst

these nations ... their relative power is constantly fluctuating according to
the character of their rulers'[65]. Indian states were in too great a state of flux
for a stable concert of India to be created. Nicolls was in full agreement,
arguing that 'To hope that the Natives of India will attend to promises is in
vain. The first argument they quote is that of Power and in fact it is the only
one.'[66]

The strategic threats with which the British had to contend were frequently divided into internal and external challenges, or ones within its
borders and ones from without. As will be seen, the two forms were not
conceived of as mutually exclusive. With hindsight the most likely external
threat was Imperial Russia. Traces of the Great Game which so preoccupied mid- and late-Victorian proconsuls can be found in the 1820s and
1830s.[67] Amherst commissioned in the mid-1820s a report on Russian designs, partly in response to Russia's war with Persia. While this report did
not identify an immediate threat, it certainly argued that the potential was
there in the not too distant future.[68] Wynn was somewhat receptive to alarmist reports from India.[69] On the other hand, there were others like Bishop
Heber who argued that, 'Russia is regarded as so distant a danger, that,
during the latter years of Lord Hastings' government, and in fact to the
present moment, the army of India has been allowed to melt away.'[70] While
the latter part of this statement is an exaggeration, for the army had not
been cut back that much, Heber's assessment of how the administration
viewed Russia at this time is accurate. By the early 1830s, however, this had
changed considerably. There was an explosion of articles dealing with a
Russian threat in the specialized military press.[71] Moreover, in the person
of Lord Ellenborough who had taken over the Board of Control, we find an
individual much more receptive to the spectre of the Russians descending
through the Khyber Pass.

Other potential troublespots beyond the Company's territories include
Nepal, the Punjab and the Burmese empire. In 1814–15 a brief but bloody
war with Nepal had secured British India's northern frontier. The unan-
ticipated ferocity of Nepali resistance coupled to British mismanagement
not only made for a war that was longer than the British had anticipated, it
also dissuaded local officials from annexing the mountain kingdom.[72] The
Punjab was to become a much more pressing problem. By the beginning of
the nineteenth century the strategic value of the area was recognized. The
fertile plains of the Punjab lay astride the most likely invasion routes from
Central Asia: domination of the region was considered by many to be the
best security against an attack coming down through the passes of the Hindu
Kush. Yet Ranjit Singh's large, well-trained and well-motivated army dis-

suaded most officials from pressing for its annexation, at least for the present. Diplomacy was therefore the preferred method of dealing with this kingdom.[73] British India's eastern frontier with Burma was prior to 1824 largely ignored by decision makers in Calcutta. Although there were frequent flare ups of violence along the frontier, Burma in itself was not viewed as a significant threat, nor were there any anticipated commercial or revenue benefits to be achieved from eastward expansion. Most importantly, from a geopolitical perspective, Burma was seen to lie beyond British India's natural frontiers.[74] Hence, strategic arguments for a more vigorous policy towards Burma were lacking.

The idea of a 'natural frontier' was not new as the term or ones similar to it had been bandied about for the past fifty years. But the early nineteenth century saw a greater commitment to pinning it down more accurately for British policy was then being shaped by a combination of deeper local knowledge and stronger strategic imperatives. A natural frontier in contemporary eyes was one where human and physical geography converged to demarcate clearly between two separate spheres. Topography was certainly the most important determinant, with rivers, mountain chains, or other physical barriers providing the clearest definition. Even this search for a natural frontier was taken to be another sign of the difference between British statecraft and indigenous forms. Walter Hamilton, in his introduction to his gazetteer of India, claimed that, 'no native has yet been brought to understand the advantages we are accustomed to see in a compact territory and uninterrupted frontier.'[75] To the northwest the search for a natural frontier normally involved a choice between the Indus River or the Hindu Kush mountains. The Himalayas were the unquestioned barrier to the north, while to the east, physical obstacles could not be fixed with the same precision. The jungled highlands north and east of Chittagong established a zone, but not a line. Those determined to establish a natural frontier in this region had to call upon social characteristics to fix the boundary between India and Burma with greater precision. It was the different social, political and cultural composition of peoples to the eastwards of these hills that ultimately confirmed it to be a natural frontier, yet it still remained a zone rather than a fixed line.

Implicit within Anglo-Indian militarism was the assumption that expansion was ultimately unstoppable, at least until India's 'natural' frontiers were reached, though there was considerable difference of opinion as to how quickly such expansion should take place. Each push forward established contact with new foes who could not be contained by geography and who appeared even more resolutely opposed to the British than were their previous neighbours. 'Every year has given us an extension of territory and brought us more closely in contact with a more warlike class of neighbours; and though there is a momentary lull, the storm will burst.'[76] The turbulent frontiers that marked out British territory were particularly pronounced in the northwest. History was called upon to demonstrate that in that area the British were 'surrounded by warlike, enterprising and numerous nations; they have been accustomed to look upon India as their prey, and the high road to fortune.'[77] One Indian commentator explained to his British audience that the militarization of north India was the consequence of Mughal rule whose character made it a 'swarming place for the military surplus population of their northern hives.'[78]

Despite the romance of the northwest frontier, internal threats were the most pressing concern for British administrators in India in the aftermath of the campaigns against the Marathas and Pindaris (1817-1819): 'more than half our army is required to preserve internal tranquillity, and support our civil administration'.[79] The British were acutely aware of their alienation from the bulk of the people, particularly in the newly-conquered areas of central and northern India. Few believed that India's domestic tranquillity could be provided for by legislative and administrative actions; India required the 'vigorous street constableship' that only the army could provide.[80] Throughout the first half of the nineteenth century the British had to contend with a great number of risings and demonstrations against their authority. Insurrections in Chota Nagpur in 1820-21, demonstrations in Patna in 1829, and the Kol insurgency of 1831-33 all testified to the turbulent state of Indian society at this time.[81] Anand Yang's recent study of Bihar has calculated that in that province there were 56 riots between 1819 and 1821, 101 between 1822 and 1824, and a further 39 between 1831 and 1833.[82] According to one witness before a parliamentary select committee, 'There is not a large city in India that cannot pour forth, when excited by any cause, a military population of from 5000 to 15,000 armed men.'[83] The same witness cited an incident in Bareilly in 1816 when a crowd of ten to fifteen thousand successfully pried a field piece away from a Company regiment sent in to subdue them. Similar sized crowds could be raised in Benares.

Of great importance in the construction of Anglo-Indian militarism was the insistence that external and internal threats could not be separated, which was precisely what officials in India argued that their counterparts in London tended to do.[84] India's security could only be considered within a broad framework: 'the actual state of our political and military power in India renders it requisite to regard our defence of that country as a whole.'[85] Any challenges from without threatened to trigger revolts in newly-annexed territories. The case for considering external and internal threats as necessarily enjoined was put forth with particular insistence by David Ochterlony: 'the distinction ... between foreign and civil war in India where factions generally extend thro' several states must ever prove virtually nugatory.'[86] Britain's newest acquisitions were fertile grounds for the breeding of discontent, particularly among the local elites who saw their status and power decline.

This commonplace notion that India could only be retained by the sword was confirmed for many by contemporary understandings of Indian society. The model of oriental despotism, with its rigid and arbitrary ordering of society, was advanced to discredit the application of enlightenment values to India. Indian society was viewed as inherently violent and uninformed by European notions of justice and civil society. Contemporary European ideas had little relevance in the eyes of Anglo-Indians, surrounded as they were by 'half-civilised natural antagonists.'[87] War was viewed as the natural state of Indian society; 'plausible and justifiable causes of warfare can never be found wanting in a region so fertile of turbulent and enterprising men as Hindoostan.'[88] In reaching this conclusion about the nature of Indian society the British reaffirmed their arguments by pointing to the nature of the Mughal state. 'The common system of the monarchs of the East, of trusting for support to their despotism, rather than their subjects, was duly admitted and received in India.'[89] Political power was therefore seen as inextricably bound up with military power. It was believed by many that Indian society had no long-standing tradition of civil institutions. To introduce them was an admirable goal, but such a goal was unthinkable unless an impression of overwhelming British strength sufficiently cowed the warlike and turbulent peoples of India. Thomas Munro devoted a great deal of attention to elaborating on how a militarized form of rule could best be implemented. He started with the assumption that civilians were conceived of as 'inherently soft', and therefore more likely to display weaknesses which would only call British legitimacy as well as British resolve into question. 'When the civil officer is in camp it encourages the rebels to hold out — because they always hope that from him they will get terms.'[90]

The violence believed inherent in Indian society was evident in Company territories as well as in the lands of their neighbours. Travellers' accounts attest to the danger lurking throughout rural India thus undermining British claims of having pacified areas under their rule. Susan Bayly has estimated that in the small state of Travancore there were still 150,000 men under arms in 1780.[91] Bishop Heber was advised to arm his servants when he travelled through the northern plains.[92] He found on his travels that rural India had not been demilitarized. Country-made arms were readily available; in Monghyr Heber found that a musket could be purchased for Rs.20 and a brace of pistols cost Rs.16.[93] The situation was even worse in the nominally independent kingdom of Awadh.[94] En route from Allahabad to Kanpur in 1824, Heber reflected that, 'the nation is still one of lawless and violent habits, containing many professed thieves, and many mercenary soldiers, who, in the present tranquillity of the country, are at any instant ready to become thieves.'[95] From Mhow, Heber proclaimed that: 'We were now, indeed, in a country where, till very lately, a fort was as necessary to the husbandmen as a barn in England.'[96] Stronger proof of the level of armed resistance to British rule is offered by the frequent raids made on contingents of British troops marching through Company territories. One officer noted that his European regiment was continually threatened by *dacoits* [gangs of bandits] as it marched from Kanpur to Ghazipur, and that regiments on the march needed further protection from local *chaukidars* [local watchmen].[97] Thefts of jewellery, cash and firearms from European cantonments also attest to the brazen nature of rural opposition to the European presence. It was reported that when Company regiments were temporarily called away from their billets in Awadh, several battalions of troops had to be borrowed from the local ruler to prevent villagers from plundering and torching the vacant barracks.[98]

Ironically, this so-called demilitarization of India tended to have the opposite effect. The conquest and subjugation of Indian states threw many soldiers out of work, while the reduction of the armies of Indian princes reduced employment opportunities in their armies. While we have no accurate figures on just how many ex-soldiers and prospective soldiers existed in India, one contemporary estimated that a half million soldiers were thrown out of work following the defeats of Mysore in 1799 and the Marathas between 1817 and 1819.[99] Later, Sleeman calculated in 1841 that the British were only employing ten per cent of the available military manpower. 'The nine-tenths, who have been disbanded, together with all their families and dependents ... remain for a generation or two in a state of painful transition, longing for some change that may increase the demand for soldiers.'[100] Bishop Heber encountered a Muslim in 1824 who 'had been, after the late pacification of India by Lord Hastings, completely thrown out of work.'[101] Aware of the large numbers of ex-soldiers scattered throughout central and northern India, the government began to try and recruit some of them into their armed forces. It became common policy to take into the army, and particularly into provincial battalions and irregular cavalry units, 'a portion of the vast floating military population of central India', and thereby try and divert these individuals away from a likely career of brigandage and into channels more conducive to the maintenance of British authority.[102] The armies of the princely states were also crucial in sopping up these unemployed soldiers; in fact, the propping up of independent and semi-independent states was partly justified as providing refuges 'to which turbulent and bad spirits may resort, and find some employment.'[103] The princely states of India were in other words a vital safety valve. This policy was only partly successful for supply always outran demand: British armies in India, and those of their Indian allies, could only absorb a small fraction of these ex-soldiers. Furthermore, the irregular cavalry units and provincial battalions which took the majority of these individuals were usually the first corps to be reduced when Company finances dictated economies. Many areas of rural society in India were to remain militarized until much later in the nineteenth century.[104] While this was particularly true for northern and central parts of India, research has also shown that in South India a considerable number of men remained under arms, operating as brigands as well as serving as retainers.[105] The presence of large numbers of disbanded soldiers in areas afflicted with increasing levels of violence, particularly *dacoity* and *thagi*, is certainly not a coincidence.

A militarized form of rule was further justified on the basis that army officers were particularly well-placed to see and understand Indian society. Officers were exposed to Indian society in cantonments and on the march and hence were provided with a window that allowed them to assess local conditions more thoroughly. As Ellenborough put it in a letter to Wellington, 'there is no understanding this country without seeing it; and I am convinced that if it were possible, the Government should be carried on [in] a camp, constantly in movement.'[106] One of the clearest indications of the influence of the army on the daily operations of the colonial state is found in those officials appointed to serve as residents at the courts of Britain's Indian allies or as ambassadors and envoys to independent states. Commonly known as politicals, a great number of these representatives were seconded from the army. Michael Fisher's *Indirect Rule in India* shows clearly how army officers gained the upper hand in many of these appointments.[107] Civilian appointees had only the slightest majority of these posts in 1815; by the late 1830s, the accelerated use of military officers gave the army a clear preponderance of residency appointments. The popularity of army officers in such postings also rested on their cost; military officers could be had at cheaper salaries than civilians.[108] Aside from these pragmatic considerations, the increasing use of military officers can be tied to the shifting ideologies of Company rule. It was no coincidence that the increasing num-

bers of military officers serving as Residents first became noticeable during
the administration of the Marquess of Hastings who was very favourably
predisposed to the army. Favouritism became even more apparent in Madras during Munro's governorship.[109] Munro was a strong advocate of the
despatching of military officers as ambassadors and residents for he believed that military officers were more likely to command the respect of
Indian rulers and their subjects. Even William Bentinck, who was one of
the least susceptible officials to such arguments, justified the employment
of military officers in civil positions in remarkably similar terms. He argued in a letter to Charles Grant that a military officer was a good choice
because he was of a 'mature age ... more active and more accustomed to the
management of natives, and can be sent back to his regiment in case of
misconduct or inefficiency.'[110]An interesting twist to this advocacy of the
army's claims to civilian positions was offered by one writer who argued
that the civil service was 'stimulated by the powerful competition of military aspirants for civil employ.'[111]

Pacification did not rest solely on either the application of force or the
absorption of potential opponents. Even the most militarized administrators realized that there were limitations to what the army could achieve. By
the 1820s a consensus had emerged that set parameters as to where and
when the army could be employed in dealing with local disturbances. In a
city such as Benares, where religious feelings and economic pressures provided considerable potential for rioting, the army was never called for 'except in affairs of real war, or when an active and numerous police is visibly
incompetent to provide for the public safety.'[112] Hence, the emphasis was
on making the army appear as omnipotent as possible. It had to impress
both conquered peoples and neighbouring states of its readiness to act
quickly, vigorously and effectively. Writing to Elphinstone, Munro confided that 'you know that I like a strong force in all new countries not so
much to put down opposition as to prevent it, and to give confidence to all
classes of people.'[113] In particular, the British had to counteract the widespread transmission of rumours and reports of their difficulties. In attest-
ing to the rapidity with which news circulated in India, Heber wrote that
'the leading events of the late war in Europe (particularly Buonaparte's
victories) were often known or at least rumoured among the native merchants in Calcutta before Government received any accounts from England', and he further claimed, perhaps apocryphally, that Londonderry's
suicide was known in Calcutta's bazaars two weeks before official news was
received.[114] Circular letters, rumours and tracts in local dialects were reportedly 'dispersed with a celerity that is incredible'.[115] Sepoys were attentive

to these rumours and 'anything injurious to the fortunes of the Government is listened to with the keenest interest.'[116] The Anglo-Indian community was amazed at just how widespread expressions of discontent were and how difficult it was to counteract them. One guidebook suggested the following to check unflattering impressions of British strength. 'It is considered good policy to create in the natives a profound persuasion of our invincibility, by making much of the notification of a victory obtained by our armies in India or elsewhere.'[117]

Image was just as important as ability. As one officer put it, 'Our strength is in the high opinion the natives entertain of the European character; weaken that opinion and you undermine the foundation of our power.'[118] Few Europeans in India were so deceived as to think that their total population of approximately 30,000 (c.1830) could hold out against a continent-wide revolt, particularly as their army contained five times as many Indians as Europeans. In and of itself, naked force was insufficient to protect the British position in India. This same dilemma was to confront colonial officials later on in Africa and elsewhere in the expanding empire where they too had to concede the impossibility of relying solely upon brute force to secure their aims. And before anyone noticed that the empire had no clothes, it was necessary to construct a new rationale of rule — the 'empire of opinion'. Indians had to be persuaded either of the benefits of colonial rule or the futility of resistance. While there were some Europeans in India who sought safety in the former, it was more commonly the latter that was advocated, at least during the first half of the nineteenth century. As convinced as many officials were of the advantages Indians derived from being placed under their care (which usually numbered security of person and property, exposure to enlightened social, legal, political and economic forms and customs, and the stamping out of barbaric practices), they were not persuaded that the bulk of the Indian population was aware of these advantages. It would take time before Indian opinion accepted these 'truths'. In the meantime, India would have to be treated as a precocious adolescent, with firmness and discipline applied when and where necessary. Hence, this so-called 'empire of opinion' was invoked in a very precise way — that of awe generated by the appearance of military strength. In the words of one pamphleteer, the 'empire of opinion' only has meaning if 'we translate the word opinion into the knowledge that the natives possess of our superior military skill and power.'[119] Any undermining of that fear and respect would dangerously weaken British authority. One of Elphinstone's most severe criticisms of Lord Amherst was that Amherst was too pacific: 'The only grounds we have for fearing disturbances is the particularly mild and quiet character of

Lord Amherst's government.'[120] Perhaps the clearest expression of the importance attached to a constant state of military preparedness was offered in a military report which had been commissioned by Hastings.

> The army in India must always be on a war establishment [because it is needed] to bear up against the barbarous violence — the natural prejudices — and above all, the habitual treachery of the powers with whom we are in a state of constant moral and physical contact.[121]

This commitment to maintaining an image of unquestioned military superiority was frequently used to defend existing army strengths, and where necessary, to advocate for increases. During the 1820s the government in Bombay, faced with constant deficits and pressed to reduce their army as the quickest economy measure, argued that present strengths must be kept up, even if no enemies were apparent, for the simple reason that the size of their army was the surest sign of their strength and resolve.[122] This emphasis on military needs and imperatives should not be interpreted as signifying that officials could not see any further than the immediate safety of Britain's Indian possessions. They were militarized in so far as they believed that there was no other possibility in the short run, but individuals such as Munro, Metcalfe, Elphinstone, Malcolm, Adam and Ochterlony also envisioned a future role for political and social reforms.[123]

The premises which underlined the empire of opinion were also derived from social, political and cultural developments in Britain. Those sent out to India brought with them as part of their baggage the cultural and ideological predispositions of a politically and economically triumphant society. Of these the sacredness of 'character' was repeatedly emphasized. Character in this sense drew heavily upon the ideals of landed British society: it was conservative, loyalist, deeply convinced of the necessity for social hierarchies and suspicious of reform. Service in India catered to the needs of those who could not afford to live as gentlemen in Britain, yet considered themselves to be part of this class. India not only provided the financial means of securing such status, it also opened up the political and military avenues through which the mores and attitudes of this class could be publicly affirmed. Contemporary curricula in the great public schools and the universities of Oxford and Cambridge tended to reinforce these values. 'The emphasis on Greek and Roman authors and ancient history meant a constant diet of stories of war, empire, bravery and sacrifice for the state.'[124] In this cold war of impressions, where the awe and respect of the subjected people was considered crucial, great emphasis was placed on the

British displaying proper and noble behaviour. In this regard both Amherst and Bentinck were unfavourably compared with their predecessors who all projected a proconsular image more successfully. Elphinstone, Prinsep and even the alleged radical reformer John Shore complained of the plainness of Amherst's banquets and the insufficient attention he paid to the pomp with which governor-generals were expected to envelope themselves.[125] The emphasis placed on the symbolic manifestation of character was also transmitted further down the hierarchy.

One of the more interesting developments of this 'empire of opinion' was that peace, if it lasted too long, could prove harmful to British interests. Warfare was increasingly viewed in a proto-Darwinian way. For officers such as Thomas Munro war was credited with positive benefits for it prompted the vitality necessary to growth and survival. 'War is to a nation what municipal government is to particular cities, it is a grand police which teaches nations to respect each other, and humbles such as have become insolent by prosperity.'[126] As well, war was necessary to maintain the army's fighting qualities. Ellenborough recollected after a conversation with Mountstuart Elphinstone that the latter 'seems to dread a long peace in India. We hold everything together by the native army, and we cannot retain them unless we retain the affections of the European officers.'[127] Thomas Munro also subscribed to this view, arguing that because the Indian army was primarily a mercenary force, the need for active service was doubly important for the material rewards of booty and extra pay were often the chief incentives to military service.[128]

Yet the emerging paramountcy of the army was hedged in by carefully crafted safeguards. When the structure of the Company's administration was being set out in the eighteenth century, the possibility of a military takeover was taken very seriously and measures were taken to limit military influence and autonomy. Kegwin's rebellion of 1684, in which Captain Kegwin, commander at Bombay, rallied his troops to bring down the governor after the latter had cut military pay and allowances, was the first instance of overt military resistance to civil authority. In Madras in the 1770s there had been a coup against the government of Governor Pigot in which several army officers were implicated.[129] And while Anglo-Indian society had grown more orderly and less fractious by the beginning of the nineteenth century, apprehensions were still being expressed over the army. One army officer noted that 'there are a great many reasons why the Civil Government in India should have a greater control over the military power than in the other foreign dependencies of Great Britain.'[130] The situation was particularly volatile in Bengal, prompting Elphinstone to observe in

1832 that 'the great problem there has been always to maintain the subordination of the military power to the civil, and to prevent clashing between the Governors and the Commanders-in-Chief.'[131] During Amherst's tenure, reports circulated, later proven to be unfounded, that he was at odds with two successive commanders-in-chief, General Paget and Lord Combermere.[132] While these reports were untrue, later rumours of Bentinck's struggles with his commanders-in-chief were well-founded.

The difficulties of maintaining the subordination of the army constantly irritated the Court of Directors as an overly militarized colonial state in India threatened their political and financial authority over Indian affairs. Statements such as Thomas Munro's 'we always are, and always ought to be prepared for war' were thought to be thinly disguised agendas for expansion.[133] One director reflected that, 'our reliance upon [the army] had induced us on many occasions to adopt measures we should not otherwise have dared to resort to.'[134] The Court was also well aware that many of the arguments of the army and its supporters were wrapped up with hopes of private gain. 'The Indian Army ... naturally looks forward to war and its advantages as a time of promise.'[135]

To maintain at least the appearance of civil supremacy in India, the governor-general was vested with supreme authority over matters both civil and military in India. The commander-in-chief was firmly subordinated to the governor-general; all orders issued by the former were issued 'with the sanction of the governor-general'.[136] To consolidate civilian control even further, the commander-in-chief, despite ranking second in the local hierarchy, was denied the right of succession should the governor-general be prevented from exercising his authority.[137] The governor-general was also invested with the command of the troops at the presidency capital. In the latter case, however, we can clearly see just how complicated civil-military relations could be as discussions continued for several years over whether the governor-general's command over the presidency fort's garrison also covered the king's troops included in it. There was also a considerable difference of opinion over just what constituted the actual extent of the garrison: did it for example also include those troops forming part of the fort guard but cantoned beyond the walls of the fort? For a time, each of the three presidencies devised its own solution to this question.[138] Eventually a compromise was forced on them by Wellington that determined that the governor-general (and governors) were to have command over all troops forming the garrison, no matter where quartered, but that this command was not to include the right of ordering courts-martial.[139]

One solution to this potential conflict between military and civilian authorities was to unite the two offices, making the governor-general the commander-in-chief as well. This was an office often called captain-general. In the past this had been attempted on two occasions — Lord Cornwallis and the Marquess of Hastings — and Bentinck was also made commander-in-chief during the latter part of his term in Calcutta (1833-35). While this provided some temporary relief to the ongoing tensions between the two offices, as a long-term solution it was looked upon with distaste by the Court of Directors and to a lesser extent the Board of Control. Fears were expressed that by uniting the two most powerful offices in one person, the governor-general's natural inclination to pursue an aggressive and expansionary foreign policy would go unchecked.

> From the personal éclat which attaches to the governor-general, as real, or supposed mover of the machine and director of its operations, a stimulus is produced which excites him to military enterprise, and which neither prudence nor principles are always able to check.[140]

[1] Francis Rawdon Hastings, Marquess of Hastings, *The Private Journal of the Marquess of Hastings*, 2nd ed. London: Saunders and Otley, 1858, II, 113-14
[2] Walter Hamilton, *A Geographical, Statistical and Historical Description of Hindostan and the Adjacent Countries*, London: John Murray, 1820, I, xxxix
[3] One recent study of the Company bureaucracy has stressed its divergence from British patterns and priorities, but has also assumed, incorrectly in my mind, a consensus between London and India that was derived from an emphasis on the Company's commercial heritage. As I argue in this chapter and elsewhere in the book, this commercial heritage had been largely jettisoned by the 19th century. Jacob Thiessen, 'Anglo-Indian Vested Interests and Civil Service Education, 1800-1858: Indications of an East India Company Line,' *Journal of World History*, 5(1994): 23-46
[4] Malcolm to Maloney, 8 April 1822, *The Life and Correspondence of Major General Sir John Malcolm*. J.W. Kaye, ed. London: Smith, Elder and Co., 1856, II, 335-36
[5] Malcolm, *Political History*, II, 76
[6] [anon], 'The Military Constitution of our Indian Empire,' *United Services Journal*. (1845, no.3): 237
[7] John Malcolm, *A Political History of India*. II, 245
[8] Munro to Canning, 14 Oct 1820, G.R. Gleig, *The Life of Major General Sir Thomas Munro*, London: Colburn and Bentley, 1830, II, 52
[9] Metcalfe's Memo, nd. (1815/16?), J.W. Kaye, *Life and Correspondence of Lord Metcalfe*. London: , Smith, Elder and Co, 1858, I, 442n
[10] The most recent survey of the history of the East India Company emphasizes the importance of self-interest in perpetuating the militarized forms of rule that were developing in India. While this is an important point, and will be returned to later, too much emphasis on self-interest obscures the even more important

appreciations of Britain's position in India that encouraged and legitimated this emphasis on the army within the broader sphere of the Company's activities. Philip Lawson, *The East India Company; a History*, Harlow: Longman, 1993, 128-31

[11] Hardinge to Walter, 4 March 1846, Henry Lord Hardinge, *The Letters of the First Viscount Hardinge of Lahore to Lady Hardinge and Sir Walter and Lady James, 1844-1847*, Bawa Satinder Singh, ed., Camden fourth series, vol. 32, London: Royal Historical Society, 1986, 157

[12] Scottish Record Office [SRO], York to Melville, 30 Dec 1811, GD 51/3/491

[13] OIOC, Nicolls' Diary, 6 June 1825, MSS Eur F175/32

[14] Section 9, 33 Geo III, c.52

[15] Section 12, 33 Geo III, c.52

[16] The principle legislation which governed troops in the period under review here was most clearly set out in the Mutiny Act of 1824, 4 Geo IV c.81

[17] S.C. on the East India Company, PP, 9(1831/32): 35

[18] Southampton, Wynn to Wellington, 27 Oct 1825, WP1/829/16

[19] OIOC, Nicolls' Diary, 29 March 1823, MSS Eur F175/31

[20] OIOC, Minutes of the Secret Committee, 25 Sept 1822, L/PS/1/13

[21] J.M. Bourne, *Patronage and Society in Nineteenth Century England*. London: Arnold, 1986, 84-5

[22] National Library of Wales, Wynn to Buckingham, 30 Dec 1821, Coedymaen Bundle 21

[23] Malcolm to Major Stewart, nd [1818-1821?], J.W. Kaye, *The Life and Correspondence of Major-General Sir John Malcolm*, London: Smith, Elder and Co., 1856, 2, 360

[24] Southampton, Dickson to Somerset, 24 July 1823, WP1/767/8

[25] OIOC, Nicolls' Diary, 1 July 1824, MSS Eur F175/31

[26] Southampton, Wellington to Bathurst, 26 Jan 1824, WP1/783/10; Wellington to Wynn, 3 Nov 1823, WP1/832/3

[27] S.C. on the East India Company, PP, 13(1831/32): 393-4, 420

[28] S.C. on the East India Company, PP, 13(1831/32), 9

[29] Public Record Office [PRO], Palmerston to Taylor, 2 July 1825, WO 80/1

[30] SRO, Lord Dalhousie, Patronage Book, GD 45/5/90

[31] Evidence of Major General Thomas Pritzler, S.C. on the East India Company, PP, 13(1831/32): 394

[32] OIOC, 'Relative Powers of the Governor-General and Commander-in-Chief in Military Matters,' 29 March 1774, H/MISC 86/23, p.739

[33] Nottingham, Malcolm to Bentinck, 24 Jan 1828, PwJf 1404

[34] OIOC, Gardiner to Nicolls, 10 Nov 1825, MSS Eur F175/49

[35] Nottingham, Barnes to Bentinck, 5 Aug 1832, PwJf 2681

[36] Paget to Lady Paget, 1825, Edward Paget, *Letters and Memorials of General the Honourable Sir Edward Paget*. London: privately printed, 1898, 176-77

[37] Samuel Whittingham, nd, Paget, *Letters and Memorials*, 28-9

[38] OIOC, Nicolls' Diary, 6 Oct 1825, MSS Eur F175/32

[39] Heber to Wynn, 21 March 1826, *Journey*, II, 457

[40] Wellington, quoted in Richard Glover, *Peninsular Preparations*. Cambridge: Cambridge University Press, 1962, 345

[41] Sir Corbet Corbet, quoted in A.I. Shand, *Wellington's Lieutenants*. London:

Smith, Elder and Co., 1902, 413; Nottingham, Combermere to Newcastle, 31 Dec 1827, NeC 5340

[42] OIOC, Nicolls' Diary, Jan 1830, MSS Eur F175/35

[43] While this argument has been around for some time, its most vigorous proponents of late have been L. Davis and R. Huttenback. *Mammon and the Pursuit of Empire: the Political Economy of British Imperialism, 1860-1912*, Cambridge: Cambridge University Press, 1986, and P.K. O'Brien, 'The Costs and Benefits of British Imperialism 1846-1914,' *Past and Present*, 120(1988): 163-200.

[44] Section 87, 53 Geo III c.155

[45] Southampton, Taylor to Wellington, 16 Dec 1824, WP1/807/17

[46] PRO, 'Sketch of the Distribution of Royal Troops,' March 1826, WO 80/1

[47] S.C. on the East India Company, PP, 13(1831/32): 7

[48] For a fuller discussion of this, see Peter Burroughs, 'The Human Cost of Imperial Defence in the Early Victorian Age,' *Victorian Studies*. 24(1980): 7-32; and Philip Curtin, *Death by Migration*. Cambridge: Cambridge University Press, 1989

[49] Metcalfe to Court, 6 March 1830, J.W. Kaye, *Metcalfe*, 2, 104.

[50] Nottingham, Thomas Campbell Robertson, Memo on the Bengal Army, 13 Dec 1827, PwJf 2584

[51] Malcolm, *Political History*, 2, 201; T.H. Beaglehole, *Thomas Munro and the Development of Administrative Policy in Madras, 1792-1818*. Cambridge: Cambridge University Press, 1960, 116

[52] OIOC, Metcalfe to Amherst, 8 June 1824, MSS Eur F140/93

[53] Wellington's Letter, 13 Oct 1803, G.H. Francis, *Maxims and Opinions of Field Marshal the Duke of Wellington*. London, 1845, 86

[54] NLW, Wynn to Southey, 27 Oct 1823, 4815D

[55] Kaye, *Malcolm*, II, 394-95

[56] Kaye, *Malcolm*, I, viii

[57] P.J. Marshall, 'British Immigration into India in the Nineteenth Century,' *European Expansion and Migration*, P. Emmer and M. Mörner, eds., Leiden: Brill, 1992, 182

[58] John Lang, 'Starting a Paper in India,' *Household Words*, 7(26 March 1853): 94-6

[59] OIOC, Nicolls' Diary, 21 May 1820, MSS Eur F175/25

[60] Hardinge to Sarah, 6 Feb 1847, *Letters of the First Viscount Hardinge of Lahore*, 207

[61] This same trend has been noticed for Britain's elite during the same period. See Linda Colley, *Britons*, 185-87

[62] C. Lushington, *A Short Notice of the Official Career and Private Character of the Late John Adam*. Calcutta: privately printed, 1825, 4

[63] Evidence of David Hill, S.C. on the East India Company, PP, 12(1831/32): 32

[64] BL, Minute by Munro, 31 Dec 1824, Add MS 22074

[65] Southampton, Munro to Wellington, 9 Jan 1826, WP1/846/8

[66] OIOC, Nicolls' diary, 31 may 1817, MSS Eur F175/20

[67] There has been a great deal of recent scholarship on the so-called 'great game'. In particular, see Malcolm Yapp, *Strategies of British India: Britain, Iran and Afghanistan, 1798-1850*. Oxford: Oxford University Press, 1980; as well as Edward Ingram's now-complete trilogy. *Britain's Persian Connection, 1798-1828;*

Prelude to the Great Game in Asia, Oxford: Clarendon, 1992, *Commitment to Empire: Prophecies of the Great Game in Asia, 1797-1800*. Oxford: Clarendon, 1981, and *The Beginnings of the Great Game in Asia, 1828-1834*. Oxford: Clarendon, 1979. A useful summary has recently been provided by Malcolm Yapp, see his 'British Perceptions of the Russian Threat to India,' *Modern Asian Studies*, 21(1987): 647-65

[68] OIOC, Lt. Col Macdonald, 'Memo on the Designs of the Russians,' nd, MSS Eur F140/96(b)

[69] NLW, Wynn to Henry Williams Wynn, 4 Oct 1826, 4816D

[70] Reginald Heber, Bishop of Calcutta. *Narrative of a Journey through the Upper Provinces of India, from Calcutta to Bombay, 1824-1825*. London: John Murray, 1846, II, 198

[71] The *United Services Journal* (the successor to the *Naval and Military Magazine*) in particular ran many articles on potential invasions from the northwest. See for example, [anon], 'On the Russian Conquests in Asia,' *United Services Journal*. 3(1830): 28-31; [Alfred], 'Russia and British India,' *United Services Journal*. 9(1832): 14-16; (J.M.), 'On the Overland Invasion of India,' *United Services Journal*. 12(1833): 145-67; [a Company's Officer], 'India, Russia and Persia,' *United Services Journal*. 16(1834): 1-16

[72] For a detailed study of this war, see John Pemble, *The Invasion of Nepal; John Company at War*, Oxford: Clarendon Press, 1971.

[73] For a fuller discussion of this, see Yapp, *Strategies of British India* and the essays in Edward Ingram, *In Defence of British India; Great Britain in the Middle East, 1775-1842*, London: Cass, 1984

[74] H.T. Prinsep, *A Narrative of the Political and Military Transactions of British India, under the Administration of the Marquess of Hastings, 1813-1818*, London: John Murray, 1820, 448

[75] Walter Hamilton, *Geographical, Statistical and Historical Description of Hindostan*, I, vii

[76] [anon], 'The Military Constitution of our Indian Empire,' *United Services Journal*. (1845, no.3): 244

[77] Lt. Col Walker to B.S. Jones, May 1818, S.C. on the East India Company, PP, 14(1831/32): 322

[78] [James Silk Buckingham], 'The British in India,' *Westminster Review*, 4(1825): 285

[79] Evidence of Captain Macan, S.C. on the East India Company, PP, 13(1831/32): 151. Captain Macan had served as interpreter to the commander-in-chief

[80] [W.D. Arnold], *Oakfield, or Fellowship in the East*. 1854, reprint, Leicester: Leicester University Press, 1973, I, 118

[81] K.K. Datta, *Anti-British Plots and Movements before 1857*, Meerut: Meenakshi Prakeshan, 1970, 23-38

[82] Anand Yang, *The Limited Raj: Agrarian Relations in Colonial India, Saran District, 1793-1820*, Berkeley: University of California Press, 1989, 213

[83] Evidence of Captain Macan, S.C. on the East India Company, PP, 13(1831/32): 151

[84] Malcolm, *Political History*, II, 70

[85] S.C. on the East India Company, PP, 13(1831/32), 454

[86] Ochterlony to Court, 1825, David Ochterlony, *Selections from the Ochterlony*

Papers (1818-1825) in the National Archives of India, Calcutta: University of Calcutta, 1964, 434

[87] British Library [BL], Col. Young, Military Report, 1820/21, Add MS 38518. The long-term ramifications of these ideas for British rule have been discussed in Bernard S. Cohn, 'Representing Authority in Victorian India,' *The Invention of Tradition*, Eric Hobsbawm and Terence Ranger, eds., Cambridge: Cambridge University Press, 1983

[88] B.S. Jones, *Papers relative to the Progress of British Power in India*, London: 1832, 196

[89] [anon], 'Memoirs of the Emperor Jahangueir,' *Colburn's United Services Journal*. 2(1829): 203

[90] OIOC, Munro to Elphinstone, 12 Dec 1824, MSS Eur F88/9/F/26

[91] Susan Bayly, 'Hindu Kingship and the Origins of Community: Religion, State and Society in Kerala, 1750-1850,' *Modern Asian Studies*, 18(1984): 376.

[92] Heber, *Journey*. I, 135

[93] Heber, *Journey*, I, 135

[94] Heber, *Journey*, I, 207

[95] Heber, *Journey*. I, 193

[96] Heber, *Journey*, II, 23

[97] [A King's Officer], 'Sketches of Military Life in India,' *United Services Journal*, 24(1837): 342

[98] Evidence of Captain Macan, S.C. on the East India Company, PP, 13(1831/32): 152

[99] [G.R. Gleig], 'The Indian Army,' *Edinburgh Review*, 97(1853): 195

[100] Major W.H. Sleeman, *On the Spirit of Military Discipline in our Native Indian Army*. Calcutta: Bishop's College Press, 1841, vi-vii

[101] Heber, *Journey*, I, 198

[102] BL, Col. Young, Military Report, 1820/21, Add MS 38518; OIOC, Minute by the Commander-in-Chief (Paget), 15 Dec 1824, H/MISC/665/2

[103] Evidence of W.B. Bayley, S.C. on the East India Company, PP, 12(1831/32): 45

[104] Evidence of this is provided by William Sleeman's accounts of his tours through Awadh, see William H. Sleeman, *Rambles and Recollections of an Indian Official*, 1844 Reprint. V.A. Smith, ed. Karachi: Oxford University Press, 1973

[105] See Dharma Kumar, 'The Forgotten Sector: Services in the Madras Presidency in the First Half of the Nineteenth Century,' *Indian Economic and Social History Review*, 24(1987): 367-93

[106] Law, Edward, Lord Ellenborough, *A History of the Indian Administration of Lord Ellenborough*, Charles Abbot, Lord Colchester, ed. London: Bentley, 1874, 343

[107] Michael H. Fisher, *Indirect Rule in India: Residents and the Residency System, 1764-1857*, Delhi: Oxford University Press, 1991, 75

[108] Fisher, *Indirect Rule*, 76-77

[109] Fisher, *Indirect Rule*, 87

[110] Bentinck to Grant, 21 Dec 1832, *Correspondence*, I, 979

[111] J. Keane, 'Anglo-Indian Mufasal Life in the Last Generation,' *Calcutta Review*, 66(1878): 714

[112] Heber, *Journey*, I, 183

[113] OIOC, Munro to Elphinstone, 5 Aug 1821, MSS Eur F/88/9/F/26

[114] Heber, *Journey*, II, 228

[115] S.C. on the East India Company, PP, 9(1831/32): 290

[116] Sita Ram, *From Sepoy to Subedar; being the Life and Adventure of Subedar Sita Ram*, 1873, reprint, James Lunt, ed. London: Macmillan, 1970, 73

[117] [Anon], *The Subaltern's Logbook*. London: 1828, 225

[118] S.C. on the East India Company, PP, 13(1831/32), lv

[119] [Colonel Firebrace], 'A Chapter in the History of John Company,' *United Services Journal*, 3(1844): 34

[120] OIOC, Elphinstone to Grant, 2 Feb 1824, MSS Eur F88/9/E/25

[121] BL, Col. Young, Military Report, 1820/21, Add MS 38518

[122] OIOC, Elphinstone to Adam, 4 March 1825, MSS Eur F109/E; Elphinstone to William Elphinstone, 13 June 1821, MSS Eur F89/1/B/10

[123] The less pragmatic aspects of the Wellesley kindergarten's programme for India has been thoroughly explored in Martha McLaren, 'From Analysis to Prescription: Scottish Concepts of Asian Despotism in Early-Nineteenth Century British India' *International History Review*, 15(1993): 469-501

[124] Linda Colley, *Britons*, 167-68

[125] OIOC, Elphinstone to Adam, 26 May 1823, MSS Eur F109/F; Prinsep's Diary, nd, MSS Eur C97/2; Shore's Diary, 17 March 1827, MSS Eur E307/2

[126] Munro to sister, 4 Oct 1795, quoted in: 'The Life of Sir Thomas Munro,' *Colburn's United Services Journal*. 4(1830): 592

[127] Ellenborough, *Political Diary*, II, 62

[128] OIOC, Thomas Munro, Draft Notes on the Strength of the Madras Army, 1820, L/MIL/5/390/132a

[129] H.D. Love, *Vestiges of Old Madras*. London: John Murray, 1913, III, 84-112. Madras would continue to be perplexed by civil-military conflicts that would peak in 1783. See G.J. Bryant, 'The East India Company and the British Army: the Crisis at Madras in 1783,' *Journal of the Society for Army Historical Research*, 62(1984): 13-27

[130] [An Old Indian]. 'The Indian Army,' *United Services Journal*. 18(1835): 310

[131] Elphinstone to Villiers, 19 Aug 1832, T.E. Colebrooke, *Life of Mountstuart Elphinstone*. London: John Murray, 1884, 320

[132] Chester Record Office, Wynn to Combermere, 21 Dec 1827, CR/72/29/161; Amherst to Combermere, 7 June 1827, CR/72/29/160

[133] Munro to Canning, 14 Oct 1820, Gleig, *Munro*, II, 52

[134] Nottingham, Ravenshaw to Bentinck, 8 Aug 1829, PwJf 1910

[135] Capt. J. Sutherland, *Sketches of the Relations Subsisting between the British Government and the Different Native States*, London: London: 1833, 1

[136] [anon], 'The Military Constitution of our Indian Empire,' *United Services Journal*. (1845, no.3): 413

[137] Section 30, 33 Geo III c.52

[138] Southampton, Wellington to Wynn, 21 Aug 1824, WP1/799/7

[139] OIOC, Courtenay to Dart, 13 May 1825, F/2/8

[140] William Huggins, *Sketches in India Treating on Subjects Connected with the Government, Civil and Military Establishments*, London: John Letts, 1824, 11

4. THE MILITARY RESOURCES OF THE GARRISON STATE

> The Indian Army forms, perhaps, the most extraordinary spectacle on which the eye of the philosopher has ever rested. Composed almost exclusively of natives, none of whom are ever permitted to rise to offices of rank or trust, it has ensured to England, for not less than seventy years, the undisputed sovereignty over a tract of country incalculably more extensive than herself.[1]

The army in India, despite being outwardly similar to most contemporary European armies, was indeed an 'extraordinary spectacle'. It was not only one of the largest armies in existence, numbering well over 200,000 when all the various corps are tallied together, but the bulk of the fighting forces was composed of local Indian volunteers who served under officers recruited and paid for by a commercial company. Contemporaries who looked upon the Indian army were carefully warned to shed any preconceptions that they might have had. 'The military constitution of India, its field of action, its prejudices and its wants, are so different from those of the army of any other nation, that persons who reason upon analogy in judging of its operations must be continually leading themselves into error.'[2]

The term 'Indian army' is somewhat of a misnomer for the British in India had several armies to call upon. Each of the three presidencies had its own army; there were king's troops serving in all three presidencies; and there were the armies of British client states in the subcontinent. There were very real and substantial differences between each of these armies. As Wellington noted about the presidency armies, 'All three armies differ in their discipline, appearance, mode of doing duty, etc., not only because they are different armies and paid at different rates, but because they are composed of people of different nations.'[3] Each of the armies had its own unique genealogy and reflected its local conditioning both in terms of the troops it recruited and its internal organization. While the differences between the three armies were for the most part pragmatic responses to local conditions, these differences would over time consolidate into well-protected traditions, emphasizing peculiarities at the expense of any overall unity. The differences between Company and king's forces were equally real and were kept alive by mutual jealousy and suspicion. Social differentiation was at work here. Company officers exchanged better financial prospects for reduced prestige while king's officers, though possessing greater social and professional status, envied the prosperity of Company officers. There was, however, one aspect common to all components of the army in India. European soldier and Indian sepoy, Company officer and king's officer, they all were united in the pursuit of personal gain, whether that meant private fortune or improved social standing. The army in India was therefore a mercenary army to a much greater extent than most other contemporary armies. In the past, self-interest had noticeably interfered with the army's efficiency as officers and soldiers placed their own needs above those of their employer. While such traits had not completely disappeared in the nineteenth century, they were very much on the wane.[4] In effect, a compromise had been worked out. The worst excesses of self-interest had been exchanged for better conditions of service, and when coupled to the officers' emerging sense of a professional calling, the needs of the service and that of the individual had begun to converge. These then are the fundamental characteristics of the army in India. It was impressive in terms of numbers and generally successful on the battlefield. Yet it was plagued by internal dissent and contradictions, thus calling into question explanations for imperial dynamics that stress a common outlook and unity of purpose. It was also, as many suspected, a two-edged sword, capable of wounding its master as easily as it could hurt the enemy.

That the Indian army was divided into three separate Presidency armies was in part the consequence of historical traditions; that it was perpetuated was a strategic decision. Despite the greater efficiency and economic savings that could be achieved by integrating the three armies, the military forces of India would continue to be divided up until 1895 as a safety measure. By keeping three distinct armies the British hoped to forestall dangerous pan-Indian combinations by 'using one to bridle the other.'[5] For many, this strategy was shown to be farsighted in the rebellions of 1857–58 when outright mutiny did not erupt in the Madras and Bombay armies.

The European component of the military forces available consisted of Europeans serving as officers in sepoy regiments, and the officers and rank and file of the approximately twenty-four regiments of European infantry (eighteen king's regiments and six Company regiments) plus two regiments of king's heavy cavalry. Standard rates of pay had been established to ensure that officers and soldiers would receive the same basic pay no matter what presidency they served in or whether their commission came from the king or from the Company. Despite these precautions European officers and soldiers in the subcontinent were riven by faction. Besides the social distinctions between Company and king's commission holders, inequalities were introduced through differential access to military offices and the varying scales of allowance offered in each presidency to the Europeans serving there. Bengal was the most generous, offering field pay (*batta*) in some cantonments as well as more lucrative command, lodging and transport allowances. These were to prove a constant source of irritation for European officers in Madras and Bombay, especially as the cost of living was less in the Bengal presidency.[6] The mutiny of some Madras officers in 1809 was caused in part by their resentment of what they believed to be the preferential treatment given to their counterparts in Bengal.[7]

Relations between Company officers and king's officers were especially strained. A sense of social inferiority pervaded the Company's officer corps, largely due to their association with a commercial company. King's officers played on this, with one of them summarizing their perspective in very clear terms:

Now, I need scarcely to observe, that the servants of His Majesty, putting it out of the question that they are more efficient or useful, must always be of a higher rank than those of a body of *mercantile subjects*, however respectable.[8]

The idea that Company's officers were not as respectable as king's officers was carried over into domestic society. Company officers could not compete with king's officers as far as status was concerned. This was made very clear in contemporary writings. For example, in Thackeray's *The Newcomes*, we are told that, 'Rosey's father was a King's officer, not a Company officer, Thank God.'[9] The diminished status of Company officers was also the result of what was commonly viewed as their less respectable origins. Officers in the Company service were more likely than king's officers to be drawn from the middling classes: only four per cent of officers in the Company service could claim an aristocratic background, nineteen per cent hailed from the landed gentry and the remainder were from the middling and professional classes. In contrast, twenty-one per cent of king's officers were members of the aristocracy, thirty-two per cent came from the landed gentry and only forty-seven per cent were from middle class or professional backgrounds.[10] Company officers tended to be the sons of the minor gentry, professionals, merchants, and Company officials. This trend was reinforced by the custom of officers' sons following their fathers into the Company's army.

Tainted by their commercial association Company officers were further insulted by what effectively amounted to a disbarment from the various awards and honours open to king's officers. Only in exceptional circumstances were Company officers ever elevated to important field commands, and it was extremely rare to find any of them being made commander-in-chief. Such honours as the Bath were only grudgingly extended to Company officers, and even then they were only eligible for the two lowest grades.[11] Their grievances were further aggravated by the custom of a king's officer outranking a Company officer when they each held the same nominal rank. Company officers were constantly being reminded of their dubious pedigree; one complained that, 'we are deemed military quacks, unlicensed pretenders to the science of war.'[12]

The Company officer's sense of inferiority was partly alleviated by his realization that there were more avenues of personal gain open to him. Prospective Company officers were informed by one handbook that 'in no service of the world are the pay and allowances upon so liberal a scale as that of the East India Company.'[13] For example, if a captain was appointed deputy assistant commissary general, he could more than double his base salary (from just under £40 per month to over £90). Even more lucrative positions were available with the armies of the Company's Indian allies. These were only open to Company officers. Captains in Hyderabad commanded what amounted to brigades and received Rs.2750 a month instead of the Rs.411 that was paid to captains doing regimental duty in Bengal.[14] The exclusion of king's officers from most administrative postings was not simply done to placate Company officers. The Company knew that their officers were more committed to staying on in India; king's officers could be reposted at any time. Furthermore, the Company in theory could depend more upon the loyalty of their own officers, as well as their familiarity with Indian conditions, than they could from king's officers.

Despite their enhanced social and professional standing, king's officers had their own set of grievances. Foremost among these was the sense that they were excluded from the most lucrative employments in India, particularly staff postings and service in the armies of the Company's Indian allies. Complaints were made that 'the opportunity for officers of the King's army becoming rich from service in India are rare to those that formerly presented themselves'[15] Some solace was given in the form of divisional and field commands; king's officers had a near monopoly on these.[16] The three choicest ones in terms of political importance and numbers of troops under their command, Meerut, Kanpur and Fort William, were nearly always in the hands of king's officers. Furthermore, service in India, despite restrictions on the posts open to king's officers, was still viewed as lucrative. Nicolls' comment that 'five years in India would be worth ten years anywhere else' could just as easily have been uttered by any other king's officer serving in India.[17] The resentment of king's officers in India was relative; they were certainly better off than their colleagues elsewhere in the empire though they chaffed at what they saw were the even more rewarding opportunities for Company officers. Discontent was to remain high within the king's army, and their grievances played an important role in shaping Horse Guards' intrigues against the Company.

The often derisive comments directed at Company officers by their counterparts holding the king's commission not only reflect the latter's acute consciousness of status, but it was also an attempt to mask over the impression that the Company officers treated their responsibilities in a more professional way, especially after the reforms of the late eighteenth century.[18] Arguably service in the Company's army was more of a career than that of the king's army. Officers enlisting in the Company's service did so in the knowledge that this was a long-term commitment to serving in India. Once in India officers of even relatively junior rank, captains for example, could find themselves exercising independent field command. Certainly officers in India tended to have much more responsibility thrust on them than was the case in the king's army. This led to arguments that Company officers were more phlegmatic than their counterparts in the king's service. 'He enters the army to be paid, not to spend money. He enters the army to serve, not to display a gaudy uniform and lounge away his life in country quarters or at a club.'[19] The pursuit of private fortune and military professionalism were not necessarily antithetical. Self-interest might on occasion undermine military efficiency, but it can be argued that good salaries and the prospects of better appointments encouraged officers to do their jobs better, just as prize money was considered to incite troops and officers to be more aggressive.

King's officers, on the other hand, often arrived in India with attitudes and assumptions that were not well designed for Indian service. Their baggage generally included European military and social preconceptions. Many proved to be insensitive to the very different conditions that they encountered, and thus they tried to superimpose their European-inspired expectations upon an unyielding environment. As early as 1810 the president of the Board of Control was complaining of this mental inflexibility. 'There exists in the minds of both his Majesty and the late commander-in-chief, and perhaps I may add the whole of the king's officers, violent prejudices and very exaggerated opinions with regards to the Indian army.'[20] Western strategical, tactical and organizational doctrines were applied with disappointing results. Particularly common amongst king's officers was their inability to conceive of sepoys in terms other than those with which they understood their own British rank and file.[21] In the long run these prejudices would encourage the growing tendency to disparage sepoys.

In spite of all these differences between king's and Company officers, there were several striking similarities. Chief among these was that both chose to serve in India for mainly pecuniary reasons. A level of financial desperation or avarice was necessary to persuade officers to suffer exile to such an inhospitable climate, especially when the average tour of duty was up to twenty years in the case of king's officers and even longer for those in the Company's service. Self-interest, embracing officers of both services, figured prominently in such descriptions of Anglo-Indian military life as *Oakfield; or Fellowship in the East*.[22] The other pronounced similarity was that officers in both services demonstrated on numerous occasions wilful streaks of independence. Officers were quick to take offence at any slight, real or imagined, and in the very fluid structure of political authority, tended to act upon their grievances. General Edward Paget warned the Select Committee that, 'a spirit of independence prevails amongst the officers which is totally inconsistent with our ideas of military discipline.'[23]

In seeking their fortunes in India, officers were unwittingly helped by the Court of Directors. The Company's reluctance to send sufficient numbers of officials to India meant that a large number of officers were continually having to be seconded from their regiments to fill staff postings. The incentive to take up non-regimental offices was encouraged by the better rates of pay attached to these offices as well as the slowness of promotion and sheer monotony of regimental duties. The Company army operated on a strict policy of promotion by seniority. While this overcame many of the difficulties associated with the purchase system in use in the king's army, it also meant that officers could wait years before they stood any chance of promotion. Statistics prepared for the Board of Control substantiated Company officers' grievances at the slowness of promotion. They revealed that on average it took fourteen years to rise from lieutenant to captain, twelve more years for a majority, and a further five and a half years to make lieutenant-colonel.[24] Ten years' later the prognosis was even more bleak. In 1831 forty-eight years was considered to be the time between initial appointment as an ensign and arrival at a colonelcy.[25] By that time an officer had not only lost out financially, he might also be physically worn out, even senile. Staff or political service were therefore easy ways to escape the promotion trap. Charles Napier complained in 1853 that 'the officers looked at their regiments merely as stepping stones to lucrative civil employment.'[26] When an officer was appointed to a political or staff position his vacancy was not filled and he continued on the regimental establishment from whence he drew his basic salary.

While this system obviously saved the Company money by subsidizing their administration through regimental budgets, it stripped many regiments of considerable numbers of their officers and in part counteracted the growth of professionalism as far as regimental duties were concerned. The situation at times became critical: in 1823, one regiment in Bengal was so short of officers that six of its ten companies were commanded by native officers (the regulations had intended that each company would be under the command of a European captain).[27] Looking at the army as a whole, only thirty-five per cent of the officers in the Bengal army were with their regiments in 1820, and though efforts to improve this situation resulted in forty-nine per cent of the officers serving in the regiments in 1825, it had fallen back to forty per cent by 1830.[28] While some of these absences were no doubt due to officers away on furlough, the clear majority of cases were caused by secondment from the regiment. The same problem existed in the other armies: in Bombay roughly forty-three per cent of its officers in 1828 were performing staff or political duties, and a further seventeen per cent were ill or on furlough.[29]

To British eyes the principle source of their strength in India lay in the European rank and file. Even though the bulk of the troops serving in India were locally raised, persistent doubts about the loyalty of Indian troops, as well as a growing belief in the inherent superiority of European soldiers, meant that ultimately it was the Europeans who were looked upon as the bedrock of British power. There were some dissenting voices, but as the nineteenth century progressed, they tended to be drowned out by a chorus of racial characterizations that rendered British troops both morally and physically superior to the Indian sepoy. It was argued that the sepoy 'will be found inferior, as a skirmisher, in boldness, activity and energy; but, perhaps, he surpasses [the European soldier] in intelligence.'[30] Claims that the sepoys were inferior in terms of their military skills to the European soldiers are not borne out by the records. Detailed reports on ball practice at the large cantonment at Meerut in the late 1820s indicate that some sepoy regiments were as proficient as their European counterparts. The top four scoring regiments included two native infantry regiments as well as one European and one Gurkha regiment.[31] Nevertheless, prevailing assumptions about the superiority of Europeans took an increasingly tighter hold on officers and administrators in India. Even the staunchest defenders of the sepoys conceded that sepoys were not the equal of Europeans, and that ultimately this was to Britain's advantage: 'I well know the superiority of my countrymen, and hope it may ever continue, as on that, indeed, hinges the permanence of our rule.'[32] As this last quote suggests, belief in the alleged 'inferiority' of the sepoy emerged in part as a means of reassuring the British in India that their superiority was unchallenged for the time being.

One issue that continually bedevilled military and political authorities in India was what should be the safe ratio between European troops and Indian sepoys. Despite the generally passive loyalty of the sepoys, the British were conscious that as mercenaries the sepoys' loyalty could not be taken for granted. In 1800 it was thought that one European to every four or five sepoys was sufficient.[33] Twenty years later growing fears of sepoy disloyalty, fed in part by the mutinies in 1806 at Vellore and 1816 in Java, led to arguments that tended to cluster around a ratio of one European for every three sepoys.[34] Neither of these figures, however, proved to be practical. The cost of bringing in substantially more European rank and file was more than the Company was willing to bear. Europeans were on average twice as expensive as sepoys, and because of their higher mortality rate they had to be replaced more frequently. It was estimated that in Bengal a European soldier annually cost £60 whereas a sepoy only cost £30.[35] There were also limits on the numbers of Europeans who could be brought immediately into service for reinforcements from Britain were at least eight months away. In an emergency a sepoy regiment could be raised and made fit for service in just over half that time.

As the army's elite force European soldiers were carefully controlled, partly to preserve their health and fighting qualities and partly to maintain their discipline, European troops were rarely deployed on harassing duties or menial tasks, such as internal policing, protecting revenue collectors, or guarding treasure convoys. These were left to sepoy regiments. Edward Paget declared:

The fact is that our European troops are kept from necessity as well as from choice with all the fare and management of a racing stud, only to be brought forth when a King's plate or gold cup is at stake, all the posting and ploughing and the laborious drudgery is executed by the native troops.[36]

Fear for the discipline of European troops was an important restriction on their use. Concern was expressed over the possibility that European troops, if let out of their barracks, would run amok in local villages. This meant that not only were they barred from performing many duties, but they were also closely guarded in their barracks by sepoy regiments stationed close by for that purpose. One respondent to the enquiry into corporal punishment in the army that was conducted in Britain reported that 'all European troops have native troops to watch them, and to prevent their going out of their cantonments.'[37] Consequently European troops rarely saw much activity unless a war broke out.

European soldiers took two forms: regiments provided out of Britain's military establishment and those regiments raised specifically by the East India Company. The largest number was supplied by the king's regiments stationed there. The 1813 charter obliged the Company to pay for the services of at most twenty-thousand king's troops, unless more were specifically requested. Sixteen regiments, including two regiments of dragoons intended to supply India's need for heavy cavalry, were normally deployed to India. At the end of the eighteenth century the majority of these regiments were stationed in the Madras presidency owing to the increased likelihood of conflict in its territories. However, with the subjugation of Mysore (1789-99), British India's most vulnerable frontier shifted northwards to encompass the Maratha territories of Central India and any potential challenger emerging along the northwest frontier. Madras, however, continued to be a popular place to station European troops mainly because of its more salubrious environment. The European mortality rates in Madras were only 4.5 per cent per annum as compared with 7.6 per cent in Bengal.[38] As a result there was by 1823 a rough parity in the numbers of king's regiments stationed in Bengal and Madras. The number of European regiments stationed in Bombay was never as great, partly because of Bombay's more troubled finances, but principally because its territories were not deemed to be as threatened.

King's regiments sent to India normally went there on a twenty year tour of duty. Given the high mortality rates in India these regiments had to be constantly replenished. While some were brought up to strength by drafts sent from Britain, a great number of regiments were repopulated with volunteers agreeing to stay on when their own regiments were reposted either to Britain or other colonies. It was estimated by one king's officer that among regiments ordered to leave India three quarters of their troops willingly volunteered to transfer to those king's regiments staying on in India.[39] Aside from a bounty of £3, the chief incentive for some soldiers to volunteer appears to be the fact that many had contracted either marriages or more casual liaisons with local women. The Indian mistresses and children of those soldiers who chose to leave India faced a very bleak future. There was no provision to let them travel to Europe or to another colony, and many were forced by poverty to look to other Europeans for support. Bentinck lamented that in most cases 'they were turned over en masse to the relieving regiment.'[40] Those few soldiers who were married to European women also appear to have been reluctant to leave for their wives were 'little disposed to exchange their present life of ease and idleness for labour and privation at home.'[41]

The other European troops stationed in India were the two Company infantry regiments and numerous artillery units located at each presidency. These troops were obtained by the Company's own recruiting depots in England, Scotland and Ireland. These regiments were chronically under strength and the two regiments at each presidency could rarely muster more than seven hundred troops between them, less than a single king's regiment. With only two small regiments per presidency the direct military value of the Company's European rank and file was always suspect. However, they did fulfill two important functions. They provided a reservoir from which European non-commissioned officers could be drawn for service in artillery and sepoy regiments. They also asserted the Company's autonomy, and the Company's right to raise and maintain these regiments was strenuously defended in the face of the efforts by the British government and king's officers in India to replace the Company's European regiments with king's troops.

The soldiers of the king's and Company service differed not only in their organizational details but also in their military culture. If one can argue in general terms that king's officers were superior to Company officers in terms of class status, the reverse was true for the rank and file of the two armies. The common impression of the early nineteenth-century private soldier as an unambitious, drunken, uncivilized lout, while partially true for the king's army, cannot be extended as well to the Company's soldiers.[42] From the 1820s it is clear that recruits for the Company service were increasingly drawn from the petty artisan and clerical classes in Britain. Many of these joined the Company in the expectation that they could better themselves by putting their trade or literacy to use in India. Sergeant George Carter, for example, found lucrative opportunities when he used his spare time to carry on his trade as a bookbinder.[43] Others took advantage of opportunities to transfer to civil positions or purchased their discharge to pursue their crafts in India. Not all Company recruits were as respectable as this, however. One new recruit complained to his wife that the other recruits who were travelling to India with him were 'the scum of society, nearly the whole of them Irish labourers and Scotchmen of the lowest classes imaginable.'[44] The clerks and petty artisans who enlisted in the Company's service were joined by a broad range of recruits fleeing poverty, the law, or domestic circumstances in Britain and Ireland. As a consequence the Company's European regiments were a polyglot mixture of individuals drawn from a variety of classes and regions. This was very apparent in the language of the barracks where a mixture of 'good Irish, bad English, indecency and blasphemy' prevailed.[45]

The major difficulty in maintaining a sizeable number of European troops in India was the high mortality rates they encountered. Disease, made worse by the poor diet and abundance of cheap liquor, annually stripped many regiments of upwards of ten per cent of their soldiers. European regiments in India needed to have their ranks regularly replenished. This added greatly to their already considerable costs. In a survey of European regiments serving in the Bengal Presidency in the second half of 1816, Jasper Nicolls found that on average one in every six Europeans was ill; the situation in Madras and Bombay was considerably better with one in nine sick in the former and one in seventeen in the latter.[46] If we look at one European regiment in a year of peace, we can see the tremendous replacement cost involved. In 1820 the listed strength of the Bengal Artillery Regiment was 2472: of this number, 218 died, 29 were discharged, 7 deserted, 22 were invalided to the invalid station at Chunar, 17 were invalided to Europe, 7 became sub-conductors, 30 were transferred to sepoy regiments, 4 became town majors, 19 transferred to other corps, 6 insane soldiers were sent to England, and 2 died insane in India.[47]

Because of this high mortality rate and with the fear of the turbulent nature of the European troops in mind European soldiers were frequently confined to barracks for long stretches. 'In many parts of the country he is not allowed to go outside the door of his barrack-room during six months of the year, from eight or nine o'clock in the morning until five in the evening.'[48] Even drill and other daily duties were considered to be too threatening to the soldier's constitution. During peak summer months contemporary medical knowledge limited outdoor exposure to two and a half hours per day, normally in the early morning and late evening.[49] Soldiers as a result were forced to find amusement within the restricted confines of the barracks. This only aggravated their physical deterioration and loosened their discipline. Nicolls complained that 'Discipline of any valuable degree cannot be supported in banishment. Even our own corps are demoralized by ten years service in this climate.'[50] Locally distilled alcohol, palm toddy or fermented cane juice, known as arrack, were available everywhere at very cheap prices. Drunkenness not surprisingly was one of the chief outlets for the soldier's boredom. One writer claimed that 'I am sorry to say that an old soldier, and a great drunkard, are synonymous terms.'[51] This was a situation that was apparent to the rank and file as well. One soldier informed his mother that 'the reson of so many dying in India is becaus the liquer being so chepe - port wine 6 pence 1 quart and fruite is so rich and plentiful the yere round that men get tipsey and eat so much fruite and lye down in the sun witch brings the brane fever.'[52]

Alcohol not only caused health problems — it also contributed to very high rates of crime within the European component of the Indian army (see Appendix A). Officers were very conscious of this relationship, but were for the most part powerless to do anything about it. 'The causes which militate against our discipline are two-fold — discontent and drunkenness. The former superinduces recklessness, a wish for change no matter what, insubordination and probably violence.'[53] Even with the low liquor prices in India, many soldiers fell into debt. Indebtedness was so widespread that payday, which fell on the twenty-fifth of each month, came to be known as 'long face day' because of the expressions on all those creditors who arrived too late to get their claims in.[54] The majority of crimes committed in the army were done under the influence of alcohol. Crime rates in European regiments stationed in India were considerably higher than for regiments stationed in Britain, largely because of this combination of cheap liquor and inescapable boredom. The 13th Light Infantry for example held more court-martials within its first four months of service in India than it had in the previous twenty years.[55] The same situation prevailed in the Company's Europeans: the First Bengal European regiment was faced with 1317 defaulters in the first seven months of 1828 yet their total strength was only five hundred rank and file.[56] Many of these recorded crimes were acts of theft and larceny, crimes for which liquor was largely responsible. Not all crimes were as petty as these; European barracks were acknowledged to be very violent places. In many cantonments European officers could not enter the barracks after dark without an escort.[57]

The largest source of military manpower in India was provided by the conquered peoples of the subcontinent. Given the great numbers of unemployed, or underemployed soldiers in India, and that they were cheaper than Europeans, it is not surprising that the Company turned to them. Sepoys performed the widest variety of tasks in India, ranging from escorting treasure to rural patrolling to regular military duties such as garrisoning forts and outposts and participating in offensive operations. Sepoys were generally given those tasks that could not be entrusted to Europeans, namely, any of those where sobriety and honesty were required. Their greater resistance to local diseases also made them more useful in such a debilitating climate. Sepoys were generally considered to be fit for service for upwards of twenty-five years, long past the twelve years accorded to Europeans.[58]

The native officers of the East India Company's armies occupied the middle ground between the European officer and the sepoys, though they possessed little influence and were given barely any respect from either their officers or the sepoys beneath them. Their situation was primarily the result of two decisions. First, with the memory of Yosuf Khan's rebellion in the 1760s still current, only a minimum of authority and responsibility could be entrusted to their native officers.[59] From 1784, regulations required that all sepoy companies be commanded by a European officer. A second impediment arose because these ranks were designed to reward long and faithful service. This meant that they were filled by strict seniority and like the situation prevailing with the Company's European officers, though even worse, native officers only reached their office at a time when their physical and often their mental faculties had become impaired. Native officers were in an anomalous situation. Their rank suggested a degree of authority, and there had at least once been the intention that they would serve as the link between European officer and Indian soldier. Yet they were never given any real responsibility and were looked upon with a mixture of suspicion and loathing by their European officers. One British veteran described them as a 'set of worn-out, puffy, ghee-bloated cripples.'[60] At the same time it was all too apparent to the sepoys that their native officers were superior only in title. Denied authority and with the sepoys very much aware of their disabilities, native officers often sunk into a depressed state. Legal records from Madras indicate that of those native officers brought before courts-martial, by far the greatest number, 127 of the 267 convicted between 1800 and 1830, were charged with drunkenness on duty — a very surprising statistic given the rarity of drunkenness among sepoys as a whole.[61] The ineffectualness of the native officers, which had been caused by a lack of foresight on the part of the British, was to have grave repercussions. With no effective link between European officer and Indian sepoy, the native rank and file were better able to assert their own traditions and customs. In some cases, native officers who were aggrieved at their treatment would emerge as ringleaders in the protests and mutinies that punctuated the nineteenth century. Other native officers sank into such a state of apathetic resentment that they did not inform their British officers where and when troubles were brewing in the sepoy lines.

One of the most outstanding characteristics of the Indian sepoys was that aside from spectacular but infrequent acts of collective protest, their regiments were generally much better disciplined than the European rank and file (see Appendix A). One explanation for this is that sepoys were not as likely to be driven into the army as a refuge from poverty or the law and hence they proved to be more amenable to military discipline. In the words of one contemporary, 'when he [the sepoy] enters the service of the Company, he has not emphatically 'gone for a soldier".[62] Sepoys were attracted to the Company's service by the respectability that such service conferred; this was particularly true for those communities in which military service had become customary such as the Rajputs of North India. The attractiveness of military service also lay in the rates and regularity of pay that were offered. Sepoys also joined up with the knowledge that such service entitled them and their families to preferential treatment by colonial institutions. The sepoy's acceptance of military life is attested to most clearly by the generally low rates of desertion. While there were exceptions, such as during unpopular wars or amongst the most newly recruited, sepoys in general did not tend to desert. Statistics from the 60th regiment of Bengal Native Infantry indicate that while this regiment lost five per cent of its troops per year through desertion during the Burma War, this rate fell to 0.5 per cent once peace was restored.[63] The legal records of the native armies of the three presidencies indicate that with rare exceptions sepoys were rarely engaged in acts that threatened to undermine the discipline of their regiments. The crimes that were most frequently reported for sepoy regiments were 'quarrels about women for the greatest part, jealousies, and occasional thefts and insubordination', none of which posed a distinct threat to the army's cohesion or efficiency.[64] This led to comments such as 'native troops, from their quick and regular habits, do not require the same number of officers as Europeans'.[65] Jasper Nicolls, reflecting on his service as the commanding officer of the Meerut Division, proclaimed that 'No general officer could control 32,000 men so placed (an area one-half the size of Ireland) were they Europeans, but the Native Army is so easily managed that it is practicable.'[66] Nevertheless, British officers were always conscious of the vast gap between themselves and their Indian troops, a gap that had increased with the decline of the native officer. 'In no army but the Company's were the natives of the conquered countries ever placed at so vast a distance below their foreign masters', and they knew that ultimately the sepoy's loyalty was given at his discretion.[67] As G.R. Gleig warned his readers, the Indian army 'must ever be regarded in the light of a powerful, but most dangerous instrument.'[68]

To explain the apparent willingness of Indians to serve foreign masters, the British generally employed the 'empire of opinion' argument — it was British character that induced sepoys to serve, and to serve loyally and effectively. This argument stemmed from the belief that 'personal attachment is the strongest tie in Asia.'[69] This position was taken up by many officers, but it was never stated quite so bluntly as in the writings of Brigadier John Jacob who attributed the survival of the entire imperial edifice to the presence of British officers in India: 'It is indeed only because the European officer is a superior being by nature to the Asiatic that we hold India at all.'[70] Jacob went on to describe the relationship between sepoys and their officers in an homologous manner: 'they are the bones and muscles of the whole frame, of which the Europeans are the brains and the nerves; and when the latter are healthy and vigorous, the former will always be perfectly obedient, and strong only to do our bidding.'[71] By denying the sepoys any independence or autonomy, observers like Jacob helped to perpetuate British assumptions about the centrality of character to the maintenance of British rule while simultaneously obscuring the deepening grounds for discontent felt by the sepoys.

With some exceptions the recruiting of sepoys proved to be relatively easy, mainly because at least initially the British operated within existing Indian military traditions. The Company's service drew from those classes of Indians that had traditionally taken up arms, thus making recruiting self-perpetuating and self-regulating. One British officer claimed that 'there are, in all parts of India, thousands and tens of thousands who have lived by the sword, or who wish to live by the sword, but cannot find employment suited to their tastes.'[72] The family and village ties of sepoys already in the service were then exploited to gather more recruits. Direct recruitment was only turned to on those occasions when military necessity required a sudden and drastic increase. That the British tended to operate within precolonial military traditions is further confirmed by the fact that in the Bengal army, sepoys' families did not accompany them into service; in the Madras army, the opposite was true, for soldiers in the south had customarily been joined by their families.[73] Recruits initially signed on for three years, but the available evidence suggests that the vast majority of sepoys willingly extended their contracts for much longer periods. In all three armies, between thirty and forty per cent of those in the ranks had served between ten and seventeen years.[74]

The definition of what constituted the ideal recruit differed between the three presidencies. These discrepancies were mainly the result of historical accidents and the unique characteristics of their local labour pool. Bengal had more stringent requirements as far as the caste and physical appearance were concerned. Over time this preference became codified into a particular Bengal discourse on which north Indian communities were 'natural' soldiers, but it did not originate in a clearly articulated policy of selective recruitment. When the Bengal army was in its formative stages, the British took into it what soldiers they found around them, troops whose homelands lay in north central India. As one official reflected, 'we found that the profession of arms at that time almost hereditary; a loose population of perhaps two millions of military men floated on the surface of society.'[75] It was the nature of the pre-colonial military labour market that initially determined the composition of the Bengal army; it was not a deliberate colonial policy. By the 1790s British official policy in Bengal confirmed these pre-colonial characteristics as they deliberately excluded the lower castes from enlisting in the Bengal army. Instead they deliberately tried to attract the higher castes, from Awadh and neighbouring areas, as a means of conciliating rural elites.[76] Despite problems in identifying exactly what constituted a caste — a confusing range of criteria was used including occupation, region and ritual ranking — the Rajputs and Brahmins of Awadh were quickly deemed more martial and hence provided the prototype for what would later become the theory of 'martial races'.[77] The higher castes had the added advantage of possessing characteristics dear to the hearts of army officers; for example the higher castes' observations of ritual purity satisfied 'the great military virtue of cleanliness'.[78] On the other hand, the shorter stature of peoples of southern and central India made the armies of Bombay and Madras employ a set of height and weight requirements that were not as rigorous as those used in Bengal. Moreover, as indigenous armies had recruited from a broad range of communities in the south, the Madras and Bombay armies never exhibited the prejudices for high caste recruits that were so apparent in the Bengal army. There is also some evidence to suggest that at least in the early nineteenth century some of the sepoys were the offspring of European officers and local women.[79]

North central India, particularly the quasi-independent state of Awadh, was the most fertile recruiting ground for the Bengal army.[80] Although it was officially set aside to meet Bengal's needs, the armies of Madras and Bombay also occasionally tapped into this area. Unfortunately there are no systematic and army-wide statistics on recruits for the Bengal army. This in itself is suggestive for it shows the extent to which the Bengal army delegated recruitment to sepoys already in its ranks. There is, however, considerable impressionistic evidence on the nature of Bengal recruits, as well as some scattered breakdowns for individual regiments. The chief recruiting areas were found in southern Awadh, eastern portions of the northwestern provinces and western Bihar. Baiswara district alone was believed to have provided upwards of thirty thousand sepoys in the 1820s.[81] Baiswara, like many surrounding districts, was undergoing profound economic and political changes in the early nineteenth century. This district had been transformed from a rich agricultural zone in the 1700s to an impoverished and overpopulated region by the 1820s.[82] It was a region wracked by anarchy and conflict, a situation that obliged the peasantry to farm 'with their swords and spears ready for defence or plunder, as occasions offered.'[83] The large pockets of Rajput (and spurious Rajput) and Brahmin cultivators in this area were particularly hard hit by deteriorating economic conditions and diminished political opportunities.[84] Heber provided a very detailed description of its political topography: 'The stronger Zamindars built mud-forts, the poor Ryuts planted bamboos and thorny jungle round their villages; every man that had not a sword sold his garment to procure one, and they bade the king's officers keep their distance.'[85] The result was 'swollen proprietary brotherhoods of petty landholders' who saw in the East India Company's army an opportunity to preserve their way of life and status.[86]

Officers in the Bengal army took great pride in the fact that their recruits were gathered from the 'Brahmin and Rajpoot Yeomanry of the Upper Provinces', a class of individuals ranked as the 'middle order of the agricultural classes'.[87] The description of these sepoys as north India's yeomanry clearly indicates British biases for these sepoys were presented in romanticized terms strikingly similar to those used on Scottish Highlanders, another allegedly martial race. Both groups were depicted as sturdy independent farmers, physically and morally well-equipped to deal with the privations of military service. Such troops were best suited to what British officers saw as the model association between officer and soldier, the 'ideal, if often mythical, relationship between the landlord and his tenant.'[88] Officers in the Bengal army took great pride in what they saw as the more respectable character of their recruits. The more enthusiastic of them dismissed the idea that the Bengal sepoy was 'a common mercenary', arguing instead that he was usually 'a small landholder, who has an interest in good order and in the permanency of a government.'[89] By imposing upon these communities British conceptions of martial qualities and rural society, the British also strengthened their own dominant position for their officers had to be sufficiently strong in character to command the respect of these subjects.[90]

Recruits were not looked for in Bengal proper. 'No good men are to be got below Behar', mainly because they were considered to be contaminated by the influences of a more commercialized economy.[91] The lower castes, no matter where they came from, were deliberately excluded. Muslims were recruited though never in great numbers [see Appendix B for breakdowns on some representative Bengal regiments]. While this partly reflected Muslim resistance to service in the Company's army, officials in Bengal were wary about taking in too many Muslims. It was argued that 'The Mahomedans are good soldiers, though they seldom become so attached to the service as the Hindoo, and their private conduct is much less moral, and their private habits much more prone to dissipation.'[92] There were also fears that Muslims, having only recently been dislodged from their positions of command and influence in North India, were more reluctant to submit to British rule. Religion also played a role; the historical tendency to view Muslims as more fanatical was frequently put forth as an objection to relying upon them for military service. They would not only resent their British officers but would also come into conflict with the Hindu sepoys.[93] However, British fears for the most part were exaggerated. There were only a few recorded instances where Hindu and Muslim sepoys in the same regiment came into conflict over ostensibly religious issues. At Muttra in 1855 Muslim sepoys' attempts to erect a mosque on the main street of the regimental bazaar led to vigorous protests by the brahmins in the regiment.[94] This episode was peacefully resolved by moving the mosque onto a side street.

The popularity of service with the East India Company can be attributed to a variety of factors. The pay was respectable enough, at least when it was set out in 1796, and it was paid regularly. These salaries played an important role in maintaining the extended families of rural Awadh for sepoys generally remitted most of their salary to their families. William Sleeman recounted a discussion he had in 1819 with a village elder who had four sons serving in the Bengal army. 'Their wives and children lived with him; and they sent home every month two-thirds of their pay, which enabled him to pay all the rest of the estate'.[95] Sepoys were also entitled to a pension after fifteen years of service. There were also important legal benefits given over to sepoys; for sepoys recruited from Awadh, they and their families were entitled to call upon the Resident's assistance in any legal issues in which they were involved. Contemporaries noted that most sepoys came from families with landed interests, either in direct holdings or as co-parcenaries.[96] If the family had one of its members in the army, his status as a sepoy allowed the family to adjudicate any civil suits much more quickly. Any fears that their religious and social customs might be threatened were usually, though not always, put to rest by a policy of non-interference. The army was especially careful to insulate sepoy regiments from the activities of missionaries. A minor scandal erupted in Meerut in 1819 when a missionary baptized a sepoy in the 25th Bengal Native Infantry. His fellow sepoys viewed this as a threat to their religion and to reduce tension the divisional commander ordered that the sepoy be removed from the corps.[97] The only Christians normally found in a regiment, aside from the European officers, were those taken on as drummers. Christians were excluded from the fighting companies of Bengal regiments.

Bengal officers' acceptance of their sepoys' sense of caste translated into a commitment to fostering their troops' claims of superiority and exclusivity. Their officers allowed them privileges denied to other soldiers — mainly over religious rites and observations — and most significantly, rarely employed the lash on them. They were convinced that the character of their high-caste recruits would be broken if corporal punishment was used too frequently.[98] By way of contrast the lash was heavily used on Europeans as well as being applied more frequently to the backs of Madras and Bombay sepoys (see Appendix C). European troops and the sepoys in these two presidencies were not considered to be driven by ideas of prestige and respectability and hence brute force was deemed more suitable to maintaining their discipline. Yet this privileging of caste and status was not accepted unanimously. Most officers outside the orbit of the Bengal army, as well as a tiny minority within, looked upon the concessions made to sepoys in Bengal as excessive and potentially explosive.

> In the Bengal army there is a constant studying of men's castes, which the Europeans appear to think as much of, and to esteem as highly, as do the natives themselves; and the sepoys, instead of looking on the European officers as superior beings, are compelled to consider them as bad Hindoos![99]

Nicolls recorded an instance when two British officers were present at a *sati* in 1820 and because of their commitment to non-interference, they did not act quickly. On two occasions the victim tried to flee, only to be returned to the pyre. It was only on the third attempt that the officers intervened to rescue the woman.[100]

The sepoys of the Madras army were markedly different from their colleagues in Bengal. There was not the same slavish devotion to restrictive recruitment in Madras. The use of caste as a standard for recruitment had been tried in Madras in the eighteenth century though with little success. The incessant warfare in which the Madras army found itself required a constant supply of manpower that could only be obtained by relaxing recruiting standards. Moreover, the Madras army recruited in an area where linguistic and other cultural differences were more obvious and appeared to be more significant than caste. Hence, the few surviving lists and reports on recruiting tend to categorize on the basis of 'country' rather than caste. Nevertheless, the Madras army never completely opened itself up to all prospective recruits. For example, efforts were made in the late eighteenth century to prohibit the employment of Telugu-speakers from the Circars, a community then thought to be insufficiently warlike.[101] This attempt failed and Telugus formed a large part of the army. Their reputation as non-martial died out at least for the first half of the nineteenth century. The lowest castes were also discouraged from joining the army — following the Vellore mutiny of 1806, orders were issued prohibiting the recruitment of untouchables.[102] Madras may not have exhibited the same rigid prejudices as were common in Bengal, but they did try to keep their army free from the lowest castes.

As a consequence of their less exclusive recruiting standards, a regiment in the Madras army tended to take on the characteristics of the region where it had been raised. Depots were generally established in the region where most of its recruits had been secured, thereby allowing the regiment to maintain its local links.[103] Samples taken from sixteen regiments in 1824 substantiate this impression (see Appendix D). The two regiments with the highest proportion of Muslims, the 35th and 36th, were raised in Mysore. Those regiments raised in the Circars, such as the 34th and 37th, show the highest proportion of Telugu-speakers, while those from the Carnatic, the 18th and 46th for example, contained a more mixed population, reflecting the more heterogeneous nature of society in that area. The overall trend in Madras was for mixed regiments with Muslims being the largest single group, Telegu-speakers coming second, Tamil-speakers running a distant third, with the remainder either being drawn from North India or having indeterminate origins. It was only in the native officer corps that we find any group dominating — Muslims were preferred as native officers, but not because of any alleged superiority.[104] Muslims were favoured for linguistic reasons. Whereas most Hindus were Telugu or Tamil speakers, languages which few European officers could speak or understand, the Muslims were mainly Hindustani-speakers, the lingua franca of the army.[105]

The Madras army can also be distinguished from the Bengal army because its officers were directly involved in the day to day lives of its sepoys. It was a more intrusive army and this was seen most clearly in the attention it paid to the sepoys' material welfare. Unlike the situation in Bengal, Madras sepoys were entitled to the payment of 'hutting' money whenever they were ordered to change their station. They also received more liberal furloughs and more generous pensions. The sepoys' families were also better cared for, in most cases by accompanying their husbands and fathers to cantonments. If sepoys were sent away on foreign duties, the interests of their families were attended to by a 'careful and respectful' senior native officer who was charged with ensuring their welfare.[106] The Madras government was also willing to intervene when the price of rice rose, offering to arrange for subsidized rice to be sold to the sepoys and their families. The Madras army also maintained a proportionately larger invalid establishment than did Bengal. Even the methods of recruitment used in Madras displayed this paternalistic attitude. Each regiment had on its strength eighty 'boys', mainly orphans of those sepoys who had died on service.[107] These apprentices were trained and paid a nominal wage until they were old enough to be absorbed into the regular establishment. Advocates of this system, including Thomas Munro, stressed the paternalism inherent in it. It was calculated to cement the bonds between the sepoys and the state by guaranteeing employment for the sepoys' sons. The success of this paternalism in meeting the sepoys' expectations is suggested by Madras having the reputation for the lowest rate of sepoy desertion of the three armies.[108]

The Bombay army was the most cosmopolitan of the three. The Bombay army had historically experienced great difficulties in recruiting from its heartland, aside from the Konkan, and therefore had to make its regiments out of whatever could be recruited from their own territories and from further afield. Eventually the Bombay army would incorporate into its ranks a very diverse range of peoples, including Africans, Bene Jews and Arabs (see Appendix E).[109] Caste was certainly not a pressing concern; two of the favoured communities, the *dhers* (a depressed caste in what is today Rajasthan) and the *moochees* (leather-workers) would not have even been considered in either Madras or Bengal. Only the most depressed castes, such as scavengers, sweepers and hangmen, were excluded. Jews were extremely popular, especially as native officers on account of their reputation as being 'commonly drunk but invariably brave.'[110] All told, in the words of one Bombay officer, that presidency had a 'most salutary mixture of castes.'[111]

The chief difficulty faced by the Bombay army in manning their army was that they were often forced to go outside the presidency to gather troops, especially after 1816 when their demands escalated. The Bombay cavalry, in particular, was mainly kept up to strength with foreign recruits — approximately eighty-five per cent were taken from territories beyond Bombay's boundaries. In most instances this meant taking recruits from the same northern areas in which the Bengal army was recruiting. Not only did this antagonize Bengal authorities who saw this as poaching on their preserve, but the Bombay army was never that happy with having to depend on recruits from beyond their frontier. Recruits from northern India showed a greater tendency to desert, and they were also suspected of having introduced the high-caste prejudices that were common throughout the Bengal army, but were considered disruptive in the very polyglot conditions found in the Bombay army.[112] Distaste at taking these northerners into the army also sprung from economic considerations. Recruits taken from territories outside the boundaries of the Bombay presidency would likely remit their salaries out of the presidency. By the end of the 1820s the Bombay army introduced regulations designed to set an upper limit for Hindustani recruits at two hundred per regiment.[113]

The governments of Madras and Bombay successfully managed to check any tendencies towards combination with their armies. Bengal, on the other hand, because of its restrictive recruiting policies and the tacit encouragement given to the caste biases of its troops, saw its army becoming progressively more disaffected and the gulf between sepoy and officer was widening. Evidence of the latter is widespread, but one particularly telling example is offered by a surgeon of the East India Company. Each regiment of native infantry had a British surgeon on its establishment, but such surgeons were generally avoided by the sepoys who preferred to seek medical help from indigenous sources.[114] The depth of dissatisfaction was difficult to plumb as the native officers, who were best placed to interpret the situation, were effectively excluded from all positions of trust and authority. In ideal regiments the gap between sepoy and officer was bridged by the latter taking it upon himself to deal directly with the sepoys. Such situations were rare.[115] The Bengal army had largely forfeited control over its troops and allowed the Bengal sepoys to become effectively self-regulating. Alarm bells were ringing in London and elsewhere, but little was done to check the deterioration of the Bengal army. The exclusivity of the Bengal army ultimately proved to be its greatest weakness. By imposing such high expectations, the British soon found that they could not always attract the same class of recruits. By 1820 concerns were already being expressed about the shortages of proper high caste recruits. Several explanations were advanced to account for this. Some claimed that Rajputs were offended at not being promoted on the basis of merit; others argued that the peasants were too contented to take up military service; conversely, others declared that conditions were so bad that families could not spare any of their menfolk for military service, and lastly, expansion had forced many corps to serve too far from their families to allow regular furloughs. In assessing these explanations, Nicolls sided with the second, believing that British rule had produced a more secure environment for agriculturalists. While Nicolls was largely incorrect in reaching this conclusion, his explanation deserves quoting: 'it is the Agriculturalist that hangs back, not the idle, dissolute Mussalman'.[116] The reality was quite different: fewer high caste recruits were coming forward because the benefits of service had deteriorated. As sepoy salaries declined relative to the cost of living, and campaigning opportunities — in which salaries could be supplemented by extra pay and booty — dried up, fewer recruits were taken up from traditional sources.[117] There were few individuals who recognized that the standard of living issue was becoming central to sepoy grievances; even those who did tended to set it out in very general terms.[118]

The exclusivity of Bengal recruitment policies had a further and more far-reaching effect. By targeting what the British believed to be the minor landed classes of the country, an army was created in which loyalty was horizontally directed (connecting members of the same social order) rather than vertically directed (tying soldiers to the officers above them). One observer reported that 'on parade there is a daily communication between the European and the natives, but not in their quarters' and 'when not on duty, or preparing for it, there is little or no interference on the part of the English officers with the sepoys.'[119] There was a sense that many of the alleged traditions and practices in the Bengal army had been invented by the sepoys. One observer wrote that while 'we should respect their castes', there was no need to encourage 'things not meant or demanded by their faith but assumed or imposed on our weakness and mistaken liberality.'[120] The insistence in the Bengal army that brahminical restrictions be followed, for example regarding types of duty to be performed or how messing arrangements were to be made, was not the practice among brahmins in the Madras and Bombay armies. Metcalfe, Munro and Elphinstone all doubted the wisdom of giving in too much to the sepoys' invented culture, a suspicion that was shared by the author of *Oakfield*. 'I think that the way in which sepoys are belauded, and bebuttered and bebattaed after a campaign ... is the grossest as well as the most impolitic thing in the world.'[121]

Until the arrival of a regiment of king's dragoons in 1783, the Company's need for cavalry had been satisfied by forces lent to them by their Indian allies. With the extension of the Company's territorial responsibilities, it was realized that the Company needed its own cavalry to police its lands. The Company never raised its own European cavalry; the lack of suitable mounts in India precluded heavy cavalry and there were plenty of opportunities to raise light cavalry from disbanded Indian armies. Light cavalry was also better suited to the Indian environment.[122] However, the cost of a European-style cavalry regiment — three times that of a similarly-sized infantry regiment — persuaded the Company to turn to the indigenous practice of raising cavalry units from volunteers who provided their own horses and saddles. Known as the *silladar* system or irregular system (and made famous in such regiments as Skinner's Horse and Gardner's Horse), it proved to be very popular in Bengal and Bombay because it was cheap and there was a ready supply of recruits at hand in recently subdued central India. Irregular cavalry and infantry units (the latter will be looked at below) had been in use for some time in various guises, but the surge of interest in *silladar* cavalry can be dated to the 1820s and 1830s. Cost was the principal attraction, but the British were also drawn to these units after having grown disillusioned with Indian corps styled along European lines.

> The irregular cavalry is of particular importance in India; it is the favourite arm of the natives, it attaches him to our service by the strong ties of interest and affection, it prevents him from being engaged against us, and if the system was sufficiently extended it would, at a trifling expense, afford us all the advantages, moral and military, which the Russians have derived from the Cossacks.[123]

There were five such regiments in Bengal in 1824, growing to thirteen by 1846 when conditions along the northwest frontier called for more cavalry. The *silladar* system was never as popular in Madras for that presidency could always call upon a steady supply of excellent Mysore cavalry, placed at their service by a treaty with that state.

Under this system, not only was the Company spared the costs of providing remounts, *silladar* corps required fewer officers (three rather than twenty) thus saving the Company the expense of keeping up a large establishment of officers. It was estimated that an Indian trooper (or *sowar*) in a regular cavalry regiment cost Rs.82 per month; a *silladar* trooper was paid only Rs.35 a month (Rs.20 in some regiments) out of which he was expected to meet all his costs, save ammunition.[124] British officers appreciated the dash and élan that surrounded these regiments as well as the greater discretionary powers given to their European officers. Until the mid-1840s regimental commanders even had the final say over the choice of weapons, style of dress and internal promotions. The *silladar* system's value also lay in what contemporaries saw as its ability to cater to the natural desire among Indians for distinction through its emphasis upon individual action and bravery. Such an outlet was particularly important for those Indians of 'good birth' who were thought to be more susceptible to this 'love of distinction.'[125] Discipline was not as systematically or rigorously enforced, prompting one observer to emphasise that *silladar* cavalry were marked with a 'certain elasticity (not laxity) in their discipline.'[126] It was argued that such units captured the cream of India's military manpower through offering promotion by merit to positions of real authority, and that this was particularly attractive to the 'descendants of the aristocracy and gentry of the old regime', making such regiments the social equivalent of British yeomanry formations.[127] The number of Muslim recruits for *silladar* regiments attests to its success as Muslims were generally reluctant to join regular infantry or cavalry regiments. Native officers in such regiments not only exercised real authority, but also stood to profit from their office. Native officers were entitled to have, depending on their rank, between two and five berths (*asami*) in the regiment.[128] They would provide the horses for such berths and then lease them to recruits (known as *bargirs*). The *bargir* in return was required to turn over two-thirds of his *silladar* pay. One contemporary figured that in some *silladar* regiments, nearly one-half of the troopers were *bargirs*.[129] *Asamis* became a valuable commodity, passed down generation to generation and often winding up in the hands of widows. When sold they could fetch prices of up to Rs.250 each. This commodification of military service meant that the *sowars* and their native officers were able to perpetuate at least some of the customs and traditions of the military entrepreneurship that had marked pre-colonial military culture in India.[130]

The popularity of *silladar* cavalry also stemmed from its ability to conform to the orientalized readings of India that were gaining currency within British circles. Such regiments were depicted as more authentically Indian with their use of Indian dress and their shunning of courts-martial in favour of *panchayats* [adjudication by five native officers who served in rotation on such bodies].[131] This preoccupation with an orientalized image of India was not simply harmless romanticism for *silladar* cavalry were also singled out as demonstrating those traits that made the English natural rulers. With so few European officers attached to each regiment, those who were in charge could and did argue that it was sheer force of character that allowed them to retain control over such fine specimens of military manpower. One such officer described his position and that of the other European commanders as 'the patriarch, chief of the clan.'[132] Hence it was a system well calculated to appeal to proponents of the 'empire of opinion'. It is no coincidence that one of the most vocal advocates of the *silladar* system was John Jacob, who as we saw earlier was one of the most vigorous advocates of a militarized rendering of this theory.

Artillery was considered to be Britain's greatest edge over its rivals. The European near-monopoly on the most advanced manufacturing techniques and the methods they had devised to best exploit these weapons were viewed as the core of British military strength. For this reason the Court of Directors regularly issued orders to their governments in India to cease recruiting Indians for this service.[133] However, the chronic shortage of sufficient numbers of European recruits meant that this order was observed more in spirit than in practice. Opinions on the efficiency of the artillery varied. A recent study has concluded that while it was poorly used and maintained at the beginning of the Nepal War it greatly improved through the course of the Maratha and Pindari wars when the Marquess of Hastings took a personal interest in the state of the artillery.[134]

In addition to British India's standing armies there was also a considerable number of local and provincial formations. These local units, mainly of infantry, could be found throughout British India (especially in Bengal) and were similar in purpose, if not in appearance, to the militia of Great Britain. Their terms of service generally limited them to the region where they had been raised; their weapons were of poorer quality than the line infantry (in some cases they were not even equipped with muskets), and they received little in the way of formal training. There were two broad categories, 'local' and 'provincial' and the difference between the two was not always clear. Generally, local battalions were better officered and trained than the provincial battalions that had to make do with invalided European sergeants as their officers and were only given the most rudimentary training.[135] Low rates of pay, minimal supervision and poor training meant that these units could not always be depended upon. Some observers saw them as nurseries for vice, charging irregulars with abusing their positions and plundering local communities, and generally undermining British authority.[136] Despite their obvious limitations, these irregular battalions performed the valuable service of policing rural areas on the cheap. They were particularly popular in wartime as they could free up regular troops for service elsewhere. The number of irregulars in Bengal rose dramatically from 22,391 in 1813 to 38,112 in 1824 after so many regulars were called away to serve in central and northwestern India.[137]

When calculating the size of Britain's military force in India, it is easy to overlook all those troops maintained by Britain's Indian allies that were effectively under British control. The treaties that bound these states to the East India Company normally contained provisions for military assistance. This military obligation could take one of two forms. In the first instance the ruler of a kingdom under British suzerainty was required to maintain a certain number of troops that were placed at the disposal of the East India Company. This arrangement was known as the contingent system. Most of these contingents were commanded by officers seconded from the Company's army. The second type of treaty stipulation was one that required the ruler to provide a guaranteed subsidy that would meet the costs of an agreed upon number of Company troops. The subsidy in many cases took the form of a cession of lands to the British. The financial benefits extracted through these arrangements was considerable; when the combined revenues from cessions and subsidies are totalled together (having first deducted the costs of providing for the administration of the ceded lands), the Bengal treasury gained £4,689,049 in 1828.[138]

The contingent and subsidiary forms of military alliance provided several advantages to the British. They gave the British a reserve force at no cost to the Company's treasury; they provided lucrative employment for a considerable number of Company officers, and they also positioned an armed force loyal to the British in kingdoms whose loyalty could not be taken for granted. The security provided by these hidden armies was proven at the outbreak of the war with the Marathas in 1817 when the Peshwa's troops chose to follow their British officers and not their sovereign. On the other hand, the subsidiary system proved to be particularly popular as it provided cash reimbursement for Company troops who were obviously even more dependable than the contingents. Residents in states that did not have subsidiary arrangements were encouraged by the government in Calcutta to try and persuade the local ruler to accept them.[139] The number of potential troops placed at Britain's disposal was not inconsiderable; in 1832, the total came to 23,850 cavalry and 12,700 infantry. There were a further four regiments of Company cavalry and sixteen battalions of Company infantry that were fully paid for by the princely states.

[1] [anon], 'The Indian Army,' *United Services Journal*. 19(1835): 311-12
[2] [anon], 'The Military Constitution of our Indian Empire,' *United Services Journal*. (1845, no.3): 238
[3] Wellington to Wynn, 7 Aug 1826, *Letters, Correspondence and Memoranda*, III, 341
[4] The army reorganization of 1796 addressed the most significant grievances of the officers and laid the cornerstones for a more professional service. See R. Callahan, *The East India Company and Army Reform*, Cambridge, Mass.: Harvard

University Press, 1972, for a fuller treatment of this period.

[5] *Bengal Hurkaru*, 17 Sept 1842

[6] [An Old Mulligatawny], *United Services Journal*, 2(1829): 755

[7] John Malcolm, *Observations on the Disturbances in the Madras Army in 1809*, London: 1812. The only recent account of these protests is Alexander Cardew, *The White Mutiny*, London: 1929.

[8] AEO to Editors, *United Services Journal*, 2(1831): 232. Attitudes such as this, which were widespread at the time, suggest that the 'gentlemanly capitalism' model does not give adequate attention to the divisions between gentlemen and capitalists.

[9] William Makepeace Thackeray, *The Newcomes*, London: 1892 edn., 728

[10] Data taken from P.E. Razzell, 'Social Origins of Officers in the Indian and British Home Army; 1758-1962,' *British Journal of Sociology*, 14(1962): 249-53

[11] There was also a ceiling on the number of Company officers who could be recipients, a qualification not levied against the king's army. PRO, Taylor to Bathurst, 4 May 1825, CO 323/202

[12] [anon], 'Groans of the Bengal Army,' *East India United Services Journal*, 1(1833): 264

[13] J.H. Stocqueler, *The British Officer*, London: Smith, Elder and Co., 1851, 284

[14] Nottingham, 'Patronage of the British Resident at Hyderabad,' 1 July 1830, PwJf 140

[15] [anon], 'The Subaltern's Logbook,' *Naval and Military Magazine*. 4(1828): 164

[16] S.C. on the East India Company, PP, 13(1831/32): xxii

[17] OIOC, Nicolls' Diary, 13 March 1825, MSS Eur F175/31

[18] For a fuller discussion of the often overlooked professionalism of Company officers, see Lorenzo Crowell, 'Military Professionalism in a Colonial Context: the Madras Army, circa 1832,' *Modern Asian Studies*, 24(1990): 249-73

[19] [anon], 'The Military Constitution of our Indian Empire,' *United Services Journal*. (1845, no.3): 243

[20] National Library of Scotland [NLS], Melville to Dundas, 19 Oct 1810, NLS 1060

[21] Nottingham, Nicolls to Taylor, 29 Nov 1826, PwJf 2743/I

[22] W.D. Arnold, *Oakfield; or Fellowship in the East*, reprint, 1854, Leicester: Leicester University Press, 1973

[23] Evidence of General Paget, S.C. on the East India Company, PP, 13(1831/32): 169

[24] OIOC, Board of Control, Memo on Promotions, 1821, L/MIL/5/404

[25] Evidence of William Cabell, S.C. on the East India Company, 13(1831/32): 498-99

[26] Charles Napier, *Defects, Civil and Military, of the Indian Government*, London: Charles Westerton, 1853, 195

[27] OIOC, Bengal Military Letter to London, 28 July 1823, L/MIL/5/385/86

[28] Data taken from S.C. on the East India Company, PP, 13(1831/32): Appendix 'a', no. 3

[29] OIOC, Col Frederick, Memo on Bombay officers, MSS Eur F765/4

[30] 'Apology for the Indian Army,' *United Services Journal*, 1(1832): 37

[31] OIOC, Nicolls' Diary, April 1830, MSS Eur F175/35

[32] [S.S.]. 'An Apology for the Indian Army,' *United Services Journal*. 8(1832): 40

[33] Dundas to Wellington, 30 Dec 1800, Edward Ingram, ed. *Two Views of British India*, 318

[34] Evidence of Thomas Munro, S.C. on the East India Company, PP, 13(1831/32): xxx-xxxii. For the Vellore Mutiny, see R.E. Frykenberg, 'New Light on the Vellore Mutiny,' Kenneth Ballhatchet and John Harrison, eds., *East India Company Studies: Papers presented to Professor Sir Cyril Philips*, Hong Kong: Centre of Asian Studies, 1986.

[35] 'The Indian Army.' *Asiatic Journal and Monthly Register*, 10(1833): 223

[36] Nottingham, Paget to Bentinck, 29 Nov 1826, PwJf 2863/iv

[37] 'Report from His Majesty's Commissioners for Inquiring into the System of Military Punishments in the Army,' PP, 22(1836): 284. See also BL, Diary of Lieut Blackwell, 1822/23, Add MS 39811

[38] Joseph Ewart, *A Digest of the Vital Statistics of the European and Native Armies in India*. London: Smith, Elder and Co., 1859, 178

[39] [Barbarossa], 'Sketches of Military Life in India,' *United Services Journal*, 28(1838): 74

[40] OIOC, William Bentinck, Military Minute, 5 July 1834, MSS Eur E424/9

[41] [Barbarossa], 'Sketches of Military Life,' 74. Only about twelve per cent of king's soldiers were allowed to bring their wives out to India. P.J. Marshall, 'British Immigration into India,' 183.

[42] For a fuller discussion of the social characteristics of the early Victorian army, see Edward Spiers, *The Army and Society, 1815-1914*. London: Longman, 1980. For the Company army, see Peter Stanley, 'Dear Comrades': Barrack Room Culture and the 'White Mutiny' of 1859-60,' *Indo-British Review*, forthcoming

[43] OIOC, Sergeant George Carter's diary, nd, MSS Eur E262

[44] OIOC, Gunner A. Wilson to Fanny Wilson, 25 Sept 1818, Photo Eur 333

[45] *Bengal Hurkaru*, 14 Dec 1839

[46] OIOC, Jasper Nicolls, 'Memo on the Proportion of Sick to Healthy in HM Regiments', Dec 1816, MSS Eur F175/19

[47] OIOC, Muster Roll for the Bengal Artillery, 1820, L/MIL/10/142

[48] [anon], 'The Military Constitution of our Indian Empire,' *United Services Journal*. (1845, no.3):239

[49] BL, Diary of Lieutenant Blackwell, 1822-23, Add MS 39811

[50] OIOC, Nicolls' Diary, 15 April 1827, MSS Eur F175/33

[51] [Anon], *The Subaltern's Logbook*, London: 1828, II, 266

[52] OIOC, Gunner Luck to his mother, 13 Oct 1813, MSS Eur E339

[53] [Turk], Letter to the Editor, *Mofussilite*, 24 July 1849

[54] [Anon], *The Subaltern's Logbook*, II, 272-73

[55] BL, Diary of Lieutenant Blackwell, 1822-23, Add MS 39811

[56] OIOC, Nicolls' Diary, February 1828, MSS Eur F175/36. A fuller range of criminal statistics can be compiled from William Hough, *A Case Book of European and Native Courts Martials, 1801-1821*, Calcutta: 1821

[57] William Hough, *Precedents in Military Law*, London: W.H. Allen, 1855, 81

[58] Evidence of Robert Scott, S.C. on the East India Company, PP, 13(1831/32): xxxii

[59] Khan, a very distinguished and competent Indian commander, had taken advantage of the chaos in Madras territories to use troops under his command to try and carve out his own kingdom. He was hanged as a rebel by the British in

1764. See S.C. Hill, *Yusuf Khan; the Rebel Commandant*, reprint, New Delhi: Asian Educational Services, 1987

[60] Anon, 'Indian Irregulars,' *Household Words*, 16(1857): 244

[61] Lieut. Col. John Briggs, *Letter*, London: privately printed, 1836, 29

[62] [anon], 'Jack Sepoy,' *Bentley's Miscellany*, 32(1852): 78

[63] OIOC, Nicolls' Diary, January 1831, MSS Eur F175/35

[64] 'Report from His Majesty's Commissioners for Inquiring into the System of Military Punishments in the Army,' PP, 22(1836):279. See also National Army Museum, Returns of the 14th Madras Native Infantry. 1832-1847, Acc 6012/65

[65] [An Old Indian]. 'The Indian Army,' *United Services Journal*. 18(1835): 306

[66] OIOC, Nicolls' Diary, 14 Feb 1828, MSS Eur F175/34

[67] [An Old Indian]. 'The Indian Army,' *United Services Journal*. 18(1835): 314

[68] G.R. Gleig, 'The Indian Army,' *Blackwood's Edinburgh Magazine*, 21(1827): 565

[69] Nicolls to Combermere, 27 Oct 1827, *Letters*, iv, 156. The sacrosanct nature of British character in commanding Indian troops has been explored in greater depth in Douglas M. Peers, 'The Habitual Nobility of Being': British Officers and the Social Construction of the Bengal Army in the Early Nineteenth Century,' *Modern Asian Studies*, 25(1991): 545-69

[70] John Jacob, *Tracts on the Native Army of India, its Organization and Discipline*. London: Smith, Elder and Co., 1858, 107

[71] Jacob, *Tracts*, 111

[72] Sleeman, *Rambles and Recollections*, 287-88

[73] Kolff, *Naukar, Rajput and Sepoy*, 27

[74] Nottingham, William Bentinck, Memo on the Native Army, nd [1830 ?], PwJf 2862/vi

[75] Evidence of Captain Macan, S.C. on the East India Company, PP, 13(1831/32): 153

[76] James Walsh, *Military Reminiscences: Extracted from a Journal of Nearly Forty Years Active Service in the East Indies*, London: Smith, Elder and Co., 1830, I, 15

[77] It is now clear that what defined a Rajput was not simply caste as commonly understood, but also the taking up of the customs, traditions and occupations of the warrior. See Kolff, *Naukar, Rajput and Sepoy*. Further discussion of the consolidation of martial race theory in the late 19th century can be found in Omissi, *Sepoy and the Raj*.

[78] [W.D. Arnold], 'Jack Sepoy,' *Fraser's Magazine*, 54(1856): 360

[79] [Gabion Fuze], 'The Indian Army for Thirty Years,' *Colburn's United Services Journal*, 1849(3): 33

[80] James Hoover of the University of Wisconsin is presently conducting the most detailed study to date of recruiting in this area. A preliminary version of his findings can be found in his article, 'The Recruitment of the Bengal Army: beyond the Myth of the Zamindar's Son,' *Indo-British Review*, forthcoming

[81] Rudrangshu Mukherjee, *Awadh in Revolt; 1857-1858; a Study of Popular Resistance*, New Delhi: Oxford University Press, 1984, 77

[82] C.A. Bayly, *Rulers, Townsmen and Bazaars*, Cambridge: Cambridge University Press, 1983, 278

[83] Hamilton, *Description ... of Hindostan*, 339. Historically, many of the peasants in this area had served as recruits for pre-colonial armies. See Kolff, *Naukar, Rajput and Sepoy*

[84] The term Rajput is particularly problematic for it is often erroneously taken as indicative of an exclusive and static community. As C.A. Bayly has pointed out, 'At best Rajputs were a broad grouping of endogamous castes with life-styles and perceived status alone as common features.' Stokes, *Peasant Armed*, 230. The fluidity of the Rajput label was not lost on all contemporary British observers. See Francis Buchanan, *An Account of the Districts of Bihar and Patna in 1811-1812*, Patna: Bihar and Orissa Research Society, 1936, 327. For a fuller description of the origins of these 'Rajputs', see Kolff, *Naukar, Rajput and Sepoy*. Elliot estimated that in the 1860s, the Rajput and spurious Rajput population of the Northwest Provinces (including Awadh) amounted to ten per cent of the population, while brahmins totalled a further twelve per cent. H.M. Elliot, *Encyclopedia of Caste, Customs, Rites and Superstitions of the Races of Northern India*, 1870. reprint. New Delhi: Sumit, 1985, 178 and 182

[85] Heber, *Journey*, I, 222. See also Rudrangshu Mukherjee, *Awadh in Revolt* for a fuller description of the social and economic conditions of this area.

[86] Eric Stokes, *The Peasant Armed; the Indian Rebellion of 1857*, C.A. Bayly, ed., Oxford: Clarendon, 1986, 51

[87] Nottingham, T.C. Robertson, Memo on the Indian Army, 1827, PwJf 2584

[88] G. Harries-Jenkins, *The Army in Victorian Society*, London: Routledge & Kegan Paul, 1977, 52-3

[89] [S.S.], 'An Apology for the Indian Army,' *United Services Journal*, 8(1832): 31

[90] A good discussion of the martial race phenomenon, and its relationship to the definition of the imperial 'self' is provided in Lionel Caplan, 'Bravest of the Brave': Representations of 'The Gurkha' in British Military Writings,' *Modern Asian Studies*, 25(1991): 571-98

[91] Evidence of Holt Mackenzie, S.C. on the East India Company, PP, 13(1831/32): 166

[92] [anon], 'The Military Constitution of our Indian Empire,' *United Services Journal*. (1845, no.3): 240

[93] Thomas Twining, *A Letter to the Chairman of the East India Company; on the Dangers of Interfering in the Religious Opinions of the Natives of India*. 3rd ed., London: Ridgeway, 1807. Historical evidence of the unreliability of Muslim soldiers was also circulated, see Colonel G. Fitzclarence, 'On the Employment of Mahomedan Mercenaries in the Christian Armies,' *Naval and Military Magazine*, 2-3(1827-28)

[94] OIOC, Lt. Col Bradford to Lt. Col Salter, 7 July 1855, MSS Eur D1057

[95] Sleeman, *Rambles and Recollections*, 641

[96] [anon], 'The Military Constitution of our Indian Empire,' *United Services Journal*. (1845, no.3): 241. The extent to which sepoys took advantage of the offices of the Resident has been shown by Michael Fisher's research to be very great. On average, the Resident in Awadh handled 1,366 petitions from sepoys per year. Michael Fisher, *A Clash of Cultures; Awadh, the British and the Mughals*. Riverdale, Md.: The Riverdale Company, 1987, 186

[97] OIOC, Nicolls' Diary, 18 Dec 1819, MSS Eur F175/24

[98] See the statistics that compared the frequency of corporal punishment in the Bengal army with the armies of Madras, Bombay and Great Britain. *Report from H.M. Commissioners for enquiring into the System of Military Punishment in the Army*, PP, 12(1836)

[99] Jacob, *Tracts*, 7

[100] OIOC, Nicolls' Diary, 29 Jan 1820, MSS Eur F175/24

[101] Evidence of Colonel J. Munro, S.C. on the East India Company, PP, 13(1831/32): vi

[102] Lieut. Col. John Briggs, *Letter*, London: privately printed, 1836, 20

[103] OIOC, Munro, Memo on Recruiting, 1 July 1825, MSS Eur F151/96

[104] Unlike the Bengal army, the Madras army (and the Bombay army) appointed their native officers on the basis of 'merit'. This then permitted Muslims to be appointed in numbers out of proportion to their strength in the overall army.

[105] John Briggs, *A Letter on the Indian Army*, London: W.H. Allen, 1857, 18

[106] General Order of the Governor, 26 March 1824, *Abridged General Orders*, Madras: 1840, 219

[107] H.H. Dodwell, *Sepoy Recruitment in the Old Madras Army*, Calcutta: Government Press, 1922, 30

[108] Evidence of John Malcolm, S.C. on the East India Company, PP, 13(1831/32): 344

[109] OIOC, Colonel Frederick, Memo on the Bombay Army, 1828, MSS Eur F765/3

[110] Evidence of James Grant Duff, S.C. on the East India Company, PP, 13(1831/32): 484

[111] Ibid.

[112] OIOC, Adjutant General to Frederick, 11 Sept 1828, MSS Eur F765/3

[113] Nottingham, Malcolm to Bentinck, 27 Nov 1830, PwJf 2801/1

[114] See for example OIOC, Henry Spry to Edward Spry, 30 December 1827, Photo Eur 308/3

[115] [An Officer of the Bengal Army], 'The Indian Army,' *United Services Journal*, 11(1833): 86

[116] OIOC, Nicolls' Diary, 29 Jan 1819, MSS Eur F175/23

[117] While salaries were fixed in 1796, they were never changed despite considerable increases in the cost of essentials. For example, the cost of grain in the Delhi area rose by fifty per cent between 1810 and 1824. Asiya Siddiqi, *Agrarian Change in a North Indian State, United Provinces, 1819-1833*, Oxford: Oxford University Press, 1973, Appendix 2. See also PRO, 'Changes to Native Troops, nd [1829 ?]', PRO 30/9/4/21

[118] See for example, [S.S.], 'An Apology for the Indian Army,' *United Services Journal*, 8(1832): 31

[119] *Asiatic Journal and Monthly Register*, new series, 10(1833): 214

[120] 'Carnaticus', *Asiatic Journal*, 11(1821): 65

[121] *Oakfield*, 2, 116

[122] Indian Light Calvary was very light. An armed and dressed Indian trooper weighed in at between 12 and 13 stone — British Light Dragoons topped the scale at 20 or 21 stone. Anon, 'Indian Irregulars,' *Household Words*, 16(1857): 245

[123] William Bentinck, Minute on Military Policy, 13 March 1835, C.H. Philips, ed., *The Correspondence of Lord William Cavendish Bentinck*, Oxford: Oxford University Press, 1977, II, 1454-55 [hereafter cited as *Correspondence*]

[124] Lieutenant G. Malcolm, 'Remarks on Sillidar Cavalry,' *Colburn's United Services Journal*, 1847(2): 585

[125] Malcolm, 'Remarks on Silladar Cavalry,' 581

[126] Anon, 'Indian Irregulars,' *Household Words*, 16(1857): 244

[127] Malcolm, 'Remarks on Silladar Cavalry,' 584

[128] J. Wheeler, 'The Irregular Cavalry,' *Calcutta Review*, 5(1846): 183-4

[129] Wheeler, 'Irregular Cavalry,' 185

[130] The nature of this pre-colonial military labour market is set out most clearly in Kolff, *Naukar, Rajput and Sepoy*. Considered more broadly, military entrepreneurs together with political and commercial entrepreneurs exerted a powerful force on the emerging colonial state, helping determine not only its nature but also the timing and direction of its expansion. See C.A. Bayly, *Indian Society and the Making of British Empire* for an extended treatment of this relationship.

[131] The 1845 Articles of War, which for the first time embraced the irregulars, discontinued the practice of panchayats.

[132] Anon, 'Remarks by an Officer of the Scinde Irregular Horse,' *Colburn's United Services Journal*, 1847(2): 231

[133] See for example, OIOC, Military Letter to Bengal, 8 Nov 1814, L/MIL/5/484

[134] Pemble, *Invasion of Nepal*, 102-6

[135] OIOC, Mackenzie to Adam, 4 July 1823, MSS Eur F109/D/16

[136] Walter Badenach, *Inquiry into the State of the Indian Army*, London: J. Murray, 1826, pp. 7 and 106

[137] S.C. on the East India Company, PP, 13(1831/32): xiii

[138] S.C. on the East India Company, PP, 14(1831/32): 25

[139] Fisher, *Indirect Rule in India*, 197

5. THE ARMY AND THE FINANCES OF BRITISH INDIA

> The rigid principles of economy and the precise form of our civil rule should both yield to the establishment of this cornerstone [the army] of our strength.[1]

Once the principle that the army was the cornerstone of British rule had been accepted, it logically followed that the army should have first call on the Company's treasury. The Company's finances were dominated by the army for the Company's and king's military forces together made up the single largest item of expenditure. Sentiments such as Charles Metcalfe's that he was 'for every increase of the army that our finances will bear' were common throughout India.[2] The result was military fiscalism or the collection of revenues by a centralizing state with the army being granted a priority over its redistribution. Crucial to the idea of military fiscalism was that war could even be made profitable, both for the state and for the individual. While individuals expected to gain from booty and prize money, the state could hope to acquire revenue-rich territories. Unlike European wars which often ended with the *status quo ante*, it was believed possible, in the words of a one-time Bengal military auditor general, to end a war in India with 'the accession of territory and revenue, and sometimes with pecuniary indemnification for the expenses incurred.'[3] Though these expectations generally proved illusory it was difficult to shake off memories of the windfall following the battles of Plassey and Buxar. This military fiscalism was certainly not new to India; its existence has been traced back to several eighteenth-century Indian states.[4] However, the British were able to develop a more sophisticated version and employ it over a much greater extent of territory.

Although this development was certainly in keeping with the plans and priorities of most officials in India, it did collide with the Court of Directors' financial intentions. Put simply it resulted in a conflict between security and profitability. The Court of Directors' perspective was determined by a balance-sheet interpretation of profit and loss. In their eyes Indian revenues should be sufficient to provide for all the normal costs of administering India, including those spent in Britain on its behalf, while still leaving a sizable surplus that would help finance the Company's trading activities from whence ultimately the Company's dividend would be paid.[5] Not all directors were united in defending this position — one of their number criticized the Court for taking this 'very narrow commercial spirit' to extremes and argued that it 'sometimes prevailed over the view of the statesman.'[6] In general the directors were ill-disposed towards money being spent on the army for it rarely provided a return on their investment. London's efforts to impose controls over expenditure, particularly military charges, either through direct intervention or through the construction of an elaborate system of checks and balances, largely failed. Costs escalated, the army dominated fiscal planning, and the Company's territorial administration in India became increasingly subsidized by commercial profits. This was diametrically opposed to the Company's intentions as the renewal of the Company's charter in 1813 had attempted to separate territorial from commercial finances. It was estimated in 1830 that twenty-two per cent of the Company's debt that had been registered in Britain since 1815 was paid off by advances from the Company's commercial profits.[7] Instead the Court's financial policies and directives meant that war was made more expensive through the introduction of an unwieldy administration, and officials in India were prompted to become more belligerent in their defence of Anglo-Indian militarism and its adjunct, military fiscalism.

The highest level for financial decision-making was in London. The same dual government that existed for the management of political and military affairs also supervised Indian finances, though with one important exception: the Company's commercial operations were strictly a Company responsibility. However, the distinction between what was territorial and what was commercial was not easy to define, and the Board of Control frequently had to consider the Company's commercial accounts when they were dealing with the Indian debt. In examining the Company's accounts the Board of Control was frustrated by its not having as much expertise at hand as was the case with the Court of Directors. The shortage of trained clerks, with the exception of James Cumming and Thomas Courtenay, was compounded by the general lack of interest in financial questions that was common to most presidents of the Board of Control. Neither Canning or Wynn displayed any significant interest or understanding of the complicated bookkeeping methods of the Company and tended to rely upon their assistants for information. Ellenborough was the exception; his papers at the Public Record Office display not only a deep concern over Company finances but an ability to master the intricate details of their accounts. The Court of Directors were far better placed to deal with complicated questions of imperial finance. Not only did they have a much larger staff to work with, many of whom like James Mill possessed considerable experience of the Company's financial affairs, but the Court could count among its members many individuals who would have had prior personal or business experience in India.

Controlling authority over Company finances in India was vested in the office of the governor-general. Once again this authority was more nominal than real for very few governor-generals possessed the skills necessary to contend with the sheer volume of financial reports or demonstrated any commitment to developing such skills. Financial discussions bored the Marquess of Hastings and confused Lord Amherst.[8] On those few occasions when Hastings did participate in financial discussions, his contributions, according to one official, showed an almost complete failure to appreciate the workings of the Indian economy.[9] Only William Bentinck showed any strong commitment to the examination of Indian accounts and this likely stemmed from the intense pressure he was under to bring Company expenditures under control. Members of the Council, whose prior Indian experience would suggest their suitability for this task, generally demonstrated a similar reluctance to become mired in financial reports. By default the overseeing of Company finances in India passed into the hands of officials further down the official hierarchy, and in particular the territorial secretary and the members of the boards of trade and revenue associated with his office. While this arguably resulted in the entrusting of financial questions to individuals better equipped to answer them, it also meant that parochialism would surface in financial planning. These officials had their sights set firmly on their own presidency and its agendas. Very often they were either unable or unwilling to consider the opinions and objectives of either the metropolitan government or the other presidencies.

The central authority in India for financial planning was the territorial department, presided over by the territorial secretary. It had been formed in 1815 through the merger of the fledgling financial department with the well-established revenue department.[10] In conjunction with the Accountant-General, an independent office, this department was charged with supervising nearly all of the government's financial activities, including revenue, loans, civil expenditure — in essence 'the whole financial business of the government.'[11] The only exceptions to its responsibilities were the Company's commercial operations which fell to a different office, and military spending over which it shared authority with the military secretary and the military board. Given the importance of finances to the government's operation, this department was considered to be a most powerful one and its head, the territorial secretary, was often described as the most influential official in Bengal after the governor-general. So powerful was this department known to be that the Court of Directors urged the governor-general to monitor its activities closely for it was reputed to tell the government only what it wanted the government to know.[12]

Holt Mackenzie held the position of territorial secretary for most of the period under review here. Amherst especially turned to Mackenzie for guidance through the labyrinth of Indian accounts and soon began to rely on him for advice on matters unrelated to Company finances. His relations with Hastings were more ambivalent. First appointed in 1817, Mackenzie had the reputation of being extremely bright and well-informed — Thomas Malthus, Mackenzie's instructor at the Company's college at Haileybury, singled him out as his brightest student.[13] The great volume of evidence Mackenzie was called upon to present to Parliament's Select Committee on East India Affairs (more than anyone else) attests to his reputation.[14] Nevertheless, Mackenzie was thought by many to be too inclined to theory. The Court of Directors were often annoyed by Mackenzie's dogmatic advocacy of lowering internal customs and duties in the hopes of stimulating internal trade.[15] Malcolm praised his intelligence, but cautioned that he demonstrated 'too great a reliance on the principles of political economy.'[16] Yet with further scrutiny Mackenzie's use of political economy theories was always subject to pragmatic considerations. Like most other officials in India Mackenzie never questioned British India's ultimate dependence upon the Indian army.

Working alongside the territorial secretary was the accountant general, perhaps the most shadowy office in the Company's bureaucracy. It was in this office that the actual accounts and estimates were drafted, based upon the statements sent to it by those departments involved in collection and expenditure. The accountant general was also expected to provide the government with financial advice. It is very difficult to come to any precise conclusion as to where this office was placed within the administrative hierarchy for it was not formally attached to any government department. The ambiguous positioning of the accountant general proved to be his greatest shortcoming for he could not on his own authority command the statistics and reports upon which his accounts and estimates depended. He could only secure the necessary information through the territorial secretary, thus placing a premium on the ability of these two officers to strike up a congenial working relationship. Such a relationship was largely lacking in the 1820s for the accountant general, Henry Wood, did not get on well with Holt Mackenzie. Mackenzie complained that Wood was too rash and hasty in preparing his estimates while Wood criticized Mackenzie for failing to send him the information that he needed.[17]

The problems inherent in the working relationship of the accountant general and the territorial secretary were symptomatic of a larger handicap to the efficient operation of the Company's financial machinery — the absence of a workable hierarchy of control. There were too many individuals and committees involved, all of whom were imperfectly linked. This frequently meant that when the government was required to respond to a particular development, its actions were not coordinated across its departments. The lack of a common treasury is but one example of this. There was no one place where receipts could be tallied against outgoings. Many sums remained unadjusted, creating almost insuperable difficulties for auditors. There was also a noticeable failure to integrate properly the finances of the three presidencies. The only formalized linkages were at the top, between governors, yet it was essential that the territorial department and the accountant general could keep in touch with their opposite numbers in Madras and Bombay to prepare the India-wide accounts and estimates that were expected of them. Securing the information needed for these reports proved to be even more difficult than acquiring similar data from departments in Bengal. The absence of regular channels of communication meant that officials at the various presidencies often worked at cross purposes. In one instance a large sum of money (Rs. 5,00,000) was taken off Madras's books with the intention that it would then be listed in Bengal's accounts, but it never appeared in the latter's ledgers. This was only picked up much later when clerks in London compared the accounts of the two presidencies.[18] Remittances from Bengal to the lesser presidencies were also reported rather haphazardly. While Bengal's records indicate that between 1815 and 1829 a total of £20,626,883 was sent to Bombay and Madras, the accounts of the two recipients can only account for £20,205,088 of this amount.[19] Just over £400,000 was missing from Company records and there was no explanation. Coordination between presidencies also suffered because there was no consensus over what categories were to be used in listing incomes and expenditures. Madras, for example, employed many large aggregate categories in place of the more specific breakdowns used in Bengal.

Between and within presidencies the strong traditions of departmental autonomy, originally designed as part of an elaborate system of checks and balances, conflicted with the need for timely financial information. Commercial activities, often used to move territorial funds, were kept entirely separate from the normal conduct of financial affairs. Some political charges were paid out of the governor-general's secret fund and were thus removed from the scrutiny of financial officers. The biggest dilemma though was trying to come to grips with military spending. Military expenditures were to a large extent obscured from the territorial secretary and the accountant general. Mackenzie complained that his 'being consulted in regards to such [military] charges depended chiefly on the personal discretion of the [military] secretary.'[20] Yet military charges were the largest single expense for the government and were prone to sudden increases during wartime. Mackenzie reckoned that if the military department could be persuaded to submit half-yearly estimates, then the uncertainties that arose from sudden fluctuations in military spending would be avoided. His recommendations came to naught for while the government agreed in principle, the military department blocked their implementation for fear of falling under greater government scrutiny.[21]

The most important mechanisms in the management of the East India Company's finances were the estimates and accounts that were regularly prepared. Accounts and estimates came in various forms and were prepared at staggered intervals. Estimates consisted of predictions of future financial positions while accounts attempted to provide a yearly balancing of revenues and expenditure. Not unexpectedly for a commercial corporation, their accounting procedures were superior to those in use by the British government. As one contemporary reported, 'the accounting branch of India was on a better footing than that of England until 1840.'[22] Some of the advances that marked out the Company's accounting procedures included the use of a common financial year in all their offices and standardized double-entry bookkeeping, neither of which was yet enforced in departments of the British government.[23]

In theory the estimates prepared by the accountant general should have been the essential tool employed by the Company in forecasting its future financial position. Estimates came in two forms, sketch and regular. The sketch estimate was produced at the beginning of the financial year and its predictions were set out in a very indeterminate way. The regular estimate provided a much more accurate forecast of Company finances, but it frequently came too late in the year to be of much assistance in financial management. Neither of these forms of estimate correspond to what we know today as budgets. True budgets consist of the advanced allocation of resources on the basis of calculated receipts. Estimates in India were much cruder affairs and were intended merely to provide information. Estimates were almost entirely based on previous years' accounts and were adjusted with only the most minimal attempt at forward projection. The accountant general took the most recent accounts and amended only those figures he knew for certain would change. The weakness of this system was most vividly exposed when accountant generals tried to prepare estimates when the previous years' accounts were still not available. In one instance the accountant general in Madras warned the governor in 1825 that his estimates were particularly haphazard as he had been forced to base them on accounts from three years before.[24] The shortcomings of the Company's estimating procedures became most apparent in wartime when previous years' accounts could give little indication as to the eventual costs during a period of extraordinary expense. As Bengal shouldered most of these wartime costs, it is not surprising to find that their estimates were the most inaccurate. Over a ten year period (1820-1830) Madras's estimates were on average only two per cent off the actual accounts. In Bengal estimates fell short of actual accounts by anywhere from six to thirteen per cent.[25]

The culmination of all these weaknesses in the Company's financial apparatus was that long-range planning became frustrated. Disputes between London and the presidency governments over spending priorities were aggravated by the very uncertainty of the data that each marshalled in support of its arguments. Once a course of action was decided upon, institutional weaknesses became even more apparent. The ad hoc development of financial machinery in India, having as its first priority the imposition of checks and balances, had created a cumbersome bureaucracy, flawed accounting procedures, and an overall lack of integration. These were serious handicaps in peacetime; in wartime they would lead to profound financial embarrassment for officials were not placed in a position from which they could deploy Indian resources effectively.

The government's attempts to square their revenue demands with their expenditures were further constrained by their having to operate within an underdeveloped economy. The British had to contend with an economy that was marked by a general depression in prices for its principle agricultural products.[26] The Indian economy was largely and increasingly centred on agrarian production; other sectors, once vigorous, were in many cases choking because of an inability to adjust to the changes unleashed by colonial rule. Manufacturing in India had to contend with the serious shocks that had been triggered by penetration of British interests into the interior and the destruction of many traditional markets. Changing rulers had led to altered consumption patterns; many items that were traditionally sought after by Indian ruling classes, particularly luxury items and military supplies, were no longer as marketable, either because the Courts that had hitherto purchased them were no longer able to do so, or because the new rulers had considerably different demands.[27] The changed fortunes of the former ruling classes were apparent to British observers. One subaltern wrote of the once powerful ruling court in Delhi that 'those who were formerly the chief nobility around the power of the emperor are now poor wretches who have no remnant of their former nobility left but a great deal of pride.'[28] The same could be said to hold true for other courts in the northern plains and with their diminution went much of the vigour of the traditional North Indian economy.

The progressive demilitarization of North Indian society also carried with it profound economic changes. It has been estimated that fifteen to twenty per cent of North India's population had been dependent upon military spending.[29] The importance of the army as a consumer is further attested to by fluctuations in North Indian grain prices. The price of grain only rose above its 1813 level on four occasions between 1813 and 1833, and in three of these four years (1818–1820 and 1826) there were large Company armies operating in the region.[30] Compared with pre-colonial times, there was no longer the massive armies that needed to be supplied, nor were the remaining troops distributed as widely as had hitherto been the case. The seventy per cent of their salaries that troops could be expected to spend in their immediate neighbourhood was consumed more and more within the new and larger cantonments that the British had established, thereby skewing consumption patterns away from traditional routes.[31] The extremely rapid growth of Kanpur during this period, from approximately five thousand people in 1798 to thirty thousand in 1830, is an excellent example of the role of the army in the emergence of new economic centres for Kanpur had become one of the Bengal army's major garrisons and depots in north India.[32]

British operations in India were also hampered by the uneven integration of the many regional economies in India. This was largely due to the underdeveloped state of India's transportation and communication networks. Most areas of India were deficient in roads, and the British were only just beginning to invest in roadbuilding, but with the important proviso that Britain's strategic needs took precedence over local economies. Hence economic development in India tended to follow navigable rivers such as the Ganges. Transportation costs on land were estimated to be twenty-eight times more expensive than on the rivers.[33] Even then the British had only an imperfect knowledge of India's river networks. It was reported that as late as 1881 the waterways of eastern Bengal were only known in the sketchiest detail.[34] The frailty of these routes of communication had a major bearing on the difficulties of Indian commerce. Transportation costs in India obstructed the development of long-distance trade in many items. Even on the Ganges, which served as the most economical route in India, transport costs were three times that of London to Calcutta.

India's very restricted money market served as a further hindrance to the East India Company's financial operations. There were very few sources of readily accessible capital in India and the Company had to compete for access to these with private traders, European as well as Indian. The most obvious absence were European-style banks; the few in existence only controlled a small portion of India's capital. Each of the presidencies had its own quasi-governmental bank and there were also the investment houses that were tied to the Agency Houses. Compounding the absence of European-style financial institutions was the fact that a considerable portion of the European capital in India did not stay in India for very long. Company officials and private Europeans in India tended to remit as much of their money back to England as they could. Henry St George Tucker, one-time auditor general in Bengal, estimated that as much as three million pounds was remitted home from private sources.[35] The absence of an interconnected banking network, with ready access to large pools of capital, as well as a reliance upon metallic currency, often forced the British to rely upon slow-moving and expensive treasure columns when moving funds from place to place. There was also the difficulty caused by too many different currencies in circulation. Upwards of eighty different rupees were present in Bengal alone. The two most common coins were the *sicca* and *sonaut* rupees, the former was the main currency of commerce while the latter, for unknown reasons, was used by the army. Company accounts, aside from those of the military, frequently employed an imaginary currency, known as the current rupee, to track their transactions. Further afield, various 'country' rupees, remnants of the pre-colonial era, were in circulation. To cope with this proliferation of currencies, the Company tried to simplify their bookkeeping by employing fixed exchange rates and thereby get around the problem of coins being debased and discounted.[36] While this procedure was no doubt useful to the accountants, fixed exchange rates masked over important fluctuations in the value of the different coins with one another. The East India Company extended the use of the fixed exchange rate to govern sterling conversions. All of their accounts presented in Britain were based upon a static rate of exchange, notwithstanding the fact that on the open market the rate fluctuated. Hence Company accounts were not always the most accurate barometer of the Company's financial performance. Repeated efforts were made by the Court to persuade the Board to allow for regular readjustments of this rate but to no avail.[37]

Aside from European financial institutions there were the Indian *shroffs* [moneychangers or moneylenders] and *banians* [merchants or managers] who were able to tap into indigenous capital, though Indian capitalists had no institutions similar in organization and operation to western joint-stock banking firms.[38] Moreover, Indian investment strategies often diverted Indian funds away from European activities. British capital normally sought a safe haven in overseas trade and looked to the European Agency Houses to manage its operations; Indian capital preferred to invest in internal trade, moneylending or landholding. There was some cooperation between British and Indian capitalists for they recognized each other's strength. The Agency Houses were well situated to handle overseas trade and transfers of funds while Indian financiers were better placed to exploit indigenous money markets. The latter skill proved to be particularly crucial in wartime when British funds had to be moved to armies in the field more quickly and efficiently than treasure columns would admit.[39] During Wellesley's campaigns, for example, it was the Indian banking houses of Benares that moved much of the government's money to where it was needed.[40]

European Agency Houses occupied a crucial yet highly ambivalent position within the Anglo-Indian political economy.[41] While William Bentinck would argue to London that these houses should be treated as partners in empire, when money markets tightened the government found itself competing with these houses for whatever capital was available. In the 1820s there were approximately fifty Agency Houses in Calcutta with smaller numbers in Madras and Bombay. The working capital of these institutions comprised for the most part the deposits of Company officials, civil and military. The size of these deposits was often considerable; Lord Combermere invested £60,000 of prize money in Alexander and Company while John Adam put just over £30,000 into McKintosh and Company.[42] Ties of an even more personal nature reinforced these financial connections between the government and the Agency Houses. Henry Thoby Prinsep, a member of the all-powerful central secretariat, had two brothers in the employ of Palmer and Company, one of the largest houses in Calcutta. These close personal links between the government and the Agency Houses put pressure on the administration to take under consideration the interests of the Agency Houses when drafting their financial plans.[43]

Financial planning in India was also seriously undercut by an almost chronic shortage of specie. This was particularly problematic in a species-based economy such as that operating in India. The supply of specie was threatened by several developments. A net loss of silver was occasioned by a drop in the amount imported from a high of Rs. 4,94,91,605 in 1818/19 to Rs. 1,26,00,153 in 1826/27.[44] The decreasing amount of imported silver was further exacerbated by the failure of the British to reinvest their revenues back into the areas from whence they had been collected. Instead specie tended to collect in the presidency capitals, or in a few instances it was remitted back to Britain to reimburse expenses paid there on India's behalf. This failure to ensure the circulation of silver reinforced tendencies to hoard precious metals. This was one of the side-effects of having a metallic economy — the medium, being so liquid, was often stashed away to meet later needs. Indian rulers and wealthy capitalists were particularly suspected of hiding their specie. It was estimated that the Nawab of Awadh had annually set aside as much as £500,000 worth of precious metals, while it was discovered after the fall of Bharatpur that its ruler was hiding over £100,000 in treasure.[45]

The revenue base from which the Company drew to meet its numerous demands was characterized by inelasticity, instability and often unreal expectations. Revenue sources can be broken down into three broad categories: commercial trade, land and other revenues that were derived from the Company's exercise of sovereign rule in India, and loans raised in either London or India. The constitutional provisions of the 1813 charter, which had legislated the separation of the Company's commercial activities from its territorial operations, also dictated how commercial proceeds were to be distributed. Bills of exchange in London were the first demand that had to be met, followed by the interest payable on the Company's commercial debt in London, and then the fixed dividend of £630,000 was to be paid out. Any remaining was to be used to reduce the debt principal.[46] However, given the growing costs of the Company's territorial operations, commercial profits were often called upon for assistance.

The greatest difficulty faced by the Company in the 1820s, with respect to its ability to remit commodities to satisfy either its commercial or territorial accounts, was volatility in commodity prices. One can see that through the 1820s there was generally a declining return on these goods. By 1820 much of the Company's trade was already operating at a loss, especially direct trade between India and London (in 1818 and 1819 the surplus commercial profits exceeded £1M, by the end of the 1820s they had fallen to just over £100,000). Yet the need to ensure a cash flow meant that trade had to be continued, though it was narrowly focused on four principal items: indigo, silk, opium and cotton.[47] All of these items experienced great fluctuations in demand and consequently their prices varied from year to year. Cotton, upon which the triangular trade with China partly depended, was in an especially sensitive state in the 1820s; its price fell by fifty per cent between 1819 and 1823.[48] The chief problem with cotton was that demand in China was determined by Chinese domestic production and this could never be predicted with any accuracy. Cotton, however, was slowly being ousted from its commanding position by opium. Opium prices oscillated in the 1820s as well (see Appendix F). High expectations led to excess production, supply exceeded demand and prices plummeted. Bengal was forced to warn London in 1823 that it was impossible to predict with any accuracy what prices opium would fetch in China.[49] Opium prices were made even more unpredictable when it was declared to be contraband in China, thus obstructing access to Chinese markets. In the two years between 1824 and 1824, opium sales realized one and a half crore for the Company's treasury, yet in the following year sales had plunged to eighty-five lakhs.[50] Indigo was a commodity that had by the 1820s come to play a crucial role in the remittance trade between India and London. It too was highly unpredictable in terms of its price (which ranged from a high of £312 in 1823 to a low of £193 in 1830). Sugar was a commodity that the Company considered using to meet remittance demands, but they were unsuccessful as duties on East Indian sugar were raised one hundred per cent to protect West Indian production.[51]

Table 5.1

Five Year Averages of Revenue Sources in India in thousands of £ and in brackets as a % of the total revenue collected.[52]

Source	1817–22	1822–27	1827–32
Land	13,263 [66.2%]	13,567 [62.0%]	13,112 [61%]
Salt	2,256 [11.3%]	2,603 [12.0%]	2,590 [12%]
Opium	1,090 [5.5%]	1,641 [7.0%]	1,747 [8.1%]
Post Office	85 [0.4%]	118 [0.4%]	124 [0.6%]
Stamps	234 [1.2%]	329 [1.0%]	381 [1.8%]
Customs	1,667 [8.3%]	1,663 [8.0%]	1,747 [8.1%]
Mint	57 [0.3%]	35 [0.2%]	37 [0.2%]
Miscellaneous[53]	1,392 [7.0%]	1,986 [9.0%]	1,789 [8.3%]

Territorial revenues across the three presidencies were largely dependent upon the taxes that the British could levy against agricultural production (see Table 5.1). There were other taxes and charges to which the Company could turn, but these made up but a small portion of the Company's income.

Land revenue, the most important revenue source in India, was subject to powerful constraints. The three most important of these were the poverty of the land, the deficiencies in British understandings of how land revenues were traditionally collected, and an underlying fear that if the British moved too rapidly, they ran the risk of setting off a rebellion. Land revenues in Bengal provided sixty-three per cent of that presidency's income. Bengal was the most fortunate presidency in its revenue collection for its soils were generally more productive than those of the other presidencies. Bengal had a further advantage in that most of its territories were taxed under the *zamindari* system. By farming out revenue collection to large landholders, the number of civil servants needed to collect revenues was reduced. The alternative revenue systems (*ryatwari, taluqdari, mahalwari*, etc.), which were based on collections from the actual cultivator, village or co-parcenary holders and were argued by some to be more in keeping with indigenous traditions, were not as efficient in the short-term because they were dependent upon a more extensive network of collectors. It was estimated in 1831 that £23,877 was collected by each civil servant in Bengal, compared to £20,749 and £11,262 in Madras and Bombay respectively.[53] *Zamindari* did, however, have one major drawback. By fixing the land tax in perpetuity, it was impossible to readjust with ease revenues to meet demands. Only through opening up of waste lands to cultivation or the abolition of tax-free lands could the government be assured of additional land revenues. In Madras (and Bombay to a lesser extent) the prevailing but by no means complete use of *ryatwari* did cost more to operate because of higher staffing levels, but it also offered more opportunities to adjust tax assessments to meet exigencies.

All three presidencies in the 1820s saw their costs of revenue collection increase faster than the amount of revenues collected. The land revenues collected annually in Bengal between 1815 and 1826 increased by nearly twenty per cent — largely on account of the annexations of land made following the end of the Maratha War, yet collection costs went up by twenty-five per cent. The worst results appeared in lower Bengal. This mystified many for it was here that *zamindari* was most entrenched, and it was assumed that collection costs would have at least remained the same, if they had not dropped.[54] Over-assessment was a further hindrance to the efficient collection of revenues, in Bengal as well as in the other presidencies, for overassessment depressed local economies by depriving farmers of disposable income and by encouraging many cultivators to leave their plots in search of less heavily taxed lands. Not only were British expectations too high, but revenue officials were often told quite bluntly that their careers rested on securing as much revenue as possible.[55] It has been estimated that British revenue demands in Bengal were some twenty per cent higher than those imposed by their predecessors.[56] Objections were made to this over-assessment, but they were overruled by the Court who feared that any relaxation would depress revenues even further.

The amount of land revenues realized was also frequently interrupted by environmental factors. Given the dependence of much of India's agriculture on the monsoon, Indian farmers were particularly vulnerable to the failure or late arrival of the monsoon rains. This was particularly true in the early stages of Company rule, when local economies were increasingly disrupted by the demands of British capitalism, an efficient transportation grid had yet to be assembled, and British famine policy was still a long ways off.[57] While not all areas of India were equally dependent upon the monsoon, and there were regional variations in the dependability of the monsoon, droughts and famines were frequent, especially in the Deccan where much of the Bombay and Madras presidencies were located. Famine swept through the Deccan in 1823–25, affecting according to contemporary estimates some eighteen million people. Land revenues dropped by six per cent in parts of Madras and by up to eight per cent in the exposed portions of the Bengal presidency. In the worst afflicted regions of Bombay, revenues fell by twenty-five per cent. Writing from eastern Bengal in 1824, Heber noted that 'our people complain of the dearth of rice. The last harvest was not a very good one, and the famine in Malabar has in some degree occasioned scarcity in Bengal. At least rice is now more than half the price.'[58] The figures for Bombay are particularly staggering for this was a presidency that pressured its collectors to take as much revenue as the cultivators could bear.[59]

The second most important source of revenue for governments in India was provided by their monopoly over the production and sale of salt (see Appendix F). Some two million pounds was on average raised in Bengal by the sale of government salt every year.[60] However, the salt monopoly was more labour intensive than land revenue collection; the direct costs of managing the salt monopoly amounted to twenty-seven per cent of the gross revenues.[61] There was a further drawback to the salt monopoly and that was the frequency with which it was evaded through smuggling and illicit manufacturing. In the ceded provinces of northern India, it has been estimated that anywhere between one-third and one-half of the salt consumed was smuggled in from territories outside the Company's control.[62] Inland customs and duties, though only providing about six per cent of Bengal's total revenues, were an attractive revenue source on account of their being cheap to administer. The costs of collecting duties and excise taxes varied be-

tween ten and seventeen per cent of the sums realized, well below those
associated with land revenues or the salt monopoly.[63] The remaining sources
of revenue, such as the mint or the post office, made little impact upon the
Company's finances for they at best broke even and more commonly operated at a loss.

When revenues in India fell short of expenditure, as was generally the
case during wartime, two alternatives surfaced. If the deficit occurred in
Madras or Bombay, then Bengal was expected to help them out as it normally ran a surplus (see Appendix B). However, loans had to be turned to
on those occasions when either Bengal's surplus was insufficient to cover
Madras or Bombay or both, or when expenditures exceeded revenues in
Bengal itself. Loans raised through local money markets were the most
popular recourse; between 1814 and 1828, some seventy per cent of India's
overall territorial deficit was funded this way.[64] The remaining thirty per
cent of the deficit was realized through internal indebtedness or the transfer of money from the Company's commercial operations. Internal indebtedness was the practice of holding salaries in arrears, or the Company's use
of monies temporarily entrusted to it such as the prize funds deposited
with the Company prior to pay out. The latter particularly provided much
needed respite to the Company treasury for the prize fund for the Deccan
campaigns of Hastings alone was worth £2,128,115.[65] These forms of internal indebtedness, listed as debt at no interest, were the only forms of
credit to which the presidencies of Madras and Bombay were entitled.

The seeking out of loans from local investors was a popular and proven
strategy in India. The government could raise capital quickly and secure
some political advantages as well. Investors were attracted by the security
of their investment for the government's credit rating was considered to be
very good. The rate at which the government could raise loans from the
public hovered between four and five per cent by the beginning of the 1820s.[66]
Moreover, the government had succeeded by the end of the 1820s in keeping their debt servicing charges to just under ten per cent of their annual
expenditure (see Appendix H). This was a notable success when compared
with developments in Britain where the loans raised during the Napoleonic
Wars eventually consumed some seventy per cent of government expenditures.[67] Investors, both Europeans and Indians, were attracted to government loans because they were one of the few openings for low-risk investment. In some cases government loans offered the added advantage to European investors of the option of having interest paid in London at favourable rates of exchange, though not surprisingly the Court of Directors
frowned on this.

The Company's credit worthiness, at least in the eyes of Indian capitalists, is demonstrated by the increasing number of Indian subscribers to Company loans (see Table 5.2). More and more Indian investors turned to the Company as a safe shelter for their capital and by 1831 it was estimated that twenty-five per cent of the government's debt was held by Indians. The flow of Indian capital into Company paper was also accelerated by the disillusionment apparent among Indian capitalists with one of their traditional investments — European private trade conducted through the Agency Houses. As will be seen later in this study, the crash of several Agency Houses drove many Indian capitalists away for Indian creditors generally suffered more than did the Europeans.

Table 5.2
European and Indian Subscriptions to Bengal Loan Issues (Sicca Rupees).[68]

Loan	Europeans	Indians	Total
Six percent of 1822	7,03,43,500	43,68,700	7,47,12,200
Five percent of 1823	7,09,87,800	2,06,39,700	9,16,27,500
Four percent of 1824/25	3,13,000	5,86,200	8,99,200
Five percent of 1825/26	5,32,74,800	4,08,79,500	9,41,54,300
Four percent of 1828/29	6,03,600	5,84,100	12,47,700
Five percent of 1829/30	19,51,700	7,01,300	26,53,000
Total	19,75,34,400	6,77,59,500	26,52 93,900

Colonial officials emphasized the political advantages that could be derived from these loans; a connection between Indian economic and political elites and the colonial state was considered to be a crucial bridge between the conqueror and the conquered. It was claimed that by the 1820s these 'bonds of connexion between the monied classes of natives and the British government' had penetrated 'every corner of Hindustan.'[69] The advantage of securing Indian capital was held to be especially true when the Indian creditor happened to be an Indian ruler. As the secretary of the Board of Control wrote, 'it is a good policy to have a bond of connection between the opulent natives and even native princes and the British government.'[70]

The belief that these rulers hoarded vast amounts of treasure and specie was widespread; there was also the realization that such funds should not be difficult to secure if the resident leaned sufficiently hard on the ruler. The Nawab of Awadh was a particularly tempting target owing to his reputed wealth and the constraints the British had already established upon him. The Marquess of Hastings was proud of three loans, totalling two and

a half crores, that were achieved 'voluntarily' from the Nawab.[71] Two contemporaries who observed the negotiations rejected Hastings' claim that
the Nawab gave the money willingly, with one insisting that one of the
loans was an 'abominable extortion'.[72] Because Indian princes were politically dependent upon the British, creditors who happened to be princes
could also be pressured to accept alternative forms of repayment, thus reducing the Company's debt load. Under pressure from Hastings, the Nawab
of Awadh agreed to forget one loan of one crore in favour of a land grant.
The land itself had been taken from Nepal in 1815 and was 'either unproductive - or populated by people who would only pay under compulsion -
which the Nabob could not provide.'[73] Another portion of these loans was
partly repaid when Hastings persuaded the Nawab to accept in lieu British
recognition of his independence from the Mughal emperor. Hastings' ea-
gerness to tap into the treasuries of his ostensible allies can also be glimpsed
in the pressure he placed on the Nizam of Hyderabad to convert the *chauth*
demands he had hitherto paid to the Marathas into a subsidy to be paid to
the British.[74]

Set against the Company's rather precarious revenue situation were the
expenses that these revenues were required to meet. The average annual
cost in the 1820s of the Company's administration of India was about twenty-
three million pounds, of which twenty million was spent in India with the
remainder forming the 'home charges', expenses paid out in England that
were chargeable to India.[75] Of the twenty million pounds consumed in India, about half was paid out for military expenses, a further forty per cent
was directed at civil charges and the remainder was used for debt servicing.
Debt servicing was an expenditure peculiar to Bengal for the governments
of Bombay and Madras had transferred their debts to the former government.[76] The charter of 1813 had also set out the priority with which territorial revenues were to meet territorial expenditures, though it should be noted
that the costs of revenue collection were deducted from the accounts at the
start. Military costs were to come first, followed by payment of any interest
on loans raised in India, and then by civil charges. Military charges were
given priority for the British were well aware that the absence or irregular-
ity of pay had been the undoing of pre-colonial armies. In such situations
the discipline of Indian armies rapidly collapsed as sepoys took their services to whomever seemed most likely to be forthcoming with their wages.
Should any revenues remain after this distribution, it was to be used to
reduce the principal of the debt taken up in India.[77]

The home charges of the East India Company have long been a source
of controversy. These funds were used to pay for the office establishments

of the Board of Control as well as the Court of Directors, the Company's training establishments at Haileybury (civilians) and Addiscombe (military), the pensions and furloughs of soldiers and officers in Britain (including a pro rated sum for king's officers pensions), the rental of military and naval forces from the Crown, supplies sent to India from England, and the servicing of debts raised in Britain. The costs of services, establishments and stores normally amounted to about two and a half million pounds per year though it fluctuated from year to year, largely because of either a Company request for extra military forces from the Crown or because an exceptionally large shipment of stores was sent to India. Debt charges also varied with creditors from India sometimes seeking repayment in Britain.

There were several methods used to meet these home charges. The shipment of Indian goods to Britain for resale was one method; funds could be directed back to England through the tea and opium trades, or occasionally it could be sent back in the form of bullion. Remittances to England fell short of meeting the actual home charges every year between 1814 and 1823 and the Company was forced to turn to their commercial accounts to subsidize their territorial operations. However, as the Company's commercial profits were plummeting through this period, this was an option very much to the distaste of the Court of Directors. As a consequence, relations between London and Calcutta through the 1820s were marked by acrimonious exchanges between an increasingly economy-minded Court of Directors and an Indian administration that held security uppermost in their thoughts. These exchanges were further sharpened by a considerable divergence between them as to how they each defined a surplus. On occasions when Bengal receipts exceeded expenditures, local officials pressed for the use of the excess either to build up the army even further or subsidize reductions in those areas of revenue collection deemed harmful to the Indian economy such as internal customs.[78] The Court reacted vigorously and informed officials in Bengal that local governments were in no position even to determine whether a surplus existed. A surplus could only be declared by the Court of Directors once they had examined the Company's complete financial situation, including territorial and commercial balances as well as those of their local and metropolitan operations.

In managing their finances, authorities in India had very little control over the home charges. Not only were these expenses a considerable burden on territorial revenues, they were also imposed with little or no consultation.[79] Calcutta was expected to provide for costs over which they had very little control and even less warning. Particularly controversial were the charges imposed for supplies sent out from India. These supplies consisted mainly of items for the army such as saddles, armaments, and accoutrements. These supplies were not only expensive, but the charges in any given year were prone to dramatic fluctuations, ranging from £241,653 in 1822 to £935,235 in 1827.[80] When Ellenborough queried Britain's Master General of the Ordnance about these costs and their fluctuations, he discovered that the average yearly expenditure of the Company on military stores in Britain between 1818 and 1828 (£562,000) was five times that of the rest of the empire combined, including Britain.[81]

The Court of Directors virtually ignored suggestions from Calcutta that many of the stores were of dubious value, or that some items sent out could be provided more cheaply in India. Instead they persisted with a system that benefited them personally (many had investments in companies involved in the manufacture and transport of such goods), but ultimately lumbered India with expensive and not always appropriate equipment. Canvas and cordage had been found at much cheaper rates in India as early as 1813 though in 1829 the Company was still looking to British suppliers.[82] Arguments for using Indian manufacturers could point to more than simply saving money; local suppliers could provide items better suited to Indian conditions and by having supplies closer to hand, large and expensive inventories could be avoided. Given India's climate many articles deteriorated more rapidly than they would have in Britain, especially items made of leather. This was certainly the case with 20,321 ammunition pouches sent to Madras in 1814; of this number, only 8260 were serviceable when they were taken out of the warehouses three years later.[83] Despite the obvious financial benefits of switching some of their suppliers to India, the Court of Directors proved to be unmoved by the arguments arrayed against them.[84] They weakly countered by claiming that by keeping production in England, they could prevent Indians from acquiring skills in the production of strategic materials. While this would hold true for some artillery pieces and firearms — though the quality of some muskets produced by indigenous gunsmiths indicate that the skills were already there — the Court's arguments were not relevant to the bulk of the items shipped to India. Accoutrements and accessories were hardly strategically vital commodities. The most likely explanation for the Court's dismissal of Indian manufacturers was that owing to their personal investment portfolios in manufacturing and shipping, many of the directors had a stake in perpetuating British production and supply of needed materials.

Many contemporary critics and nearly all modern historians have tended to become fixed on the army as the reason for the Company's financial embarrassments. They have argued that the army was the principal drain on the Company's treasury. While it is obvious that the army was the single largest category of expenditure, and that wartime was particularly expensive, the very visibility of the army and its costs has tended to obscure the unceasing growth in the Company's civil charges. However, there were some who recognized that the poor state of the Company's finances was due to the 'continued and progressive augmentation in every department.'[85] If we average out military and civil expenditure between 1815 and 1823, military expenditure only increased by eight per cent; the costs of India's civil administration had in the meantime grown by forty-six per cent and even then the figures are misleading for many civil offices were filled by army officers who drew much of their salary from military paymasters.[86] More alarming data were provided by the Board of Control whose enquiries revealed that while civil charges were up by nearly fifty per cent, revenues had only grown by thirty-seven per cent.[87] The Board followed up their findings with orders to the Court of Directors to direct their officials in India to review and report on the many unexplained increases in civil spending.[88] The outbreak of war with Burma delayed this report, but when Bentinck finally issued a preliminary brief on civil spending, he held the Marquess of Hastings responsible for most of the increases.[89] Hastings' impatience with details, well attested to by others, had allowed his subordinates to build up their own bureaucratic empires. During Hastings' years in India the size and allowances of Bengal's civil administration had increased by twenty-four per cent.[90]

Within India, the most pressing concern for the Company was the seemingly unstoppable growth in all categories of territorial spending. Amherst was warned in 1825 that growth in the size of the Company's bureaucracy was the major difficulty they faced.[91] Not only was expenditure increasing in absolute terms, but more alarmingly it was outpacing the much smaller increases in revenue collection. In the post office, expenditures had overtaken receipts by 1825. Even the cost of revenue collection was growing rapidly: these costs (expressed as a per centage of total revenues collected) rose from eighteen per cent in 1815 to nearly twenty-four per cent in 1826.[92]

In examining the financial performance of the East India Company during this period, it is important to bear in mind that there were important differences between the three presidencies (see Appendix G). Madras managed best to keep expenses within its resources. Bombay, on the other hand, was faced with a chronic revenue shortfall, despite all the promises of a rosier future that followed Bombay's acquisition of territory after the Pindari war. Madras's ability to live for the most part within its means was made even more impressive by the fact that Madras provided most of the military and many of the civilians needed to administer Bombay's newly acquired territories. The success enjoyed by Madras in balancing its books was partly attributable to the very careful attention given to the presidency's accounts by Thomas Munro, its governor from 1819 to 1827. Even such minor charges as tents and doolie corps were carefully scrutinized by Munro.[93]

Contemporaries were baffled by what was happening — or not happening in the case of revenues — in Bombay. An examination of Bombay's accounts for the years between 1823 and 1827 reveals that in spite of these being years of peace, and with no responsibilities being added to the presidency, total expenditure grew by twenty-three per cent. More alarming was the eight-fold increase in Bombay's civil charges between 1815 and 1823.[94] When queried over these costs, Bombay did not provide any explanation.[95] Examination of the Bombay government's financial consultations does not shed much further light on these increases. The most likely explanation is that the increases in civil and military spending were made in anticipation of the revenues that Bombay would accrue from territories recently seized from the Marathas. At the conclusion of the Pindari War in 1819, many anticipated that Bombay would become financially independent.[96] These expectations were never realized and because of its swollen expenditure, Bombay became even more dependent on Bengal for financial relief.

Despite the obvious importance of military spending within the Company's financial operations, there has been surprisingly little work on this topic. Although one recent scholar has claimed that 'War finance, an art still wrapped in mystery, was unknown in the Company's India', a closer examination of the institutions and policies that governed military finance in India reveals that officials were very much preoccupied with this alleged mystery.[97] This is not to say, however, that Company officials were able to decipher the 'mystery', but they were certainly trying. Many of their difficulties in smoothing over the transition from an army geared to a peacetime economy to one for service in wartime stemmed from the structural and institutional handicaps that have already been noted. Beyond that, the army's financing operated under several unique afflictions. It is therefore necessary to consider in some detail the specific details of the composition and operation of the army's own financial machinery, as well as the demands with which it had to contend.

The complexities of military spending required special skills, skills usually lacking in those who in theory had the major voice in military affairs, the governor-general and the commander-in-chief. One exception to this was Thomas Munro, whose combination of military experience and financial acumen allowed him to examine military accounts with an expert eye. In his evidence before the select committee, the Court of Directors' military secretary, Colonel J. Salmond, reported that when it came to military finance, governors and commanders normally had to reply upon the experience of the military auditor general and the military secretary.[98] However, as Mackenzie warned Amherst, such dependence did bring with it the danger of falling prey to officers whose interests lay in a strengthened and expanded army.[99] The commander-in-chief laboured under the added disadvantage of being blocked from inquiring too deeply into financial matters by the constitutional provisions that had placed questions of military expenditure under the supervision of the military department of the central government. The only route through which the commander-in-chief could hope to direct military funds was through his interpretations of Britain's strategic situation. There were those who suspected that this was learned quickly by incoming commanders-in-chief, and consequently changes in the deployment of the Indian army, especially in times of intended retrenchments, were determined by his desire to secure more funds for the army.[100]

Each presidency had its own military department, supervised by the military secretary, that was intended to oversee all military spending. Members of this department were drawn from the army for it was felt that expert opinion on technical matters was required. This had been particularly true in the eighteenth century when the provisioning and equipping of the army had been rife with corruption. Their military background gave them an appreciation of military problems and priorities, but it also tended to convince them of the fundamental wisdom of a strong militarized presence in India. The expectation that they would act as a watchdog on the army was never really satisfied. The military department rarely questioned military spending; instead, they devoted their time to petty struggles over how such funds should be distributed within the army itself, and more particularly, over the relative shares to be enjoyed by the king's and Company armies.

The combination of conditions in India and the numerous checks and balances imposed by the East India Company made the transport and supply of the army difficult tasks. The two departments in India that were charged with supporting the army were the commissariat and the ordnance. As already noted, the Court of Directors had carefully isolated these two departments from the army and placed them instead under the Military Board which reported through the Military Secretary to the Supreme Council. This way civilians could keep a closer eye on military expenses. Economy was achieved at the expense of efficiency by 'vesting the chief controul of a department of which celerity and prompt decision are the life, in a Board, the judgments and actions of which, from its construction, are, and must remain slow.'[101] The end result was a conflict between economy and efficiency that could not be easily reconciled. The initiative and independence of commissariat and ordnance officers was stifled by a cumbersome procedure that obliged them to submit all their expenses to the Military Board for prior approval. Multiple receipts were required for all transactions — as one officer complained, 'to repair a doolie to the extent of sixpence or a shilling requires two military committees and two reports in triplicate'.[102] Orders were given to officers in these two departments to disregard all personal requests from army officers for supplies and only distribute what had previously been sanctioned.[103] Inventories of essential items were never maintained; the only concession was a recommendation to commissariat officers to prepare lists of what was available locally. This emphasis on the teeth rather than the tail of the army did result in considerable savings, but at the cost of rendering mobilization a very haphazard and incomplete operation. As will be seen later, these shortcomings were all too evident in the early phases of the war against the Burmese. The only notable campaign in which mobilization proceeded quickly and effectively was that against Bharatpur in 1825. On that occasion the army was fortunate that not only were supplies of needed material already up to strength on account of the war against Burma, but the army sent to reduce this stronghold operated close by the major storehouses and arsenals in the cantonments of Kanpur, Agra and Allahabad.

The military auditor general (the Indian equivalent of the British secretary at war) assisted the military secretary in the management of military spending. This office was viewed by many as one of the key military positions in India, and if the salary of the office is any indication, the Court also looked upon it as vitally necessary. Only the commander-in-chief had a higher salary.[104] In an attempt to ensure that this office was subordinated to the supreme government and removed from the direct influence of the army and the commander-in-chief, appointments to it could only be made from the Company's army and were to be decided upon by the governor-general and not the commander-in-chief. Despite these safeguards, and in part because of them, there were serious problems with how the military auditor general conducted his business. By being removed from the army, the military auditor general, like the accountant general in the civil line, could not gain easy access to the books of those military departments that received military funds. In some cases, the military auditor general was forced to build his estimates upon accounts that were three or more years out of date.[105] In wartime, the accuracy of his forecasts became even more suspect. There was also the suspicion that the military auditor general deliberately underestimated his accounts in a bid to placate the government.

As with any other army, the key variable in determining the cost of the Indian army was that of its intended use. The cost of the army was directly related to strategic demands; its size, deployment and internal organization reflected the perceived threats to British India. Self-serving, personal motives cloaked under the guise of objective analysis must also be taken into account. Certain deployments and missions, like those into prosperous regions, were all the more enticing because of the prospect of prize money, promotion or personal fame. Underlying all these were the pressures exerted by the military ethos that subordinated public finances to the need to ensure the security of British India.

The dominant strategic position was that internal and external threats to British rule could not and should not be separated. The beauty of this argument was that a potential challenger could always be discovered, and that having tied internal and external threats together, an army of sufficient size to deal with both was always required. Hence the army could insist that a well-equipped field force must always be maintained ready for service. Loud voices demanded that 'the army in India must always be on a war footing.'[106] If taken to their logical conclusion, these strategic imperatives meant that the army's growth could only be constrained by the available resources in British India. If revenues were increased, for example by annexation, the extra funds should be used to 'maintain the increased forces of which the necessity has been admitted.'[107] Authorities in London were criticized for failing to recognize these characteristics of Indian rule and for putting trade before territorial defence. Nowhere was this made more apparent than in London's expectations that with a prolonged period of peace, reductions could be made to the army.[108] A very different argument was made in India. Increased territorial responsibilities meant that an even larger sized army was needed for in addition to the troops actually stationed in the new lands, the British also had to have sufficient reserves to put on a show of force when needed.

The most expensive item of military spending under peacetime conditions was the pay and allowances of the officers, soldiers and sepoys of the Company's and king's forces at each presidency; in 1823 the number of soldiers and sepoys in Bengal stood at 129,473, with 71,423 in Madras and a further 36,475 in Bombay (see Table 5.3).[109] Costs were greater in those branches that had a high proportion of expensive European officers.

Table 5.3
Sizes and Costs of the Various Branches of British Forces in India in 1823
Expressed as a Percentage of the Whole.[110]

Branch	% of Force	% of Expenditure
European Artillery	2.6	4.2
European Cavalry	1.2	2.1
European Infantry	7.3	6.9
Indian Artillery	2.6	.8
Indian Regular Cavalry	5.6	8.1
Indian Irregular Cavalry	1.9	1.9
Indian Infantry	57.7	31.0
Indian Irregular Infantry	13.4	3.6
Staff	.3	6.0
Commissariat	.1	7.1
Medical	.4	1.4
Engineers	.4	.7
Total[112]	93.4	73.8

The most expensive troops were easily those in European regiments; a king's regiment was reckoned to cost £51,475 per year whereas a sepoy regiment which had approximately the same number of troops was only £24,492 per year.[111] Even cheaper were those locally-raised forces that required a minimum complement of European officers, such as the irregular infantry or irregular cavalry. Sepoy and irregular corps had the added advantage that they could be broken up more easily should India's financial state make savings necessary.

For those who audited the Company's accounts, the most alarming costs as well as those most difficult to explain were the pay and allowances of the army's staff. Nowhere was the army more generous than in the financial perquisites granted officers in either departmental or divisional staff postings. In theory the growth in staff positions should have slowed after these offices had first been established, assuming that they would have been able to cope with increases to forces in the field. At worst the staff should have kept pace with the overall growth in the army. Instead the ratio of field officers to subalterns in the field went from five for every forty in 1796 to three for every seventeen in 1829.[112] Bloated staff establishments were most apparent in Bengal where despite a slight fall in the size of the army between 1814 and 1830, the number of staff appointments was eighty-four more than it had been at its height.[113] The cost of the staff in Bengal grew even more dramatically: it nearly doubled between 1814 and 1830.[114] All this happened despite the Court's concerted efforts to impose thrift on army spending. The Court even tried to require their officials to submit all projected staff positions to London for prior approval, a requirement that was generally evaded though the Court did on at least one occasion reject a proposed appointment to a staff position.[115]

The most expensive items of expenditure in wartime were associated with the commissariat. The supply and transport of foodstuffs and essential material was the responsibility of this department. Figures from Bombay show that in peacetime the commissariat could expect to pay Rs. 35 per regiment of sepoys per month whereas in wartime the amount was Rs. 1702.[116] The cost of keeping Europeans in the field was considerably greater, as much as Rs. 13,051 per regiment. Field service also increased the amount disbursed as pay and allowances. When sepoys and soldiers were serving outside their own territories, they were entitled to a form of extra pay known as *batta*. To keep logistical expenses as low as possible, the army was expected whenever possible to turn to the marketplace for victualling. Sepoys in particular were expected to provide for themselves by buying their foodstuffs from local merchants. The dietary customs of European troops prevented that option from being used on them; they instead were provisioned by the state following deductions from their salary. The European soldiers were provided with 1 lb of bread, 1 lb of meat, 1/3 oz tea, 2 oz of sugar and 2 gills of arrack.[117] Anything beyond that was to be secured and paid for by the troops themselves. Sepoys were expected to provide for all their needs out of their pay packets. Although we have very little direct evidence of sepoys' private economies, comments by British officers can shed some light on this area. According to Jasper Nicolls, sepoys were able to save a considerable portion of their pay for he estimated that Hindu sepoys only spent Rs. 2 per month on food (out of a monthly pay of Rs. 7) while Muslim sepoys spent Rs. 4.[118] The difference here can be attributed to dietary customs and traditions as Muslims tended to consume more meat.

Local merchants were deliberately encouraged to set up shop within the army's lines, no matter whether the troops were in the field or in cantonments. In effect these bazaars came to resemble compact and mobile cities, capable of providing the troops with a vast range of products and services. The army in the field also looked to the *brinjaras* for logistical support. *Brinjaras* were an itinerant community of long distance traders, handling for the most part wheat, rice and other bulky foodstuffs. They had historically maintained armies in the field and in the sparsely populated regions of central India, no army could operate without them. Brinjaras, however, were a mixed blessing. The British had no direct control over them and could not, therefore, completely depend upon them. Criticisms were also levied against them owing to reports that *brinjaras* were also guilty of plundering along the line of march.[119]

The use of market forces for supplying the army with its needs was one that was at least initially successful in India where it built upon indigenous traditions. However, serious shortcomings were to emerge over time as British forces pushed further and further outwards. While merchants willing to supply the army could usually be found within India, this was not the case as the British began to push their armies outside India's frontiers. In campaigns where the British were operating in areas of low population and fierce local resistance, such as Afghanistan and Burma, the army was forced to take on a more direct responsibility for its logistics. Lacking the infrastructure needed for this, and still hampered by an unyielding bureaucracy, supplying the army in these campaigns became a major difficulty.

Despite all the precautions introduced by London to try and keep their army and its expenses under control, the army grew relentlessly and without appearing to follow any rational plan (see Appendix I). The weak point in London's financial calculations was that they failed to make sufficient provision for war and the growth in civil and military institutions in their long-term planning. Peace was assumed to be norm, leaving local authorities with little room to manoeuvre. When war did break out the Company's failure to provide for it in their calculations became evident as London could only offer desperate pleas for thrift. As one observer noted, 'if British India could carry on an expensive war upon her income, she would be very unlike any other country in the world, and especially unlike England.'[120] Furthermore, the Company's assumptions regarding Indian finances were based upon an unreal appreciation of India's resources. Years like 1822/23, which were highlighted by the directors as the ones to which all accounts were to be compared, were exceptional (see Appendix G). The inelasticity of Indian revenues was generally overlooked as was the underdeveloped nature of the Indian economy. Most worrying for the Company was that expenditure seemed to be continually outpacing revenues. War certainly exacerbated the situation, but civil charges were in the long run growing even more rapidly. Military charges, because they were easier to detect, came under the most criticism.

Nevertheless, the Court's suspicions of unchecked military expenses were in part well founded. Piecemeal additions were constantly being made to the army, even during peacetime, much to the dismay of authorities in London. While few doubted that wartime required extra troops, most in London expected that these increases would be rolled back after the war. This was not the case. Only the Madras army approximated this pattern. The overall trend in the Bombay and Bengal presidencies was that despite occasional reductions their armies would continue to grow. While London argued that once an enemy was subdued the army could be reduced, officials in Bengal and Bombay insisted that their armies needed to be kept up to wartime strength to provide sufficient force to pacify conquered territories and overawe any new challenger. This becomes more apparent when we compare the sizes of the armies of these presidencies before and after the annexations of territories from the Maratha states.

Table 5.4
Sizes of the Armies of Bengal, Madras and Bombay, 1813/14 and 1822/23.[121]

Presidency	1813/14	1822/23	Difference	Per Cent Change
Bengal	99,769	129,743	29,704	30.0
Madras	66,389	71,423	5,034	7.5
Bombay	28,274	36,475	8,201	29.0

Once we take into account the extra numbers of troops required to garrison newly-acquired territories, Madras's ability to live within its limited means becomes apparent. Bengal's acquisitions in Rajasthan, along the Narbada and in Mhow forced them to secure the area with 32,256 troops which was more than they had raised during this period. Nearly 3000 troops had to be redeployed. The Madras army was called upon to provide troops for lands that had been acquired in Berar and the southern Maratha lands, the latter under the jurisdiction of the Bombay presidency but garrisoned by the Madras army. A total of 14,603 troops were needed which, when considering that their army had only increased by 5,034, forced the Madras government to shift some nine and a half thousand troops from their existing territories into new stations. Only in Bombay was the army left in 1822 with more troops than needed by the annexations. Acquisitions made in Cutch and Kathiawar needed 3,929 troops — Bombay had meanwhile raised just over eight thousand which left them with approximately four thousand troops surplus to their immediate requirements.

The most heated conflict lay between the Court's vision of the army's position in India and that held by officials in India and followed from the ending of the wars against the Marathas and the Pindaris. The Court of Directors argued that the last significant internal challenge to British hegemony had been extinguished and therefore tranquillity and its consequences — reductions to the size, cost and influence of the army — could be anticipated.[122] With these hopes in mind, the Court proposed that the army be restructured in such a way as to convert what had been a field army into something akin to a colonial gendarmerie. Such a revised army would be better equipped to deal with internal unrest. They concluded their review with the statement that:

> It appears that our position ought to be wholly defensive and precautionary, and the army, should now be organized principally with a view to internal security and reduced to the lowest practical scale consistent with a reasonable provision for that object.[123]

One of the economy measures ordered by the Court of Directors was that a number of Bengal cantonments be put on half-batta and that further reductions be made to allowances traditionally granted to European officers in India. Batta had initially been intended as a field allowance to help cover the costs experienced by officers going on campaign. It had, however, in Bengal come to be paid to all officers below the rank of colonel, except those at Fort William, no matter whether they were in the field or in garrison. The Court's plans were quite limited; only the three garrisons closest to Calcutta (Berhampore, Dinapore and Barrackpore) were to be put on half batta. The savings anticipated by changing full batta for half batta for these few garrisons was in itself quite small compared to the overall costs of the army. For the individual officer, however, the financial consequences of going over to half batta could be quite serious. A lieutenant colonel on half batta would receive £74 per month; on full batta he was entitled to £92. Captains saw their pay drop by £4 to £33 and for lieutenants used to £22 per month, they would have to make do with £20.[124] These paycuts were aggravated by the fact that most officers were deep in debt as they tried to live up to the lavish lifestyle that had become customary for officers in India. Mess bills, numerous servants, horses, wines and spirits all added up.[125]

The Company's plans to introduce half batta as well as other savings had been in the offing for some time. The original orders had come out in 1814, but owing to the government of India's preoccupation with the war in Nepal and later struggles against the Marathas and Pindaris, Hastings had managed to defer the implementation of these orders.[126] The Court's determination to secure the passage of the half-batta regulations was only partly due to economies. They were also sensitive to the grievances of officers in Bombay and Madras who were not entitled to any batta unless they happened to be actually in the field. There were some indications that the mutinous behaviour of some officers in the Madras army in 1809 had been prompted by resentment over the better allowances paid in Bengal.[127] Concern over these inequities resurfaced in the 1820s when Charles Wynn was informed by Bishop Heber that officers in Bombay and Madras still resented what they saw as an injustice.[128]

Hastings worked to prevent the implementation of these new economies. His tactics at the beginning were those of prevarication and a polite request to London to reconsider its decision. In private, however, Hastings instructed the council in Calcutta to disregard the Company's instructions regarding military savings. Hastings also tried to use the wars with Nepal and the Marathas as an excuse for delay The Court was not deflected by these tactics and repeated their orders in 1817. London's obstinacy over these instructions forced Hastings to attempt a different tactic: he referred the Court's instructions to a committee for further consideration. This infuriated the Court for not only were their orders not subject to discussion, but the committee assembled by Hastings, comprising eight senior army officers and three civilians, could hardly be deemed neutral. The Court angrily wrote to Hastings that 'on no pretence whatever shall our orders be hereafter referred for report to a Committee of our servants, how many be more or less interested in their non-execution.'[129] The other argument that Hastings raised in support of the Bengal officers' claims, the higher cost of living in Bengal, was quickly disproven by the Court of Directors.

Underlying the struggle between the Court and the army (with Hastings at its head) was a substantial difference of opinion over how India should be governed and by who. Hastings' argument that 'the first duty of the government is to fix the amount of military force necessary for the maintenance of India' was a stark reminder of just how deeply military fiscalism had become entrenched. He pushed his argument even further by stating that 'if reductions be then necessary to square the receipts and expenditure of India; it must fall upon the civil charges of government.'[130] By strenuously advancing the cause of the army in India, Hastings was able to placate the growing apprehensions in the army that their personal interests would soon suffer with the return of peace. One subaltern wrote of these fears to his uncle in England, 'we are therefore likely to have a long peace, which tho[ugh] advantageous to our employers is not the thing for an army so exceedingly backward in promotion.'[131] Were any regiments to be broken up in order to reduce army expenses, promotions would become even more delayed. By defending the size and perquisites of the Indian army, Hastings was appealing to the officers' self interest. As a consequence, one officer noted, 'a spirit of reasoning, and a fervour of writing' was encouraged in the army and officers were seduced by 'mistaken notions of their own independence.'[132]

While his acts were certainly well designed to appeal to the European officers, they also began a long and acrimonious struggle between London and Calcutta, a struggle that typified the contest between the Anglo-Indian militarism of the periphery and the commercial priorities of the metropole. The Court protested to Hastings that his recommendations 'seem to be to render India a military government.'[133] The Court of Directors' suspicions that their Indian administration was becoming increasingly militarized under Hastings was well-founded, for Hastings confided to William Elphinstone that 'the subjection of the military to the civil power is a most just principle, but in its application advertence should be made to local peculiarities.'[134] Hastings also left a difficult legacy for his successors. If they wanted to secure the respect and support of the military, they would have to maintain his line on economies.[135]

The vigour with which Hastings pressed his arguments, when coupled with the Court of Directors' fears for the discipline of the Bengal army, persuaded the Court to amend the order in 1823.[136] The planned abolition of some of the smaller allowances was scrapped, and the impact of the half batta order was to be delayed until after the next rotation of regiments between stations in Bengal. The Court also tried to placate the officers by ordering the reorganization of the army from regiments of two battalions to single battalion regiments. By splitting regiments, the number of colonelcies and captaincies was increased, therefore holding out the promise of quickened promotion. House rent was also offered to officers placed on half batta, though this did not make up the entire difference. The cumulative effect of these amendments was to reduce by half the expected annual savings, from £12,000 to £6,000. Moreover, the expense of splitting the regiments was estimated to be £22,840 per year.[137] Half batta ceased to be an issue of economies and became instead one of principle.

Despite all the potential faultlines in the Company's finances that have here been identified, the beginning of the 1820s saw widespread confidence in the future profitability of British India. This optimism owed much to the Marquess of Hastings' persistent efforts to portray his administration in as positive a light as possible. Unreal expectations were fostered by his constant lobbying of the Company, the Prince Regent and the Board of Control. Hastings bombarded his metropolitan correspondents with inflated predictions, perhaps to counteract the adverse publicity that surrounded him following the exposure of his involvement in certain questionable dealings of the House of Palmer at the Nizam of Hyderabad's court.[138] Hastings even boasted of Bombay's glowing and profitable future, a prediction that was questioned in private by the governor of that presidency.[139] Mountstuart Elphinstone's survey of newly annexed lands, written in 1821, concluded that owing to the desolation of the countryside following years of warfare, rural prosperity would take many years to recover.[140] Elsewhere in India a heady atmosphere prevailed. His successor was warned by Holt Mackenzie that in the prevailing mood 'it is next to hopeless in any person in a subordinate position to force upon the government of Bengal a due sense of the duty of economy.'[141] Sceptics like Elphinstone were quickly dismissed. Hastings advised the Company's chairman, 'Don't be misled by croakers [Elphinstone] who talk at random' and reaffirmed his belief in India's future profitability: 'I confidently avert to you a great surplus.'[142] This chorus of approval was joined in by members of his administration, eager to improve their own reputations in London. Even Bengal's resident scholar, H.H. Wilson, succumbed to the enthusiasm. Wilson wrote:

At no previous period in the history of the country was the prospect of financial prosperity more promising than at the commencement of 1823, when the Marquess of Hastings retired from the guidance of the pecuniary interests of India.[143]

London's attention was also drawn to Hastings' efforts to reduce the Indian debt. Between 1820 and Hastings' departure in early 1823, £4,538,046 had been paid off.[144] Few, however, dwelt on how this had been accomplished, namely, through the dispatch of a large amount of specie to Britain which was intended to lure creditors to accept payments in Britain. This created a bullion shortage that would handcuff his successor. Nor did Hastings consider that even these reductions to the debt had not brought it down to what it had been when he arrived in India.

The boosterism engaged in by Hastings and his supporters was certainly not to everybody's taste, and a few individuals forecast correctly some of the trials ahead. Henry St. George Tucker, whose earlier experience as military auditor general in Bengal gave him a uniquely well informed perspective, demolished the claims made for Hastings' years of financial management. He argued that whatever improvements had occurred in Indian balances were the consequence of the economies of Hastings' predecessor, the Earl of Minto.[145] Minto never received due credit for establishing the government's credit on a safe and secure footing. There were others, including Thomas Courtenay of the Board of Control, and two directors of the East India Company, John Loch and J.G. Ravenshaw, that expressed misgivings about the state of the Indian economy.[146] Contrary to Hastings' boasts, Bombay's financial position had not improved with the annexation of new territories; instead, as can be seen in Appendix G, Bombay's deficit had grown even larger. A report on the Company's military expenditure charged Hastings with paying too little attention to the details of expenditure and, most significantly, for failing to take advantage of the return of peace to institute substantial reductions.[147] The latter lay at the heart of the Company's looming financial crisis — expenditures were growing more quickly than revenues, and given the inelasticity of Indian revenues, balanced budgets could only be secured through more rigorous controls on administrative and military costs.[148] Hastings' successor, Lord Amherst, was not in a position to do much about this for he was pinned down by an expensive war with Burma. It was up to Bentinck to effect economies, but to do so, he had to contend with Hastings' legacy — a bloated administration and an army that jealously guarded their autonomy and perquisites.

[1] Evidence of John Malcolm, S.C. on the East India Company, PP, 13(1831/32): 346

[2] Kaye, *Life of Metcalfe*, 149. Colonel Young's report for the Marquess of Hastings argued that the military must have first priority on Indian finances, and if need be, on extra-Indian finances as well. BL, Colonel Young, Military Report, 1820, Add MS 38518

[3] Henry St. George Tucker, *Review of the Financial Situation of the East India Company in 1824*, London: np, 1825, 15

[4] Burton Stein, 'State Formation and Economy Reconsidered,' *Modern Asian Studies*, 19(1985): 390-91

[5] 53 Geo III c.155. See also the Court's instructions to Madras, OIOC, Court to Madras, E/4/911

[6] Tucker, *Review*, 190-91

[7] S.C. on the East India Company, PP, 10(1831/32), Pt 1, xiv-xvi

[8] OIOC, H.T. Prinsep's diary, nd, MSS Eur C97/2, p.100.

[9] OIOC, Mackenzie to Adam, 17 Jan 1822, MSS Eur F109/D

[10] B.B. Misra, *The Central Administration of the East India Company, 1773-1834*, Manchester: Manchester University Press, 1959, 87

[11] S.C. on the East India Company, PP, 9(1831/32): 305

[12] PRO, Sullivan to Ellenborough, 23 Nov 1830, PRO 30/9/4/11/II

[13] S. Ambirajan, *Classical Political Economy and British Policy in India*, Cambridge: Cambridge University Press, 1978, 160

[14] See S.C. on the East India Company, PP, (1831/32): volumes 9, 10, and 13

[15] Percival Spear, 'Holt Mackenzie — Forgotten Man of Bengal,' *Bengal Past and Present*, 86(1967): 24-7

[16] Nottingham, Malcolm to Bentinck, 24 Jan 1828, PwJf 1404

[17] OIOC, Mackenzie to Adam, 17 June 1822, MSS Eur F109/D; Mackenzie to Amherst, 11 Jan 1825, MSS Eur F140/143; Accountant General to Government, 3 June 1825, Madras Financial Consultations, P330/49

[18] OIOC, Financial Letter to Bengal, 1 Mar 1826, L/F/3/676

[19] S.C. on the East India Company, PP, 10(1831/32): Pt 1, xv

[20] S.C. on the East India Company, PP, 9(1831/32): 4

[21] OIOC, Consultations, 28 April 1825, Bengal Financial Consultations, P/161/42. It should be noted that this predicament was not unique to India. In 1847/48, the British Treasury was also complaining that required information was not forthcoming from the War Office, the Foreign Office and Horse Guards. Henry Roseveare, *The Treasury 1660-1870; the Foundation of Control*, London: Allen and Unwin, 1973, 69

[22] PP, 46(1861): 97

[23] Roseveare, *The Treasury*, 69-70

[24] OIOC, Accountant General to Government, 3 June 1825, Madras Financial Consultations, P/330/49

[25] OIOC, Figures for Madras are taken from Madras Military Accounts, L/MIL/8/93-103 and those for Bengal are from Bengal Military Accounts, L/MIL/8/29-38

[26] 'Price figures and contemporary comment leave no doubt that all parts of India experienced a significant downward drift of prices of food grains and export cash crops between about 1818 and 1845.' C.A. Bayly, 'State and Economy in India over Seven Hundred Years,' *Economic History Review*, 38(1985): 590

[27] C.A. Bayly, *Rulers, Townsmen and Bazaars; North Indian Society in the Age of British Expansion, 1770-1870*, Cambridge: Cambridge University Press, 1983, passim but especially chapter 7

[28] National Army Museum, Lieut. Hutton Watkins to James Hutton, 10 Dec 1810, Acc 7510-38

[29] Bayly, *Rulers*, 54

[30] Siddiqi, 'Money and Prices', 262

[31] Bayly, *Rulers*, 54

[32] Bayly, *Rulers*, 215

[33] John Crawfurd in K.N. Chaudhuri, *The Economic Development of India under the East India Company, 1814-1858*, Cambridge: Cambridge University Press, 1971, 237

[34] G.H.P. Livesay, *Notes on Military Transport on the Northeastern and Eastern Frontiers of India*, Calcutta: 1881, 4

[35] Henry St. George Tucker, *Remarks on the Plans of Finance lately Promulgated by the Honourable Court of Directors and by the Supreme Government of India*, London: 1821

[36] John Crawfurd in Chaudhuri, *Economic Development*, 258

[37] OIOC, Board to Court, 6 July 1824, L/AG/29/11/1; see also the correspondence between Ellenborough and the chairs in PRO 30/9/4/1/2

[38] A.K. Bagchi, 'Transition from Indian to British-Indian Systems of Banking,' *Modern Asian Studies*, 19(1985): 501-19

[39] Ward, 'Industrial Revolution and British Imperialism', tends to underestimate the importance of Indian capital and Indian capitalists during wartime.

[40] Bagchi, 'Transition', 508

[41] For an overview of Agency Houses, see Bagchi, 'Transition'; Tripathi, *Trade and Finance*; and S.D. Chapman, 'The Agency Houses; British Mercantile Enterprise in the Far East, c.1780-1920,' *Textile History*, 19(1988): 239-54

[42] S.K. Basu, 'The House of Palmer and Company,' *Indian Journal of Economics*, 15(1934): 6; OIOC, G. Wellesley to M.E. Elphinstone, 2 Oct 1824, MSS Eur F88/C/16

[43] See for example, OIOC, Bengal financial Letter to London, 17 Feb 1825, L/F/3/16

[44] H.H. Wilson, *Review of the External Commerce of Bengal*, Calcutta: 1830,

[45] John Crawfurd in Chaudhuri, *Economic Development*, 264

[46] Section 57, 55 Geo III c.155

[47] S.C. on the East India Company, PP, 10(1831/32): Pt I, xxxii

[48] Asiya Siddiqi, *Agrarian Change in a North Indian State: United Provinces, 1819-1933*, Oxford: Clarendon, 1973, 150-51

[49] OIOC, Financial Letter to London, 19 June 1823, L/F/3/15

[50] East India Accounts, PP, 24(1825); East India Accounts, 20(1826/27)

[51] K.N. Chaudhuri, 'Foreign Trade and Balance of Payments (1757-1947),' *Cambridge Economic History of India, Vol. 2, c.1757-c.1970*, Dharma Kumar and Tapan Raychaudhuri, eds. Cambridge: Cambridge University Press, 1982, 323

[52] Statistics taken from Frederick Hendriks, 'On the Statistics of Indian Revenue and Taxation,' *Journal of the Statistical Society of London*, 21(1858): 223-96

[53] Miscellaneous sources of revenue would include excise taxes on alcohol and tobacco, marine fees, and a range of smaller items.

[54] S.C. on the East India Company, PP, 10(1831/32): Pt I, 412

[55] PRO, Ellenborough, memo on land revenues, nd, PRO 30/12/20/9; Loch to Ellenborough, 17 Nov 1829, PRO 30/9/4/43

[56] F.J. Shore's diaries continually make reference to the pressures in Bengal on collectors to maximize their returns. OIOC, MSS Eur E307. The same was true in Bombay, see Guha, 'Society and Economy in the Deccan', 391-94

[57] P.J. Marshall, *The New Cambridge History of India: II.2. Bengal, the British Bridgehead*, Cambridge: Cambridge University Press, 1988, 144

[58] An extensive body of literature is available on famines and famine policy in India. See for example, Michelle McAlpin, *Subject to Famine: Food Crises and Economic Change in Western India, 1860-1920*, Princeton: Princeton University Press, 1983

[59] Reginald Heber, Bishop of Calcutta. *Narrative of a Journey through the Upper Provinces of India, from Calcutta to Bombay, 1824-1825*. London: John Murray, 1846, I, 82

[60] OIOC, Madras Financial Letter to London, 8 July 1825, Madras Financial Consultations, P/330/49; Mackenzie to Amherst, 11 Jan 1825, MSS Eur F140/145; S.C. on the East India Company, PP, 11(1831/32): 275. A description of the ruthlessness of Bombay collectors is provided in Guha, 'Society and Economy in the Deccan', 391-94

[61] PRO, memo on Indian revenues, c.1829, PRO 30/12/20/9

[62] Ibid.

[63] Bayly, *Rulers*, 260

[64] Ibid.

[65] S.C. on the East India Company, PP, 10(1831/32): Pt I, xiv-xvi

[66] Conflicts over how the Deccan prize money was to be apportioned out delayed its disbursement by more than ten years. Normally, however, borrowing from prize money deposits was a more short-term expedient for prize monies were

normally paid out within five years of the campaign from which they had been acquired. S.C. on the East India Company, PP, 10(1831/32): Pt I, 196

[67] OIOC, Henry Wood, memo on government loans, 11 March 1824, MSS Eur F140/141

[68] Norman Gash, *Pillars of Government and other Essays on State and Society, c.1770–c.1880*, London: Arnold, 1986, 31

[69] S.C. on the East India Company, PP, 10(1831/32): Pt I, xxi

[70] Hamilton, *Description*, xi

[71] BL, Courtenay to Herries, 17 Sept 1823, Add MS 38411

[72] Tucker, *Review*, 31

[73] Chatterji Nandalal, 'Colonel Baillie and the Oudh Loans,' *Journal of Indian History*, 31(1953): 9, OIOC, comment by H.T. Prinsep, nd, MSS Eur C97/2, pp.74-5

[74] Heber, *Narrative*, I, 222

[75] OIOC, Nicolls' Diary, 30 Nov 1818, MSS Eur F175/23

[76] Averages computed from figures in an undated and unsigned memo in the Ellenborough Papers. PRO, memo, nd, PRO 30/12/31/2. By way of comparison, annual government expenditure in Britain between 1817 and 1854 hovered between fifty and sixty million pounds. A.W. Acworth, *Financial Reconstruction in England, 1815-1822*, London: P.S. King and Sons, 1925, 25

[77] OIOC, Note by Holt Mackenzie, 1823, MSS Eur F140/142

[78] Section 55, 53 Geo III c.155

[79] OIOC, Mackenzie to Adam, 26 Feb 1825, MSS Eur F109/D

[80] OIOC, Mackenzie to Amherst, 1823, MSS Eur F140/142; Lieut. Col. Frederick, *Report on the Military Expenditure of the East India Company*, London: 1831, 80

[81] Data taken from S.C. on the East India Company, PP, 6(1831/32): 640-41

[82] PRO, Hardinge to Ellenborough, 30 Aug 1828, PRO 30/9/4/1/2

[83] PRO, Ellenborough to Chairs, 26 Sept 1829, PRO 30/9/4/27 Pt III

[84] PRO, Ellenborough to Chairs, 26 Sept 1829, PRO 30/9/4/27 Pt III

[85] OIOC, Chairs to Ellenborough, 4 Sept 1829, E/424/3

[86] S.C. on the East India Company, PP, 10(1831/32): Pt I, xi-xii

[87] Statistics compiled from S.C. on the East India Company, PP, (1831/32), volumes 8, 10, 11, and 13.

[88] S.C. on the East India Company, PP, 10(1831/32): Pt I, ix

[89] OIOC, Court Circular to India, 1 April 1824, L/PS/5/585, no.553

[90] Nottingham, Bentinck to Auber, 6 May 1830, PwJf 198

[91] OIOC, Mackenzie to Amherst, 11 Jan 1825, MSS Eur F140/143

[92] OIOC, Mackenzie to Amherst, 11 Jan 1825, MSS Eur F140/143

[93] PRO, Ellenborough, Memo on Indian Revenues, nd, PRO 30/12/20/9

[94] See his lengthy memos on expenditure in the Munro Papers, OIOC, MSS Eur F151/95

[95] Statistics taken from S.C. on the East India Company, PP, (1831/32): vols 8, 10, 11, and 13

[96] OIOC, Mackenzie to Amherst, 11 Jan 1825, MSS Eur F140/143

[97] Nottingham, Financial Letter to Bombay, 12 Dec 1827, PwJf 2575; H.T. Prinsep, *History of the Political and Military Transactions in India during the Administration of the Marquess of Hastings*, London: John Murray, 1820, II, 444

[98] Tripathi, *Trade and Finance*, 214

[99] Evidence of Colonel J. Salmond, S.C. on the East India Company, PP, 13(1831/32): 316

[100] OIOC, Mackenzie to Amherst, 15 Oct 1827, MSS Eur F140/85

[101] OIOC, Salmond to Bentinck, 16 Jan 1831, MSS Eur E424/5

[102] 'Remarks on the Constitution and Efficiency of the Bengal Commissariat,' *East India United Services Journal*, 1(1833): 268

[103] Col Burlton, quoted in Humphrey Bullock, *History of the Army Service Corps*, Aldershot: 1952, 57

[104] OIOC, Instructions to Ordnance and Commissariat Officers, 24 April 1824, Bengal Military Consultations, P/30/48

[105] OIOC, See salary tables in Bengal Military Accounts, 1825, L/MIL/8/33

[106] OIOC, Accountant General to Government, 28 May 1825, Madras Expeditionary Consultations, P/330/45

[107] BL, Report by Colonel Young, 1820, Add MS 38518

[108] Charles Metcalfe in J.W. Kaye, *The Life and Correspondence of Lord Metcalfe*, London: Smith, Elder and Co., 1858, I, 185

[109] OIOC, Military Letter to Bengal, 25 Nov 1823, L/MIL/5/468

[110] S.C. on the East India Company, PP, 13(1831/32): vii

[111] Data compiled from the appendices to S.C. on the East India Company, PP, 13(1831/32)

[112] Those numbers unaccounted for in the list above were made up of various labour parties while the remainder of the budget was for the purchase of military stores and expenditure on military buildings.

[113] S.C. on the East India Company, PP, 13(1831/32): 242-43

[114] PRO, Ellenborough, memo on staff appointments in the Indian Army, 1829, PRO 30/9/4/3

[115] S.C. on the East India Company, PP, 13(1831/32): lxxix

[116] From £546,053 to £1,103,725, Ibid, 240

[117] OIOC, Military Letter to Bengal, 5 Dec 1826, L/MIL/5/386/98

[118] OIOC, Colonel Frederick, Calculation on Commissariat Expenses, c.1829, MSS Eur D765/2

[119] [King's Officer], 'Comparative Pay and Allowances of King's Officers in India and England,' *United Services Journal*, 12(1833): 223

[120] OIOC, Nicolls' Diary, 2 July 1816, MSS Eur F175/19

[121] Capt. John Briggs, 'Account of the Origin, History and Manners of the Race of Men called Bunjaras,' *Transactions of the Literary Society of Bombay*, 1(1841): 170-97

[122] [R.D. Mangles], 'Ministerial Misrepresentations Regarding the East,' *Edinburgh Review*, 77(1843): 289

[123] Statistics taken from S.C. on the East India Company, PP, 13(1831/32): passim

[124] SRO, Ramsay to Dalhousie, 10 Nov 1824, GD 45/5/4; OIOC, Military Letter to Bengal, 25 Nov 1823, L/MIL/5/468

[125] OIOC, Draft Letter to Bengal, 1823, L/MIL/5/385/88

[126] This table has been calculated on the basis of a 30 day month with an exchange rate of 2s2d per sonaut rupee. Data taken from S.C. on the East India Company, PP, 13(1831/32): 280

[127] Contemporary memoirs frequently refer to officers living well beyond their

means. W.D. Arnold's *Oakfield* offers a particularly damning indictment of these tendencies.

[128] OIOC, Military Letter to Bengal, 26 Feb 1814, H/MISC/552. The other cuts that were ordered by the Court included reducing the allowances given for such expenses as stationery and small arms repair. OIOC, Military Letter to Bengal, 5 May 1815, L/MIL/5/368

[129] J. Malcolm, *Observations on the Disturbances in the Madras Army in 1809*, London: 1812

[130] OIOC, Wynn to the Duke of York, 25 Dec 1823, F/2/7

[131] OIOC, Military Letter to Bengal, 25 Nov 1823, L/MIL/5/468

[132] OIOC, Hastings to Court, 6 Jan 1820, L/MIL/5/386/98

[133] National Army Museum, Lieut. Hutton Watkins to James Watkins, 8 Aug 1818, Acc 7510-38

[134] General Samuel Ford Whittingham, 24 June 1825, *A Memoir of the Services of Lieutenant-General Sir Samuel Ford Whittingham*, London: Longmans, Green and Co., 1868, 352-53

[135] OIOC, Draft Reply, 1823, L/MIL/5/305/88

[136] OIOC, Hastings to William Elphinstone, 20 March 1820, MSS Eur F89/2/A/1/4

[137] SRO, Ramsay to Dalhousie, 18 Nov 1824, GD45/5/4

[138] OIOC, Military Letter to Bengal, 25 Nov 1823, L/MIL/5/392/139

[139] OIOC, memo on financial savings, L/MIL/5/401/199

[140] Hastings to Bloomfield, 20 June 1821, A.A. Aspinall, ed., *The Letters of George IV, 1812-1830*, Cambridge: Cambridge University Press, 1938, II, 438; OIOC, Hastings to W.F. Elphinstone, 13 May 1821, MSS Eur F89/2/A/1/4. For a discussion of Hastings' involvement with the scandals surrounding the House of Palmer in Hyderabad, see Peter Wood, *Vassal State in the Shadow of Empire: Palmer's Hyderabad, 1799-1867*, unpublished Ph.D. dissertation, University of Wisconsin-Madison, 1981

[141] OIOC, M. Elphinstone to W.F. Elphinstone, 11 May 1822, MSS Eur F89/9/E/23

[142] OIOC, Mountstuart Elphinstone, *Report on Territories, Conquered from the Peishwa*, Calcutta: 1821, L/PS/20/F52

[143] OIOC, Mackenzie to Amherst, 15 Oct 1827, MSS Eur F140/86

[144] OIOC, Hastings to Campbell Marjoribanks, 11 Nov 1819, MSS Eur F206/84

[145] H.H. Wilson, *History of British India*, London: 1840, VI, 564

[146] Indian Accounts, PP, 23(1859): cmd 201

[147] Tucker, *Review*, 31-3

[148] BL, Courtenay to Herries, 17 Sept 1823, Add MS 38411; PRO, Loch to Ellenborough, 17 Nov 1829, PRO 30/9/4/43; OIOC, Ravenshaw to Munro, 5 Jan 1823, MSS Eur F151/78

[149] OIOC, Lieut. Col. Frederick, Report on Military Finances, MSS Eur D765/1

[150] A survey of Company finances undertaken by the Court in 1828 revealed in unquestionable terms that expenditures were growing at a much quicker rate than revenues, and had been doing so since 1794/95. See OIOC, 'General Results of the East India Company in their Political Capacity from 1794/95 to 1826/27,' L/F/5/83

6. THE GARRISON STATE IN ACTION: THE BURMA WAR AND THE CAMPAIGN AGAINST BHARATPUR

William Pitt Amherst arrived in India in 1823 as Hastings' successor and found an administration still very much drugged by the heady cocktail of conquest and promises of future profits that had been served up by the Marquess of Hastings. Nearly everybody around him had bought into this rhetoric. Few realized just how precarious Indian finances were at that time or how many fault lines had begun to disturb the surface of the army. All it would take to topple the Raj's finances and unsettle its army was for an unforeseen and expensive war to break out. India's military and financial resources would be stretched to the breaking point in such a situation. Yet in 1823 a war seemed to be nowhere in sight. Reminiscing on his own arrival in India in that same year, Edward Paget, the newly-installed commander-in-chief, sarcastically commented:

> It may be your lot as it was mine to be borne down by the precious dogma ... that the wisdom of Lord Hastings had so conciliated the minds of the whole population of India ... that nothing but the remote contingency of a Russian invasion was ever likely again to find occupation for the Indian army.[1]

Delusions were shattered in early 1824 when the Burma War erupted, quickly followed by a campaign to seize the Jat fortress of Bharatpur in 1825. The Burma War was to prove to be the costliest war fought to date as well as the most controversial, for not only did it fail to secure any tangible benefits for either the colonial state or the troops and officers in the army, but it demonstrated very clearly that despite the very militarized nature of British rule, the regime was shot through with so many flaws and inconsistencies that effective military operations were made less certain. The war's

very notoriety can be gauged from the outpouring of books at its conclusion and the sustained effort made by the Court of Directors to secure the
recall of the governor-general.[2] At least fifteen books and articles, nearly all
the product of actual service in Burma, were written in years following,[3]
and the war figured in two spectacles mounted in London theatres.[4] The
ultimate accolade, however, came in 1897 when this first war with Burma
was used as the setting for a Henty novel.[5]

The source of this interest and controversy lay in the conditions of fighting on Bengal's eastern frontier. Those who served in this war were faced
with little prospect of prize money, very little loot and seemingly endless
desultory fighting in an inhospitable climate. It was a war very different
from those to which the British had grown accustomed, one in which the
standard strategies, tactics and logistical arrangements were unsuited. Authorities in India were baffled by these developments and, as the war dragged
on, they quickly became disillusioned. Exasperated by the difficulties in
bringing the war to a successful conclusion, Munro wrote to Wellington
that 'I wish it were well over and bed time.'[6]

When Lord Amherst arrived in India as Hastings' successor in the autumn of 1823, barely four months before the Burma War broke out, neither
he, nor officials in London, nor the members of his administration, anticipated that conflict would break out on India's eastern frontier, or anywhere
else for that matter. London looked forward to a period of peace and retrenchment. The Court's willingness to accept Amherst as governor-general was in part due to their expectation that Amherst would not be inclined to obstruct their economy drive. Unlike Hastings, Amherst was considered to lack initiative and ambition and hence he would prove more receptive to Company directives to reduce Indian expenses. These characteristics, however, were ill-suited to presiding over an arduous war. As one
director ruefully wrote later, 'Lord Amherst is unfortunate, he certainly
was never calculated for a war governor.'[7]

The Court of Directors and the Board of Control were united in the
conviction that there were no foreseeable threats to disturb the peace in
India. Amherst was sent to India with two accounts of its current state; one
was prepared by Thomas Reid on behalf of the Court and the other was
drafted by B.S. Jones of the Board of Control.[8] Though these two reports
were drafted independently of each other, they both reached the same conclusion — there was nothing likely to disturb the peace in India and that
the time was perfect to begin to effect reductions in Indian expenditure.
These points were reiterated in verbal communications between the Court
and Amherst. He was warned that the 'extension of territory [is to be]

deprecated' and that 'financial surpluses [were] applicable to the reduction of debt.'[9] The Court particularly impressed upon Amherst their expectations that he would bring the army's costs and influences under control, largely through the introduction of their amended half-batta orders.[10] His official instructions concluded: 'There is no power, nor any combination of powers, which could make head against us or furnish reasonable grounds for attack.'[11]

Lord Amherst arrived in India intent upon meeting London's expectations of peace and profitability.[12] Indeed his conscientiousness struck many onlookers, who were used to flaunting the Court, as ludicrous. Writing shortly after a flood had damaged the governor-general's residence at Barrackpore, Paget sarcastically described Amherst as being more troubled by the 'house and furniture of the Honourable Company having experienced this disaster, than if they had been his own. I fear I entertain no such feelings.'[13] Amherst set about introducing the expected economies shortly after he landed in Calcutta. Reductions in civil expenditure were ordered and the half-batta order was resurrected. Economic conditions, at least on the surface, seemed to confirm the optimism that had been expressed in London. Interest rates were low and capital appeared to be abundant. The fiscal year that had just ended (1822/23) was one of the most successful the Company had ever experienced, further encouraging optimism [see Appendix G].

What most upset Amherst's hopes of implementing economies was that conditions in India were not like those he had been briefed to expect. Paget had warned Amherst shortly after the governor-general had arrived to discount the 'fashionable persuasion that the tranquillity of India is fixed on a basis so solid as to render the prospect of its being disturbed very remote.'[14] In his private correspondence, Amherst would later reflect upon just how unfounded were the reports he had been given prior to departure. Most importantly he had not been warned of the simmering tensions along Bengal's eastern frontier, tensions that would provide the rationale for the British capture of Rangoon in May 1824.[15] However, even before the prospect of a war with Burma had appeared, relations between London and Calcutta were troubled by a fundamental difference of opinion over how Indian finances were to be employed. Conflict between the Court and their officials in India broke out over what should be done with surplus revenues. Officials in Bengal argued for one of two destinations, either build up the army, or after having seen to India's security, surpluses could be used to kindle the economy by relaxing internal customs and lowering tax burdens on the agricultural sector. A strong proponent of the latter, Holt Mackenzie, triggered a heated debate with London when he recommended that in light of anticipated surpluses, the government of Bengal should lower its internal customs duties from 7.5 per cent to 2.5 per cent.[16] The Court dismissed the latter and refused even to consider the former, arguing that not only did it exceed Bengal's discretionary authority, but that officials in India were not competent to decide when a surplus existed.[17] The Court insisted that only they had the power and ability to declare a surplus and sought to reassert their control over Indian finances. More importantly, as seen in their instructions to Lord Amherst, the Court had planned to use any surplus to try and reduce the Indian debt.

Tensions between the British and their eastern neighbours had existed for years, only counteracted by Calcutta's traditional apathy towards their eastern frontier. Northeastern India lacked the attractions that areas in central and northwestern India possessed, particularly the potential of a secure revenue base and a healthy environment in which troops could be stationed. Moreover, there did exist an embryonic notion that Burma lay beyond the natural frontiers of British India, and hence should play no part in the Company's strategic policy.[18] The consequence of this disinterest was that when faced with turbulence along the frontier, the British had historically done their best to ignore it. Warnings and evidence of Burmese expansionary pressures were disregarded in the hope that they would go away.[19] Amherst's predecessors, especially Minto and Hastings, had deliberately chosen to overlook provocations that elsewhere in India would have likely led to war. Minto did, however, feel that a war was likely to break out in the future.[20] Hastings, on the other hand, insisted that 'there is not the remotest apprehension of a rupture' between the British and the Burmese.[21] According to one observer, Hastings and Minto both felt that a war was justifiable, but that it was not warranted because there were no obvious economic or military benefits to be gained.[22] Formal contacts between the supreme government and the Burmese Court were therefore kept to a minimum and British officials confined their dealings with Burma to a series of half-hearted ambassadorial overtures.[23] These embassies failed to reduce tension for once the British had established that their European rivals, particularly France, had not established a toehold in Burma, they let relations with Burma lapse. Not one embassy was sent during the whole of Hastings' period in office.

These border tensions had arisen largely as a consequence of the internal dynamics of the Burmese state, hence supporting those recent scholars who have seen British Imperialism as the consequence of a complex interaction between British and indigenous developments.[24] This argument, put simply, insists that the conditions which gave rise to the British empire in India had as much to do, if not more, with what was happening within local political, economic and social circles. British relations with Burma confirm this line of argument. Similar to the British empire in India, Burma was an expanding power and much of its momentum was directed at territories contiguous to the frontier with British India.[25] Beginning in the mid-eighteenth century, the Burmese had broken out from their traditional power base in the central drylands of Burma and began the process of subjugating their neighbours, starting with the neighbouring state of Pegu to the south. This was followed by their conquest of Tennasserim in 1759 and moves into the Arakan peninsula in 1785 (see map 3). The potential for a collision with Britain increased greatly with the extension of Burmese influence into Manipur and Cachar in 1812, and peaked in 1817-22 when the Burmese invaded Assam. While these moves did not always lead to annexations (the Burmese only established client states in Manipur and Cachar) it did bring British and Burmese interests into direct contact.

A more immediate source of misunderstanding was provided by the presence in British territories of large numbers of refugees who were fleeing from the Burmese. In particular, the Burmese annexation of the Arakan peninsula had driven thousands of Magh refugees into the Chittagong district of eastern Bengal. The Maghs were not content to reside within British territories and from their camps along the border mounted armed raids into Burmese territory. Relations with the Burmese deteriorated further as the Burmese began to suspect, with good reason, that the British had no serious intention of controlling these people, nor would the British permit Burmese parties to pursue raiders back across the border. Thomas Robertson and others argued afterwards that British officials in the frontier areas were both incapable of and often unconcerned with bringing the Maghs under control.[26] The British realized too late just how annoyed the Burmese were by what appeared to them to be British complicity. Adoniram Judson, a missionary working in Rangoon at this time, believed that it was this insensitivity on the part of the British that was mainly responsible for the complete collapse of relations between India and Burma.[27] Later, the Burmese occupation of Assam also gave grounds for alarm as it was feared that this would allow them to unleash their dreaded warboats on the Brahmaputra and perhaps even threaten Calcutta. From Dhaka, Heber echoed contemporary British fears of these warboats: 'Had the Burmans really possessed any considerable force of warboats in the neighbourhood of Teak Naaf [Tek Naf], Dacca might early have fallen their prey, and alarm excited lately was very great, and with some better reason than I had supposed.'[28]

Tensions were certainly high along the frontier in 1823, but no higher than they had been between 1809 and 1816 when Hastings, who one would expect to have reacted promptly to such challenges, did his best to ignore any signs of trouble. In 1822-23, dynastic rivalries in Manipur, encouraged by the Burmese, spilled over into Cachar thus bringing Burmese influences closer to Calcutta. In Arakan, the Burmese made a claim to the hitherto insignificant island of Shapuri in the Naf River. They also began to impose taxes on Indian traders operating along the river. The British response was to back up their claim to Shapuri by stationing a small garrison on the island. This garrison was attacked by a much larger Burmese force on the night of 24 September 1823 and the British force suffered several casualties before being driven off.[29] While these incidents do point to an escalation of tensions, they do not in themselves account for the British decision to mount an expensive amphibious operation to seize Rangoon.

An obvious way of explaining this decision would be to turn to the often used argument of expansion being driven by economic needs or desires. One of the most persistent arguments in Indian historiography is that wars of expansion in India were determined by British commercial and or manufacturing interests. Traces of this interpretation have also been advanced to account for the outbreak of the Burma War.[30] Contemporary evidence, however, does not support such a conclusion. In 1824, there was very little interest in Burmese markets, nor was there much belief in the future profitability of Burma. Burma's chief commercial attraction, teak, had lost most of its appeal with the depression in the Indian shipbuilding industry.[31] One Calcutta merchant who had plans of penetrating Burmese markets, Henry Gouger, noted that merchants in Calcutta did not hold many hopes for a profitable trade with Burma.[32] Theories have also been put forward concerning British designs to secure either an overland passage to China or better protect the existing seaborne route.[33] Neither of these explanations carries much weight in the period prior to the outbreak of the war. British interests in overland routes to China only emerged later and even then government encouragement was limited to sanctioning a few underfunded survey parties.[34] The thesis that Burma was invaded so as to strengthen British control over the sealanes to China appears to be equally unfounded. The only two possible threats to this route, the French and the Dutch, had largely been neutralized by 1824. The French were not active in the area, and relations with the Dutch had improved with the treaty of 1824.

With the absence of any commercial or economic motive to go to war, and considering that border tensions had existed for years, the decision to declare war on Burma seems somewhat perplexing. It is made even more curious when one considers that Lord Amherst was extremely reluctant to take India into war. Like his predecessors, he sought to avoid conflict with Burma and even after the incident at Shapuri, Amherst looked for a peaceful solution. On that occasion, Amherst wrote to the Burmese Court to complain of what had happened, but carefully phrased his letter so as to ensure that the Court itself was not being blamed. Instead, and to provide the Burmese Court with a means of saving face, Amherst suggested that the attack on Shapuri could only have been an impetuous act by a local official.[35] Lady Amherst wrote to their son in England of her husband's reluctance to adopt a more aggressive policy, claiming that Amherst was 'very anxious having tried in vain by every conciliating means in his power to preserve peace.'[36] Amherst reminded his college friend George Canning that 'I remember well it being said most justly before I left England that if a conqueror was wanted in India, I was not the man who would have been selected to go there.'[37] Unlike Wellesley, whose expectedly grandiose claim was to accomplish all his 'grand financial, political, military, naval, commercial, architectural, judicial and political reforms', Amherst sought a quiet term of office, one marked by cautious stewardship rather than aggressive and dynamic leadership.[38] The last thing that Amherst wished to be associated with was an extension of British rule in India.

Why then did war break out? What had changed was that in 1823 conditions within India made the British government more inclined to respond vigorously to threats from outside. Put another way, war arose because Anglo-Indian militarism demanded it. A more hawkish foreign policy surfaced in 1823 when fears were raised that subjugated peoples in India would take their cue from the Burmese and rise up against their foreign rulers. Any signs of discontent in India were very quickly tied to Burmese intrigues, though never with any substantiating evidence.[39] There were allegations that Ranjit Singh had sent agents to Ava to seek an alliance, and that unrest in Kittur and among the Gujars of the Doab had been sparked by rumours of British setbacks at the hands of the Burmese.[40] Some even speculated that the Russians were somehow behind all this.[41] Amherst's private reservations notwithstanding, those advising him were adamant that war needed to be declared. They insisted that war was 'necessary to the honour of the government, and murmured greatly against Lord Amherst for not being more ready than he was to commence it.'[42] Amherst was confronted with a very different situation in India than for what he had been prepared. Not only were conditions in India less stable than he had been led to believe, but the Anglo-Indian strategies of rule were ones he found difficult to master. Confronted with a 'Queen Bee [who] is too full of European ideas and prejudices', the drones who surrounded Amherst set out to govern the hive.[43] Fortunately for these drones, Amherst was quickly brought under control. It is ironic that the one characteristic which secured for Amherst his appointment to India, the Court's hopes that he would be sufficiently pliable to concede to their demands, meant that once he was in India he readily placed himself under those officials he considered more expert than himself. To Thomas Munro, who would quickly become Amherst's principal mentor, Amherst wrote: 'These are matters on which I feel a great deal of anxiety to form a right judgment, for I think the opinion which I lean to is at variance with the opinions of the majority perhaps of those with whom I am in frequent consultation.'[44] Amherst particularly felt the lack of prior military experience. Correspondents in Britain sympathized, one lamented that 'Notwithstanding your hereditary claims to military science [his uncle and guardian had been commander-in-chief in Britain], the practice with the St. James Volunteers can scarcely have been sufficient to give you any part of the confidence which the urgency ... must have required.'[45]

The dominant opinion in India was that the British must respond with a vigorous display of force. Whatever they may have thought in the past, officials in India were nearly unanimous now in insisting that Burmese aggressions must be countered as swiftly and as convincingly as possible. Otherwise, the British would inadvertently give an impression of having gone soft. This was viewed as a potentially fatal mistake in an empire of opinion where opinion was read as being the fear and respect generated by British arms. When the Burmese had previously threatened the frontier, the British had been occupied in other wars which gave them plenty of opportunities to display their strength and resolve. In 1824, however, India had gone through six years of peace and there were worries that the British and their army were slowly being sapped of their potency. It was argued that 'it was well to bring it [affairs with Burma] to a point now when we have nothing else to do.'[46] From members of the secretariat to officials serving in Arakan and Assam, the demand was made that the British must visibly retaliate against the Burmese.[47] As Nicolls' recorded in his diary, 'We are in the position of Champion of England; we must fight whenever neighbouring nations think proper to throw down the gauntlet.'[48]

Once the decision was made that a show of force was required, discussions then turned to what type of war should be fought. A limited defensive action along the frontier was quickly ruled out. While such an operation might have countered Burmese incursions, it could not satisfy the broader imperative of demonstrating British might and determination.[49] The strategy that was decided upon was a spectacular display of force through an amphibious attack on Rangoon; it was expected that 'debarkation at Rangoon would act like a blister upon the Burmese, and oblige them to withdraw all their force from the frontier [with eastern India].'[50] This attack was to be supported by an overland invasion of Burma through the Arakan peninsula as well as the despatching of smaller forces to Assam and through Cachar to Manipur [see map 2]. One of the principle advocates of this plan was Captain Canning. Canning had not only served as an envoy to Burma in 1809, he was also an old family friend of the Amhersts' and hence possessed a great deal of influence over the governor-general.[51] Canning stressed repeatedly that Rangoon would welcome the British as liberators and that the invading force could count upon the locals to provide them with all necessary foodstuffs.

By focusing their attentions on Rangoon, the British revealed their ignorance of Burmese politics. The British laboured under the assumption that Rangoon was vital to the rulers of Burma and that by seizing it the Burmese would quickly succumb to British demands. In British eyes, Rangoon was the 'great emporium of the enemy's commerce ... the supplies of rice and other grains and remittances, even of tribute, were said to find their way to the capital by Rangoon.'[52] Losing such an emporium could not but force the Burmese to seek terms. The one official with any first-hand experience of Burma, Captain Canning, confidently predicted that 'When Rangoon shall be in our possession, I think it probable that the Court will accede to the terms that will be offered.'[53] In such a scenario, British terms were kept quite limited: no territorial demands were made, Burma itself was to be left intact, and an indemnity was to be paid to the British to reimburse them for the costs of the war.[54] In the expectation of a short war — two months was the consensus[55] — the British concluded that any further demands would only embroil them in the tangled politics of Southeast Asia. A cowed but independent Burma would serve British interests by preserving the balance of power in the region.[56] Drawing on his earlier experiences as the head of an unsuccessful embassy to China, Amherst was particularly worried lest any larger British presence in the region bring them into conflict with the Chinese. It is significant that throughout the war Amherst regularly requested that the Company's agents in Canton monitor Chinese official actions for any indication of hostile responses from Beijing.[57]

The one major dissenting voice against the optimistic predictions of a short and successful campaign was that of the commander-in-chief. Paget was unique in foretelling the disasters that could befall such an ambitious plan.[58] He correctly predicted that the loss of Rangoon was not sufficient to force concessions out of the Burmese. More prophetically, Paget questioned the assumption that the inhabitants of Rangoon would willingly assist the invading force with provisions and transport. Without such assistance, Paget forecast — correctly as it turned out — that the army would only find 'jungle, pestilence and famine.'[59] However, Paget's scepticism made very little impression for he was not properly plugged into the government. Paget did not return to Calcutta from an upcountry tour of inspection until April 1824, even though British plans were being discussed as early as the previous October. Even when he was informed of what had been proposed, Paget tried to extend his tour so as to avoid the heat and intrigues of Calcutta and enquired of Amherst in February whether there was any chance that the Burmese might seek terms.[60]

Once the broad parameters of British strategy had been decided upon, the details of the British attack had to be worked out. Here, the British laboured under a crippling shortage of timely and accurate intelligence. As one participant would later reflect, 'the first thing to arrest my attention ... was the mutual ignorance of the contending parties, as to each other's objects and designs.'[61] Ignorance of Burma was complete at all levels of the government. Even the officers ordered to begin the preparations had no real sense of what lay ahead. One later recounted the scenes in the mess when the attack was announced, 'Rangoon!' we all exclaimed, 'where is Rangoon?' Books and maps were consulted in vain, for Rangoon had not then acquired its fatal celebrity.'[62] There were no translators attached to the expedition and the commander was forced to employ a Chinese youth. This did not prove very satisfactory as the youth could not read or write Burmese and only possessed a rudimentary knowledge of English.[63] The strength and capabilities of the Burmese army were almost entirely unknown. Knowledge of Burmese politics and economy was equally deficient. In place of accurate information, the British relied upon hearsay and the very dated and biased reports of the embassies of Symes, Cox and Canning. All of these individuals had been personally snubbed by the Burmese court and vented their frustrations in tirades against the Burmese government. In particular, they dwelt on the alleged tyranny and wanton cruelty of the Burmese monarchs. To buttress their arguments, they cited the depopulation of lower Burma which they attributed to Burmese avarice and terror.[64] It was concluded from these reports that the British would be welcomed as liberators by the mass of the population. This in turn led to two fundamental miscalculations: the war would be a short one and that the local population would only be too willing to supply the British with whatever they needed.

Given the limits and biases in what was known about the social and political conditions in Burma, planning then turned to addressing known obstacles, most significantly climate and geography. Here again British shortcomings became obvious, particularly in the absence of reliable maps and marine charts. Munro complained that the only information that he had at hand regarding Burma was the published memoirs of Symes and Cox.[65] The commanders sent to lead the expeditions into Burma had to make do with the same information. As the travels of Symes and Cox had been limited to the route between Rangoon and the capital at Ava, everything beyond the Irrawaddy river was 'all mystery and conjecture.'[66] The timing of the attack on Rangoon demonstrates the poor state of British intelligence: working from Symes' observations of some thirty years before, the expedition was despatched in the spring, at the height of the monsoon, in the belief that at this time the Irrawaddy River was at its highest and would therefore allow the force to move north if the Burmese did not submit after Rangoon had fallen.[67] When the fleet arrived at Rangoon, they found that indeed the river was high, but it was also 'rushing towards the ocean at eight or ten miles an hour'.[68] Even if the force had been prepared to push upriver, which as we shall see was not the case, their boats would not have made much headway against such a current. The shortage of proper maps from which a campaign could be planned was partly the result of restrictions imposed by the Company. Concerned to save money as well as prevent accurate surveys from falling into the hands of Britain's potential enemies, the Court would not allow sufficient numbers of large-scale maps to be distributed to its officials in India. Instead the few good maps were safely stored in London. Valentine Blacker, the surveyor general of India, did not even have a copy of Rennell's atlas of Bengal at hand.[69] Yet the Court of Directors' efforts to prevent maps of India from falling into the hands of potential opponents were not that successful. It was reported that on a visit to the Dépôt de la Guerre in Paris, Bentinck saw on open display a secret British map of their troop deployments in India.[70]

The force sent to capture Rangoon comprised units from the Bengal and Madras establishments. The former sent two regiments of king's troops and some detachments of native infantry and foot artillery, totalling 2858 soldiers. Madras provided a further four regiments of European soldiers and eleven regiments of sepoys, 9691 men in total, which with the 69 artillerymen from Bombay made for a total land force of 12845 men. Madras was chosen to provide the bulk of the troops for two reasons. Much of the Bengal army was already busy securing the frontiers and providing troops to counteract what appeared to be a restless society in North India. There were also some underlying worries that because of their caste restrictions on undertaking sea voyages, Bengal sepoys would react badly to being ordered to Rangoon. In addition to these troops, there was also a sizeable naval commitment from both the Royal Navy and the Company's own Bombay Marine.[71] Command of this force was entrusted to Brigadier Archibald Campbell — described as a 'gallant but hard-headed insensible man' — who was also given the authority to negotiate with the Burmese.[72] Captain Canning accompanied the expedition as the governor-general's political agent.

Following a rendezvous in the Andaman Islands, troops from the two presidencies descended on Rangoon [see map 2]. The Burmese had made little effort to secure the city against attack and the British captured it with deceptively little resistance on May 10. Once they were lodged in the city, the British were struck by their true predicament. Not only was there no sign of willingness on the part of the Burmese to admit defeat, but the fall back plan of beginning to move up the Irrawaddy to force a settlement on the Burmese Court was clearly impossible for the time being. Such a plan hinged upon the British ability to find adequate transport and provisions in Rangoon. Neither were forthcoming for the local population had fled from the city taking their boats and draught animals with them. And there was no sign of their returning once the British had become established. Nobody involved in the planning of the expedition had foreseen this possibility, so confident were they that the local population would receive them warmly. Rangoon had become in the words of one participant a 'Scotch prize.'[73] The possibility that the locals could be encouraged to trade with the British was considerably weakened once the expeditionary force began to ransack the town in search of loot. Many of the British officers, including Campbell, were not only aware of these 'midnight antiquarians', but actively participated in the pillaging of Burma.[74] Most serious of all was the sacking of the many Buddhist temples in Rangoon, including the giant Shwedagon pagoda from which a giant bell was taken. It was no wonder then that the local population showed little inclination to participate with the invaders.[75] Troops went so far as to try and extract the talismans made of precious stones and metals from under the skins of some of the fallen Burmese.[76] The search for loot was stimulated by the widespread belief that the war would end with little hope of prize money in a land where 'there were many gilded pagodas but little gold'.[77]

It also became apparent that Campbell was a poor choice to lead this expedition. Eager to portray his operations in as complimentary a light as possible, Campbell persistently underestimated the difficulties facing him

— especially his supply problems. Meanwhile he constantly exaggerated his successes. His bombastic despatches soon became topics of ridicule in London, Calcutta and Madras. Wynn sarcastically said of him, 'If pompous and inflated despatches were all that is requisite, he certainly is superior to most commanders.'[78] Newspapers were even more scathing in their criticism; the editor of the *Oriental Herald* wrote that: 'Sir Archibald Campbell calls one of his successes such a prodigy future ages will scarcely believe it. What right has Sir Archibald to anticipate that our great-grand-children will be more incredulous than ourselves.'[79] Campbell also held strong and unfounded prejudices against some of the corps under his command. He favoured the king's army in particular and it was their officers who formed most of his staff even though few had any Indian experience.[80] Of the Company's forces in India, Campbell showed a marked preference for the Bengal army over the Madras army even though it was the latter establishment that provided most of his fighting forces. Officers of the Madras army were offended by the slights they received and strongly protested Campbell's failure to acknowledge their contributions. Even more obvious was Campbell's hostility towards Indian sepoys, and as most of these were from the Madras establishment, it only furthered their officers' sense of alienation. Throughout the war, Campbell sought to limit sepoy participation in the campaign, relegating them for the most part to serve as pickets and guards along his lines of communication. When his urgent request for more troops to help his advance was met by a hurriedly despatched force of 1500 Madras sepoys, these troops upon arrival were left to languish in Rangoon as Campbell plodded northwards.[81]

The British position in Rangoon became even more precarious with the onset of the monsoon rains. Deprived of adequate provisions, and forced to contend with incessant rains, the expeditionary force was soon beset by disease. By July the British lines were described as 'one vast hospital' with one regiment, the Madras Europeans, having already lost two-thirds of its original complement to disease.[82] The total casualty figures for the entire expeditionary force over the three years would confirm the debilitating effect of disease on the soldiers. The overall casualty to strength ratio for European soldiers was calculated to be forty-five per cent and that for sepoys at twenty per cent.[83] Casualties that resulted from enemy actions were far less frequent, less than ten per cent for the sepoys and European combined. These conditions compared unfavourably with previous campaigns. For the Madras army the deaths per thousand during the Burma War stood at 119; in peacetime it hovered between 56 and 70, and even at the height of the Maratha War of 1801-1805, deaths only reached 88 per thousand. [84]

Climate, though a contributing factor, was not the sole reason behind these losses. Diet was the chief factor; the inadequate rationing of the soldiers weakened them and left them prey to diseases. A reasonable stock of provisions was not sent with the expedition owing to the impression that local supplies would be adequate.[85] When this did not materialize, troops were forced to improvise. One seemingly attractive solution lay close at hand — vast fields of ripening pineapples — yet overindulgence only furthered the spread of diarrhoea.[86] However, there was very little else but pineapples in the area. The inhabitants had not only fled, but they had taken with them their livestock and many of their crops had been destroyed in a deliberate attempt to deny the British any assistance. An unprecedented demand was placed without warning upon the Bengal commissariat. Everything from rice, meat and other foodstuffs to smaller items like tobacco and betelnut had to be collected in Bengal and then shipped by sea to Rangoon. While this provided a windfall for shipowners in Calcutta, the commissariat itself was not sufficiently geared up to meet these demands. Very few items could be acquired in lower Bengal for most of the government's arsenals and storehouses had been allowed to run down after many years of peace. Private suppliers hoarded their stocks in anticipation of the Company eventually being forced to pay higher prices. Cultivators stashed away their livestock and produce out of fear that the government would soon be forcibly requisitioning such items.[87] Eventually the search for supplies would take the commissariat into areas far removed from Calcutta. Cattle, for example, were brought in from as far afield as the banks of the Narmada, some one thousand miles away.[88] The delays occasioned by these extensive searches for provisions and then the journey to Rangoon (anywhere between ten and thirty days[89]) ensured that many of the products were inedible when they finally arrived. Although the commissary general claimed that 'weevil does not render biscuit unserviceable', many in Burma begged to differ, especially those who took to throwing their biscuits at walls so as to try and dislodge some of these insects.[90] A partial solution to this supply crisis was sought from the private merchants of the Calcutta area. They were encouraged to open up shops in Rangoon. This only induced a small trickle of supplies, most of which were priced far out of the average soldier's reach. Chickens were sold for as much as Rs.8, equal to a sepoy's monthly salary, while bread fetched Rs.2 a pound.[91] The poor dietary state of the soldiers was rendered even more crippling by the failure to provide them with dry and sanitary shelters. In spite of torrential rainstorms, Campbell never requested Calcutta to send a supply of raincoats and proper footwear and the construction of sentry boxes was not ordered until the war was nearly over.[92] Medical facilities in Rangoon were woefully under-equipped to deal with the flood of casualties. As with the rest of the campaign preparations, the hospital sent with the expedition had calculated on a short and successful war. It had enough supplies and personnel to handle 450 casualties over a period of six months, yet within three weeks, more than seven hundred casualties had passed through the hospital.[93]

The Burmese troops waiting in the surrounding jungle realized the British predicament and began to subject the invading army to constant and wearing harassments. Campbell and his troops were stranded in Rangoon for six months; having set siege to the town they soon found the situation reversed with the British becoming the besieged. With such restricted mobility, the British were forced to limit their operations to what Campbell called 'boating and stockading.'[94] This consisted of sending small detachments along the many rivers and creeks surrounding Rangoon in an attempt to drive the Burmese out of the stockades in which they were entrenched. It was not a particularly successful strategy: Burmese troops rarely defended a stockade to the last man and chose instead to withdraw and build another one.[95] Given the limited means at their disposal, the Burmese were able to grind the British down slowly. The British grudgingly came to respect their enemy and his skill in using the environment: 'The enemy, rarely to be seen in the open field, continually harassed the outposts, under cover of an impervious and incombustible jungle; and in the defensive system of stockades and breastworks, displayed no little skill and judgment.'[96] It was a style of war for which the British and the sepoys were not prepared by their prior service in India. Consequently, morale deteriorated. One participant wrote that of 'all species of warfare, jungle or bush fighting is the most unpleasant, the most discouraging to soldiers, and the most effectual method of trying their discipline, order and steadiness.'[97] The British situation was fittingly compared by one observer to Gulliver's encounter with the Lilliputians.

> An armed man, unprovided with the means of moving, may not be inaptly compared to a giant chained to the ground, but still having his limbs at liberty, thereby retaining the power of lashing out at all within his reach.[98]

Reports of the British thrashing about in Rangoon, trying to strike an enemy that refused to expose himself, were soon followed by even more distressing accounts from Bengal's eastern frontier. A detachment of troops commanded by Captain Noton had been sent to Ramu to ward off any

Burmese attacks from that quarter. The Burmese attacked his post on 17 May 1824, causing the deaths of some two hundred and fifty sepoys out of a force of one thousand as well as mortally wounding the commanding officer. The shockwaves were felt throughout India. Panic was clearly evident in Calcutta where many feared that the Burmese would soon be marching on the city. Even in Hyderabad reports circulated of the imminent demise of the Raj. One rumour current in the city's bazaars, which even had the Resident seeking reassurance, was that Calcutta had been sacked and the governor-general forced to commit suicide.[99] There were other indications as well that British power was no longer as respected as the British believed it had been. In one instance approximately three hundred armed peasants attacked Company boats carrying ammunition to the eastern frontier.[100] As Company vessels were rarely attacked by *dacoits*, local authorities viewed the attack as a harbinger of further resistance to their authority. To quell the alarm as well as check any Burmese threats from the Arakan peninsula, reinforcements were rushed to the frontier. Yet given the publicity generated by these setbacks, and with the ever-present imperative of maintaining proof of British omnipotence, such reverses had to be met with an even more vigorous display of force. The suggestion that Campbell's force be recalled and used instead to defend Arakan was quickly rejected by the government as smacking too much of panic.[101]

On the Arakan front, defensive operations yielded to plans for an overland invasion of Burma that was intended to link up with British forces pushing north up the Irrawaddy.[102] A force of nearly twelve thousand Europeans and sepoys was ordered to invade the Arakan peninsula. Owing to the harshness of the climate and the difficult terrain that would have to be traversed, such an operation was questionable from a military point of view. However, it was justified on the political grounds that the British must be seen as having responded vigorously to these challenges. Once the British forces crossed the frontier, they encountered little resistance from the Burmese Army. Most of the Burmese Army, along with Maha Bandula, Burma's most successful general (nicknamed the 'Sable Bonaparte' by British soldiers) had been pulled back to defend against the British expeditionary force which had recently landed at Rangoon.[103] By the end of April 1825 British forces under General Morrison had taken possession of most of Arakan. However, in doing so their numbers had been greatly reduced by the twin scourges of disease and malnutrition. Supply lines with India were nearly non-existent, food was scarce, and the increasingly weakened army was hit by a cholera epidemic. Troop returns from September 1825 reveal just how badly decimated was this army. There were only 3240 effective troops; a further 5505 were either ill or on convalescent leave.[104] This rapid deterioration of the army and a profound ignorance of local geography prevented the Arakan force from reaching its next objective — forcing its way across the Arakan mountains into the Burmese heartland where it was expected to join forces with the columns moving up the Irrawaddy River. The best route into Burma was over the Aeng pass, and though the British vaguely knew of its existence, Morrison instead chose to listen to his chief engineer, an officer only recently arrived from England, who insisted upon undertaking a time-consuming and ultimately unproductive survey of the Talak pass.[105] The delays occasioned by this survey allowed disease to weaken the army to such an extent that it was in no fit state to press on any further.

Meanwhile Campbell was ordered to strike at whatever targets lay within reach. He was still unable to move up the Irrawaddy because a shortage of draught animals prevented the despatch of a column to secure one bank of the river, necessary to protect those troops travelling by boat. He chose instead to despatch forces to capture Burmese territories along the Tennasserim coast. The taking of Martaban, Mergui and Tavoy in the autumn of 1824, while doing little to hasten the war's end, did secure welcome places for convalescent depots. The main force did not begin its voyage up the Irrawaddy until February 1825 and then it moved in three columns. Campbell commanded the largest force and it ponderously travelled overland, its course roughly paralleling the river from where it could be resupplied. A smaller column under command of Brigadier Willoughby Cotton travelled in boats and it was intended to secure the vital communications link with Rangoon. Colonel Sale led the third column around the coast to Bassein. Its objective, aside from seizing that port, was to discover a route through the delta through which he could rejoin the main force. Sale managed to capture Bassein, but it proved impossible, given the existing state of knowledge, to find a way through the delta especially as they were running short of supplies.[106] The remainder of the expeditionary force was left in Rangoon to secure it against any Burmese attacks. The main army's movement upriver was handicapped by logistical shortcomings. One officer who accompanied the force claimed that 'in fact, from the disasters encountered by the Commissariat Department, it had more the appearance of a retreat than an advance into the enemy's country.'[107]

Campbell's progress up the Irrawaddy was impeded by the numerous stockades erected by the Burmese. The largest of these stockades was at Danubyu and it proved to be the most difficult to crack. The river column attempted to drive through it on its own but with no success. Campbell's column, which had progressed considerably further north and was running critically low of supplies, was forced to retrace its steps and join up with Cotton's troops in early April 1825. Embarrassed by this setback, Campbell employed the interesting strategem of trying to blame it on the Burmese who in his eyes had failed to act according to the rules of war. Campbell argued that the defenders of Danubyu should not have tried to retain Danubyu once Campbell's column had appeared to the north for that meant that the British had outflanked the Burmese.[108] Observers in India like Thomas Munro were not convinced by Campbell's argument. The Burmese may not have known the rules of the game, but they were somehow managing to play it better than the British. Danubyu eventually fell to this combined force, but only after a fortuitous cannon shot had decapitated Bandula, the Burmese general.[109] Enthusiasm for this British victory was dampened when it was revealed that the entire surviving garrison, estimated at ten thousand, had managed to escape.[110]

The British encountered little resistance after Danubyu and by the end of April their troops were able to capture Prome in time to use that town as a cantonment when the wet season burst. With the approach of the dry season, peace overtures were received from the Burmese Court. Envoys were exchanged in September 1825, but neither side seems to have pursued these talks with any enthusiasm. Instead they each used the truce to build up their forces and strengthen their supply lines in time for the next campaign. By December the British were at Meaday, close to the capital at Ava. Another attempt at negotiations was made but it too collapsed. In January 1826 British forces had pushed the Burmese to within five miles of the capital and here at Yandabo on February 26 a treaty was signed to end the war.

The difficulties the British experienced and the setbacks they encountered in bringing the Burmese to terms did not result in any diminution of British resolve. Rather, the opposite was the case. As the war became more prolonged and the government became more desperate for an impressive victory British demands hardened. This sense of frustration became very apparent in the governor-general. By October 1824 he had conceded that 'we must conquer a peace with the Burmese.'[111] Even more extreme was Thomas Munro who consistently advocated a more aggressive military plan as well as harsh terms for the Burmese. He impressed on Amherst the need for British troops to fight on 'until our armies are in a position to dictate the terms.'[112] By early 1826, with no end of the war in sight, Munro was even recommending the forcible dismemberment of the Burmese empire. He advised the government to try and establish an independent government in Pegu.[113] Munro's recommendation to make Pegu's independence a priority was seconded by Campbell, who added a military argument to the political ones supplied by Munro — an independent Pegu would assure the British of a more reliable supply of provisions.[114] Eventually even Amherst began to consider this option. Amherst tried to persuade Munro to take on the responsibility for setting up such an arrangement, but the end of the war intervened before this could be acted upon.[115]

Why the independence of Pegu was viewed as so simple to attain is a bit of a mystery. Thomas Campbell Robertson, who had replaced Canning as the governor-general's political representative, poured scorn on the idea that Pegu's independence was imminent, writing that it was the 'darling project of almost every Englishman ... that the independence of Pegu, which, after an interval of seventy-seven years, had in three days been accomplished.'[116] There were others who were opposed to any commitment to an independent Pegu. John Adam and Mountstuart Elphinstone both doubted whether its independence could be maintained without an expensive investment by the British.[117] Campbell was on the spot and could see that there was no sign of any claimants to the Pegu throne, nor in 1824-25 was there any apparent willingness on the part of the population to rise up against the Burmese who had ruled over them for three generations. Campbell was likely fishing for any measure that would hasten the end of what had become an inglorious, unpopular, and unprofitable war. The fact that Munro maintained his support for this policy for so long, and in the face of contradictory evidence, is less easy to explain. Perhaps the best explanation that can be offered is that of sub-imperialism. Should Pegu be set up as a client state, Munro was well aware that its supervision and garrisoning would likely be entrusted to Madras. Faced with the presidency's declining fortunes, an expanded overseas role would restore some of its past glory.

The eventual terms imposed upon the Burmese by the Treaty of Yandabo, while not as severe as Munro might have liked, were harsh enough to satisfy Calcutta's desire for a salutary lesson to be inflicted. Arakan and Tennasserim were annexed by the British; the Burmese were also forced to relinquish their claims to Assam (formally added to British India in 1831) and they were expected to pay a substantial indemnity as well. This indemnity was originally set at two crore of rupees, but it was later reduced to one crore when it was realized that Burma's limited resources could not be stretched to the former. It was meant to serve partly as a punishment and partly to repay the vast sums expended by British India over the three years of war.[118] The annexation of Arakan, though disliked by the Court of Directors for it was looked upon as an area with little prospect of revenue or exploitable resources, was justified to the Board of Control on strategic grounds. Possession of Arakan, it was argued, would provide India with a naturally more secure eastern frontier.[119]

The British decision to retain Tennasserim after the war came about more by default than by design. Four options suggested themselves in 1826 as to what could be done with these coastal lands. The first was to declare the area independent, but this was quickly rejected when it was pointed out that the area would not likely long survive tucked between Burma and Siam. A suggestion was made that Tennasserim could be exchanged with Siam for territories elsewhere on the Malay Peninsula. This was the Court of Director's preferred option for it held out the promise of an improved trading position in Southeast Asia.[120] Calcutta quickly dismissed it as they did not trust the Siamese for they recalled their earlier unsuccessful attempts to secure military and material cooperation from Siam in their fight against Burma.[121] A third possibility was to return it to the Burmese. This suggestion made little headway. Underlying the official reason that the local inhabitants would suffer from a return to Burmese tyranny was the belief that such an act would send out the wrong signals. Britain's opponents in India would only see it as an act of weakness.[122] This only left the option of retention. There were no economic reasons at work here for even the most forceful proponents admitted that the area possessed little economic value and its revenues might barely cover the costs of a reduced administrative establishment.[123] Nevertheless, economic arguments were forged to defend the decision and so head off the Court's criticisms. The government in Calcutta was shrewdly advised that 'there is nothing that will be so popular in England ... as the establishment of a commercial post in the vicinity of the Burmese and Siamese dominions.'[124] Officials from Madras lent their support to calls for retention when they realized that the personnel needed for the new territories would be taken from their establishment.

In the midst of their struggle with Burma the Bengal Army also took on the short but successful siege of Bharatpur. Although it was described as 'a mere party of pleasure' by an officer serving in Burma, the capture of Bharatpur in January 1826 was at least as important as the successful conclusion of the Burma War for the government in Calcutta, if not more so.[125] The immediate catalyst for this war was a succession crisis in Bharatpur which together with Dig and Hatras was one of the major Jat principalities in the area just south of Agra. In August 1824 the then ruler of Bharatpur, Buldeo Singh, sought from David Ochterlony, the British resident in Delhi, a British guarantee that his six year old son Bulwant Singh would be confirmed as raja following Buldeo's death. Ochterlony strongly recommended that the government agree to this, but Amherst and the council were unwilling to declare themselves without further information, particularly as they were uncertain as to whether Bulwant's claim was better than that of Durjan Saul, a twenty-five year old nephew of the late raja.[126] There were some doubts as to whether Bulwant was Buldeo's biological son for Calcutta had received reports that he was only a nephew who had been adopted by Buldeo as his son. If that was the case then according to the British preference for primogeniture Durjan Saul's claim must also be considered.[127] A firm decision had yet to be reached by 6 March 1825, the day that Buldeo died, largely because Ochterlony had still not forwarded to Calcutta the necessary information.[128] The court in Bharatpur immediately recognized Bulwant as his successor with one of Bulwant's uncles acting as regent on his behalf. This succession was soon challenged by Durjan who with the backing of most of the state's army removed the regent and placed himself in that office. Durjan's act set off a struggle with his brother, Madheo Singh, who gathered his troops and established himself at Dig. Confronted with what he saw as an illegal usurpation of the throne, and apprehensive that the turmoil would soon inflame neighbouring territories, Ochterlony acted quickly. Proclamations were issued to the local population that declared Durjan a usurper and called on the people to support their rightful ruler. Ochterlony backed up his declarations by mobilizing forces that could if necessary be used to restore Bulwant. When Calcutta was informed in July of Ochterlony's plans, and in particular his orders for troops to be readied to take the fortress, they quickly countermanded them and by overturning his decisions brought about Ochterlony's resignation.[129]

Yet within a few months Calcutta had reversed its position and was engaged in planning a much larger military campaign than that conceived by Ochterlony. Calcutta's decision to retreat from its policy of non-interference can only be understood within the context of what the British were then reading into Indian affairs. The commitment that the Council undertook to restore Bulwant had very little to do with the legitimacy of the claims of either contender, nor did it really have much to do with the state of Bharatpur itself. Instead Calcutta was prompted to act out of fear that any sign of passivity on its part would ultimately prove disastrous to British rule throughout India. News of British setbacks in Burma were believed by the British to have unleashed hopes throughout India that the Company Raj was in terminal decline. Heber reported from Awadh that local rumours predicted that the British were on the brink of abandoning India.[130]

Alarmed officials in Calcutta could also point to the recent court revolution (1824) at Kittur, a fortified town in the province of Bijapur located about nineteen miles northwest of Darwar, that required the intervention of five thousand troops from Madras to restore order.[131] Kittur was another example of a disputed succession in a nominally independent kingdom and once again the British decided to act out of fear that the rebellion would spread. The panic of local officials was palpable; the local commissioner wrote to the government of Bombay, 'For God's Sake send a force immediately without delay to Kittoor.'[132] The areas surrounding Kittur, parts of the old Maratha confederacy, were thought to be particularly hostile to British rule. Added urgency was provided by the rebels having captured part of the force that was initially sent, including Thackeray (the principal collector of the Southern Maratha Territories) who died in captivity. This was interpreted as a major blow to British prestige in such a volatile area. While the immediate crisis was dealt with by the reinforcements sent in after Thackeray's death, it would not be until 1827 that discontent was brought completely under control.[133] Interestingly, the rebels' communications with the British forces sent to restore order emphasized their loyalty to the British and drew attention to their valiant service under Wellesley and Munro during previous wars against Mysore and the Marathas.[134] It can be argued that the rebels did not see themselves as rebels; rather they were trying to re-establish relations with the British on an older pattern, one that emphasized the mutual interconnectedness of British and Indian institutions and resources. Unfortunately for the rebels, such a system was incompatible with the now-dominant ideology of Anglo-Indian militarism.

Rural violence throughout India was also thought to be on the increase as the peasantry, convinced of the decline of British authority, resorted to anarchy and plunder. From the conquered territories northeast of Delhi came reports of spectacular acts of banditry. In one pitched battle over two hundred *dacoits* squared off against a sepoy regiment.[135] An even more alarming report was received of a millenarian prophet, believed to have been a Jat, whose promises that foreign rule would soon be extinguished had drawn to him 'a multitude of credulous followers, with some armed Akalees [armed ascetics, likely Sikhs]'.[136] Although the prophet and many of those with him were easily subdued, thousands of his followers continued to bathe in a tank that had been identified as particularly auspicious. Even more worrying were some isolated episodes that hinted that the sepoys were inclining towards the crowd. One observer reported an incident in Bharatpur before the siege when the *diwan* [chief minister] was attacked by a mob who were accusing him of aiding the British; the mob included several sepoys.[137]

Incidents like those noted above convinced already jittery officials in Calcutta that North India was a tinderbox and that Bharatpur was, in the words of one officer, 'the nucleus of rebellion and intrigue and how can we be Master of Hindoostan till it is subdued?'[138] Bharatpur by itself was a significant threat. Its defences in 1804 had withstood four British attacks, thereby offering up one of the greatest humiliations that the British had experienced to date. Prior to the beginning of the campaign, Heber reported that in a local carnival he had witnessed a play in which red-coated actors were beaten down: the red coat clearly symbolizing sepoys.[139] The local population prided themselves on their martial qualities, 'the only people in India who boast that they have never been subdued either by the Mughal emperors or the English.'[140] Bharatpur was also home to a large army; it was estimated in 1816 that it had some twenty-five thousand men under arms, proof that the demilitarization of this part of India had not proceeded very far.[141] There were also sizeable parties of armed Jats attached to the rulers of Dig and Hatras. Ochterlony's threat to invest Bharatpur persuaded Durjan Saul to raise even more forces for its defence, many of whom came from the neighbouring territories of Jaipur, Gwalior and Alwar. These forces had by early summer 1825 reached a critical mass and if not kept under control threatened to plunder surrounding districts and render British authority even more precarious.[142]

Bharatpur's military resources, as well as the memory of earlier embarrassments suffered there, persuaded British officials that Bharatpur had become the focal point of a conspiracy that united a diverse range of states and subjugated peoples against them. Heber wrote from Allahabad in September 1825 that 'there are rumours of war in this part of the world, and people talk of armies and invasions from the Seiks, Nepal and Nagpoor.'[143] From a newswriter at Ranjit Singh's court came news that the Sikhs had begun to lay in a supply of grain and military stores in the strongholds of the Punjab.[144] A small affray at Kalpi which Sindia was alleged to be involved in was taken as a signal that a rejuvenated Maratha confederacy was in the offing.[145] There were also suspicions, never substantiated, that the Burmese had been intriguing with Durjan Saul.[146]

Charles Metcalfe, Ochterlony's replacement as Resident in Delhi, fully subscribed to his predecessor's trepidations. One only has to remember his advice to Amherst in early 1824, that British India is 'undermined by any reverse, however trifling, and would not long withstand any serious indication of weakness', to realize that Metcalfe was certainly not the man to reverse Ochterlony's policies.[147] The two were in agreement over the very limited applicability of the ideals of non-intervention in India. The only substantial criticism that Metcalfe made of Ochterlony was that he had tried to move too quickly and without a sufficiently strong force to guarantee victory (Ochterlony's force was only eight thousand strong). Metcalfe was true to the first principle of Anglo-Indian militarism: for the 'empire of opinion' to be upheld, quick and unquestioned success must be guaranteed. This was a perspective shared by most officials in India. 'Should he [Combermere] fail, it is unhappily but too true, that in all northern and western India, every man who owns a sword, and can buy or steal a horse, from the Sutlege to the Nerbudda, will be up against us.'[148] Even those who doubted whether there really was a lurking anti-British conspiracy still maintained that an uncontested victory was essential to the consolidation of British rule. Bharatpur may lack immediate allies, but the rest of India was keenly watching from the sidelines. 'I do not believe a single state will openly assist them tho[ough] all undoubtedly and heartily wish them success in proportion as we are hated and detested.'[149] Similar views were echoed in London with one writer claiming that defeat at Bharatpur would mean, 'India, if retained at all, would be retained at an expense of blood and treasure infinitely greater than was expended during the whole course of its gradual subjugation.'[150] Another writer declared that 'Our object is not only to subdue the fort; but as a political measure to shew the natives we can, and will take it, in any way we choose.'[151] This conviction that the fate of British India hinged on the unconditional surrender of Bharatpur was still being repeated eighty years later.[152]

Only Amherst needed to be reminded of the strategic imperatives of British India. In August 1825 he was still reluctant to sanction operations against Bharatpur. He referred in a council minute to the legalities of the situation, claiming that the existing treaty (1806) with Bharatpur had not provided the British with any justification for interference in the state's internal affairs. He also questioned the strategic benefits of such an operation: 'I am not aware that the existence of this fortress has occasioned us the slightest inconvenience.'[153] Amherst concluded by stating his hopes that Metcalfe would defuse the crisis. The council itself was split over what to do. Fendall and Paget advocated a more aggressive policy — if not the capture of Bharatpur then at least a show of force. As Paget cynically noted, 'negotiations are very apt to thrive, when backed by a good army.'[154] Harington, however, agreed with the governor-general that a more moderate course of action was to be preferred. Amherst's reservations were slowly undermined by the persistence of Metcalfe's arguments. The point that Metcalfe pushed most insistently was that European ideals of non-intervention were of little use in India. Instead the British had to consider the more abstract responsibilities conferred on them by their paramount status. 'We are bound, not by any positive engagement to the Bhurtpoor state, nor by any claim on their part, but by our duty, as Supreme Guardian of

General Tranquillity, Law and Right.'[155] Such arguments eventually wore down Amherst's defences and in September 1825 he conceded that his perspective was still not sufficiently attuned to Indian realities. He deferred to Metcalfe's recommendations and preparations for the taking of Bharatpur were set in motion.[156] This time the British were determined not to be embarrassed as they had been in 1804 — nearly 30,000 troops were deployed in 1825 together with a large artillery park, about triple what Ochterlony had organized and four times larger than the force Lake brought to Bharatpur in 1804.[157]

Combermere arrived in Agra on 1 December, several months after preparations ordered by Paget had begun, and a week later he was on the march to Bharatpur [see map 3]. Bharatpur's fortifications were formidable, and comprised four interlocked fortresses contained within two sets of walls that were approximately eight miles in circumference and were between seventy-four and eighty feet high, studded with outworks and towers, all of which were enclosed by a ditch thirty feet wide and twenty yards deep.[158] Surrounding the walls was a belt of forest. Cavalry was sent ahead to secure control over the sluices that linked the ditches surrounding the fortress with a nearby reservoir. By cutting the supply of water and keeping the ditches dry, the defenders were deprived of one their best defences, and the one that had proven impossible for Lord Lake to surmount in 1804. British troops established themselves within cannon shot of the walls on December 10-11 and after setting up positions for their artillery, they began a long and laborious preparatory bombardment on 24 December. Constructed of mud, the fortress's walls were able to absorb much of the shelling with considerable impunity. Consequently, mining was employed to enlarge the few breaches that were being carved out and, like the rest of the British preparations, it was carried out on a grand scale with some mines containing as much as 1500 pounds of gunpowder.

The forces within Bharatpur were in a particularly difficult position. Unlike the defenders of 1804, those holed up in the fortress in 1825 were largely cut off from outside help. Supplies and reinforcements were difficult to acquire once the British had encircled Bharatpur. Further afield, the British had since 1806 acquired a series of military positions across North India which allowed them to isolate Bharatpur from potential allies.[159] British spies reported that the shelling of the town together with food shortages had led to a great loss of life within the walls.[160] The defenders also had problems with their ordnance. Despite the number of artillery pieces within Bharatpur (estimated at two hundred pieces[161]) and the intensity of their fire, counter-bombardment caused comparatively few casualties among their besiegers. According to British observers, Bharatpur's guns were difficult to traverse and depress and hence their shots tended to fall within well-defined and easily avoided areas.[162]

On 17 January the attack began, but as with the rest of the siege it proceeded quite ponderously. Two and a half hours were taken up moving the troops one and a half miles to their assembly points.[163] The mines were then ignited and the attack began. Aside from the panic and casualties caused when one overcharged mine blew debris back into one of the advancing columns, the capture of the fortress was achieved very quickly and with comparatively little loss of life on the British side. Bulwant was returned to power, the cost of the campaign was charged to his court, and the British set about destroying the fortifications to curb any future threat from Bharatpur.[164] British casualties during the whole of the siege totalled just under one thousand soldiers and sepoys; the defenders on the other hand lost an estimated fourteen thousand killed or wounded.[165]

The campaigns in Burma and against Bharatpur together were to have serious consequences for the Bengal army. Writing in late 1825, one officer commented that the two wars 'have certainly caused great dissatisfaction, and if they continue, God only knows what can become of the army.'[166] The sepoys' reputations deteriorated. Even Bishop Heber, normally known for his measured assessments, took on the prevailing attitudes when he wrote that 'our new enemies are in everything but arms and discipline far from despicable, and decidedly superior in courage and bodily strength [to the sepoys].[167] Bengal sepoys in particular were looked upon with reservations. Their reluctance to serve in Burma was taken as proof of their unreliability.

Looked at from the sepoys' perspective, it is clear that military service during the Burma War was viewed with misgivings by many sepoys. It was not only the climate and living conditions that the sepoys disliked; they were also annoyed by the preferential treatment meted out to the sepoys from the Madras establishment. Unlike the Bengal sepoys the latter were paid full *batta* for foreign service as well as receiving their rations at public expense. Full *batta* was only belatedly and grudgingly awarded to the Bengal sepoys once their grievances became more assertive and persistent. Bengal sepoys were further antagonized when they witnessed civilians recruited for service as labourers (and often of a lower caste) being paid much more generously than themselves.[168] The unpopularity of service in Burma can also be ascribed to the behaviour of the expedition's commander. Campbell not only had very little experience of sepoys, but from the very beginning he demonstrated strong prejudices against them. Reports circulated in Calcutta and London that Campbell personally ordered some particularly offensive punishments to be dealt out to sepoys under his command. The most controversial of these was to tie pieces of rancid pork around the necks of some Muslim sepoys.[169] Campbell also publicly denounced Indian sepoys, claiming that they were cowards when faced with the Burmese, conveniently overlooking that the army which had driven the Burmese out of Assam was composed exclusively of sepoy regiments.[170] It should also be remembered that most of the sepoys with Campbell were left in Rangoon and therefore had little opportunity to prove themselves in battle. While no doubt Campbell found these conclusions useful in accounting for the army's setbacks, they also tended to reinforce growing British scepticisms about their local army, and the Bengal sepoys in particular.

This relationship between the war in Burma and the morale of the Bengal army is clearly evident in the experiences of the 60th Bengal Native Infantry. Between 1824 and 1826 this regiment had an annual desertion rate of approximately 5.5 per cent per annum; following the end of the war the desertion rate fell to only 0.5 per cent per annum.[171] In some regiments desertion rates were even more spectacular. One regiment marching to the eastern frontier reported that it was losing anywhere between twenty and thirty men per night.[172] Even regiments stationed in the upper provinces were finding it difficult to maintain their strength. Too many sepoys were seeking their discharge at the same time as the pool of recruits was shrinking. Some potential recruits were probably drawn back to the land when they found that local grain prices had been pushed up by the commissariat's wartime purchases. Nicolls noted that in the brigade under his command one half of the sepoys had served less than five years with the British and one-quarter had under two years' experience.[173] Moreover, Nicolls also noted that desertions were increasing at an alarming rate; in his brigade there had been sixty deserters in the first three days of January 1825. Apprehensions that they might be sent to the eastern frontier also induced many prospective sepoys to seek service elsewhere. Not surprisingly the Bombay army was faced with a sudden influx of Hindustani-speakers.[174] In light of this reluctance to enlist in the Bengal army, it was forced to resort to direct recruiting, something it had not hitherto been forced to undertake.[175] Direct recruiting had its costs; the quality of the troops was not so certain, and veteran sepoys were alarmed at what they saw as a looming threat to their monopoly if recruits from non-traditional sources became more common.

The most spectacular expression of discontent was the outbreak of a mutiny in 1824 at Barrackpore, then serving as a transit stop for troops bound for the eastern frontier. During their stopover at Barrackpore, troops of the 47th regiment (plus two companies from the 62nd regiment and 20 men from the 26th) placed a list of grievances before their commanding officer. His response was to refer their demands to Calcutta. When the commander-in-chief was apprised of the situation, he went personally to Barrackpore with additional troops, European artillery as well as infantry. The sepoys were ordered to turn over their arms and fall into ranks before Paget would entertain any petitions. When they hesitated Paget ordered the assembled troops and artillery to open fire. No warning shots were fired and the order was given, 'no prisoners — no quarter.'[176] The sepoys of the 47th Native Infantry were hunted down relentlessly and evidence suggests that their pursuers were not too discriminating in who they cut down. The troops 'shot down and bayoneted all that they could reach ... never stopping to satisfy themselves that the blackmen they saw were sepoys or not.'[177] One doctor called upon to treat many of the wounded reported that he found many injured civilians among his patients, including women, children, and even a gardener from the governor-general's home at Barrackpore.[178] News of the mutiny spread quickly. Robertson reported that the sepoys on the march in Arakan knew of the mutiny sooner than their officers.[179] The total number of casualties has never been ascertained, but there seems to be a consensus that more than three hundred were killed.[180] Of those sepoys captured alive, a further forty were sentenced to death by a court martial held on the same day. Six of these were hanged two days later, their bodies suspended in chains beside the parade ground, with the remainder having their sentences commuted to fourteen years hard labour.[181] The tremors from this mutiny spread even further than those caused by the war and arguably had a more lasting impact in the suspicions they raised about the loyalty of their army. In Calcutta 'a most indescribable gloom seemed to descend upon the whole community.'[182]

The mutiny came about for a variety of reasons, most of which were not immediately recognized by British authorities who were far more concerned with dealing with what they feared was the touchstone of an army-wide revolt. Their emphasis was on suppression rather than comprehension. While it is true that sepoys were upset at being ordered on unpopular service, a stronger sense of resentment stemmed from the failure of the army to fulfill the sepoys' expectations that carriage would be provided for them. In the past such assistance had been customary when draught and carriage animals were in short supply, and sepoys viewed it as essentially part of their contract with the state. Significantly, just prior to the outbreak of protest among the sepoys of the 47th regiment, a European regiment has passed by, lavishly equipped with carriage and draught cattle that were carrying the European soldiers' belongings.[183] The grievance that the British had failed to live up to their contractual obligations was also warranted in the eyes of the sepoys by the British failure to provide the new knapsacks and assorted other accoutrements that the sepoys would need in Burma and for which deductions were already being taken from their pay. Added to this was the sepoys' concern that the elite character of the army (principally grounded on the practice of respecting their 'caste') would soon be diluted by the arrival of lower caste recruits. One other observer claimed that the sepoys of the 47th regiment had been seduced by a rumour that the Arakan Peninsula was populated with sorcerers and evil spirits.[184]

To some extent there are similarities with the events of 1857. On both occasions the immediate cause appears to have been the sepoys' fear that the respect with which they were held by the British was deteriorating and as a consequence their service was not as valued nor as advantageous as it had once been. A near mutiny in the 40th Native Infantry that was part of the Arakan force in 1825 testifies to the jealousy with which the sepoys of Bengal guarded their prerogatives. On this occasion troops from Bengal were serving alongside Madras sepoys, and the former were ordered to help construct huts as the Madras sepoys were already doing. The 40th refused, and were initially supported by their commanding officer who agreed with them that such tasks as hut construction or trench digging were beneath their dignity. Unlike Barrackpore, this crisis was peacefully resolved: the officer was relieved of his command, and the 40th were persuaded to return to duty.[185] In all these cases conflict was triggered when the British tried to change without prior arrangement the terms of the contract that bound the sepoy to the state. In 1824 the lack of carriage provided part of the spark; in 1857 it was partly the General Service Enlistment Act with its requirement that sepoys were obliged to serve wherever they were sent. Sepoys had hitherto joined the army on the tacit condition that they would not be obliged to serve overseas unless they volunteered to do so, and that those who did proceed on foreign service were rewarded with extra *batta*. When confronted with what they deemed a British breach of faith, on these occasions as well as others, the sepoys' normal response was to take industrial action, down tools, and refuse to obey orders — mutiny in military parlance. In some cases this tactic was successful; their grievances were acknowledged and the perpetrators were either never punished or their punishments were comparatively lenient. However, in 1824 their labour protest brought a swift and brutal response from the commander-in-chief. In 1857 the sepoys expressed their grievances, at least in the very beginning, in the traditional manner, that is by downing their tools. Yet in 1857 the situation was much more explosive and their grievances could not be contained. These grievances affected the entire army, not just a single regiment. The frustration of the sepoys was also matched by growing popular discontent, especially in their homeland of Awadh, and this convergence of the army and the peasantry, together with some discontented elites, allowed the conflagaration to sweep across northern India.[186]

Misgivings about the sepoys that circulated after Barrackpore were further reinforced by reports from Bharatpur that the sepoys had hung back from the assault.[187] These reports, however, seem to be without foundation and tell us more about how the British wanted history to be recorded. Writing the sepoys out of the record only made British valour and success that much more obvious. A much different perspective is offered by one participant who wrote that not only was it impossible for the sepoys to be in the forefront as Combermere had lined up the three columns with Europeans heading each, but it was the sepoys who were on the receiving end of the debris and shrapnel thrown up by the overcharged mine. Another observer wrote that 'In the column to which the writer was attached, not the slightest symptom of backwardness was evinced by the native troops; the assault was perfectly successful, every thing went on smoothly, and all mounted the breach and ramparts in the order they were placed in the trenches.'[188] Such attempts to restore the sepoys' reputation were largely unsuccessful. British rhetoric was not only demanding that sepoys be seen as inferior, but there were also clear indications that sepoy morale and loyalty were becoming strained. At Bharatpur the 15th Bengal Native Infantry was briefly rocked by unrest. It began when a Muslim sepoy in that regiment suffered a head wound on 3 January 1826. Surgeons apparently resorted to bleeding the victim though without success for he died four days later in the field hospital.[189] When his colleagues claimed the body for burial, they discovered the holes in the temple where he had been bled and a rumour quickly spread that he had been murdered in the hospital. Soldiers of the 35th Bengal Native Infantry which was encamped nearby also became agitated. British officers concluded that 'It is impossible not to couple this with some latent causes — either fear of defeat, and death in the approaching assault, or disloyalty to the government, or to as superstitious belief that Bhurtpoor was not to be taken.'[190] Eventually the only punishment awarded (aside from private admonitions) was that one native officer was dismissed for having failed to report the discontent to the regimental commander. A formal investigation was decided against for it was privately feared that such an enquiry would only reveal what many suspected, but did not want publicly announced — that the mutiny broke out because the European officers had failed in their duty of maintaining morale and discipline in the regiment.[191] The regiment was also spared further punishment because of its steady performance in the attack on January 18.

The complacency and corporate spirit of the army was also threatened by factions that quickly emerged following the ending of the Bharatpur campaign. Officers who had served in Burma resented their opposite numbers in northern India who, after a shorter and less punishing campaign, emerged with greater fame and fortune.[192] Compared with the war with Burma, the conquest of Bharatpur came off very easily. Unlike Campbell, Combermere had several advantages working for him. The march to the objective was short and over easy terrain, British supply lines were well secured, the troops were fighting in the coolest season, and they were well furnished with everything they required for fighting as well as for their personal comfort. Combermere's troops could also look forward to a share of Bharatpur's reputed riches. It was far different in Burma. Campbell's second in command complained that 'our prize money will turn out to be a trifling and here is Lord Combermere's luck — gets himself and his army an immensity for six weeks' champagne campaign in the trenches.'[193] Grievances were even more apparent between king's and Company officers who had served at Bharatpur. Mutual jealousies had been sparked by the ways in which the campaign had been narrated to British audiences. The first report to be published in Britain, written anonymously by G.R. Gleig, had made the most of the king's officers, stressing their valour and dedication.[194] Company officers, alive as ever to any intimations against their skill and honour, quickly mounted a defence of their service. Articles were written protesting against what they saw as a poorly informed article, 'full of aspersions and calumnious insinuations against that great portion of the army, whose skill, talent, and heroic exertions contributed, no less than that of their fellow-soldiers in His Majesty's regiments, to its glorious termination.'[195] Yet in mounting this defence, Company officers found themselves in the paradoxical position of defending their own role in the siege while still trying to maintain the unflattering picture of the sepoys, who comprised most of the troops that they themselves had led.

The beginning of March 1826 found the Company's military forces victorious in two campaigns, one a long drawn out punishing affair in Burma and the other a short and spectacular seizure of one of India's most famous fortresses. These successes had not been easily achieved and in consequence serious shortcomings were exposed in the capacity of Britain's garrison state to wage war. At the same time the strength of Anglo-Indian militarism was undiminished. When coupled to the financial costs incurred by these wars,

Britain's position in India appeared to many onlookers to be in a very per-
ilous state.

[1] Nottingham, Paget to Bentinck, 29 Nov 1827, PwJf 2863/iv
[2] The Court of Directors' struggle to have Amherst recalled against the wishes of
the Board of Control is explored in Douglas M. Peers, 'The Duke of Wellington
and British India during the Liverpool Administration, 1819-1827,' *Journal of
Imperial and Commonwealth History*, 17(1988): 5-25
[3] James Edward Alexander, *Travels from India to England*, London: Parbury, Allen
and Co., 1827; [Major] Bennet, 'Burmah and the Burmese in the Late War,'
United Services Journal, 31(1838): nos 1-4; J. Butler, *Sketch of the Services of the
Madras European Regiment during the Burma War*, London: Smith, Elder and Co.,
1839; F.B. Doveton, *Reminiscences of the Burmese War in 1824-5-6*, London: Allen
and Co., 1852; Henry Gouger, *A Personal Narrative of Two Years Imprisonment in
Burmah*, London: John Murray, 1860; Henry Havelock, *Memoir of Three
Campaigns of Major General Sir Archibald Campbell's Army in Ava*, Serampore:
Baptist Mission Press, 1828; W.F.B. Laurie, *Our Burmese Wars and Relations with
Burma*, London: W.H. Allen, 1880; Frederick Marryat, *Olla Podrida*, 3 vols,
London: Longman, Rees, Orme, Brown and Green, 1840; John Marshall,
Narrative of the Naval Operations in Ava, London: Longman, Rees, Orme, Brown
and Green, 1830; H. Lister Maw, *Memoir of the Early Operations of the Burmese
War*, London: Smith, Elder and Co., 1832; Thomas Campbell Robertson,
Political Incidents of the First Burmese War, London: Richard Bentley, 1853; J.J.
Snodgrass, *Narrative of the First Burmese War*, London: John Murray, 1827; M.
Stewart, *Some Considerations on the Policy of the Government of India*, Edinburgh:
Tait, 1826; H.H. Wilson, *Documents Illustrative of the Burmese War*, Calcutta:
Government Gazette Press, 1827; H.H. Wilson, *Narrative of the Burmese War in
1824-26*, London: 1852
[4] One was titled 'War in India; or the Burmese' (*Times*, 15 May 1825) and the
other was titled 'Massacre at Rajahpoor' (*Times*, 28 March 1826).
[5] G.A. Henty, *On the Irrawaddy*, London: Blackie and Sons, 1897
[6] Munro to Wellington, 9 Jan 1826, *Letters*, III, 62
[7] OIOC, Ravenshaw to Munro, 12 March 1825, MSS Eur F151/80
[8] OIOC, Thomas Reid, 'Observations on India,' 28 Nov 1822, MSS Eur F140/
56; B.S. Jones, 'An Account of the State of India,' Nov 1822, MSS Eur F140/
60(a)
[9] OIOC, untitled scrap of paper, c.1822, MSS Eur F140/55
[10] OIOC, Notes by the Board of Control on the 1823 Arrangements, n.d., L/
MIL/5/392/240(a)
[11] OIOC, Board's Draft Instruction to Lord Amherst, 10 March 1823, L/PS/5/
585
[12] Nottingham, Paget to Bentinck, 29 Nov 1827, PwJf 2863/iv
[13] Paget to Harriet Paget, 11 Feb 1825, Paget, *Letters and Memorials*, 178. The
local press also mocked Amherst's loyalty to his employers, see *Oriental Herald*,
16(1825): 125-26
[14] OIOC, Paget to Amherst, 25 Oct 1823, MSS Eur F140/79
[15] BL, Amherst to Morley, 11 Dec 1824, Add MS 48225

[16] OIOC, Mackenzie to Adam, 26 Feb 1825, MSS Eur F109/D

[17] Ibid.

[18] Prinsep, *Narrative*, 448

[19] Robertson, *Political Incidents*, 26-8

[20] Minto to Court, 25 May 1812, Papers on Relations with the Burman Empire, PP, 24(1825): 139

[21] OIOC, Hastings to Board, 27 July 1822, L/PS/20/162

[22] OIOC, Dawkins to Clinton, 29 Oct 1825, MSS Eur D920

[23] Michael Symes was sent to Burma in 1795 and again in 1802. His first embassy was followed up by one led by Hiram Cox in 1796-98 and in 1809-10 Captain John Canning was despatched to Burma. For firsthand accounts of these missions see Hiram Cox, *Journal of a Residence in the Burmhan Empire*, 1821. Reprint, London: Gregg, 1971; Michael Symes, *An Account of an Embassy to the Kingdom of Ava in the Year 1795*, London: W. Bulwer, 1800 and Michael Symes, *Journal of his Second Embassy to the Court of Ava in 1802*, D.G.E. Hall, ed., London: Allen and Unwin, 1955. British diplomatic efforts are examined more closely in A.C. Banerjee, *The Eastern Frontier of British India, 1784-1826*, 2nd ed. Calcutta: Mukerjee, 1966; and in G.P. Ramachandra, 'The Canning Mission to Burma of 1809-10,' *Journal of Southeast Asian Studies*, 10(1979): 119-39

[24] This perspective is most clearly articulated in Bayly, *Indian Society and the Making of the British Empire*. Another scholar who makes a compelling argument in favour of this explanation is David Washbrook who particularly stresses economic aspects. For a summary of his argument, see his 'Progress and Problems: South Asian Social and Economic History, c.1720-1860,' *Modern Asian Studies*, 12(1988): 57-96.

[25] Victor Lieberman, 'Secular Trends in Burmese Economic History, c.1350-1830, and their Implications for State Formation,' *Modern Asian Studies*, 25(1991): 1-31

[26] Robertson, *Political Incidents*, 10; Arthur Phayre, *History of Burma*, London: Trubner and Co., 1883, 223; Captain W. White, *A Political History of the Extraordinary Events which Led to the Burman War*, London: Hamilton, 1827, 39

[27] Judson's deposition at the end of the war, 1826, Wilson, *Documents*, 231

[28] Reginald Heber, Bishop of Calcutta. *Narrative of a Journey through the Upper Provinces of India, from Calcutta to Bombay, 1824-1825*. London: John Murray, 1846, I, 94

[29] OIOC, Resolution of the Governor-general, 17 Oct 1823, H/MISC/660

[30] Economic explanations for the origins of the Burma War are put forward more forcefully in G.P. Ramachandra, 'Anglo-Burmese Diplomacy; September 1823 to July 1824,' *Journal of Indian History*, Diamond Jubilee Volume, Pt I, 1982, 71-107; J.S. Furnivall, *Colonial Policy and Practice; a Comparative Study of Burma and Netherlands India*, New York: New York University Press, 1942, 23-4; and John P. Halstead, *The Second British Empire; Trade, Philanthropy and Good Government, 1820-1890*, Westport, Conn.: Greenwood Press, 1983, 69

[31] G.A. Prinsep, *Remarks on the External Commerce and Exchanges of Bengal*, London: Kingsbury, Parbury and Allen, 1823, 46-7. See also Hamilton, *Description*, II, 770-71

[32] Gouger, *Personal Narrative*, 59

[33] Ma Thaung, *British Interests in Trans-Burma Trade Routes to China, 1826-1876*, unpublished Ph.D. thesis, University of London, 1955; Nicholas Tarling, *British*

Policy in the Malay Peninsula and Archipelago, 1824-1871, Kuala Lumpur: Oxford University Press, 1979

[34] See R.H. Phillimore, *Historical Records of the Survey of India*, 3 vols., Dehra Dun: Survey of India, 1950 for a history of the mapping and exploration of northeastern India.

[35] OIOC, Amherst to Captain Canning, 12 Oct 1823, MSS Eur F140/99

[36] OIOC, Lady Amherst to William Pitt Amherst, c.1824, MSS Eur F140/168

[37] OIOC, Amherst to Canning, 8 Aug 1825, MSS Eur F140/114(a)

[38] Wellesley to Grenville, 18 Nov 1798, *Memoirs and Correspondence of the Most Noble Richard Marquess Wellesley*. Robert Pearce, ed. London: Richard Bentley, 1846, I, 83

[39] Hamilton, *Description*, II, 787

[40] OIOC, Paget, minute on the defence of India, 15 Dec 1824, H/MISC/665/20; Amherst to Wynn, 13 Dec 1824, MSS Eur F140/104(b); [Anon], 'Sketches of the Burmese War,' *United Services Journal*, 8(1832): 168

[41] OIOC, M. Elphinstone to Adam, 4 March 1825, MSS Eur F109/E

[42] Reginald Heber, Bishop of Calcutta. *Narrative of a Journey through the Upper Provinces of India, from Calcutta to Bombay, 1824-1825*. London: John Murray, 1846, II, 230

[43] OIOC, Adam to Swinton, 14 Dec 1824, MSS Eur F109/J

[44] OIOC, Amherst to Munro, 11 June 1825, MSS Eur F140/168. Prior to his departure for India, Amherst had been recommended by one of the directors to seek out Munro's assistance. OIOC, Reid to Amherst, 24 Jan 1823, MSS Eur F140/55. Through the course of the war, Amherst maintained a fortnightly correspondence with Munro.

[45] OIOC, Morley to Amherst, 28 Dec 1824, MSS Eur F140/11/a

[46] OIOC, Adam to M. Elphinstone, 31 May 1824, MSS Eur F88/9/F/27

[47] See for example, OIOC, Notes by Metcalfe, 1824, MSS Eur F140/93; Robertson, *Political Incidents*; and Nirode K. Barooah, *David Scott in North-East India, 1802-1831*, New Delhi: Manoharlal, 1971. Even F.J. Shore, one of the least militant officials in India, was all in favour of an attack on Burma. OIOC, Shore to Charles Shore, 17 Sept 1827, MSS Eur E307/2

[48] OIOC, Nicolls' Diary, 5 July 1824, MSS Eur F175/31

[49] OIOC, John Adam, Paper on the Means of Proceeding, 1 July 1824, MSS Eur F109/J

[50] [Anon], 'Sketches of the Burmese War,' *United Services Journal*, 8(1832): 174

[51] OIOC, Sarah Amherst to William Pitt Amherst, 3 Sept 1824, MSS Eur F140/168

[52] OIOC, Amherst's Memo, Sept 1824, MSS Eur F140/115(g); Adam to Swinton, 21 Oct 1824, MSS Eur F109/J

[53] OIOC, Captain Canning to Amherst, 11 Jan 1824, MSS Eur F140/118(c)

[54] OIOC, Adam to Amherst, 26 March 1824 and 1 July 1824, MSS Eur F109/J

[55] OIOC, Supreme Council Proceedings, 1 March 1824, Bengal Military Consultations, P/30/43

[56] OIOC, Amherst to Urmston, 22 Sept 1824, MSS Eur F140/114(a)

[57] See for example, OIOC, Amherst to Urmstom, 14 March 1824 and 22 Sept 1824, MSS Eur F140/114(a). Amherst also informed London of his worries. OIOC, Amherst to Secret Committee, 12 Aug 1824, H/MISC/660/3

[58] Interestingly, the planning difficulties of this campaign were later used as part of the officer training programme at the Indian Army staff college. See OIOC, Indian Army, Intelligence Branch, Frontier and Overseas Expeditions, Burma, 5(1907), L/MIL/17/13/16/7

[59] OIOC, Paget to Amherst, 25 Oct 1823, MSS Eur F140/79; Minute by the Commander-in-Chief, 24 Nov 1823, L/PS/20/102

[60] OIOC, Paget to Amherst, 16 Feb 1824, MSS Eur F140/79

[61] Robertson, *Political Incidents*, 137

[62] [Anon], 'Sketches of the Burmese War,' *United Services Journal*, 8(1832): 170

[63] Gouger, *Personal Narrative*, 297

[64] This impression of a desolated and depopulated countryside is one that has continued to dog the historiography of Burma. It has, however, been convincingly overthrown by studies by Michael Adas which have shown that much of Pegu's depopulation occurred in the 16th century, a full two centuries before the Burmese conquest of lower Burma. Michael Adas, 'Imperialist Rhetoric and Modern Historiography: the Case of Lower Burma Before and After the Conquest,' *Journal of Southeast Asian Studies*, 3(1972): 175-93

[65] OIOC, Munro to Amherst, 15 April 1824, MSS Eur F140/74(a)

[66] Snodgrass, *Narrative*, 16

[67] OIOC, Amherst to Wynn, 24 May 1825, MSS Eur F140/114(a); Symes, *Account of an Embassy*, 24-8

[68] [Anon], 'A Memorial of the War in Ava,' *Colburn's United Services Journal*, (1844, no.1): 115. The officer who wrote this article speculates that had the fleet arrived in the fall, when travel upriver was possible, the war could have been kept to only six or eight months. His reasoning emphasizes that not only could the fleet have moved forward immediately, but the serious losses suffered by the enforced stop in Rangoon would have been avoided, leaving a fitter and better equipped army to take the field.

[69] Matthew H. Edney, 'The Atlas of India 1823-1947: The Natural History of a Topographic Map Series,' *Cartographica*. 28(1991): 73.

[70] Edney, 'Atlas of India,' 76

[71] Included within these naval forces was the *Diana*, the first steam powered vessel ever to serve in a naval campaign. Freed from reliance upon the wind, the *Diana* was to prove particularly valuable as it could tow barges carrying soldiers upriver. The government had been persuaded to purchase the *Diana* for service in Burma by Captain Marryat, a naval officer who would later become famous as an adventure novelist; OIOC, Frederick Marryat, Memo to the government, 6 April 1824, Bengal Military Consultations, P/30/46

[72] *Oriental Herald*, 6(1825): 262-63

[73] [Anon], 'Naval Operations of the Burmese War,' *United Services Journal*, 8(1832): 12

[74] J. Alexander, *Travels from India to England*, 18; Bennet, 'Burmah and the Burmese', 79

[75] Somerset Record Office, Doveton's Diary, 18 June 1824, DD/DP/22

[76] BL, Lieut. Blackwell's Diary, 1824, Add MS 39811

[77] Fortescue, *History of the British Army*, XI, 369

[78] OIOC, Wynn to Amherst, 1 Aug 1825, MSS Eur F140/104(d). Amherst received further reports from London that detailed just how ridiculous Campbell

looked to them. Morley to Amherst, 26 Aug 1825, MSS Eur F140/74(b)

[79] *Oriental Herald*, 5(1825): 491

[80] OIOC, Nicolls' Diary, 5 Dec 1824, MSS Eur F175/21

[81] OIOC, Munro to Amherst, 27 Sept 1825, MSS Eur F140/74(b)

[82] Doveton, *Reminiscences*, 111

[83] Statistics calculated from Medical Returns of European Troops Overseas, PP, 27(1842): 255. It is difficult to establish what were the principal diseases at work here for the tables produced by contemporaries grouped casualties according to symptoms. In Burma, 23 per cent of the deaths were reportedly caused by stomach diseases, most likely amoebic dysentery and acute diarrhoea.

[84] 'Report of the Committee of the Statistical Society of London, appointed to Enquire into the Vital Statistics of the Madras Army,' *Journal of the Statistical Society of London*, 3(1840): 124

[85] North Yorkshire Record Office, Havelock to Gardner, 22 May 1824, ZDG (H) II 2

[86] Doveton, *Reminiscences*, 43-4

[87] OIOC, Paget, Memo on the Commissariat, 21 June 1824, H/MISC/663/3; *Oriental Herald*, 6(1825), passim

[88] Herbert Edwardes and Herman Merivale, *Life of Sir Henry Lawrence*, 2nd ed. London: 1872, I, 53-4

[89] F.B. Doveton, 'The Beginning and the End of an Expedition,' *Colburn's United Services Journal*, (1847, no.2): 92

[90] OIOC, Cunliffe to Watson, 21 Oct 1825, Bengal Secret Consultations, P/333; BL, Lieut. Blackwell, diary, 1824, Add MS 39811

[91] John Marshall, *Narrative of the Naval Operations in Ava During the Burmese War in the Years 1824, 1825, and 1826*, London: Longman, Rees, Orme, Brown and Green, 1830, 127

[92] BL, Lieut. Blackwell, Diary, 1825, Add MS 39811

[93] OIOC, Supreme Council Consultations, 5 April 1824, Bengal Military Consultations, P/30/48

[94] OIOC, Campbell to Bengal, 31 July 1824, H/MISC/663/2&3

[95] British efforts to capture Burmese stockades also suffered from the relative imperviousness of these stockades to British artillery. Made of bamboo, the walls of the stockades allowed shot to pass through without causing much damage. The Burmese were also masters of guerrilla war and used terrain to their advantage. Their chief weakness, aside from a political and economic structure that did not permit the maintenance of a permanent and disciplined standing army, was that their weapons were greatly inferior in numbers and quality to the British. Most of their firearms were outdated matchlocks, crudely fashioned and generally incapable of sending their shot accurately.

[96] [Anon], 'Naval Operations of the Burmese War,' *United Services Journal*, 8(1832): 13

[97] BL. Lieut Blackwell, diary, 1825, Add MS 39811

[98] Doveton, *Reminiscences*, 260

[99] Metcalfe to Amherst, nd, Kaye, *Metcalfe*, II, 121. A remarkably similar rumour was circulating in Delhi where it was reported that Calcutta had fallen to the Burmese and that the administration had fled back to Britain. Ochterlony to Court, 1825, David Ochterlony, *Selections from the Ochterlony Papers (1818-1825)*

in the National Archives of India, Narendra Krishna Sinha and Arun Kumar Dasgupta, eds. Calcutta: University of Calcutta, 1964, 435

[100] Heber, *Narrative*, I, 102

[101] OIOC, Supreme Council Minutes, 31 July 1824, H/MISC/663/2

[102] OIOC, Minute by Amherst, 31 July 1824, H/MISC/663/2

[103] Doveton, *Reminiscences*, 293. In accounting for Bandula's victories against the British, victories that called for skills and aptitudes thought deficient or lacking in most non-Europeans, the possibility was raised that Bandula was not Burmese but a European. Some speculated that he was a deserter from the British army; others rumoured that he was the illegitimate son of the Marquess of Hastings. *Oriental Herald*, 7(1825): 567-68

[104] OIOC, Troop Returns from General Morrison, 4 Sept 1825, Bengal Secret Consultations, 21 Oct 1825, P/333

[105] Robertson, *Political Incidents*, 121-22

[106] BL, Lieut. Blackwell's Diary, 1825, Add MS 39811

[107] Major Bennett, 'Burmah and the Burmese During the Late War,' *United Services Journal*, 28(1838): 81

[108] OIOC, Munro to Amherst, 20 April 1825, MSS Eur F140/74(b)

[109] Doveton, *Reminiscences*, 305-6

[110] Doveton, *Reminiscences*, 305-6

[111] OIOC, Amherst, Memo on the State of Affairs, 4 Oct 1824, MSS Eur F140/115(h)

[112] OIOC, Munro to Amherst, 2 Feb 1825, MSS Eur F140/74(b)

[113] Munro to Wellington, *Letters*, III, 61; OIOC, Munro to Erskine, 15 Jan 1826, MSS Eur F151/145

[114] SRO, Memo by Captain Snodgrass (Campbell's secretary), 26 Aug 1825, GD45/6/521

[115] OIOC, Amherst to Munro, 7 June 1826, MSS Eur F140/79(c)

[116] Robertson, *Political Incidents*, 140. This belief in a nascent sense of Mon ethnic nationalism in Pegu has recently been explored by Victor Lieberman. His researches have shown that the many of the so-called Mons in Pegu had become assimilated to Burmese forms and institutions. Victor Lieberman, 'Ethnic Politics in Eighteenth-Century Burma,' *Modern Asian Studies* 12(1978): 455-82.

[117] OIOC, Adam to Amherst, 7 March 1824, MSS Eur F140/81(a); M. Elphinstone to W.F. Elphinstone, 4 Feb 1826, MSS Eur F88/9/E/24

[118] Robertson, *Political Incidents, 167-84*; OIOC, Consultations of the Supreme Council, 26 March 1824, Bengal Secret Consultations, P/231

[119] OIOC, Wynn to Amherst, 8 Jan 1827, MSS Eur F140/104(f)

[120] OIOC, Chairs to Amherst, 7 Nov 1826, H/MISC/680/6

[121] The brief flirtation with Siam is recorded in OIOC, Bengal to Madras, 13 May 1825, Madras Expeditionary Consultations, P/321/77

[122] OIOC, Fullerton to Amherst, 18 March 1826, MSS Eur F140/137(a)

[123] OIOC, Swinton's memo to the supreme council, 26 April 1826, H/MISC/668/13

[124] OIOC, Burney to Calcutta, 16 Sept 1825, Bengal Secret Consultations, P/333

[125] [Anon], 'Sketches of the Burmese War,' *United Services Journal*, 8(1832): 169

[126] Ochterlony to Swinton, 27 Aug 1824, *Ochterlony Papers*, 353; Governor-General in Council to Ochterlony, 1 Oct 1824, 1 Oct 1824, *Ochterlony Papers*, 354

[127] The right of succession was further complicated by a longstanding claim that Buldeo's own predecessor had adopted Durjan as his legitimate successor. Ochterlony to Swinton, 1 Nov 1823, *Ochterlony Papers*, 332

[128] OIOC, Bengal Political Letter to Court, 1 Oct 1825, E/4/116

[129] OIOC, Amherst to Secret Committee, 9 April 1825, E/4/115

[130] Heber, *Narrative*, I, 244

[131] OIOC, Memo by the Bombay Quartermaster General, 30 Oct 1824, F/4/986; Bombay Secret Letter to Court, 4 Nov 1824, E/4/507

[132] OIOC, enclosure in William Fullerton to Bombay Government, 23 Oct 1824, F/4/986

[133] OIOC, Madras Secret Letter to London, 26 July 1825, E/4/355; W. Chaplin to Bombay, 29 Nov 1827, F/4/986

[134] OIOC, Translation of a Letter from the Rebels, November 1824, F/4/986

[135] OIOC, Bengal Judicial Letter to Court, 7 Dec 1826, E/4/119

[136] OIOC, Bengal Political Letter to Court, 31 May 1826, F/4/987

[137] Anon, 'The Siege of Bhurtpore,' *East India United Service Journal*, 13(1835): 13

[138] OIOC, W.G. Gardner to Nicolls, 10 Nov 1825, MSS Eur F175/30

[139] Heber, *Narrative*. II, 233

[140] Heber, *Narrative*. II, 248

[141] Bayly, *Rulers, Townsmen and Bazaars*, 271. Hamilton in his gazetteer described Bharatpur in 1823 as follows. 'The Bhurtpoor territory was in a most flourishing condition, the villages numerous and well constructed, and the crops waving abundance, yet the peasantry *went constantly armed*.' Walter Hamilton, *The East-India Gazetteer*, 2nd ed., London: Parbury, Allen and Co., 1828, I, 233

[142] On 24 August 1825, a total of 30,000 armed retainers were reported to have converged on Bharatpur and Dig, all eager for service. The magistrate at Agra reported that these troops were more volatile than ever owing to the diminished authority of their traditional leaders. OIOC, Bengal Political Letter to Court, 1 Oct 1825, E/4/116

[143] Reginald Heber, Bishop of Calcutta. *Narrative of a Journey through the Upper Provinces of India, from Calcutta to Bombay, 1824-1825*. London: John Murray, 1846, II, 222

[144] OIOC, Murray to Swinton, 2 Jan 1826, Bengal Political Consultations, P/124/37

[145] Heber, *Narrative*, II, 7

[146] [G.R. Gleig], 'The Siege of Bhurtpore,' *Blackwood's Edinburgh Magazine*, 23(1828): 445

[147] OIOC, Metcalfe to Amherst, 8 Jan 1824, MSS Eur F140/93

[148] Heber, *Narrative*, II, 248

[149] OIOC, W.G. Gardner to Nicolls, 10 Nov 1825, MSS Eur F175/30

[150] [G.R. Gleig], 'The Siege of Bhurtpore,' *Blackwood's Edinburgh Magazine*, 23(1828): 446

[151] Anon, 'The Siege of Bhurtpore,' *East India United Service Journal*, 10(1835): 339

[152] Fortescue, *History of the British Army*, XI, 355

[153] OIOC, Amherst, Minute to Council, 6 Aug 1825, F/4/888

[154] OIOC, Fendall, Minute to Council, 23 July 1825; Harington, Minute to

Council, 26 July 1825; Paget, Minute to Council, 3 Aug 1825, F/4/888

155 OIOC, Charles Metcalfe, memo, 29 Aug 1825, F/4/888

156 OIOC, Amherst, Minute to Council, 3 Sept 1825, F/4/888; Resolution of the Governor-General in Council, 16 Sept 1825, Bengal Political Consultations, P/124/25

157 OIOC, Nicolls' Diary, 2 Jan 1826, MSS Eur F175/31

158 OIOC, Neil Campbell, Notes on the Siege of Bhurtpur, Photo Eur 73

159 OIOC, Nicolls' Diary, 2 Jan 1826, MSS Eur F175/31

160 OIOC, Lieut. William Anderson, Dairy, 4 Jan 1826, MSS Eur A9

161 OIOC, Neil Campbell, Notes on the Siege of Bhurtpur, Photo Eur 73

162 OIOC, Nicolls' Diary, 2 Jan 1826, MSS Eur F175/31

163 OIOC, Nicolls' Diary, 17 Jan 1826, MSS Eur F175/31

164 The amount settled upon as the indemnity was Rs.24,39,173. Evidence of B.S. Jones, S.C. on the East India Company, PP, 14(1831/32): 196

165 Fortescue, *History of the British Army*, IX, 365

166 OIOC, Colonel Dawkins to Henry Clinton, 29 Oct 1825, MSS Eur D920

167 Heber, *Narrative*, II, 199. This opinion has had a remarkable longevity. Fortescue's *History of the British Army* has this to say: 'The Bengali is not, at the best of times, distinguished by great courage, and he had been thoroughly terrified by the first mishap at Ramu' (vol.IX, page 297)

168 SRO, 'Observations by D. Patton on the Prospects of Officers in the Bengal Army,' 1831, GD45/5/51; OIOC, Munro to Amherst, 15 Jan 1825, MSS Eur F140/74(b)

169 OIOC, Robinson to Amherst, 12 July 1825, MSS Eur F140/69; Wynn to Amherst, 1 Aug 1825, MSS Eur F140/104(d)

170 OIOC, Amherst to Munro, 19 Feb 1825, MSS Eur F140/104(b); Butler, *Sketch of the Services of the Madras European Regiment during the Burmese War*, London: Smith, Elder and Co., 1839, 22-3

171 OIOC, Nicolls' Diary, Jan 1831, MSS Eur F175/35

172 SRO, Ramsay to Dalhousie, 10 Nov 1824, GD45/5/4

173 OIOC, Nicolls' Diary, 10 Dec 1825, MSS Eur F175/31

174 OIOC, John Malcolm, 'Observations on the Indian Army,' 1830, L/MIL/397/171

175 OIOC, Casement to government, 29 Oct 1824, L/MIL/5/388/115

176 OIOC, Deposition by Lieut Col John MacInnes, 18 Nov 1824, L/MIL/5/389/124(a)

177 OIOC, William Prinsep, diary, 1824, MSS Eur D1160/4, p.25

178 Diary of Thomas Erskine Dempster, 'The Barrackpore Mutiny of 1824,' reprinted in *Journal of the Society for Army Historical Research*, 54(1976): 3-14

179 Robertson, *Political Incidents*, 106-7

180 OIOC, Deposition by Lieut Col John MacInnes, 18 Nov 1824, L/MIL/5/389/124(a)

181 *Asiatic Journal*, 19(1825): 469-70

182 OIOC, William Prinsep, diary, 1824, MSS Eur D1160/4, p.27

183 [S.S.], 'An Apology for the Indian Army,' *United Services Journal*, 8(1932): 36

184 Ibid.

185 Anon. 'How to Deal with Sepoys; a Reminiscence of Arracan,' *Colburn's United Services Journal*, (July, 1865): 402-4

[186] There is a vast amount of material on the Indian 'mutiny', although much of it is dated, sensationalistic, polemical or narrowly focused on a particular area, group or individual. However, two recent studies of the 'mutiny' have looked at it from a broader perspective and have shown how the particular and the general and the civilian and the military all converged in this period. Eric Stokes, *The Peasant Armed: the Indian Rebellion of 1857*, C.A. Bayly, ed., Oxford: Clarendon, 1986. Rudrangshu Mukherjee, *Awadh in Revolt, 1857-1858; A Study of Popular Resistance*, Delhi: Oxford University Press, 1984.

[187] The persistent silence on the role of the sepoys is maintained up until the twentieth century. Fortescue in his history makes no mention of the sepoy regiments; instead he only explicitly notes the European regiments. Fortescue, *History of the British Army*, 353-69

[188] [S.S.]. 'An Apology for the Indian Army,' *United Services Journal*. 8(1832): 37. Another writer who defended the sepoys was an anonymous engineering officer. Anon, 'The Siege of Bhurtpore,' *East India United Service Journal*, 13(1835): 8

[189] OIOC, A.G. Watson to Military Department, 3 Feb 1826, Bengal Military Consultations, 3 March 1826, P/31/48

[190] OIOC, Nicolls' Diary, 5 Jan 1826, MSS Eur F175/31

[191] OIOC, A.G. Watson to Military Department, 3 Feb 1826, Bengal Military Consultations, 3 March 1826, P/31/48

[192] See, for example, [Anon], 'Sketches of the Burmese War,' *United Services Journal*, 8(1832): 168-70. Not only was the amount of prize money from Burma small, it was also years before it was distributed. See Anon, 'Prize Money for the Burmese War,' *United Services Journal*, 7(1831): 261

[193] Willoughby Cotton to Herbert Taylor, 19 June 1828, Herbert Taylor, *The Taylor Papers*, arranged by Ernest Taylor, London: Longman, Green and Co., 1923, 223

[194] [G.R. Gleig], 'The Siege of Bhartpore,' *Blackwood's Edinburgh Magazine*, 23(1828): 444-57

[195] [Veritas], 'Siege of Bhurtpoor,' *Naval and Military Magazine*, 3(1828): 396

7. ECONOMIES, IMPERIAL AUTHORITY AND WAR

> In India everything resolves itself into a matter of expense, and it therefore is not only the moral responsibility, but the money responsibility.[1]

The unique conditions of the Burma war and the political and military difficulties experienced in meeting them yielded unforeseen costs. Politically, the authority of the governor-general came under threat. The war was used as an excuse by the Court of Directors to try and rid themselves of an appointment that they had never liked. Their animosity was taken advantage of by members of the administration who sought to strengthen their own position by realigning political offices. The reverberations of these manoeuvres spread to India where the governor-general's authority became openly flouted. Public support was guaranteed for these intrigues by the very unpopularity of the war. *The Times* captured this mood and published the following condemnation of the war:

> Success also will, in all probability, attend our armies: but success in such cases, is like the sport of a good marksman in the midst of plenty of game in foreign regions - he can neither eat nor carry away the birds which he has shot: they turn, therefore, to no account, and his powder and shot is all wasted.[2]

Coupled to this weakening of political authority in India was the growing number of doubts attached to the efficiency and loyalty of the army in India. Difficulties in Burma combined with the mutiny at Barrackpore to encourage such doubts. Moreover, the pre-war attempts to reform the army had not only been postponed, but the war's demands led to a grossly inflated army even more in need of reduction.

184

Undoubtedly much of the financial embarrassment experienced after the war was owing to swollen military spending. This is certainly how it was interpreted at the time as well as in succeeding generations. The truth behind the financial crisis that first made its appearance in 1825 is much more complex. The British Indian economy was nowhere near as stable as the Court, the Board and many officials in India had deluded themselves into believing it was in 1823. It has already been shown that revenues were falling behind expenditure even without the intervention of the war. The war only served to accelerate the crisis, principally by redirecting what little capital was available to a single outlet — the government. The tightening of money markets, when added to existing trading difficulties and the ever present budget deficit, brought about commercial and public distress. What was really needed was a fundamental restructuring of the British Indian economy. Amherst and later Bentinck would try and tackle the problem but they were limited in what they could do. Only local expenditures were within their immediate control and here they encountered strong institutional resistance. The mere mention of economies and reductions caused widespread alarm, not only because they threatened the private interests of many officials, but retrenchments were conceived of as a threat to the dominant institutions and ideologies of colonial rule. Officials in Calcutta, Madras, Bombay and the numerous upcountry stations were disturbed by what they saw as an attempt by ill-informed metropolitan officials to impose expectations and requirements that might be suited to domestic conditions, but were deemed dangerous within the Indian context. They were especially worried lest the army, whose expenses were so massive and visible, be forced to bear the brunt of the Court's cost-cutting measures.

Before either the army or the finances of India could be tackled, there was an even more pressing problem of what could be done about the steadily deteriorating position of the governor-general. Within a year of the outbreak of the war in Burma, his authority was openly flouted. It appears that this phenomenon began in London and then spread to India. Amherst was warned by Malcolm that in London he was being compared to Napoleon Bonaparte, and that he was popularly viewed as 'the person who brought the blue flies into the butcher's shop'.[3] The disrepute that Amherst had fallen into was only partially explained by the war. The more important reason was that he had gone to India with negligible support and the outbreak of war offered the Company a chance to press for a replacement. That Hastings could recover from the equally disastrous reverses at the outset of the Nepal War is a measure of how essential it was for a governor-general to command the support of home authorities.

The complaints that the home authorities lodged against Amherst were not due to his declaration of war. Both the Court and Board agreed that the war was justified. Wynn wrote privately to Amherst to reassure him of this: 'It is perfectly clear that you have done everything to avert the war'.[4] However, for some unexplained reason, the Court of Directors later included in the charges they laid against Amherst the criticism that he should not have issued a formal declaration of war. This contradicts their position in the summer of 1824 when they pressed Calcutta to adopt an aggressive posture and drive the Burmese back from the frontier.[5] Another criticism that the Court made was that Amherst had failed to keep them regularly informed of what was happening in India. Amherst was not the sole reason for the Court's frustration at not knowing what was happening; the Board of Control also kept the Court in the dark. They deliberately withheld many sensitive documents from the Company.[6] Cut off from their governor-general in India and denied access to the Board's sources of information, which for the most part were private communications from India, the Court was forced to deliberate on what little information came through other channels. This information was mainly derived from unofficial and unsubstantiated reports and rumours from India, sources that were mainly hostile to Amherst.[7]

The public outcry against the war was orchestrated largely by the *Oriental Herald* under the editorship of James Silk Buckingham. Buckingham's motives for these attacks were largely personal for he had been expelled from India for libellous behaviour in 1823. Although Amherst was not responsible for this decision (it had been taken by Adam with the support of both the Board and the Court), Buckingham apparently linked Amherst to Adam and that was enough to start the vitriol flowing.[8] In attacking Amherst, Buckingham was soon joined by other papers who eagerly reprinted his reports as a means of attacking Liverpool's administration for Amherst was viewed as politically tied to them. Amherst experienced at first hand the difficulties of disassociating imperial from domestic politics.

The autumn of 1825 saw the most sustained campaign to have Amherst recalled. As this drama unfolded it became obvious that the key figures operating against Amherst were the Chair and Deputy Chair of the Company, William Astell and Campbell Marjoribanks; the Duke of Buckingham and his son the Marquess of Chandos, and George Canning. Intrigues began when the Court looked to Indian setbacks as a means of securing a new governor-general. News of the disastrous war in Burma, the brutal reaction to the Barrackpore mutiny and falling trading profits only further exasperated the Court and a scapegoat was looked for.[9] The charges that the Court would later bring against Amherst were suspected by most independent observers of being hastily concocted. Jasper Nicolls noted in his diary that although the Court emphasized Barrackpore, they had only had the reports from that incident for twenty-four hours before they lodged their demands — most of the directors would not have had time to look at them.[10] Morley's enquiries indicated that the Court had not bothered to formulate a cohesive set of charges. If left there the issue might have died had not members of the government breathed new life into it. The mastermind was George Canning who skillfully manipulated the Court's grievances to further his own career. An Indian vacancy could have allowed him to secure support from the Grenvillites by offering the position to the Duke of Buckingham. Failing that, Canning knew that the Court would be willing to take William Bentinck whose appointment to India would also provide Canning with more support.[11] One wonders whether it was this episode in Canning's career which inspired Thomas Love Peacock, the novelist, who as a senior employee of the Company might have been aware of these intrigues, to concoct the character 'Mr. Anyside Antijack' in Canning's likeness. In particular, the line 'My tailor is so clever, that my coat will turn for ever' seems pregnant with possibilities.[12] Amherst was eventually backed by the Duke of Wellington, whose arguments were sufficient to convince Charles Wynn, impress Lord Liverpool, and overwhelm the Company.[13]

Amherst's reputation in India was just as precarious as it was in London. In addition to being associated with a war that had gone distinctly sour, Amherst's style of leadership was not in keeping with the proconsular forms employed by his predecessors. He was too conciliatory and deferential to those around him. Officials in India took these to be a sign of weakness and indecision and berated him accordingly. Amherst's personal standing suffered a further blow when it became publicly known that his recall was being considered in London. Reports of the Company's animosity towards Amherst were leaked (Wynn thought deliberately) to India.[14] As his authority became increasingly exposed to hostile criticisms, Amherst responded by retreating more and more from public life. This only served to deepen his predicament for it confirmed what was already believed of Amherst, namely that he was not fit to be governor-general. It soon came to be feared that if the Indian press got wind of this lack of confidence in the governor-general, it could further encourage demonstrations against British rule.[15]

While Amherst's tenure was ultimately secured by Wellington's intervention and the ending of the unpopular war, he did not stay on much longer in India. The intrigues against him took their toll and the death of

his eldest son in late 1826 persuaded him to leave in early 1827.[16] Nevertheless he did begin to make some headway in reducing the Company's expenditures and returned to the much needed military reforms, though now the
emphasis lay on retrenchment. Just before the war broke out he had managed to introduce the new regimental organization called for by the Court.
This was not an especially contentious reform; the separating of regiments
of two battalions into two regiments of one battalion each commanded the
support of the army for it hastened promotion. Further reforms were shelved
for the war's duration though the Court did keep up the pressure for their
realization. By the end of the war conditions within the army and the
economy made retrenchments and reforms even more essential. The war's
experience, especially the mutiny at Barrackpore, had brought the morale
and effectiveness of the Bengal Army under suspicion. Doubts were expressed in London over its reliability. In June 1825 Wynn chose to amend
an extremely critical despatch from the Court of Directors, substituting
'alleged incompetency' for 'incompetency' so as not to needlessly antagonize officers in India.[17] When General Jasper Nicolls embarked for India in
1825, Horse Guards requested that he send confidential reports on the state
of the Bengal Army.[18] Three reports were prepared of which only two were
shown to the commander-in-chief. Nicolls' final report was so full of detailed criticisms that he decided not to show it to Combermere for fear that
the commander-in-chief might pass it on to the governor-general, or worse
yet, the Court of Directors.[19] The circulation of these reports in London
was limited to Wynn, Wellington and the Horse Guards. Nicolls' comments
on the state of the Bengal Army were reiterated to a large degree in an
equally devastating memo by Thomas Campbell Robertson.[20] The conclusions that were drawn from these reports led Wynn to write to Munro that
it appeared that 'every rank of the Bengal Service [is] inattentive to its duties and discontented'.[21]

The single most important incident which provoked these misgivings
was the disturbance at Barrackpore. The mutiny of a whole regiment, with
the suggestion that there were several others awaiting the outcome, reflected
poorly on the military system of the supreme presidency. Elsewhere there
were other worrying signs including the assassination of a European officer
in Hyderabad.[22] Officers were accused of paying less attention to their regimental responsibilities and more to their personal prospects. It was now
clear to authorities in London that the sepoys had gained an alarming degree of autonomy as a result of the absence of discipline from above. The
Bengal army's apparently unquestioned acceptance of its high-caste recruits'
insistence that their traditions and customs be respected was taken as one

of the surest signs that the officers had implicitly surrendered much of their authority over their troops.[23] Notably absent from these reports was any critique of the other presidencies' armies. Bombay was fortunate to be far removed from the glare of post-war recriminations, while Madras had emerged from the Burma War with an enhanced reputation. Its sepoys had never demonstrated any reluctance to serve outside India, and Campbell's prejudices notwithstanding, there were few harsh words said about their troops. Undoubtedly much of the praise bestowed on Madras was due to Munro's sagacious advice and the Madras tradition of officers taking a more active role in their regiments. Whereas it was assumed that Bengal had witnessed a deterioration in her army over the past fifteen years, Madras had experienced an improvement to an equal degree.[24]

A more immediate concern for the Court and the Board was the immense growth in the army (see Appendix I). It was suspected in London that the growth was not only unwarranted but lopsided. Of a total increase of 53,463 troops between 1823 and 1826, Bengal was responsible for fifty-two per cent, Madras for twenty-three per cent and Bombay for twenty-five per cent.[25] In the case of Bombay, both London and Bengal were mystified for Bombay had not experienced any great demand for troops over that period. The tables below illustrate the growth of establishments and costs over the war years.

Table 7.1
Military Establishments: 1823-26.[26]

Presidency	1822/23	1825/26
Bengal	129,473	157,250
Madras	71,423	83,829
Bombay	36,475	49,755
Total	237,371	290,834

Table 7.2
Military Charges: 1823-1826 (£).[27]

Presidency	1822/23	1825/26
Bengal	4,226,636	7,113,114
Madras	3,109,709	3,375,338
Bombay	1,781,222	2,335,647
Total	9,117,567	12,824,099

In using the figures calculated above, it must be taken into account that the spending figures for Bengal included all the transport and commissariat charges for the war with Burma. These war costs were not the chief cause for concern as they were of a short term nature. What did worry London was that Bengal's army had grown so unaccountably large when compared to Madras. Madras had not only contributed more sepoys to the war, but troops from that presidency had at the commencement of the war relieved ones from Bengal that had hitherto garrisoned Nagpur. Demands on the Bengal establishment had also been relieved by Bombay taking on the responsibility of garrisoning Mhow. Thomas Munro, with some justification for he had secured the most economical military establishment, was the most scathing in his comments. He wrote to Elphinstone that 'the Bengal government took Mhow, Assurghur and Nagpore, then raised additional regiments to maintain them and now give the places to Bombay and Madras but keep the troops.'[28] Calcutta's response to the escalation of the war in Burma was to order even more increases to its establishment.[29] Munro's critique of the Bengal establishment was welcomed in London as further justification for their efforts to bring military establishments back under control. The Court of Directors had to warn Bengal to avoid additions on such speculative grounds.[30] Munro's strenuous efforts to bring Bengal's excesses to London's attention were spurred on by the chance to put his government in the most favourable light at a time when he realized that the mood in London was distinctly anti-Bengal. The secretary to the Board of Control urged the Court to 'point out to the Bengal government the impropriety of augmenting the army without considering the disposition of the whole military force of India.'[31]

Munro blamed the inflated state of the Bengal army upon the absence of any effective check to military spending. Munro wrote sarcastically to Malcolm that 'an Adjutant General will always find very urgent reasons for increasing, and even for doubling, the army if Government is disposed to receive them.'[32] The government in Bengal needed little encouragement to increase their army. Metcalfe, Adam and Paget all insisted on more troops. They seduced Amherst into ordering increases that totalled more than that required for the immediate tasks at hand. Amherst could not counter their arguments given his lack of expertise. Increases were particularly noticeable in the irregular cavalry, provincial and local regiments, all of which could be raised much quicker than regiments of the line.[33] Average annual expenditure on the various types of irregular corps between 1810 and 1822 was only Rs. 11,24,544; by 1826 it had reached Rs. 24,18,972.[34] Few irregulars saw action during the war and spent most of their time patrolling rural areas.

In contrast to Bengal's policy of ordering blanket increases, Madras originally limited its expansion to only increasing and replacing losses in regiments sent overseas.[35] The elasticity of the Madras Army impressed even
Elphinstone in Bombay who wrote to Munro that he 'was quite astonished
at your resources.'[36] Eventually Munro reluctantly allowed small increases
to those regiments remaining in India because of the increased areas they
had to cover. In the first year of the war the only corps raised was a local
force at Seringapatam designed to release the regiment stationed there for
foreign service.[37] With increasing losses in Burma and no end of the war in
sight, there was a call for whole regiments to be raised. Munro ordered four
extra regiments to be brought into service, so-called because they were temporary formations with a stripped-down complement of officers. This allowed them to be quickly disbanded when they were no longer needed.
The rapidity with which Madras reduced its establishment after the war
also helped it avoid the Court's censure. Amherst encountered much more
difficulty in thinning out the Bengal army. With the conclusion of the war,
six of the twelve regiments raised were broken up but that still left six plus
all the irregulars, as well as the increased establishment of each regiment.[38]
Regiments were reduced to 820 sepoys from 900, but even this meant establishments larger than those of Madras.

The ease with which Madras controlled its military spending indicates
that the government maintained a closer supervision over the army. Madras officers were also less inclined to dispute the government's economy
orders. This not only reflects the respect with which Munro was held by
the army, but indicates the consequences of Hastings' decision to sanctify
the grievances of the Bengal officers by taking it upon himself to lobby on
their behalf. As a result, Amherst's attempts to impose economies were sty-
mied by a more determined and coordinated resistance. Bengal officers were
also assured of the support of many of the civilians in Calcutta.

The financial consequences of the Burma War were an even more pressing problem facing Amherst in the final year of his administration. There
has been a wide divergence of estimates as to the war's cost, ranging from
around five million pounds to a much higher figure of thirteen million
pounds. G.E. Harvey, J.L. Christian, A.C. Banerjee and John Halstead all
put the war's costs at around five million pounds, apparently basing this
figure on that concocted in the nineteenth century by H.H. Wilson.[39] An
alternative costing was presented by D.G.E. Hall who worked from the figures of W.B. Laurie. Laurie, Hall and later Dorothy Woodman and A.T.Q.
Stewart maintained that the war cost just under thirteen million pounds.[40]
Laurie's estimate is the most unsatisfactory for it is solely derived from the

increase in the Indian debt between 1823 and 1827. Such an approach lumps military costs in with various charges not related to the war, such as revenue shortfalls, trade difficulties and growth in civil expenditure. From the calculations I have made from the Company's accounts, and looking only at those charges that were directly attributable to the war effort, it would seem that the direct cost of the war was just slightly more than £4,800,000 [see Table 7.3].

Table 7.3
Military charges of the first Burma war (Sicca Rupees).[41]

Presidency	Department	Charge
Bengal	Royal Navy	4,50,000
	Staff Pay	33,45,000
	Shipping Fees	1,44,20,487
	Pay and Allowances	51,18,183
	Medical Supplies	70,734
	Commissariat	1,74,93,197
	Ordnance and Buildings	5,72,472
	Intelligence	48,901
	Miscellaneous	5,12,472
Madras	Staff Pay	3,69,799
	Pay and Allowances	43,34,599
	Commissariat	10,63,818
	Ordnance	69,804
	Medical Supplies	1,12,579
	Contingencies	1,60,456
	Total (Rs.)	4,81,32,357
	Total (Sterling)	approx. £4,800,000

This figure must be taken as a very rough attempt. A more accurate estimate is frustrated by the many anomalies and inconsistencies found in contemporary bookkeeping practices. It was impossible to produce a costing of the Maratha War of 1816–19 for the same reasons.[42] In reaching this figure of just under five million pounds, the emphasis has been on extracting extraordinary expenses, the categories of charges that were not considered to be part of the normal costs of maintaining the army. However, not all war related costs were listed as extraordinary expenses (such as increases to regimental strength), and the ordinary expenses of the army have been examined for signs of such expenditure. The difficulty in distinguishing clearly between what was normal and what was caused by wartime demand would persist in India. Thirty years after the Burma War, Indian authorities were no closer to calculating the exact costs of the Afghan War — 'as a very large proportion of the expenses is not separated from the ordinary military charges, it is not practicable, from the accounts, to form an accurate estimate of the cost of the war'.[43] Some of the specific difficulties experienced in trying to generate a figure for the total cost of the war include differences between presidencies in how and where charges were assigned, unreliable conversion rates between currencies, and the impossibility of separating the costs of increases to the army establishment brought on by the war from expansion for other reasons.[44] Hence the figure of £4,800,000 can only be taken as an approximation and does not adequately address all the indirect costs.

Of the costs incurred by the war, that spent on transport and commissariat was by far the greatest. Shipping alone accounted for nearly thirty per cent of extraordinary charges, while commissariat expenses were even higher, totalling thirty-five per cent. The extra expenses for pay and allowances were quite small in comparison. Madras calculated that the sepoy regiments sent to Burma only cost twenty-two per cent more than if they had been stationed within the presidency.[45] This figure would be less in Bengal where fewer troops were entitled to batta. The situation was different for those officers composing the staff of the forces sent to Arakan and Rangoon. Bengal's stinginess to its native troops did not extend to Campbell and his staff. Campbell himself received Rs.3000 a month on top of his basic salary of Rs.1000.[46] The total amount spent on the Rangoon staff was eight per cent of the total war costs paid in Bengal. A further Rs.3,69,799 was paid in Madras on staff officers, owing to the fact that the Madras corps took with it its own staff establishment.[47]

Transport and commissariat expenses were what made the costs of the Burma War unique. Given the tradition of extrapolating future military expenses from the accounts of previous wars, few of which had made extraordinary demands for supplies or transportation, it is no wonder that great difficulties were experienced at the beginning of the war in forecasting its ultimate cost.[48] British Indian forces in past campaigns had been more successful in living off the land and were largely independent of seaborne supply. Local market forces had been relied upon thus saving the government the costs of investing in a large and well-supplied commissariat. Though the government was aware that conditions in Burma necessitated a greater commitment on their part to the outfitting of the expedition, their anticipation of a short war persuaded them that these efforts could be kept limited, and they planned for their supply and transport requirements with correspondingly little forethought.

The maritime effort mounted by the British to transport and sustain the war effort was particularly unique and without precedent. The force that invaded Arakan, for example, was dependent upon a flotilla of ninety-five vessels manned by nearly 1600 seamen.[49] Although the earlier invasions of Java, Mauritius and Sri Lanka had given them some exposure to the complexities of amphibious warfare, these expeditions had been much more restricted in scope. Troops despatched to these places were able to live off the land much more easily than those in Burma. Shipping was required after the initial landing at Rangoon to keep the army supplied. Moreover, and again unlike previous campaigns, shipping was called upon in Burma to move troops about within the country.

The immense demand for shipping was distributed widely throughout eastern India. The Royal Navy and the Bombay Marine provided the larger armed vessels. European shipowners in Calcutta supplied most of the larger transports as Indians only owned about eight per cent of the large seagoing transports registered in Calcutta.[50] European shipowners, many of whom were linked to the Agency Houses, received about seventy per cent of the entire shipping budget.[51] Indian shipowners from Calcutta as well as from some of the other coastal communities scattered along the Bay of Bengal furnished smaller vessels for use on inland waterways. Given the size of the demand and the haste with which shipping was collected, officials in Calcutta were not in a position to impose rigorous standards nor could they properly coordinate these vessels. Many of the transports were poorly suited to ferrying troops and provisions; some had previously been used to freight sugar with the consequence that their holds were infected with vermin.[52] In other instances ship's captains failed to provide adequate supplies of water for the troops on board. There were also serious problems in the management of those vessels in use. Supplies collected in India were detained in Madras and Calcutta for want of shipping to get them to Burma. Thomas Munro complained that he could have sent five times as many cattle to Burma had there been transport available.[53] This problem arose not because there was a shortage of shipping; in fact the Company had hired too many vessels.[54] The obstruction lay in Rangoon where in the absence of any officer charged with coordinating transport many vessels lay idle. There were even reports that supplies on board vessels docked at Rangoon were allowed to rot because there was no one to take charge of their off-loading.[55] The Company was also charged far in excess of the going rates for ship hire. The average rate in the Burma War was Rs.20 per ton per month. This was considerably higher than the rates charged in previous expeditions, for example Rs.12.5 for the Red Sea expedition and Rs.17 for Java, and were especially so given that the costs of ship construction had fallen.[56] Transportation during the Burma War was not only inefficient, it was more expensive than it needed to be. This prompted one naval officer to remark later that 'the marine force collected and equipped for the expedition was uselessly expensive and far from efficient.'[57] All this made for a very expensive war by nineteenth-century standards, even with a conservative estimate of £4,800,000. The war with China in 1860 cost the Indian Treasury and the British Exchequer combined just under £4,700,000, while the cost of the Ashanti War of 1873/74 was under £1,000,000. Of those wars for which figures are available, only the Indian Rebellion of 1857-58, the Crimean War, the Abyssinian Expedition, the Second Afghan War and the Sudan War cost more.[58]

Even without the extra costs occasioned by the war with Burma, severe economic distress would have likely occurred in 1825. Trade was declining regardless of what was happening along the eastern frontier. The erratic state of the opium trade with China caused increasing concern. The value of this trade had fallen from one and a half crore in 1822/23 to eighty-five lakhs in 1823/24.[59] Returns from indigo were also unsatisfactory. The inelasticity of Indian revenues was, however, the most pressing constraint (see Appendix G). When looking at Bengal, the years after 1822/23 were ones of stagnation at best and in some areas of collection, there was a noticeable falling off (see Appendix F). Even more worrying was the inexorable growth in non-military charges. Throughout the war years, the civil costs of administering the Raj continued to mushroom [see Appendix G].

Bengal's revenues dropped by approximately seven per cent between 1823 and 1826, while there was very modest growth in Madras and Bombay of two per cent and one and a half per cent respectively.[60] Those areas of revenue collection in which the largest decreases were registered were land revenues from the provinces ceded to Britain by Awadh in Wellesley's time (from Rs. 2,41,08,718 in 1822/23 to Rs. 2,23,13,797 in 1825/26), customs (from Rs. 47,68,840 to 34,94,166), salt (from Rs. 2,55,31,957 to Rs. 2,13,94,690), and opium (from Rs. 1,49,35,545 to Rs. 93,98,910). The declining revenue returns from the ceded territories can be put down, at least in part, to the instability in the area; peasants and landlords both took advantage of local tensions to avoid their revenue payments. The falling off in customs receipts was the consequence of the disarray in local economies as colonial rule became more consolidated. Opium, as we have already discussed, was subject to wild fluctuations caused by Chinese attempts to stamp out the importation of this commodity, as well as oversupply and competition from other producers, notably cultivators and merchants in Malwa. As for salt, no explanation could be found to account for its sudden decline, though it did rebound after 1830.

No such spectacular fluctuations occurred in Madras where government receipts did not vary much over the war years, though some increases were secured in the revenue collections from lands in Tanjavur and from the sale of salt. Similarly Bombay's revenues remained fairly level with modest gains in some departments being offset by decreases in others. Yet Bombay had little reason to boast for while its revenues remained fairly constant, they were still far below what had been anticipated following the annexations of 1818 and 1819, and were not sufficient to cover the increased civil and military charges that were predicated on those expected gains being attained.

If revenues at best held their prewar position, expenditures shot upwards and many of these were unrelated to the war with Burma. After deducting all military expenses from Bengal's list of charges for the war years, we find that there was still an increase of seventeen per cent. The largest gains were reported in the costs of the civil establishment — the pay and allowances of the civil servants — where it jumped nearly one-third, from Rs. 76,72,003 in 1822/23 to Rs. 1,00,72,346 in 1825/26. And the costs associated with opium went up by a factor of five (from Rs. 10,56,786 to Rs. 56,06,727), and this at a time when opium receipts were falling. Smaller increases took place in nearly all other areas of expenditure. Not surprisingly military charges in the aggregate accounted for most of Bengal's expenditure. In 1822/23 total military charges equalled Rs.3,76,68,823; in 1825/26 military costs had risen to Rs. 6,81,40,741. While some of this increase can be put down to the war, there were also considerable sums spent in areas or departments far removed from the war effort. It would seem that civilians and soldiers alike took advantage of the government's preoccupation with the war to enhance their own little empires.

The modest revenue gains in Madras were accompanied by some success in controlling general expenditure for it was able to bring spending down by five per cent (from Rs. 1,26,82,481 to Rs. 1,42,68,458). Nearly all areas and departments kept their costs within prewar spending limits, and some (salt and revenue collection) even managed to bring them down further. Bombay was a different story. Its slight increase in revenue receipts was overwhelmed by burgeoning charges, including military charges which ought to be included here as Bombay was not contributing to the war effort. Bombay's total expenditure in 1826 was thirty per cent greater than in 1823 (Rs. 3,56,17,950 compared to Rs. 2,72,88,199). Military expenses accounted for much of this increase as they went from Rs. 1,50,02,397 to Rs. 2,10,80,404. Even discounting military expenditure, the increase in Bombay amounted to seventeen per cent. Civil expenditures bounced up to Rs. 39,85,724 from Rs. 27,46,201 and the costs of the judicial establishment rose from Rs. 5,64,607 to Rs. 8,79,857.

While the war's direct impact on the Company's finances has hitherto been exaggerated, mainly because these costs were not looked at in the context of all areas of revenue and expenditure, there is nevertheless a case to be made for the war having had serious indirect influences on the Indian economy. An already tight money market had to contend with the government's belated appetite for capital when they entered the money market in late 1824. With the benefit of hindsight, the Court of Directors would later criticize the authorities in Calcutta for not taking more aggressive financial measures earlier. The directors felt that a large loan should have been opened at the outbreak of war.[61] In Chapter five it was pointed out how the amount of available specie in India had shrunk. Bullion was leaving India faster than it could be replaced. This was largely due to London's insistence that remittances be made if necessary in precious metals. Hastings was only too willing to oblige and in 1823 a temporary glut of cash in the Company treasuries encouraged him to send a large shipment to London. The following year nearly one crore's worth of coin and bullion was sent to London and there were plans to send more.[62] Individuals were also remitting in cash some of their savings to Britain. At the same time the average annual import of gold and silver into India was only one or two crores.[63] The emerging cash shortage only came to the government's attentions when they were well into the Burma War. Having forecast a short and inexpensive war the government did not initially implement any plans for raising extra capital. Three months after the war had broken out, Mackenzie was still reassuring the governor-general that 'there was little room for apprehension' with respect to the government's financial situation.[64] Plans continued to send more bullion to Britain.[65] It was not until December 1824 that discernible signs of apprehension can be witnessed in the supreme council's financial deliberations. It was hinted to London that the Company's financial position could well deteriorate for war costs were rising at a time when revenues were sinking, and London should prepare itself for the possibility that remittances might have to be withheld temporarily.[66]

Procrastination when coupled to the new style of warfare encountered in Burma threw the East India Company's accounting procedures into disarray. We have already seen in Chapter five how the Company's estimates had many shortcomings. The war only made these worse and in the absence of timely and accurate estimates, sound financial planning was at an impasse. In his evidence before the Parliamentary Committee investigating the East India Company, Holt Mackenzie attributed the financial distress occasioned by the war chiefly to the absence of reliable estimates.[67] The first estimate of the war's cost, produced in June 1824, assumed that it would last six months at most.[68] Consequently the government miscalculated the expected costs of the war by a wide margin: their first estimate only equalled about one-third of the costs of the first year alone. Assuming a short war was not the only error made. The military auditor general, who gave the accountant general most of the raw data, had seriously underestimated the monthly charges for commissariat and shipping. Both the accountant general and the military auditor general urged in their own defence that all they had to rely upon were their records of previous wars as the departments concerned were extremely tardy in delivering up their most recent accounts.[69] By September 1824 the accountant general was beginning to comprehend the extent of the problems he faced. In the spring of 1825 he surrendered. 'Every day's experience evinces the necessity of our being prepared for new charges, of which the war having been conducted under circumstances that baffle prospective calculation'.[70]

Such inflexibility was inherent in a system modelled upon reference to past events. Had the individual departments been required to produce more regular and prompt statements of their expenses, the accountant general in conjunction with the military auditor general might have been able to provide the government with a more timely warning of what they could expect. Henry Wood, the accountant general, unsuccessfully tried to get the government to order all departments to submit half-yearly estimates.[71] Although the government agreed with him in principle, resistance from the other departments prevented its implementation. Momentary confusion was also injected by the government who failed to inform the accountant general on how Madras's war charges were to be debited, with the result that his original forecasts did not include the cost of the sizeable Madras force.[72]

The Court of Directors reacted very unfavourably to Wood's admission of defeat. They sarcastically penned the following despatch: 'The only definite opinion which you seem able to adopt is that [the costs] must greatly exceed the expenses of any former wars'.[73] Wood was later held guilty by the Court and by Mackenzie for much of the chaos enveloping the government's attempts to manage its finances.[74] However, it appears that Wood's culpability was largely determined by the need to find a scapegoat for he was handicapped by a more general failing in the Company's financial system. Moreover, as will become more evident later, Wood in association with Mackenzie sought to prevent the government's activities from impinging upon the tightening money markets. Their concern for private traders was to limit their scope for action.

The war and the ever-growing charges of civil administration were not the only demands facing the accountant general. He had also to make provision for the demands of the Bharatpur campaign which eventually totalled Rs. 25,86,518.[75] Fortunately he only had to contend here with a short war that was conducted within British-Indian territories. Bombay also gave endless cause for concern given Bengal's responsibility for underwriting its deficit. In 1825 Bengal had steeled itself for a shortfall in Bombay of Rs. 1,07,59,300. Instead Bengal eventually had to pay Rs. 1,43,47,360 as a subsidy, nearly fifty per cent more than they had anticipated.[76] Only Madras gave no grounds for worry. As has already been seen, Munro succeeded in keeping its expenditure well under control. A further charge for which the accountant general had the responsibility of meeting, but had no means of predicting, was that levied by London on India's territorial revenues. In the face of the extraordinary demands placed upon Indian treasuries between 1823 and 1827, the extra demands made by London were unhelpful. In 1825/26 there was a pronounced increase in the amount charged to India which would later prompt criticisms in the Parliamentary Committee investigating the state of India in 1831/32.[77] One of these additional charges was the annual sum of sixty thousand pounds to be debited to the Company to help finance the pensions of Royal officers. Furthermore, in 1826, the British Exchequer successfully extracted from the Company an agreement to pay the expenses of any naval units used exclusively for Indian purposes.[78]

Home charges rose by twenty per cent over the war years. Between 1814 and 1829 the annual average charge was just over £3,008,425, whereas the average between 1823 and 1827 was £3,608,000.[79] In the face of erratic and often fragile trading opportunities, bullion was often used to meet these demands. Specie shortages, however, prevented this. The Company then turned to its practice of internal indebtedness. By owing the commercial branch and through transferring any commercial profits left over after meeting all commercial charges, territorial demands were met. However, in many years, the Company's poor trading results meant that there were often insufficient profits to meet all of the territorial demand. This forced them to debit their commercial treasury. This caused the internal debt to rise from £2,769,081 in 1822/23 to £7,930,726 in 1827/28.[80] This, however, could only be a short term solution for the Court insisted that the Commercial treasury be repaid. In 1826, somewhat hastily, the Court of Directors pressed Bengal to dispatch two crores of rupees, nearly two million pounds, to meet this debt.[81] The Bengal government was expected to open up another loan to secure the necessary funds. In the face of a severe cash shortage and with the prospect of a general economic crisis, the governor-general wisely refused to implement the plan, especially as the Court of Directors had warned him to be ready to begin paying out the Deccan Prize Money from which account the government had already been borrowing heavily.[82]

The combination of all these demands and the delayed realization of what the war would eventually cost meant that the government sought extra funding at the point when the market was least equipped to give it. The demands placed upon the Treasury could only be met by opening loans and trying to control expenditure. There was little hope of increasing revenues on account of their being so inelastic. All major public works were ordered to be discontinued soon after the war was declared, and as many Company employees as possible were paid in arrears, which was shown in the Company's accounts as loans not at interest. Troops on the eastern frontier were allowed to fall seven months into arrears.[83] This option was not extended elsewhere in Bengal as it was considered too risky, especially given the signs that sepoy morale was deteriorating. Town duties at Banares, which had been set aside for the restoration of an ancient garden, were expropriated for military needs.[84] These measures quickly proved to be too little too late and loans became necessary. Loans, however, were viewed with misgivings; in the depressed state of the money market, any demands by the government could drive up interest rates and strangle the commercial sector. Bengal warned London that too much pressure on available capital could cripple the private sector, a fact that did not overly concern the Court of Directors.[85] Mackenzie was especially worried for the Agency Houses.[86] The government's anxiety over the fate of these firms contradicts what some have alleged to have been a hostility to private traders on the part of the government in Bengal.[87] However, this concern for the Agency Houses aroused the anger of the Court of Directors, who were alarmed at what they suspected to be an attempt by their officials to sacrifice the Company's interests to help out the private traders. They unsuccessfully cautioned Calcutta against any misdirected philanthropy.[88]

Unable to avoid turning to loans to assist them, the government decided in September 1824 to issue a loan at four per cent, the interest rate kept down so as to avoid driving up the rate on private lending which was currently around seven or eight per cent.[89] This rate was too low to raise the money required; by December of that year only seventy-six lakhs had been invested and twenty-five lakhs of it came from the quasi-governmental Bank of Bengal.[90] Noticeably absent from the investors to this loan were Indian capitalists. Many of them expected the government to relent and issue better terms so they withheld their funds until a better offer was made.[91] This willingness on the part of Indian capitalists to invest in Company paper, but only on favourable terms, and the government's need for such investments lends support to the arguments of Bayly and Marshall that local indigenous initiatives were crucial to British rule. The government realized that a higher rate was needed, but delayed raising its interest rates until May 1825 when it offered a loan at five per cent. Investors in the four per cent loan were allowed to transfer into the new one upon payment of an equal amount in cash.[92] This time the government were far more successful in that they raised £6,563,605. Moreover, the government raised much of this by tapping sources far removed from the shock-prone money markets of Calcutta.

To spare the commercial community of Calcutta as much as possible, the government followed Hastings' well-worn path to the proverbial wealth of the Indian princes. Residents at Indian courts were encouraged to seek these rulers' help in meeting the Company's needs. Roughly one-quarter of the total subscription to the five per cent loan was secured from Indian rulers and their entourages. Amherst justified his course of action in a letter to the Court by pointing out that much of their treasure was 'uselessly or hurtfully hoarded'.[93] Not surprisingly it was Mackenzie with Swinton's help who suggested this course of action to the governor-general.[94] The ruler of Awadh was the first to be targeted though Amherst employed more subtle tactics than did Hastings. Rather than lean on the ruler, Amherst pressured the resident. The initial negotiations with the Nawab were conducted in secret, not even the council was informed of the correspondence between Amherst and Mordaunt Ricketts, the resident, until after the loan was concluded.[95] The idea of a loan originated with the Nawab who correctly anticipated Bengal's imminent cash shortages and hinted that he would be willing to exchange some of his treasure for territory. The government would not consider the transfer of any land, but were encouraged by this indication of a supply of ready money.[96] Amherst then suggested that Ricketts try and get fifty lakhs at five per cent. The Nawab countered by offering one crore at six per cent, the interest to be paid in perpetuity as a pension to members of his retinue.[97] The government refused these terms and brought pressure on Ricketts to secure a better arrangement. Acting upon Swinton's advice, Amherst wrote to Ricketts to warn him that any failure would demonstrate a lack of influence 'greatly to be regretted'.[98] Eventually a loan at five per cent was secured, though the intended secrecy proved to be faulty for within hours of it being agreed, exchange rates between Awadh and Bengal shot up and the loan's value plummeted by eight per cent.[99] It was not a loan in the typical sense for it was never intended that the principal would be repaid. Instead the money was advanced in perpetuity in return for a guaranteed pension for a large number of the Nawabs' retainers and favourites. In 1826 a further fifty lakhs were drawn from the Nawab upon similar terms. Subscriptions to the Company's loans were also solicited from other Indian courts. While this did not bring in the same windfall that had been provided by Awadh, Metcalfe in Delhi was able to raise seven and a half lakhs from Sindhia's chief minister together with two and a half lakhs from Nawab Uhmad Buluh.[100] Twenty-two lakhs were also collected from various petty rulers in and around Bundelkhand.[101] The table below indicates the composition of the Indian debt as of 30 April 1827.

Table 7.4
Debt in India as of 30 April 1827 (£).[102]

Loan Issue	Rate	Principal	Annual Interest
Fort Marlboro	10 per cent	2,390	239
30 June 1822	6 per cent	8,666,499	519,990
1818	6 per cent	228,638	13,718
Awadh 1813	6 per cent	1,204,323	72,259
Bhow Begum 1816	6 per cent	649,418	38,965
Notes to Java Prize Captors 1817	6 per cent	37,354	2,241
Civil Annuity Fund 1825	6 per cent	130,938	7,856
1823 Loan	5 per cent	10,636,411	531,820
1825 Loan	5 per cent	6,563,605	328,180
Awadh Loan 1825	5 per cent	1,109,975	55,499
Awadh Loan 1826	5 per cent	554,987	27,749
Indian Princes Loan 1825	5 per cent	376,350	16,817
Treasury Notes	5 per cent	359,820	17,991
1824 Loan	4 per cent	273,458	10,938
Total		30,794,166	1,646,262

The Court of Directors tried to censure the government for drawing money from Awadh. Conscious of the Palmer and Company scandals in Hyderabad, scandals that not only involved the resident, but also hinted at the governor-general's involvement, the Court wished to restrict the opportunities for their servants to enrich themselves while being posted to the vulnerable courts of India's princes. The Board of Control had no such doubts and viewed the treasuries of Indian rulers as an obvious asset to be exploited.[103] The Court's misgivings were not without some foundation for in Mordaunt Ricketts, the Company had appointed a Resident of questionable ethics. Despite having been heavily in debt when first posted to Lucknow, Ricketts emerged very wealthy from his time there. In 1829 reports were sent to Bentinck that Ricketts had stashed away a personal fortune of between 2 and 3 lakhs of cash which 'was not honestly come by.'[104] When pressed for an explanation, Ricketts hastened his departure from India. The corruption was even more widely spread: a friend of Ricketts who was serving as a brigade major in Awadh was believed to have set aside four lakhs.

Only a small portion of the money raised outside the presidency was remitted to Calcutta. Most of the funds were used locally to pay demands on the British. Just over half of the Awadh loan was sent downriver to Calcutta with the rest being used to pay off the troops and civil charges in Awadh and neighbouring territories.[105] This spared the Company the cost and worry of moving large amounts of treasure and also cushioned them against losses on the exchange rates.

The Company's treasuries experienced some relief in 1826. Not only had the wars ended, but the taking of Bharatpur was followed by the discovery of vast hoards of treasure and cash within the citadel. The prize fund of Rs. 41,50,000 was deposited with the Company and though it was not theirs to keep, the distribution of prize funds was normally delayed for many years and during that time the Company could borrow from it.[106] It was much more difficult to find any optimism surrounding the state of Bengal's Agency Houses. Although the Bengal government succeeded in diverting many of its capital demands away from the sensitive money markets of the presidency, it was not enough to prevent financial disaster from rocking the Agency Houses. However, the government's loans were not the sole reason for their embarrassment. Through intemperate and short sighted actions of their own, the Agency Houses hastened their own downfall. Much has been written about the collapse of many houses of agency in the years after 1826, with most implying that the government's financial policies were to blame. Such reports tend to disregard the Agency Houses' own greed and their involvement in ruinous speculation.

The crises of the Agency Houses affected a great many people in India. William Makepeace Thackeray used it as the setting for his novel about returned Anglo-Indians, *The Newcomes*. As a member of an old Anglo-Indian family, Thackeray had insights into the operation of Agency Houses and these insights did not endear him to their method of conducting business. 'Agency House after Agency House has been established, and have flourished in splendour and magnificence, and have paid fabulous dividends – and have enormously enriched two or three wary speculators – and then burst in bankruptcy, involving widows, orphans, and countless simple people'.[107] Another critic of the Houses of Agency was William Huggins, an indigo planter in Bengal. He wrote that 'these gentlemen according to a bombastic mode of expression used in India, are called, by way of eminence, the princely merchants of Calcutta.'[108] He went on to state that 'the Calcutta agents are a class of very respectable men, very useful men, very proud men, and very selfish men'.[109] Moreover, many of the older established houses had lost their competitive edge, thereby encouraging the establishment of newer and more risky enterprises.

The initial abundance of cheap capital around 1822 had spurred the Agency Houses into hasty purchases of vast amounts of indigo. The result was an oversupply to London that drove down the price there by nearly thirty per cent.[110] This in itself need not have been catastrophic had not the Agency Houses aggravated the problem by simultaneously speculating in opium and cotton, both of which were experiencing difficulties in Chinese markets. As early as November 1824, before the squeeze on the money markets became apparent, members of the government in Calcutta were quietly withdrawing their savings from the Agency Houses.[111] The suddenly discovered shortage of capital in late 1824 therefore coincided with the Agency Houses' desperate need for cash injections. The Company's loan at four per cent had not worried them greatly for there were not many subscribers to that loan. Furthermore, many of the Agency Houses were benefiting from the war with Burma as they were in a position to lease out their shipping at very profitable rates to the Company. According to one observer the sudden demand for shipping actually helped to postpone the coming crisis.[112] However, with the opening of the five per cent loan and growing public disillusionment with their mode of conducting business, Agency Houses were faced with borrowing charges as high as fifteen or eighteen per cent.[113] As well, the five per cent loan opened by the government offered investors the option of having it repaid in England, thereby undercutting one of the chief advantages of Agency House paper. The Agency Houses' plight soon became widely known and this scared off their crucial Indian investors who either hoarded their capital or invested in the much more secure government bills. At this point partners in the Agency Houses panicked and withdrew their investment rather than use it to shore up their companies. This rush on the houses created its own momentum and several houses were forced into bankruptcy. The fact that the original partners rarely lost in these bankruptcies, unlike smaller investors (most notably Indian investors), further dampened confidence in the Agency Houses.

The government's reaction was to try and quietly advance some relief to the troubled firms. We have already seen how both Mackenzie and Wood were very supportive of the Agency Houses. Set against this support was the traditional antipathy of London towards private mercantile and financial activities in India. Therefore any aid that could be extended had to be as secretive as possible. The government in 1826 voted a loan of twenty lakhs while the Bank of Bengal, illegally but with the connivance of the government, offered a further seventeen lakhs to help the Agency Houses.[114] This aid was too little and too late to halt the collapse of many firms. After Amherst's departure for England, Bentinck was persuaded to try another rescue attempt, but it too was doomed to failure, largely because of the collapse of the whole Agency House system.

In concluding this chapter, it must be reiterated that the war's financial impact has been traditionally overestimated while the political and military ramifications have passed largely unnoticed. Although the cost of the war was larger than had been expected and extra resources had to be found, the ratio of debt servicing to total revenues was kept under control. Moreover, this was achieved despite a not inconsiderable increase in the total debt. The Burma War served as the acid test of the Company's credit and the Company had passed. The government managed to retain public confidence in their finances. As Tucker wisely noted, 'public credit cannot, like a hot house plant, be forced out of season into existence, it is the offspring of confidence and the result of experience.'[115] The administration in Calcutta only had to raise their interest rate from four to five per cent to ensure investment in government securities. However, it was at the same time conceded that economies were needed in all government departments. Unlike 1824, when any such reductions were considered impossible, in 1826 Amherst ordered that the spending habits of the Indian presidencies be examined by committees set up to review civil and military expenditure.[116] Healthy as the Company's credit was, the same could not be said about the state of the Indian economy. Here the war can be held partially responsible. The underdevelopment of the Indian economy, when coupled with a restricted money market that laboured under the extra demands imposed by the war, triggered some spectacular failings in a few crucial sectors of the economy. The psychological cost of the war was far more insidious yet harder to gauge. The coming together of economic distress, military disillusionment and uncertainty over British India's political position sparked demands for reforms. It was into this new questioning age that William Bentinck was sent as governor-general of India in 1828.

[1] Anon. 'The Military Constitution of our Indian Empire,' *United Services Journal*. (1845, no.3): 415

[2] *The Times*, 6 July 1826

[3] OIOC, Malcolm to Amherst, 31 May 1826, MSS Eur F140/137(a). I have looked at this episode in more detail in 'The Duke of Wellington and British India during the Liverpool Administration, 1819-1827,' *Journal of Imperial and Commonwealth History*. 17(1988): 5-25

[4] OIOC, Wynn to Amherst, 22 July 1824,, MSS Eur F140/104(a)

[5] OIOC, Secret Committee to Amherst, 4 Aug 1824, H/MISC/680/1

[6] See OIOC, 'List of Papers not Communicated to the Court', H/MISC/673/7 and Randall Jackson, *Substance of a Speech of Randall Jackson on a Motion of Thanks to Lord Amherst*, (London, 1827), 12

[7] OIOC, Wynn to Amherst, 12 Nov 1824, MSS Eur F140/104(a)

[8] For more information on Buckingham see: OIOC, John Adam's Papers, MSS Eur F109 and Ralph E Turner, *The Relations of James Silk Buckingham with the East India Company, 1818-1836*, Philadelphia: University of Pennsylvania Press, 1930.

[9] OIOC, Nicolls' Diary, 7 June 1825, MSS Eur F175/32; Ellis to Amherst, 22 April 1825, MSS Eur F140/112

[10] OIOC, Nicolls' Diary, 5 April 1826, MSS Eur F175/34 (Nicolls Papers); Morley to Amherst, 28 Nov 1825, MSS Eur F140/111(a)

[11] BL, Amherst to Morley, 26 Dec 1825, Add MS 48225; Harriet Arbuthbot, *The Journals of Mrs Arbuthnot, 1820-1832*, London: Macmillan, 1950, I, 433-34

[12] Thomas Love Peacock, *Melincourt*, London: Everyman editions, 1897: 294

[13] Southampton, Wellington to Liverpool, 10 Oct 1825, WP/1/830/10

[14] BL, Wynn to Liverpool, 23 Nov 1825, Loan 72, Vol 18, f 127

[15] OIOC, Wynn to Amherst, 11 April 1825, MSS Eur F140/104(c)

[16] BL, Amherst to Morley, 23 Nov 1826, Add MS 48225

[17] OIOC, Draft Letters to Bengal, June 1825, H/MISC/675/17

[18] OIOC, Nicolls' Diary, 6 June 1825, MSS Eur F175/32

[19] OIOC, Nicolls' Diary, 1 May 1827, MSS Eur F175/35. Nicolls' full report can be seen in *Letters*, IV, 148-58. An earlier version is at Nottingham in the Portland Papers where Wellington's hand can be detected in the marginal comments. Nottingham, Nicolls to Taylor, 29 Nov 1826, PwJf 2743/I

[20] Nottingham, T C Robertson, 'State of the Bengal Army', 1827, PwJf 2584

[21] OIOC, Wynn to Munro, 29 May 1826, MSS Eur F151/72

[22] OIOC, Nicolls' Diary, 17 May and 28 May 1827, MSS Eur F175/35

[23] Nicolls to Combermere, 27 Oct 1827, *Letters*, IV, 149

[24] Nottingham, T C Robertson, 'State of the Bengal Army', 1827, PwJf 2584; Nicolls to Taylor, 29 Nov 1826, PwJf 2743/I

[25] Appendices, S.C. on the East India Company, PP, 13(1831/32): 410-11

[26] Appendices, S.C. on the East India Company, PP, 13(1831/32): 410-11

[27] Ibid.

[28] OIOC, Munro to M. Elphinstone, 12 Dec 1824, MSS Eur F88/9/F/26

[29] In 1825, Wynn prepared a memo which highlighted this tendency. He showed that from 1823 to 1825, the Bengal army was inexorably increased to meet all rumoured crises. OIOC, Wynn to Chairs, 29 June 1825, F/2/8

[30] OIOC, Draft Letter, Jan 1825, H/MISC/673/17

[31] OIOC, Courtenay to Dart, 25 Feb 1824, E/2/34

[32] Munro to Malcolm, 29 Sept 1825, Gleig, *Munro*, II, 157

[33] OIOC, Metcalfe to Amherst, June 1824, MSS Eur F140/93; Paget's Minute, 15 Dec 1824, H/MISC/665/2

[34] OIOC, Court Financial Letter to Bengal, 12 Dec 1827, L/F/677

[35] In the summer of 1824, Munro ordered that only those regiments on foreign service be increased to 900 rank and file from 750. In the spring of 1825 an increase of 100 for home regiments was allowed, bringing them to 850, in the hopes of raising more volunteers for Burma and to cover for those regiments away. In September 1825, because of the great losses in Burma, regiments on foreign service were increased to 960 while their counterparts at home were brought up to 900. Nottingham, 'Notes on Changes to the Madras Establishment', 1830, PwJf 2750/xiii

[36] OIOC, Elphinstone to Munro, 16 Nov 1824, MSS Eur F151/63

[37] Munro's Minute, 31 Dec 1824, Gleig, *Munro*, II, 387

[38] Amiya Barat, *The Bengal Native Infantry; its Organization and Discipline, 1796-1852*, Calcutta: Mukhopadyay, 1962, 226

[39] G.E. Harvey, 'Burma', *Cambridge History of India*, Cambridge: Cambridge University Press, 1929, V, 560; J.L. Christian, *Modern Burma*, Los Angeles: University of California Press, 1942, 28; A.C. Banerjee, *The Eastern Frontier of British India, 1784-1826*, Calcutta: Mukerjee, 1966, 442; John P. Halstead, *The Second British Empire; Trade, Philanthropy, and Good Government*, Westport, Conn.: Greenwood, 1983, 73; H.H. Wilson, *Narrative of a War in Burma*, Calcutta: 1830, 262

[40] W.F.B Laurie, *Our Burmese Wars and Relations with Burma*, London: W.H. Allen, 1880; D.G.E. Hall, *Burma*, Oxford: Oxford University Press, 1956; 105; Dorothy Woodman, *The Making of Burma*, London: Cresset Press, 1962, 80; A T Q Stewart, *The Pagoda War; Lord Dufferin and the Fall of the Kingdom of Ava, 1885-1886*, London: Faber and Faber, 1972, 38

[41] Data compiled from Bengal and Madras Military Accounts for the years 1824 to 1829 in OIOC, L/MIL/8 and supported by reference to accounts presented yearly to Parliament and to estimates in Bengal Financial Consultations.

[42] OIOC, Hastings to W.F. Elphinstone, 28 Jan 1819, MSS Eur F206/68

[43] India Accounts and Estimates, PP, 23(1859): 81

[44] For example, much of the war's direct costs were presented in the form of arrears up until 1830 in both Madras and Bengal. Bengal kept these costs separate while Madras merged theirs into the ongoing costs of garrisoning Tennasserim. See OIOC, Madras Military Accounts for 1827/28, L/MIL/8/101

[45] OIOC, Military Accountant General to Government, 13 July 1824, Madras Expeditionary Consultations, P/321/66

[46] OIOC, Bengal Military Accounts, 1824/25, L/MIL/8/33

[47] OIOC, Madras Military Accounts, 1825/26, L/MIL/8/99

[48] For some unexplained reason, the earliest accurate prediction was provided by Henry St. George Tucker in London who had very little data at hand upon which to found his estimate. In early 1825 he predicted that the war's final cost was to be in the neighbourhood of £5 million. At the same time, those in Bengal were continuing to forecast expenses of just under £1 million. See Tucker, *Review*, 45

[49] OIOC, Commodore Hayes to Paget, Sept 1824, H/MISC/664/11

[50] S. Bhattacharya, 'Eastern India,' *Cambridge Economic History of India*, II, 274

[51] Calculated from OIOC, Bengal Military Accounts, 1824-26, L/MIL/8/34-36

[52] Doveton, *Reminiscences*, 11

[53] Munro to Amherst, 2 Feb 1825, Gleig, *Munro*, II, 140-41

[54] OIOC, Accountant General to Government, 9 June 1825, Bengal Financial Consultations, P/161/50

[55] *Oriental Herald*, 6(1825): 540

[56] From Rs.276 per ton in 1810 to Rs.218 per ton in 1823. John Phipps, *A Guide to the Commerce of Bengal containing a View of the Shipping*, Calcutta: 1823, 129-33

[57] H. Lister Maw, *Memoir of the Early Operations of the Burma War*, London: Smith, Elder and Co., 1832, 9

[58] Costs of British military campaigns taken from PRO, 'Cost of Principal British Wars, 1857-1899', WO 33/256

[59] Accounts presented to Parliament, 1822/23, PP, 24(1825); 1823/24, PP 25(1826)

[60] Financial data for this period were compiled from the accounts presented to Parliament. See PP, 24(1825); PP, 25(1826); PP, 20(1828); PP, 23(1828)

[61] OIOC, Court Financial Letter to Bengal, 1 March 1826, L/F/3/676

[62] OIOC, Bengal Financial Letter to Court, 23 Nov 1823, L/F/3/15; Bengal Government to Accountant General, 24 Feb 1825, Bengal Financial Consultations, P/161/49

[63] Wilson, *Review of the Financial Situation*, 25-33

[64] OIOC, Mackenzie to Amherst, June 1824, MSS Eur F140/142

[65] OIOC, Amherst to Court, 25 June 1824, L/F/3/15

[66] OIOC, Amherst to Court, 31 Dec 1824, L/F/3/18

[67] Evidence of Holt Mackenzie, S.C. on the East India Company, PP, 9(1831/32): 44-7

[68] OIOC, Accountant General to Government, 25 June 1824, Bengal Financial Consultations, P/161/43

[69] OIOC, Accountant General to Government, 3 June 1825, Madras Financial Consultations, P/330/49

[70] OIOC, Accountant General to Government, 17 Feb 1825, L/F/3/16

[71] OIOC, Government Resolution, 28 April 1825, Bengal Financial Consultations, P/161/44

[72] OIOC, Madras to Bengal, 12 March 1824, Bengal Financial Consultations, P/161/42

[73] OIOC, Court Financial Letter to Bengal, 1 March 1826, L/F/676

[74] OIOC, Court Financial Letter to Bengal, 11 July 1827, L/F/3/676; Memo by Holt Mackenzie, 19 May 1825, Bengal Financial Consultations, P/161/50. Mackenzie claimed that Wood had by 'relying on military estimates; and referring to expenses of former wars, grossly underestimated this one'.

[75] OIOC, Bengal Military Accounts, 1825/26 and 1826/27, L/MIL/8/34-5
[76] OIOC, Bengal to Court, 13 April 1826, L/F/17
[77] S.C. on the East India Company, PP, 10(1831/32): Pt 1, x
[78] Once the Company's reluctance had been overcome, there was considerable discussion over what formula would be applied to cost the services. Eventually, a fixed charge per man per month was applied. £5.6/man/month by three years for six vessels. The total sum was Rs.4,50,000. See PRO, Chairs to Wynn, 1 Feb 1826, Adm1/3919; Dart to Barrow, 5 May 1826, Adm 1/3919
[79] Data taken from PRO, Ellenborough, memo on home charges, (1828?), PRO 30/9/4/20, Pt II
[80] Ibid.
[81] Tripathi, *Trade and Finance*, 165-66
[82] OIOC, Court to Bengal, 25 Aug 1825, Bengal Financial Consultations, P/161/51
[83] OIOC, Consultations, 30 Sept 1825, Bengal Financial Consultations, P/161/52
[84] Heber, *Narrative*, I, 188
[85] OIOC, Bengal Financial Letter to Court, 17 Feb 1825, L/F/3/16
[86] OIOC, Mackenzie to Adam, 10 Jan 1824, MSS Eur F109/D
[87] See for example, S.B. Singh, *European Agency Houses in Bengal, 1783-1833*, Calcutta: Mukhopadhyay, 1966, 265-6
[88] OIOC, Court to Bengal, 1 March 1826, L/F/3/676; Nicolls' Diary, 4 June 1826, MSS Eur F175/34
[89] OIOC, Advertisement of 4 per cent Loan, 17 Sept 1824, Bengal Financial Consultations, P/161/44
[90] OIOC, Bengal financial letter to Court, 31 Dec 1824, L/F/3/15; Evidence of Holt Mackenzie, S.C. on the East India Company, PP, 9(1831/32): 44, 59
[91] *Oriental Herald*, 6(1825), 325-26
[92] OIOC, Bengal financial letter to Court, 4 Aug 1825, L/F/3/16
[93] OIOC, Amherst to Chairs, 25 Aug 1825, MSS Eur F140/114(a)
[94] OIOC, Mackenzie and Swinton to Amherst, 3 June 1825, MSS Eur F140/146
[95] OIOC, Amherst's Minute, 27 Oct 1825, Bengal Financial Consultations, P/161/53
[96] OIOC, Ricketts to Amherst, 27 Nov 1824, MSS Eur F140/95
[97] OIOC, Ricketts to government, 14 July 1825, Bengal Financial Consultations, P/161/53
[98] OIOC, Swinton to Amherst, 3 June 1825, MSS Eur F140/146; Amherst to Ricketts, 22 July 1825, Bengal Financial Consultations, P/161/53. Ricketts appears to be universally unpopular in India. There is no readily apparent reason for this other than perhaps his habit of constantly reminding people that Lord Liverpool was his cousin. See for example, OIOC, Ricketts to Amherst, 25 Aug 1823, MSS Eur F140/95
[99] OIOC, Ricketts to Amherst, 13 Aug 1825, MSS Eur F140/146
[100] OIOC, Metcalfe to Government, Oct 1825, Bengal Financial Consultations, 1 Dec 1825, P/161/54
[101] OIOC, M. Ainsle to Government, Nov 1825, Bengal Financial Consultations, 1 Dec 1825, P/161/54
[102] PRO, Ellenborough, 'Debt as of 30 April 1827', PRO 30/12/31/2
[103] OIOC, Board to Court, 28 May 1827, L/PS/3/117

[104] OIOC, Nicolls' Diary, Nov 1829, MSS Eur F175/34

[105] OIOC, Ricketts to Political Department, 29 Nov 1825, Bengal Financial Consultations, P/161/54

[106] OIOC, Nicolls' Diary, 12 April 1826, MSS Eur F175/32

[107] William Makepeace Thackeray, *The Newcomes*, London: Everyman edition, 1892, 692

[108] William Huggins, *Sketches in India Treating on Subjects Connected with the Government, Civil and Military Establishments*, London: 1824, 71

[109] Ibid, 75

[110] From £16.2.2d per lb to £12.6s per lb; Tripathi, *Trade and Finance*, 258n

[111] OIOC, Lushington to Adam, 13 Nov 1824, MSS Eur F109/F

[112] Robertson, *Political Incidents*, 230

[113] Tripathi, *Trade and Finance*, 164

[114] OIOC, Government Resolution, 31 May 1826, Bengal Financial Consultations, P/161/56; Amiya Kumar Bagchi, 'Transition from Indian to British-Indian Systems of Money and Banking,' *Modern Asian Studies*, 19(1985): 515

[115] Tucker, *Review*, 31

[116] OIOC, Bengal financial letter to Court, 6 Feb 1824, L/F/3/15; Notes by Metcalfe, 1828, MSS Eur F140/149; Mackenzie to Amherst, 11 Jan 1825, MSS Eur F140/143

8. ANGLO-INDIAN MILITARISM IN AN AGE OF RETRENCH-MENT AND REFORM

This illustrious despot and his no less illustrious deeds were constantly affording matter of speculation to the powerless pygmies over whom he ruled ... One day his Lordship would be reported ill or mad; the next he was sane; and in proof of this it would be affirmed that he was on the eve of embarkation for England ... There was a mystery about him which none could unravel; one thing, however, was sufficiently apparent — ill or well, the ability to do mischief and to annoy was never impaired.[1]

Bentinck came to India in 1828 with a reputation for dynamism, liberalism and reform, and with such credentials he could expect a warm welcome from the many officials who were weary of Amherst's dithering style. One army surgeon wrote to his brother in England that 'people here look forward to the arrival of Lord William with great pleasure — the present man is thought very little of and his abilities estimated at a low rate.'[2] Bentinck left India seven years later as one of the most loathed governor-generals ever. The surgeon mentioned above who had been so enthusiastic was three years later referring to Bentinck as 'that most infernal scoundrel'.[3] It was said that he added the 'treachery of the Italian to the caution of a Dutchman.'[4] This animosity came about largely because Bentinck trampled upon the delicate feelings and undermined the vested interests of those beneath him in his pursuit of retrenchments (and to a lesser extent reforms). The reforms that he did achieve were rarely discussed; instead it was his attacks on perquisites and his failure to conform to the traditional way of conducting business that were the cause of much dissent. Contemporaries did not dwell on Bentinck the reformer; to them he was the 'clipping Dutchman', a mean spirited martinet who sacrificed them to placate the Court of Directors. And if the Anglo-Indian press is anything to go by, it was a reputation that clung to Bentinck for decades afterwards.[5]

Yet it is the former impression that we find most common today — Bentinck, the committed utilitarian and modernizer, responsible for ushering in an Age of Reform.[6] The most recent history of the Company depicts Bentinck's years in India as those of a full-fledged Anglicizing assault on Indian tradition as well as an attack on the established forms of Company rule.[7] Here was no conservative and romantic reactionary determined to maintain British rule by force if necessary. Instead Bentinck was pictured as a governor-general who sought to introduce an improving administration that would ultimately bind the rulers and the ruled together in a much more empathetic relationship — 'the clipper of salaries had become the planter of the seeds of modern India'.[8] Such an impression certainly has much to recommend it; one only has to list some of the reforms that were introduced: the abolition of *sati*, the crackdown on *thagi*, the prospects of a new revenue settlement for the northwestern provinces, the introduction of government-funded English-language education, his advocacy of allowing European settlers into India (to implant the skills and institutions necessary for social and economic modernization), the end of Persian as an official language, the recommendation that greater numbers of Indians be recruited into Company employ, and the abolition of corporal punishment in the Indian army.[9] Reconciling these discordant themes is not easy and rather than argue about whether or not Bentinck was a reformer, I will suggest that while he certainly had reforms in mind and did successfully attain some of them, these reforms should not blind us to the more mundane details of government (particularly the need to effect economies), the limited impact of his much-vaunted reforms, or the extent to which Bentinck, like those before and after him, had to contend with the army.[10]

In breaking the axiom 'that ignorance and inexperience are essential qualifications for Indian office', Bentinck was a substantial departure from his predecessors who were content to be guided by local expertise and ideologies.[11] Lacking either the malleability of Amherst or the easily manipulated vanity of Hastings, Bentinck sought to impose his will and ideas upon India. Central to these was a radically different appreciation of India's strategic imperatives. Bentinck did at times promise a new imperialism, but making reality out of the rhetoric proved to be a difficult and at times impossible task.[12] The path was littered with obstacles, some of them institutional or structural, others personal. Economic demands and turbulent relations with a very independent minded administration were continually to bedevil Bentinck. No matter how much Bentinck intended on embarking upon an extensive programme of Indian development and reform, the financial resources were not at hand. Nor could he count upon much assistance, either from London or from within the Company's hierarchy in India. He was plunged into conflict with the dominant interests in India, both civil and military. He had been warned of this. John Ravenshaw, who looked after his interests in the Court of Directors, explained to him that, 'the connection between our civil and military servants and the mercantile community is to me fraught with great danger. It crosses the financial operation of government on all occasions and in all directions.'[13] Moreover, Bentinck was not always consistent. He was particularly susceptible to intellectual fashions, being the 'sounding board for every fashionable opinion, being in turns nationalist, evangelical, democrat and utilitarian...'[14]

The army was a particularly high hurdle for Bentinck to clear. By considering Bentinck's relations with the army, from his conflict with them over the half-batta issue to his final year's preoccupation with the composition and distribution of the army, we find that while Bentinck did press for some major changes to the composition and orientation of the army, Bentinck never completely broke with the tradition of Anglo–Indian militarism. As much as Bentinck wished to interpret 'empire of opinion' as winning over the hearts and minds of his subjects through a programme of progressive reforms — even he had to concede to arguments that the British had to maintain sufficiently strong forces to maintain their position in India. His adoption of the imperatives if not necessarily the rhetoric of Anglo–Indian militarism is seen clearly in his handling of the Coorg crisis of 1834. Furthermore, the changes he did propose to make to the army were ultimately dependent upon taking the military with him, winning their support and cooperation for a different role and with different establishments in place. The bitterness that lingered after the half-batta issue, when coupled to his own tactlessness at crucial points, prevented a reconciliation. When he departed India in 1835, the army was chastened but it still remained paramount within official circles. Anglo–Indian militarism had survived its most vigorous challenge.

Events in India in 1828 were already being propelled towards major changes by the precarious state of Indian finances as well as misgivings about the reliability of the Indian army. Tripathi has rightly pointed out that several initiatives commonly ascribed to Bentinck originated elsewhere, such as the greater employment of Indians which was urged on the Bengal government by London as a means of cutting establishment costs.[15] In addition, savings were already set in motion by Amherst through his major review and retrenchment of civil and military establishments. These were not enough though. The single most important and inescapable fact that Bentinck faced was, in the words of a confidential memo printed for

Wellington's cabinet, that 'the present prospect of Indian finances is, first, that, upon an average of years, an annual deficiency of resources to meet the expenditure ... is to be apprehended.'[16] Financial necessity demanded retrenchments which any governor-general would have found difficult to evade, and none more than Bentinck whose reputation with London was sufficiently weak to limit his autonomy.

Bentinck also arrived in India with painful memories of when, as governor of Madras, he had suffered the humiliation of being recalled following the 1806 Vellore Mutiny. Several regiments of sepoys had mutinied, seized the fort, and were implicated in the deaths of several civilians and European officers. The immediate cause of the mutiny was the commander-in-chief's orders for new uniforms and dress codes, including clean-shaven faces and leather cockades on their headgear. The sepoys refused to obey the new code, insisting that to do so would mean violating their religious and caste customs. Bentinck had not agreed to these changes, nor had he been adequately consulted, but he had to bear much of the blame. Together with General Sir John Cradock, the commander-in-chief, he was recalled by the Court.[17] His biographer has written that 'it was the turning-point of Bentinck's career.'[18] The recall was not only a personal slight that he was desperate not to repeat, but it made him determined to restore his reputation in India. It was also a telling lesson in the dangers of allowing the officers and the troops in the army too much autonomy. Such suspicions were further reinforced by recent correspondence from India in which the shortcomings of the army were highlighted. Events like the mutiny at Barrackpore confirmed for him the danger of allowing the sepoys to place their own customs above the needs of the army. Bentinck would also draw disturbing parallels between General Cradock's failure to discuss his orders with him, and the behaviour of the commanders-in-chief during his tenure as governor-general, all of whom fought to restrict Bentinck's authority in military affairs. Lord Combermere (1825-1829) claimed that he had absolute authority over king's troops in India; Lord Dalhousie's (1830-1831) frequent bouts of sickness kept him cranky and on the sidelines, while Edward Barnes' (1832-1833) cantankerous nature created instant animosity between the two officials and led to his eventual recall.

Bentinck's scope of action was also restricted by tortured relations with London and like Amherst his course of action was partly predicated on how he read London's possible reactions. Ironically Bentinck initially went to India with what appeared to be the firm backing of both the government and the Company — advantages denied his predecessor. Of greater political weight than Amherst, and close to Canning by virtue of his politics as well as by marriage (Canning had married Bentinck's sister), Bentinck could look as well to the support of the Court who had lobbied unsuccessfully in 1823 for his appointment. However, this support quickly dissolved. Not only was he under intense pressure to secure retrenchments throughout India, but he arrived in India to find that the mildly supportive administration of Canning had been replaced by the actively hostile regime of Wellington with Lord Ellenborough at the Board of Control.[19] Wellington's recollections of Bentinck's service in the Peninsula and later in Sicily had convinced him that Bentinck needed careful watching, for in both places Bentinck had tried to rally popular support by appeals to nationalism (popular support and nationalism were both anathema to the Duke). As an indication of Wellington's wariness, he is reported to have said, on hearing that Bentinck advocated the opening up of India to British settlers, that he 'always expected some wild measure from Lord William.'[20] Even when Wellington's government yielded to a Whig administration under Earl Grey, Bentinck still had to contend with a general lack of support.[21] Bentinck hoped that a fellow Whig at the Board would mean his policies would be given more favourable attention. He was disappointed to find that Charles Grant, 'tho' highly educated and having something of a natural feeling in favour of India, is sadly inert.'[22]

Nor was Bentinck's support within the East India Company as forthcoming as many expected. In spite of what Ellenborough identified as a 'Bentinck party in the Court', Bentinck could not confidently depend upon the directors.[23] The pressing needs for financial recovery, especially with the Company's charter coming up for renewal, made the Court more suspicious of their subordinates than ever. Bentinck was quickly apprised of the Court's ambivalence towards him. One director warned him that 'there is no great good will towards you.'[24] Confronted by reports of his weakening support within the Court of Directors, Bentinck wrote to one director to reassure him that 'as the captain of your quarterdeck, I wish to have the ship in good order and prepared for the storm.'[25] These reassurances do not seem to have had much of an effect for Bentinck was privately warned in 1833 to be extremely careful in what he wrote to the Court. The directors had become very suspicious of his plans and alarmed at the hostile reports coming back to Britain concerning his government.[26]

Bentinck's uncertain relationship with London was partly the consequence of a growing tension between the Company and the government. While the directors wished to preserve the Company's traditional posture in India (namely an emphasis on protecting investments and keeping Britain's commitments and responsibilities to a minimum), the Board, reflecting an increasing engagement with India on the part of some commercial, industrial and humanitarian interests, began to push for a more aggressive and intrusive presence in India. While some signs of this shift can be traced back to the immediate post-Napoleonic War period, they became more pronounced in the late 1820s as changes within domestic British society and economy created an environment more conducive to an altered imperial agenda.[27] Financial institutions, manufacturers and the government responded to Britain's enhanced international position and its commanding role in an expanding global economy by demanding a greater say in how India was ruled and for who. The developing great game along the northwest frontier, together with the 'eastern question' accelerated strategic interests in India, the dream of new markets in Asia stimulated commercial and manufacturing groups, while a growing commitment to Britain's divine mission of carrying civilization and Christianity to backward lands whetted the appetites of missionary, humanitarian and scientific societies. These agendas converged into what can be viewed as a 'new imperialism' and while arguably Bentinck can be seen through his commitment to modernization and reform to have shared some of their objectives, as well as their arrogance, 'new imperialism' was still very much in its formative phase. There was no clear consensus as to how India should be ruled, just a growing sense that it was being badly ruled at the moment.

In the absence of any agreement, and with the Court apprehensive about its future, Bentinck could receive little constructive guidance from London. Ravenshaw warned him to proceed very cautiously because in the 'state in which our Court and the authorities at home are at present, you must not consider anything decided on till it finally passes the Board and the Court'.[28] Wellington's choice as President of the Board of Control, Lord Ellenborough, exacerbated tensions through his disregard for the Company. Ellenborough was not persuaded that cooperation with the East India Company was in Britain's best interests. His ultimate ambition was to replace Company rule of India with direct Crown administration. Only then could India be properly subordinated to Britain's global interests. His plan 'to go quietly to work ... to substitute the King's government for that of the Company' hinged upon his ability to persuade his colleagues that India would not become a burden on the government.[29] His autocratic temperament, as well his intrigues to manipulate India into a position where it could check Russian designs, won him few friends in Leadenhall Street. Ellenborough's appointment was greeted with a sarcastic outburst from *The Times* who made the most of what Wellington acknowledged as Ellenborough's 'crotchets'.[30] 'We wish the Directors, the Government, and the country much joy of so very promising a bargain, in a situation which calls for no small quantity of good feeling, amiable manners, discretion, and good sense.'

The key to understanding Ellenborough's behaviour at the Board of Control, aptly described as 'bombastic, masterful, vain and extremely ambitious', lies in his efforts to use that office as a springboard from which he could launch a policy of containment designed to limit the growth of Russian power.[31] While Ellenborough would have preferred to pursue this plan from the Foreign Office, the Board of Control was the best alternative: 'I feel confident we shall have to fight the Russians on the Indus, and I have long had a presentiment that I should meet them there, and gain a great battle.'[32] By using the Board of Control as a surrogate Foreign Office, Ellenborough hoped 'to create the means of throwing the whole world in arms upon Russia at the first convenient time'.[33] Ellenborough wanted to see India incorporated much more tightly into the British Empire. Its military and material resources could then be used to bring pressure on Russia's southern flanks. In pursuing his ambitions, Ellenborough submerged himself in the details of Indian affairs, including Indian finances, to an extent hitherto unseen at the Board.[34] It was also imperative that the forces available in India be made more accountable to authorities in London. Ellenborough was unsympathetic to the parochial views of the Company's officers in India, as well as impatient with what he saw as the narrow commercial-mindedness of the Company's directors.

However, while Ellenborough's ultimate political ends were anathema to the Company, they were in agreement over one crucial issue — India's finances had to be brought under control. Thus the pressure on Bentinck to achieve reductions in Indian expenditures was doubly strong. James Mill privately warned Bentinck of the 'strong spirit of retrenchment sprung up at the Board of Control'.[35] Bentinck was informed by Ellenborough in no uncertain terms that his tenure in India hinged upon his ability to secure the necessary savings; if he failed to do so, 'then one will be found who is.'[36] If anything Ellenborough was even more impatient to see economies. The Court realized more fully than Ellenborough that economic reforms and an improved financial situation would take time to mature[37] They appealed to Wellington to restrain his combustible colleague. Wellington obliged by calling upon his Indian experience to convince Ellenborough that considering that India had just passed through half a century of almost constant warfare, its accounts were in pretty fair shape.[38] Subdued but not defeated, Ellenborough would continue his intrigues.

Bentinck's scope was further handicapped by conditions within India and the difficulties he had in working with the existing bureaucracy in India, civil and military. He was succeeding, in the words of one director, 'to a most amiable but imbecile governor [Amherst] and with a service that will require to get out of the effects engendered by Lord Amherst's predecessor [Hastings]'.[39] Matters were made worse by Bentinck's obstinacy and inflexibility which quickly alienated most of those with whom he was expected to work. Bentinck's military career inculcated in him an intolerance for indiscipline and disobedience, traits all too common in the civil and military servants of the Company. He tried to impose these military values, what Rosselli aptly describes as 'administrative generalship', though with little success.[40] Enemies and supporters alike conceded that Bentinck was not the easiest person to get along with. Wellington opined that Bentinck 'did everything with the best intention, but he was a wrong-headed man, and if he went wrong he would continue in the wrong line.'[41] *The Times* echoed this when they described him as a 'perfectly honest and well-meaning man but the most inflexible of all descendants from a Dutch forefather'.[42] Others noted that he became too easily bogged down in details.[43] It was commented that his 'penchant for prying into minor details is proverbial in India.'[44] Even J.C. Marshman conceded that Bentinck was too suspicious of others and tardy in placating those whose feelings he hurt.[45]

Instead of the teamwork that had marked Amherst's and Hastings' governments, Bentinck introduced secretiveness and favouritism. Dalhousie, the commander-in-chief, described the result; it was 'an every day occurrence in this presidency to find the various departments of government clashing together, reversing orders, or impeding questions.'[46] Bentinck broke with tradition and tried to reduce the influence of the central secretariat. It was said of him that 'As to the secretaries, who in Lord Amherst's time were actually the governors — he does not confide in them implicitly.'[47] Only the secretary of the department concerned was allowed to attend council deliberations and even then he was not expected to participate in discussions.[48] In place of consensus decision-making, Bentinck relied more on confidential discussions with a few favoured individuals. His determination 'not to be a puppet' like Amherst led to him becoming, in the words of one contemporary observer, 'a tool in the hands of spies and informers'.[49] There were allegations, still circulated twenty years later, that Bentinck had pressured army officers to send confidential reports to him of the loyalty and efficiency of their colleagues.[50]

The hostile response that greeted his so-called merit-fostering minute of 1834, which sought to replace promotion by seniority in the civil service with promotion by merit, should be seen in light of Bentinck's management techniques. While some have argued that opposition to merit was proof that the Company and their officials were simply unwilling to shed themselves of the eighteenth-century tradition of interest politics, and that at heart the Company's service refused to become a modern bureaucracy, when seen in the context of Bentinck's troubled relations with Company officials, the assessment of merit through annual reports smacked of surveillance and did not appear as disinterested as its later advocates suggest.[51] Contemporaries drew a parallel between Bentinck's monitoring of army discontent and his recommendation that reports be filed on civil servant performance: the latter was referred to as a system of 'universal espionage.'[52] Hence it was not simply a case of reform confronting 'old corruption'. Bentinck was not oblivious to these suspicions. Towards the end of his term, he privately lamented that 'I fear I have not as much indulgence as I ought for Indian feelings.'[53]

One other difference in India's political culture after 1828 lay in the absence of such strong figures as Munro and Elphinstone at the lesser presidencies. Munro's replacement, Stephen Lushington, was inexperienced in Indian affairs and was generally embroiled in running battles with his council. Malcolm, who replaced Elphinstone in Bombay, might have been expected to keep Anglo-Indian militarism alive within the higher levels of government. Yet Malcolm also became entangled in local infighting, particularly with the local supreme court over the extent of their respective spheres of authority. As well, Malcolm's tactlessness and incessant efforts towards enlarging his fiefdom, by continually pressing Bentinck to cede central India to Bombay, took away from the respect with which he might have otherwise been entitled. The opinion of many was summed up by Ravenshaw when he wrote 'if only he [Malcolm] would only leave others to see his merits without thrusting them before your eyes upon all occasions, he would be second only to Munro'.[54] Malcolm was also constrained by the same forces operating on Bentinck; he too needed to enforce economies in his administration. Consequently many of those who had initially rallied to Malcolm as the spokesman for their cause became disappointed at what they saw as the contrast between Malcolm the colonial troubleshooter and Malcolm the colonial governor. The army in particular was disillusioned by Malcolm's apparent readiness to follow Bentinck and impose retrenchments. One officer lamented that, 'Sir John Malcolm, on his way to the top of the ladder, had been remarked for the great liberality, if not the prodigality, of his public outlay; reaching the summit, he had now become the most inveterate economist.'[55]

The overriding concerns which faced Bentinck upon his arrival in India were the need to check burgeoning expenditure, coax a surplus out of the revenues, and subdue the restlessness of the army. To assist in securing the retrenchments required, two committees were established, one to review military expenses and the other to do the same for civil expenditure. They were composed of three members with one member from each presidency. Bentinck has traditionally been given credit for establishing these committees.[56] This is not the case for they originated with Amherst, acting upon the advice of Holt Mackenzie.[57] The military committee was an abject failure; the civil committee was slightly more successful. The military committee's mandate did not extend to considering the size, deployment or composition of the three armies. As these were the chief determinants of cost, their exclusion immediately limited the conclusions that the committee could reach. The civil committee was strengthened by being chaired by Holt Mackenzie, an expert who commanded the respect of most in the Company including the governor-general. The military committee was presided over by Brigadier Wilson, a much less influential person. The military committee was also hampered by the great detail with which it had to contend, extending from gunpowder supply to salaries to public buildings. Moreover, the military committee was hopelessly divided with each member of the committee seeking to protect his presidency's interests. Bentinck was warned that 'constituted as the committee is, it can hardly be innocent'.[58] The member on the committee from Bengal ultimately resigned in protest when the representatives from Madras and Bombay kept ganging up on him.[59]

Despite the failure of the military committee, the Bengal government did begin to enjoy some respite from ever-increasing military charges (see Appendix I). These savings, however, were largely due to Amherst and not to Bentinck. Because of the time lag between when a reduction was ordered and when it was reflected in the Company's accounts, the reduced costs listed in the accounts for 1829/30 were the result of decisions made two years earlier. The savings of approximately two million pounds that were listed in the accounts of 1828-30, years when Bentinck was governor-general, were the result of Amherst's orders to reduce the army following the end of the Burma War. The following two years only witnessed further savings of one million pounds. Most of these reductions were simply the natural result of no longer having to meet the charges imposed by war. The very slight decrease in ordinary charges stemmed from the reductions ordered by Amherst at the end of the war.[60]

Further cuts were obstructed in part by decisions taken in London. There were four more king's regiments in Bengal in 1828 than there were in 1823. Upon the advice of the governor-general in council, which significantly included the commander-in-chief, the Court of Directors tried to convince

Wellington's government that these four were no longer necessary.[61] The Company stood on their right to pay for no more than twenty-thousand troops while the cabinet searched for ways of keeping all the regiments in India and away from parliamentary scrutiny. Wellington felt that the British army was becoming dangerously understrength, but given the prevailing economic worries, Parliament was loath to approve any increases. His eventual proposal, disliked by the Court, was to retain the same number of regiments though each was to have a reduced establishment.[62] This would keep the total number of troops under twenty thousand, but the number of officers, the most expensive charge, was to remain the same. This did the Company little good, but it did provide the government with a means through which existing regiments could be maintained away from Parliamentary scrutiny.

The most contentious economy pursued by Bentinck was his imposition of the Court's half-batta order. The half-batta order for officers at Berhampur, Barrackpore and Dinapur was re-issued soon after his arrival.[63] While he personally questioned its financial value and anticipated the army's howls of protest, Bentinck clearly knew that failure to implement the long-standing order would damage beyond repair his reputation with the Court. He also recognized that if he tried to defer or delay the order, the army would interpret this as proof that their position of dominance was secure. The half-batta order became the acid test of Bentinck's governor-generalship. To retreat would weaken his position in London, and possibly lead to his recall, and just as alarmingly, it would in effect mean subordinating his office to the army. Three months before it was ordered, Bentinck wrote to one of the directors that 'I dread as much touching any civil or military allowance as much as a magazine of gunpowder.'[64] The economic benefits were so minuscule (the savings were less than one per cent of the total army budget) that he questioned whether it was worth risking the loyalty of the officers. He wrote to Horse Guards that the order 'was good for nothing, neither for its principle nor its economy; and in the mean time gives great disgust.'[65] Meetings with officers of the Bengal army convinced him that 'discipline requires to be raised in Bengal very much, and the difficulty of raising it with discontented agents will be I fear insurmountable.'[66] No matter how much he disagreed with the actual order, Bentinck concluded that if the officers successfully blocked the order, their respect and obedience would be lost forever. Ironically the Duke of Wellington for once agreed with him. Wellington felt that although the order was poorly conceived, the government was now publicly committed and could not retreat without surrendering even more authority over the army. When

London became worried over the growing signs of discontent in the army, Wellington convinced the cabinet that the only proper course would be to weather the storm and openly support the governor-general.[67]

It now appears that the army's determination to resist was fortified by the commanders-in-chief pitting themselves against the government. Combermere was easily duped into heading the resistance by his military secretary, Lieutenant Colonel Finch, while Dalhousie and Barnes appear to have had difficulties in adapting to India's style of government, having come from colonial governments where they had united the supreme political and military functions (Dalhousie had been governor and captain-general of Lower Canada, 1819-28, and Barnes had been governor of Ceylon, 1824-31). Combermere's links with the discontented appear to have been engineered by his military secretary with the help of Colonel Fagan, the adjutant general. General Whittingham informed Bentinck that Combermere 'was unable to calculate cause and effect beyond the limits of the confined circle within which his mind had been accustomed to exert its powers.'[68] It was rumoured of Fagan that 'an offer was made to [Fagan] to allow him a handsome yearly sum, and to pay his debts, if he would resign his office, and be their advocate in London.'[69] What prompted the most controversy was the leaking of a letter from Combermere to Bentinck that condemned the governor-general's decision to issue the order. This letter was reprinted in London in the *Morning Chronicle*.[70] Although Combermere was not found guilty of releasing this letter to the press, its contents and several other indiscretions he had made in India caused the Company to toy with the idea of having him recalled. Even Wellington suggested that the Company might have to take this course of action.[71] The directors eventually chose not to recall Combermere when they considered that such an action could turn him into a martyr.[72] Nevertheless, Combermere's indiscretions defeated any hopes that he might have had of future rewards in Britain.[73]

The impact of the half-batta order was not evenly spread across the army for it only applied to the stations nearest to Fort William. The artillery was hardest hit as they tended to be clustered around Dum Dum and Barrackpore, while no cavalry units were threatened for they were all stationed up country. Within the officer corps, the burden of the retrenchments were unequally shared. To placate regimental commanders, batta for colonels was untouched. Lieutenant colonels lost the most, up to twenty-five per cent of their monthly salary, with majors losing nearly the same. For subalterns, the loss was about ten per cent. However, to lessen the pain, regular rotations of regiments ensured that officers would only be on half batta for three years out of every twenty-four.[74] Furthermore, a house allowance was introduced which further lessened the financial penalty. The ratio of corps on full batta to those on half batta was six to one. In the past, when only Fort William was a half-batta station, the ratio was thirty-seven to one. In contrast, the ratio was reversed in Madras and Bombay with nearly four on half batta to every one on full batta.[75] The total saving made by the half batta order was about £6,000, which amounted to only 0.05% of a total military budget of £10,773,966. The amount saved was less than the annual pay of a councillor on the supreme council.[76]

Although the financial savings were small, the political and military consequences were enormous. The half-batta issue caused irreparable damage to relations between Bentinck and the army, and in particular with the commanders-in-chief. It was not until Bentinck was given the military command that this struggle between supreme military and supreme political authority abated, but this did not placate the wider military. Bentinck's invitations to officers to dine when he was on tour were deliberately snubbed.[77] Officers in the Bengal army, including officers in the king's service, considered sending official delegations to London to lobby the government and the Court. Seven thousand pounds were raised to fund this delegation and there were rumours that a fire in the Allahabad magazine had been deliberately set by disgruntled officers.[78] The conflict in Bengal was transferred to England when newspapers, eager to attack the government and the Company, printed exaggerated accounts of the tension in Bengal. Letters from among others the commander of artillery were used as proof of the deteriorating state of the army in Bengal.[79] It was not simply Bentinck's offensives on the army's perquisites that drew hostile fire; the animosity of much of the officer corps was further whipped up when they compared his public parsimony with what they viewed as his private indulgences: 'his expensive tents — his steam-boats to convey him to Benares — his pulling down the public buildings to erect a home for himself.'[80] Up until his departure in 1835 Bentinck was confronted with a disgruntled army whose frustration was often vented on him personally. The mood of the army was made worse by the commercial crisis which wiped out many officers' savings. A large portion of the working capital which had been employed by the Agency Houses was drawn from officers' savings. The crash of Palmer and Co., which had been considered the cornerstone of the Agency House system, was particularly distressing for the army. Two of the key military charity funds — the widows' fund and the orphans' fund — were locked up in Palmer and Company investments and were decimated with the collapse of the house. The grumblings continued, the army and the government were clearly at loggerheads and London grew worried that unless they sent out a new governor-general, the army's loyalty might be lost. Ellenborough tried to reassure Bentinck not to take their concerns personally; Bentinck was unfortunately paying the price for his predecessors' negligence.[81] The government eventually decided that to recall Bentinck would give the unfortunate impression that the army officers were in the right and so they reluctantly retained him. They were, however, clearly disappointed at how he had handled the army. The half batta issue did not die there. Ellenborough's successor at the Board, Charles Grant, briefly considered its repeal, and while the Court rejected his suggestion, they did eventually reduce still further the number of half batta stations.[82]

While military expenses were the most visible and contentious issue in the first two years of Bentinck's term, they were not the sole cause of the Company's financial embarrassment. Civil expenditures continued to give grounds for concern and Bentinck took steps to roll these back too. The retrenchments inflicted on the civil service created far less of an outcry than did those to the military, though the civilians were hit even harder. The civilians were much less united than were their colleagues in the army and could not bring strategic arguments to their defence. Moreover, the reductions in the civil service were planned with far more sophistication and the impact upon individuals was much more subtle. One of the first discoveries of the committee reviewing civil expenditure was that civil establishments across the three presidencies exceeded their officially-sanctioned number. In Bengal and Madras it was found that the numbers present were twenty-five per cent more than was actually needed; in Bombay, it was seventy-five per cent greater.[83] Several measures were introduced to reduce expenditure and restrict the sizes of establishments. Attrition took effect when London restricted the number of new recruits being sent out to India. Bentinck imposed new salary scales which were computed on average rates of pay and set ceilings on them.[84] These measures were more equitable than those inflicted on the army where reductions were made specific to named garrisons. Only the most inflated allowances, namely those of the residents at the courts of Delhi, Hyderabad, Lucknow and Nagpur, were noticeably reduced.[85] Otherwise the pain was more evenly distributed as a large number of small cuts were made. In addition, some office establishments were reduced and a large saving was made by abolishing the Provincial Courts of Appeal. The latter by itself recovered Rs. 6,73,000, just over one third of the total immediate savings of Rs.15,66,910.[86]

Reductions to civil and military expenses could only alleviate some of the Company's financial embarrassment for there were many economic problems that remained largely beyond Bentinck's reach. In looking to re-store stability to Bengal's public finances, Bentinck could not isolate them from what was happening in Britain. The 1825 banking crisis increased the plight of the Indian Agency Houses for many of their English creditors were less willing to make the necessary advances. The economic depression that was tied in with Reform Bill agitation unleashed further shockwaves on the Indian economy. Conditions in India were no less encouraging. There was a dawning realization that Indian revenues could not cover expendi-tures and still provide a surplus except under exceptional circumstances. Metcalfe gloomily predicted that 'the revenues of India are not equal to the support of its expenses, and judging from past experiences are not likely to become so.'[87] The heady expectations whipped up by Hastings were in-creasingly viewed as ill-founded. Even more worrying was the potential loss of the China trade. The Company's home finances were increasingly dependent on the profits and loans advanced from their commercial activi-ties. Purchase of the investment in India had already ceased to be profit-able.[88] Bentinck's correspondents in Britain encouraged him to assume that the China monopoly would not be retained after 1833.[89]

Economic conditions in the private sector were equally disheartening. Two years after Bentinck's arrival, the second wave of bankruptcies swept through the Agency Houses. Many firms had failed to learn from the 1825/26 crisis and continued to gamble heavily in indigo. They had not re-estab-lished their equilibrium when over-production of indigo prompted yet an-other collapse in indigo prices. Indigo, which sold for Rs.270-330 per maund in 1825, could only fetch Rs.140-158 in 1832.[90] William Prinsep, a partner in Palmer and Company, later admitted that much of the crisis was of their own making. 'I am convinced that if John Palmer had been more far-sighted and had led the way to a change of tactics altogether, the great disaster would have been avoided.'[91] Once again a shortage of specie helped to pre-cipitate the crisis. Forced by the Court to continue sending remittances to London, the government sucked up much of the available cash in a four per cent loan in early 1829 and a further loan at five per cent in early 1830. Though neither of these loans drew in capital to the same extent as the loans of 1824 and 1825, they nevertheless hampered the Agency Houses at a critical juncture by stripping Calcutta of much of its unused capital. The reductions in military and civil spending restricted another source of capi-tal. The Agency Houses' London creditors became nervous and demanded partial liquidation of their debts. Panic ensued. The principal partners in the various firms failed to unite and instead tried to remit their monies to England. This triggered a rush on the remaining Houses and several firms had to close down. Like Amherst's government, Bentinck and his council were unable to sit idly by like the Court ordered them to do. Not only did these Agency Houses owe considerable monies to many Company employees, but Bentinck was worried that if they all crashed, the Indian economy would be further weakened as he did not see any other capitalists to take their place. He reluctantly sanctioned government loans to several of the larger firms, but it was too late. It was not enough to resuscitate them and by the end of 1830 three of the seven principal Agency Houses and sixteen of the twenty smaller firms had collapsed.[92] One contemporary calculated the total bankruptcy at about twenty million pounds.[93] With each firm's failure it became increasingly difficult for the survivors to maintain the confidence of their creditors. A renewed wave of bankruptcies erupted in 1832. Indian investors were particularly hard hit; when Mackintosh and Co. failed, over half of its debts were owed to Indians.[94] The Company drew some benefits from this. After 1825 there was a significant increase in the number of Indians investing in the Company's loans. Only six per cent of the 1822 loan was held by Indians; the 1829 loan attracted far more Indians who held in total forty-seven per cent.[95]

Bentinck's hopes of nurturing Indian finances into a healthier state were only partly successful. As he informed London in late 1832, India's accounts still appeared very precarious. Capital was in short supply, expenditures had not been reduced to the levels that had been planned for upon his departure for India, and land revenues were still pitched too high to break the deflationary spiral that kept prices in India in a depressed state. Yet some breathing room had been gained.

As the economies ordered by London and introduced by Amherst and Bentinck began to take effect, and with some financial relief in sight, Bentinck could now turn to those areas of Company rule that he felt were in need of reform. Here we can detect some basic principles at work. Bentinck was more like later Victorian imperialists than his predecessors in that he was less inclined to accept indigenous institutions, including the Company's own traditions, at face value. His inclination, however ill-defined, was to 'modernize' India through the introduction of western ideologies and institutions. Indians needed to be encouraged to adopt British ideas and institutions as their own. Bentinck described India 'as a great estate, of which I am the chief agent, whose principal business is to improve the condition of the tenantry and to raise the revenues...'[96] Through the introduction of British ideas of what constituted a modern economy, together with the more tangible application of British capital and skilled labour, Bentinck hoped that the Indian economy would emerge from its underdeveloped state and provide benefits for the British Empire as well as for the people of India.[97] He was convinced that India's future development could not proceed without significant changes. The limits on the traditional allocation of capital and labour had been reached. The crises suffered by the Agency Houses had established that 'credit is at an end, and there is no means of raising a shilling upon the very best security.'[98] The solution that he advocated was to introduce more Europeans into India as well as allowing them to own land. The capital that they would bring, as well as that mortgaged from the lands they owned, would partly redress the chronic shortage of disposable capital. Meanwhile, their skills would improve output.

Bentinck's advocacy of moving British India's capital to an interior location was similarly intended to alter Britain's position in India.[99] A capital at Agra, or a similar city in north central India, would place the British closer to India's historic heartland. British control would be firmly planted in Indian soil instead of tenuously clinging to the coast in Calcutta, a seaport which was too obviously a remnant of the mercantile age. He also suggested strategic reasons for such a move for it was in those areas where the British faced off against the bravest and most independent-minded peoples.[100] In contrast, Bengal itself required little supervision for it is 'inhabited by the most submissive people in the world.'[101] In a similar vein, he also recommended that the capital of the Madras presidency be moved from its coastal enclave to Bangalore, another inland, central position.[102] Bentinck formed these recommendations on a set of assumptions that was diametrically opposed to that of the Company. His efforts to dislodge colonial rule from its commercial antecedents, while seductive to Ellenborough, were explicitly rejected by the Court of Directors. They argued that 'India is governed by a distant maritime power, and the position of the seat of government must be considered with reference to that peculiar circumstance.'[103]

At the heart of Bentinck's policies for British India lay a dramatically changed role for the army. Military reform was to preoccupy Bentinck right up until his departure from India, especially after he had gotten rid of his troublesome commanders-in-chief and personally assumed that office in May 1833. Bentinck offered a revised interpretation of the idea of an 'empire of opinion'. While he did not completely discard the imperatives and fears of Anglo-Indian militarism, he nevertheless argued that the army could only be part of the solution to British India's stability. 'If we maintain ourselves in Bengal by the sword and the sword only ... we had better give up the attempt to govern at all.'[104] Unlike most of those around him, Bentinck was not convinced of the inseparability of internal and external enemies.

He tended to dismiss the lurking internal enemy as the paranoiac ram-
blings of an over-sensitive Anglo-Indian psyche. He wrote mockingly of
the alarmist reports generated by Metcalfe, Malcolm and similarly inclined
individuals concerning the designs of India's deposed elites. 'The importance of those chiefs and states have been dressed up with a certain degree
of poetical imagery, which the daily despatches of all the political agents
residing at those durbars, seem completely to contradict.'[105] This was a theme
he would return to just prior to his departure when he still maintained that,
'of internal danger, nobody I believe entertains less alarm than myself.'[106]
He chose instead to focus his attentions on the more threatening presence
of the Russians. India's internal order was to be strengthened by economic,
legal and social 'improvement'. If sufficient Indians of the higher classes
could be convinced of the benefits of British rule, and be persuaded to
adopt some western ways, then the benefits would trickle down to the masses.
Prosperity, security of life and property, and the ending of barbaric traditions such as *sati* would eventually win over more Indians than could be
coerced by the army.

Yet if Bentinck did not stress the centrality of the army as much as his
predecessors had, he was still convinced of its importance. He was equally
certain that it was an army in dire need of reforms. Bentinck agreed with
the observation of General Whittingham that 'There is no army in India!
There is an immense military mass, numerous beyond our wants; but without shape, or form, or due proportions. Its coloration is as defective as its
composition.'[107] By breaking the link between the internal and external aspects of India's defences, separate war and peace establishments could be
envisioned. Here the need for economies coincided with his own reforming
ambitions. This placed him squarely at odds with the prevailing doctrines
of Anglo-Indian militarism. When Metcalfe's note reminded him that 'it
seems we ought to maintain all [the forces] that we can pay, and to pay we
require all the revenues we can raise', Bentinck wrote in the margin that 'I
am not quite of this opinion'.[108] Bentinck's disinclination to subscribe to
India's militarized traditions stemmed in part from his attaching less weight
to the threat of internal rebellion. He also rightly suspected the army of
self-aggrandizement. Bentinck's intended military reforms are most clearly
articulated in a minute he delivered to council in mid-1832.[109] His insistence that separate war and peace establishments be instituted was accompanied by his identification of what was to be British India's strategic priority — the securing of the northwest frontier, principally against a Russian
attack. He took for granted that within British-ruled India, British supremacy was unchallenged.

There was no single Indian prince with the ability to overthrow British rule, and an alliance between these princes was unlikely. The Madras presidency was considered to be completely secured, while the only danger facing Bombay would come from Sind and that could be easily dealt with by the Bengal army. This left Bengal as the only vulnerable presidency. Bengal's northern and eastern frontiers had been securely fastened; the only significant threat was from across the northwest frontier. Bentinck called upon what the British knew of Indian history to substantiate his conclusions. 'It is from this quarter that all the successful attacks upon India have been made, it is the only point of our immense confines whether by sea or land, by which the safety of the empire can be seriously endangered.'[110] The belief that the greatest threat to India was Imperial Russia had gained considerable currency by 1830.[111] There was a flurry of articles in English literary and military periodicals of this time that prophesied an imminent clash between the British and the Russians somewhere along India's northwest frontier. Reports from Central Asia had convinced many observers that the area was ripe for Russian intrigues and 'there can be little doubt that the Persian, the Affghaun, and Tartar tribes, would readily assist in such an invasion, — all notoriously addicted to predatory war.'[112] Bentinck's proposed military reforms were developed with the Russians in mind. The army that was required to deal with such a threat was in his eyes qualitatively and quantitatively different from the one he found in India.

If Bentinck's broad strategic perspective was to downplay internal threats and concentrate on what appeared to be a more threatening enemy from without, the one military campaign that he personally supervised, the invasion of Coorg in 1834, suggests that in practice he could not totally disassociate himself from traditional preoccupations with the enemy within. Even his closest military advisor stressed that in the last resort British rule was maintained by the sword. General Whittingham wrote that 'we are mere military occupants, and our empire rests exclusively on the superior organization of the military force by which we have conquered, and by which alone we hold possession.'[113] Nearly eight thousand troops invaded Coorg in 1834 to restore stability to a tiny kingdom beset by a succession crisis.[114] In 1808, against the wishes of the recently deceased Raja who had indicated that his daughter should succeed, the British had settled his son on the throne. The daughter and her husband then sought sanctuary in Company territory. The new ruler and his successor had difficulties in quelling internal unrest and were accused by their opponents of various atrocities. When the British tried to investigate the situation in 1833, they were rebuffed by the ruler who claimed that his treaty with the British did not provide them with any rights over his internal affairs.[115] The government of Madras might not have proceeded further, had it not been for increasing signs of turbulence in neighbouring Mysore and Canara.[116] Fearing that a successful assertion of independence in Coorg might prompt similar demonstrations in the latter areas, the government of Madras suggested to Bentinck that intervention might be necessary. Bentinck agreed with the governor of Madras's position that strong language is useless 'unless one is determined to follow it up by more vigorous proceedings', and preparations for a campaign were set in motion.[117] Rumours of an impending Russian-Sikh alliance were also cited as a further incentive to flex British muscles.[118] Eventually Bentinck decided that a military demonstration was essential and that the raja should be deposed. In defending his actions, Bentinck's rhetoric came very close to that of the Anglo-Indian militarists: 'the rajah sets our power at defiance and the course we are bound to take is equally clear'.[119] The raja of Coorg had not only insulted the British, but his example could set a dangerous precedent in a volatile area. An example must be made of him, and if a suitable heir could not be found, then the territory would have to be annexed. A short but bloody campaign followed, with three hundred British casualties (106 of them were Europeans ambushed in the jungle). Annexation was ordered after no likely successor could be found and after Bentinck was convinced by Whittingham that possession of Coorg had strategic advantages.[120] Whittingham described Coorg as a 'perfect Gibraltar' which in the hands of an enemy could disrupt British control over southern India.

Not long after his victory over Coorg, Bentinck once again faced the possibility that military force might be necessary to subdue a truculent Indian prince. Though nothing came of this, he did write the chairman of the Company that he might have to send a force to Jodhpur, and while he would rather not do so, conditions in the area may not give him any choice.[121] The raja was clearly flaunting British authority and continued displays of disobedience would only rally other discontented groups. Certainly Bentinck was not as belligerent as Hastings, nor was he duped as easily into offensive actions as Amherst, but he was none the less willing to deploy the army to sustain the reputation of British strength. He was not that naive to think that the affections of a broad section of Indian society had been won over to British rule.

The survival of separate military establishments at Madras and Bombay struck him as particularly wasteful. He questioned the 'supposition that each presidency is a distinct country, with its separate interests and separate enemies.'[122] Neither of these presidencies had in his eyes dangerous frontiers to defend and the resources expended upon them could be better employed in Bengal. He recommended that the three armies be merged together to form a grand army under Bengal's control. Bentinck agreed with the argument that 'Madras formerly was, but of late Bengal has been, and must be the fighting presidency.'[123] With the death of Munro and the eclipse of Wynn, the Madras army lost its chief defenders and its decline began. In 1833 a journalist in India taunted: 'The Madras army might now return like Alexander and weep for former conquests.'[124] Bentinck also singled out the Bombay army for criticism, noting that it was no larger than a Bengal division, yet it was equipped with a large and expensive staff establishment.[125] However, Bentinck was conscious of the strong sense of independence alive in these armies and the supporters they could call upon in London. His pursuit of army unification was therefore conducted quietly and mainly through private channels.[126] Bentinck did not succeed in securing much support for his plans and they were allowed to quietly lapse.

Bentinck was somewhat more successful in the pursuit of another of his objectives, that of deploying existing forces more effectively. By the time he left India the Bengal army was not nearly as widely scattered as it had been. This concentration of force was accomplished in part by increasing the size of regiments while reducing the overall number of regiments.[127] The regiments were also collected together into larger stations so as to permit a field army to be marshalled more quickly. The bulk of the Bengal army was also shifted westward so as to be in closer proximity to the frontier with the Punjab.[128] Roughly one half of the army was stationed in the divisions closest to the frontier in 1835. Of a total strength of 79,876 men, just over 39,000 were to be found in the Meerut, Kanpur, and Sirhind Divisions and in the Rajputana field force [see map 1]. Even more striking was the concentration of European regiments in upcountry cantonments where they would not only be better placed to deal with any attack from the northwest, but they were also moved away from the unhealthy stations further down the Ganges.

Bentinck also brought into play increased apprehensions over the reliability of the Company army, especially their Indian troops. 'I fearlessly pronounce the Indian army to be the least efficient and most expensive in the world.'[129] Indian troops were a 'two-edged sword', as likely to threaten British India as to defend it. His suspicions were no doubt influenced by his memories of the Vellore uprising and the more recent mutiny at Barrackpore. Bentinck was also persuaded by Paget's advice to 'get as many of the King's troops as you can.'[130] The efficiency and dependability of the Bengal army appeared to be rapidly declining. Sepoy morale was believed to be low, high caste recruits were no longer as forthcoming, and doubts were being raised as to whether the Bengal army was not becoming a liability.[131] There were many explanations advanced to account for the apparent deterioration of the Bengal army. A favourite one was that officers and sepoys were no longer as close as they had been. Critics could point to the fewer number of officers serving with their regiments, and these officers' loss of authority over their men. Prior to 1824, regimental commanders could order courts-martial and approve their proceedings without reference to their superiors. These powers were revoked, and regimental commanders were made more accountable to their superiors. This was viewed by many as counterproductive, especially given the widely accepted belief that the bond between European officer and Indian sepoy rested upon the European's unquestioned possession of power and authority. Warnings were issued that, 'The habits of the natives are so different from our own, that too much power can hardly be given to the officer commanding a sepoy corps, if we wish him to retain that ascendancy over their minds which is necessary to secure their respect and attachment.'[132] Sepoy officers were also charged with having disregarded the culture and ways of local society in favour of a retreat into those European communities in India that were starting to spring up. One commander-in-chief lamented: 'Woefully indeed has our thirst for civil institutions and predilections for British customs and fashions changed the nature of the relations between the European officers and the sepoys.'[133]

It was not only the sepoy's loyalty that was called into question: like many officers around him, Bentinck was receptive to racialist arguments concerning Indian character and had begun to question whether the sepoys from the Company's traditional recruiting grounds were up to a future conflict with soldiers from outside India. Sepoys from Awadh may have proved their worth in contests against other communities within the subcontinent, but Bentinck doubted whether they could stand up to the more warlike Central Asian tribes, or more ominously, a Russian army. Commentators noted that while sepoys were successfully used in establishing military control over the interior of India, their value outside of India was questioned. These questions were partly a legacy of the selective rewriting of the Burma War and the Bharatpur campaign where failings in leadership and planning were masked by references to the unreliability of the sepoys.[134] Bentinck was particularly susceptible to Whittingham's bleak prognosis that 'nothing short of 30,000 British soldiers collected at Cawnpore, Agra, Meerut, Delhi and Karnaul ... can ... ensure the safety of British India'.[135] Bentinck himself asserted that the 'defects of the natives of India are a want of physical strength, and of moral energy.'[136] Broadly similar assumptions can be detected in Bentinck's decision to reject a candidate for a staff appointment on the grounds that the applicant's mother had been an Indian woman.[137] Though in this instance Bentinck pleaded that he was not prejudiced, and only acted according to the rules of Anglo-Indian society, it is clear from his earlier comments that Bentinck was not immune to racialist influences. Not even cost-benefit arguments, which arguably account in part for his support of greater Indian recruitment into the civil service, could persuade him that India's security could be safely entrusted to an army with a high proportion of sepoys.

Bentinck's plan was eventually to have an army of 160,000 with a ratio of one European for every three sepoys — in 1828 the army numbered just over 250,000 with a ratio of one to nine. This was to be achieved by replacing two sepoy battalions with one king's regiment until the army was brought down to 160,000. The Company's European troops were to be reduced altogether. Such a plan would do little to help Bengal's struggling finances and actually contradicted Bentinck's hopes for further economies. As European soldiers were considerably more expensive than sepoys, any savings from the reduction of sepoy regiments would be more than compensated for by the costs of extra king's troops in India. Even without the implementation of Bentinck's plan, the ratio of European troops to sepoys had already grown as a consequence of the immediate post-war economies (see Appendix J). One of Amherst's parting acts had been to reduce the listed establishment of a sepoy regiment from nine hundred to seven hundred.[138] Postwar reductions had fallen exclusively on the sepoys. European troops had actually increased in number.[139] In 1822 their numbers were respectively 216,175 and 29,065; in 1833 they were 187,067 and 36,409.[140] Bentinck's intention of reducing the numbers of sepoys even further through replacing them with more king's regiments was blocked by the Court of Directors who could not accept the costs that would follow from such a plan. Nor were they willing to allow Horse Guards to assimilate their own European regiments into the king's army. Nevertheless, when Bentinck left India in 1835, the ratio of sepoys to Europeans was still much higher (7 to 1) than he would have liked (3 to 1), but it was down from what it had been when he first arrived (9 to 1).

However much Bentinck mistrusted the sepoys and wished to replace them with European rank and file, practical considerations meant that unless metropolitan authorities were to reverse themselves and fund a huge increase in European troops for India, the British would continue to depend upon Indian recruits. He then had to look for ways to raise their morale and improve their efficiency. There was the seemingly intractable problem of too many officers absent from their corps. Many attributed the declining morale of Indian troops to this. However, there were some officers who argued that this only diverted attention from more fundamental questions. 'Are we in India come to the point where it is desirable to make up in officers what the native infantry has lost in loyalty and morale?'[141] Bentinck himself was not especially worried over the apparent shortage of officers in sepoy regiments for in his opinion there were already far too many officers with regiments whose future he saw as that of a rural gendarmerie. The growing unreliability of the Indian component of the Bengal army was the result not of numbers of officers present with their corps but of a more thorough disintegration of the complex bonds between the sepoy and the state. The sheer intricacies of this problem were reflected in the Select Committee's report in 1831/32. They produced a complete volume of reports yet failed to reach any conclusions.[142]

The most important and for some the most controversial gesture made by Bentinck to restore sepoy morale and hopefully encourage the return of high caste recruits was to pass an order prohibiting the use of corporal punishments on Indian soldiers.[143] This was not the first instance in which his concern to maintain the high caste character of the Bengal army was registered. Earlier, during his deliberations on the plan to prohibit *sati*, he did not act until he had canvassed army officers as to how they felt the sepoys would react. While some officers were concerned that prohibition would be seen as an attack on caste, Bentinck was convinced by those officers who countered by insisting that the sepoys, while high caste in origin, did not come from regions in which *sati* was common.[144] With respect to corporal punishment, he argued that 'this degradation could no longer be inflicted upon the high caste sepoy of the Bengal army' and that the presence of corporal punishment dissuaded many eligible recruits from joining.[145] In reaching this conclusion, Bentinck was reflecting back on the Burma War during which time many believed that the army's ranks had been filled with undesirable lower caste recruits. While there is no firm evidence to show that this had actually taken place to any great extent, Bentinck like so many around him wished to return the Bengal army to its pristine high-caste composition. To do so in his eyes meant getting rid of any possible disincentives. It was not a completely novel idea; sepoys as we have already seen were rarely subjected to the lash in the Bengal army and Combermere had issued strict restrictions on when it could it be used. In 1827, the use of the lash on Bengal sepoys was limited to the crimes of marauding, stealing and gross insubordination, and then only after the punishment had been confirmed in writing by the general commanding the local division.[146] There was an outcry against Bentinck's blanket prohibition for notwithstanding the traditional distaste for the lash within the Bengal army, very few officers wished to see it scrapped entirely.[147] For several years to follow, pressures were exerted on the government to reconsider its position. Ultimately, opponents of this measure were successful for the lash was reintroduced for use on a few select crimes — a return to the pre-1835 status quo.[148] Bentinck's intentions were once again frustrated by the army.

We have seen so far the extent to which Bentinck's actions were determined by pressing financial needs and his own initiatives frustrated by either outright opposition or bureaucratic inertia. It has also been indicated that while many of his so-called reforms were merely retrenchments camouflaged in more appealing guises, there were also underlying assumptions that went against ideas then prevailing in India — namely Anglo-Indian definitions of security and the centrality of the army. Lord William Bentinck was caught between his own, often contradictory, instincts and the unavoidable pressures for economy, while being buffeted by metropolitan manoeuvres and facing the formidable alliance of civilians and soldiers. Bentinck was not the great reformer that he wanted to be. He was not even the great clipper railed at by vested interests. The most significant burden on Indian finances, that of maintaining a war establishment in the field, naturally retreated with the conclusion of the Burma War. Nor was the state of the army visibly improved by his attentions. In 1833 it was argued 'that there exists a deterioration in the army, it is useless, it might be deemed presumptuous, to deny'.[149] Such predictions were certainly proven correct in 1857 when most of the sepoy regiments in the Bengal army mutinied (but not regiments in the Madras and Bombay armies). The officers of the Bengal army were only momentarily chastened by the imposition of half-batta. More than ten years later, their politicization prompted an officer of the Bombay army to write: 'the normal state of the Bengal army is such as must appear, to an officer of the Royal or of the Bombay army, as a state of mutiny.'[150]

If Bentinck's administration were to be summed up in a single word, the most apt choice would be discord. Contemporaries were almost unanimous in their criticism of his government. Although one detects vested interests in the forefront, the volume of complaints is in itself indicative of the situation in British India. The government's ability to introduce positive measures was greatly restricted for they had sacrificed the cooperation of many Europeans. Ellenborough's contacts in India convinced him that no matter how well-intentioned he was, Bentinck's ability to act was frustrated by his unpopularity.[151] The army and the civilians alike were suspicious of him.

Those reforming members of the administration who had enthusiastically greeted his appointment, such as Frederick Shore, felt cheated by his preoccupation with economy.[152] For many onlookers, 'Half Batta Ben's' cutbacks appeared to be the thin edge of the wedge — the imposition of European principles of statecraft onto the British-Indian body politic.[153] The golden era of the soldier-administrator, the militarized man of action beloved of Munro, Malcolm and Elphinstone, was momentarily under threat. Malcolm's plaintive plea, 'the days of liberality are gone and we live in those of clippers and calculators and our long coats are every hour in danger of being made coatees', reflected the fears of many in India between 1828 and 1835. Such fears were exaggerated for not only did many of Bentinck's plans fail to materialize, but those that did were in the long run compromised or overturned by the persistence in India of those who still maintained militarized understandings of colonial rule. The Company implicitly and somewhat belatedly recognized this essential characteristic of the colonial regime when they lobbied (unsuccessfully) for Metcalfe to succeed Bentinck at Calcutta. In the Company's eyes, Metcalfe's greatest asset was his ability to restore harmony between the army and the government, harmony that had been bent but not broken by Lord William Bentinck.[154]

[1] [King's Officer], 'Sketches of Military Life in India,' *United Services Journal*, 25(1837): 505

[2] OIOC, Henry Spry to Edward Spry, 30 Dec 1827, Photo Eur 308/3

[3] OIOC, Henry Spry to Edward Spry, 20 Jan 1830, Photo Eur 308/4

[4] J.C. Marshman, 'Lord William Bentinck's Administration,' *Calcutta Review*, 1(1844): 355

[5] See for example Keane, 'Anglo-Indian Mufasil Life in the Last Generation,' *Calcutta Review*, 66(1878): 717 in which the rumour of Bentinck's plan to sell the Taj Mahal to a Hindu banker is mentioned.

[6] See for example Eric Stokes' classic, *The English Utilitarians and India*, Oxford: Oxford University Press, 1959 and George Bearce, 'Lord William Bentinck: the Application of Liberalism to India', *Journal of Modern History*, 28(1956): 234-46

[7] Lawson, *The East India Company*, 149-52. While Lawson later qualifies this picture by referring to Bayly's work, there is nevertheless a sense that it is change and not continuity that Lawson ultimately identifies with.

[8] Percival Spear, 'Lord William Bentinck', in C.H. Philips and M.D. Wainwright, eds., *Indian Society and the Beginnings of Modernisation*, 28

[9] Not all contemporary voices were critical. One of the earliest hagiographies to emerge, and one that clearly linked Bentinck to reform, was J.C. Marshman, 'Lord William Bentinck's Administration,' *Calcutta Review*, 1(1844): 337-71. It provides a complete catalogue of those reforms which Bentinck was credited with.

[10] Scepticism surrounding the actual impact of Bentinck's reforms is hinted at in several of the essays in C.H. Philips and M.D. Wainwright, eds., *Indian Society*

and the Beginnings of Modernisation, c.1830-1850, London: School of Oriental and African Studies, 1976. The most recent evaluation of these reforms, and one which also downplays their actual significance while judiciously asserting their importance as a barometer of changing attitudes, is to be found in C.A. Bayly, *Indian Society and the Making of the British Empire*, 120-26

[11] J.W. Kaye, *The Life and Correspondence of Henry St. George Tucker*, London: Bentley, 1854, 453

[12] Bentinck's most recent biographer carefully notes the obstacles with which Bentinck had to deal, though the importance of the army is not developed as fully as it might. John Rosselli, *Lord William Bentinck; the Making of a Liberal Imperialist, 1774-1839*, Berkeley: University of California Press, 1974

[13] Nottingham, Ravenshaw to Bentinck, 3 March 1828, PwJf 1903

[14] Eric Stokes, 'Bureaucracy and Ideology: Britain and India in the Nineteenth Century', *Transactions of the Royal Historical Society*, 30(1980): 151

[15] Tripathi, *Trade and Finance*, 175-6

[16] PRO, Ellenborough, 'Considerations Respecting the Financial Concerns of the East India Company', 26 July 1828, PRO 30/12/31/2

[17] R.E. Frykenberg, 'New Light on the Vellore Mutiny,' Kenneth A. Ballhatchet and John Harrison, eds. *East India Company Studies*, Hong Kong: Centre of Asian Studies, 1986, 220

[18] Rosselli, *Bentinck*, 45.

[19] Chester Record Office, Thomas Moody to Combermere, 18 Jan 1828, CR 72/29/165

[20] Ellenborough, 17 June 1829, *Political Diary*, II, 51

[21] Philip Harling and Peter Mandler, 'From 'Fiscal-Military State to Laissez-Faire State, 1760-1850,' *Journal of British Studies*, 32(1993): 44-70

[22] Auber to Bentinck, 24 Nov 1831, *Correspondence*, I, 718

[23] Ellenborough, 1 July 1829, *Political Diary*, II, 62

[24] Nottingham, Ravenshaw to Bentinck, 2 Dec 1828, PwJf 1906

[25] Nottingham, Bentinck to Lindsay, 28 Dec 1828, PwJf 1200

[26] Auber to Bentinck, 14 May 1833, *Correspondence*, II, 1069-70

[27] The imperial consequences of these developments are assessed in Bayly, *Imperial Meridian*, 235-47.

[28] Nottingham, Ravenshaw to Bentinck, 3 Mar 1828, PwJf 1903

[29] Ellenborough, 13 Nov 1829, *Political Diary*, II, 131

[30] *The Times*, 20 Sept 1828; Wellington to Arbuthnot, 18 Oct 1830, Gerald Wellesley, 7th Duke of Wellington, ed., *Wellington and His Friends*, London: Macmillan, 1965, 90

[31] C.H. Philips, *The East India Company, 1784-1834*, Manchester: Manchester University Press, 1961, 261

[32] Ellenborough, 3 Sept 1829, *Political Diary*, II, 92; see also entries for 11 Sept 1828, II, 217 and 29 Oct 1829, II, 122 where he expresses his admiration for a pamphlet on the Russian threat to India which he passed on to Wellington.

[33] Ellenborough, 10 Oct 1828, *Political Diary*, I, 238

[34] This can be seen most clearly in the papers of Lord Ellenborough preserved at the Public Record Office. Ellenborough's mastery of the intricacies of Indian affairs was also commented upon by others. These same characteristics would also mark Ellenborough's period as governor-general of India (1842-44). Henry

Hardinge, his successor as governor-general of India, noted that, 'Lord Ellenborough trusted no one and liked to do the inferior drudgery of every office from an insatiable necessity of being employed.' Hardinge to Walter, 17 Aug 1844, Henry Hardinge, *The Letters of the First Viscount Hardinge of Lahore*, Bawa Satinder Singh, ed. Camden Fourth Series, vol. 32, London: Royal Historical Society, 1986, 28

[35] Nottingham, Mill to Bentinck, 2 Jan 1829, PwJf 1799

[36] Ellenborough, 11 Dec 1825, *Political Diary*, II, 273

[37] PRO, Loch to Ellenborough, 17 Nov 1829, PRO 30/9/4/43

[38] Wellington's Speech to the House of Lords, 5 July 1833, *Speeches*, 644-45

[39] Auber to Bentinck, *Correspondence*, I, xxii-xxiii

[40] John Rosselli, *Lord William Bentinck; the Making of a Liberal Imperialist, 1774-1839*, New Delhi: Thomson Press, 1974, 316

[41] Ellenborough, 23 June 1829, *Political Diary*, II, 56

[42] *The Times*, 22 Oct 1829

[43] Nottingham, Ravenshaw to Bentinck, 19 Nov 1829, PwJf 1912

[44] [King's Officer], 'Sketches of Military Life in India,' *United Services Journal*, 24(1837): 465

[45] J.C. Marshman, 'Lord William Bentinck's Administration,' *Calcutta Review*, 1(1844): 371

[46] SRO, Dalhousie, Memo on Civil-Military Relations, 20 Dec 1830, GD45/5/50

[47] OIOC, Nicolls' Diary, May 1828, MSS Eur F175/34

[48] OIOC, Prinsep's Diary, MSS Eur C97/2, 129

[49] F.J. Shore, *Notes on Indian Affairs*, London: J.W. Parker, 1837, I, 221

[50] 'The Present Adjutant General,' *East India United Service Journal*, 13(1835): 5-7; [Gabion Fuse], 'The Indian Army for Thirty Years,' *Colburn's United Services Journal*, (1849, no.3): 506

[51] Thiessen, *Anglo-Indian Vested Interests*

[52] J.C. Marshman, 'Lord William Bentinck's Administration,' *Calcutta Review*, 1(1844): 352

[53] Bentinck to Metcalfe, 4 Feb 1834, *Correspondence*, II, 1200

[54] Nottingham, Ravenshaw to Bentinck, 18 Feb 1829, PwJf 1902

[55] [Gabion Fuse], 'The Indian Army for Thirty Years,' *Colburn's United Services Journal*, (1849, no.3): 349

[56] See for example Tripathi, *Trade and Finance*, 176-79

[57] OIOC, Amherst's Minute, 9 Feb 1828, L/MIL/5/398/175, p129

[58] Nottingham, Craigie to Bentinck, 17 June 1829, PwJf 2778/v; see also the papers of Lt. Col Frederick, Bombay's representative on the committee, especially his notes, OIOC, MSS Eur D765/1

[59] OIOC, Nicolls' Diary, Sept 1829, MSS Eur F175/34

[60] OIOC, Amherst's Minute, 5 Feb 1825, L/MIL/5/398/175

[61] OIOC, Chairs to Melville, 22 March 1828, L/MIL/5/487

[62] Wellington, Memo on the Indian Army, 14 Feb 1825, *Dispatches*, IV, 265-66

[63] OIOC, Minute by Bentinck, 29 Nov. 1828, MSS Eur E424/2

[64] Nottingham, Bentinck to Loch, 12 Aug 1828, PwJf 1202

[65] Bentinck to Taylor, 14 Feb 1829, Herbert Taylor, *The Taylor Papers*, 243

[66] OIOC, Nicolls' Diary, 30 July 1827, MSS Eur F175/33

[67] Ellenborough, 19 Nov 1829, *Political Diary*, II, 138; PRO, Wellington to

Ellenborough, 4 Sept 1829, PRO 30/9/4/1/2

[68] Nottingham, Whittingham to Bentinck, 18 Dec 1832, PwJf 2254. Whittingham was Bentinck's chief contact within the army, and most of Bentinck's minutes on military matters show unmistakable signs of Whittingham's presence.

[69] OIOC, Nicolls' Diary, Jan 1830, MSS Eur F175/35

[70] PRO, Loch to Ellenborough, 13 Oct 1829, PRO 30/9/4/41

[71] PRO, Wellington to Ellenborough, 17 Oct 1829, PRO 30/9/4/21

[72] PRO, Loch to Ellenborough, 20 Oct 1829, PRO 30/9/4/41

[73] Combermere had first sparked Wellington's wrath when he criticized Amherst's conduct of the Burma War. See Southampton, Wellington to Wynn, 4 Jan 1827, WP1/881/5. Wellington and Ellenborough persuaded William IV not to make him a privy councillor. The decision to deny honours to Combermere is discussed in Ellenborough, 27 June 1830, *Political Diary*, II, 283.

[74] PRO, Loch to Ellenborough, 27 Oct 1829, PRO 30/9/4/41

[75] PRO, Unsigned Memo on Reductions, 1829, PRO 30/9/4/3

[76] The *Times*, 5 Nov 1829

[77] 'They all thought it better to swallow his dinner than lose their commissions', SRO, Note by Dalhousie, 16 Dec 1830, GD 45/5/59; other insults are recorded in: Nottingham, Memo By Bentinck, 1829, PwJf 2633

[78] OIOC, Henry Spry to Edward Spry, 20 Jan 1831, Photo Eur 308/4

[79] *The Times*, 22 Oct 1827

[80] OIOC, Nicolls' Diary, Nov 1830, MSS Eur F175/35

[81] See Ellenborough, 16 Dec 1829, *Political Diary*, II, 149

[82] Nottingham, Ravenshaw to Bentinck, 10 Dec 1831, PwJf 1924; [King's Officer], 'Sketches of Military Life in India,' *United Services Journal*, 25(1837): 206

[83] S.C. on the East India Company, PP, 8(1831/32): 166-7

[84] Bentinck to Melville, 16 Dec 1828, Philips, *Correspondence*, I, 121; Government Resolution, 17 Feb 1829, S.C. on the East India Company, PP 9(1831/32): 704-15

[85] S.C. on the East India Company, PP, 9(1831/32): 717

[86] Ibid. Figures are calculated from Appendix 7

[87] Nottingham, Metcalfe, minute, 11 Oct 1829, PwJf 1522

[88] Between 1825 and 1830, direct trade with India was showing an annual loss of between £150,000 and £500,000 a year. The China trade was profiting with an average of about £1,000,000 a year. S.C. on the East India Company, PP, 10(1831/32): pt 1, 401-5

[89] Nottingham, Ravenshaw to Bentinck, 14 April 1828, PwJf 1905

[90] Tripathi, *Trade and Finance*, 309

[91] William Prinsep in A.C. Staples, 'Memoirs of William Prinsep,' *Indian Economic and Social History Review*, 26(1989): 67

[92] Bentinck, Minute on the Agency Houses, 14 May 1830, *Correspondence*, I, 435

[93] Crawfurd in K N Chaudhuri, *Economic Development*, 281

[94] N.K. Sinha, 'European Banking in Bengal, 1779-1848,' *Bengal Past and Present*, 88(1969): 18. This challenges some recent works that have suggested that the European depositors bore the brunt of these bankruptcies. See for example, S.D. Chapman, 'The Agency Houses; British Mercantile Enterprise in the Far East, c.1780-1820,' *Textile History*, 19(1988): 242

[95] S.C. on the East India Company, PP, 10(1831/32): Pt 1, 441

[96] Bentinck to Ellenborough, 5 Nov 1829, Philips, *Correspondence*, I, 333

[97] Bentinck's ambitions are situated within the broader context of British economic relations with India in David Washbrook, 'South Asia, the World System and World Capitalism,' *Journal of Asian Studies*, 49(1990): 479-508. See also his article, 'Progress and Problems: South Asian Social and Economic History, c.1720-1860,' *Modern Asian Studies*, 12(1988): 57-96

[98] Bentinck to Marjoribanks, 18 May 1833, *Correspondence*, II, 1073

[99] Bernard Cohn, 'Representing Authority in Victorian India', in Eric Hobsbawm and T.O. Ranger, eds., *The Invention of Tradition*, Cambridge: Cambridge University Press, 1983, 174-75

[100] Bentinck, Memo on Central India and the Upper Provinces, 10 Feb 1829, *Correspondence*, I, 151

[101] Bentinck, Minute on the Removal of the Seat of Government to the Upper Provinces, 15 Sept 1829, *Correspondence*, I, 285

[102] Rosselli, *Bentinck*, 230

[103] Court to Bentinck, 3 July 1829, *Correspondence*, I, 247. Ellenborough, in one of his fits of romantic fantasy, speculated aloud that perhaps the British should go further and like 'the first Turkish sovereign, have no palace but his camp and rule from his imperial stirrup.' Ellenborough to Bentinck, 19 May 1829, *Correspondence*, I, 200

[104] Nottingham, Bentinck, Memo on Barrackpore, nd, PwJf 2739/1/iv

[105] Bentinck, Minute on the Removal of the Seat of Government to the Upper Provinces, 15 Sept 1829, *Correspondence*, I, 285

[106] Bentinck, Minute on Military Policy, 13 March 1835, *Correspondence*, II, 1441

[107] Whittingham to Bentinck, 18 March 1831, *Correspondence*, I, 605. Whittingham's role in shaping Bentinck's military policies can be clearly seen in Bentinck's Minute on Military Policy, (13 March 1835, *Correspondence*, II, 1444) which was plagiarized from a report sent to him the previous year by Whittingham. Even the rhetorical device, 'From the days of Peter the Great to the present time...' was lifted verbatim from Whittingham's letter. See Whittingham to Bentinck, 18 Aug 1834, *Correspondence*, II, 1359

[108] Nottingham, Metcalfe's Minute, 11 Oct 1829, PwJf 1522

[109] Bentinck, Minute on the Defence of India, 29 June 1832, *Correspondence*, II, 846-47. The contents of this document also shows clearly Whittingham's influence.

[110] Ibid, 847

[111] The political and military developments behind this sense of alarm can be best followed in Edward Ingram, *Britain's Persian Connection*, especially pp. 272-305

[112] [W.W.], 'Considerations on the Native Army and Defence of India,' *United Services Journal*, 7(1931): 6

[113] Whittingham to Bentinck, 14 March 1834, *Correspondence*, II, 1223

[114] A personal narrative of this campaign can be found in 'The Coorg War of 1834,' *Colburn's United Services Journal*, (July, 1858): 393-400. A brief history of Coorg can be found in: Anon, 'History of Coorg,' *Calcutta Review*, 27(1856): 181-86

[115] Graeme to Adam, 29 Oct 1833, *Correspondence*, II, 1129-30 [Graeme was the representative sent by Madras to meet with the Raja who the Raja declined to meet]

[116] James Fraser to Adam, 17 June 1837, in James Stuart Fraser, *Memoir and*

Correspondence of General James Stuart Fraser, London: Whiting and Co., 1885, 29 [Fraser was the governer-general's agent on the expedition]

[117] Adam to Bentinck, 15 Aug 1833, *Correspondence*, II, 1095. See also Bentinck to Auber, 20 July 1833, *Correspondence*, II, 1088

[118] Colonel Morrison to Adam, 12 Nov 1833, *Correspondence*, II, 1140–41

[119] Bentinck, Minute on Coorg, 3 March 1834, *Correspondence*, II, 1215; see also OIOC, Bentinck, Minute on Coorg, 17 February 1834, L/Mil/5/408

[120] Bentinck to Tucker, 12 May 1834, *Correspondence*, II, 1281; Whittingham to Bentinck, 14 April 1834, *Correspondence*, II, 1241

[121] Bentinck to Tucker, 3 Sept 1834, *Correspondence*, II, 1370

[122] Bentinck to Metcalfe, 16 Sept 1829, *Correspondence*, I, 290

[123] OIOC, Combermere to Amherst, 9 Nov 1826, MSS Eur F140/86(a)

[124] 'The Editor's Tablets', *East India United Service Journal*, 5(1833): 177

[125] Bentinck, Minute on Military Policy, 13 March 1835, *Correspondence*, II, 1447

[126] Bentinck to Ravenshaw, 8 July 1832, *Correspondence*, II, 850-51

[127] OIOC, Bentinck to Court, 9 Aug 1834, L/MIL/5/401/196

[128] Comparison of troop distribution based on statistics for 1830 taken from S.C. on the East India Company, PP. 13(1831/32) and for 1835, Bentinck, Memo on Military Policy, 28 Feb 1835, *Correspondence*, II, 1434

[129] Nottingham, Bentinck to Ravenshaw, 17 Nov 1832, PwJf 2685

[130] Nottingham, Paget to Bentinck, 29 Nov 1827, PwJf 2863/iv

[131] A good indication of Bentinck's anxiety for the morale and discipline of the sepoy corps is evident in his discussions prior to the implementation of his famous prohibition against *sati*. Before the legislation was introduced, Bentinck carefully canvassed regimental commanders as to how they suspected their high caste recruits would react to what might be construed as British interference with their religions and customs. Bentinck, Minute on *Sati*, 8 Nov 1829, *Correspondence*, I, 342. Significantly, only five of the forty-two officers he polled came out strongly against the abolition on the grounds that it might antagonize Indian sepoys.

[132] [An Old Indian]. 'The Indian Army,' *United Services Journal*. 18(1835): 310

[133] Paget to Wynn, 10 May 1826, Wellington, *Dispatches*, III, 330

[134] [W.W.]. 'Considerations on the Native Army and the General Defence of India,' *United Services Journal*. 7(1831): 2-3; [add more titles]

[135] Whittingham to Bentinck, 15 Dec 1832, *Correspondence*, I, 971

[136] Bentinck, Minute on Military Policy, 13 March 1835, *Correspondence*, II, 1450

[137] Whittingham, *A Memoir of the Services of Lieutenant-General Sir Samuel Ford Whittingham*, 393

[138] OIOC, Amherst, minute on military expenses, 5 Feb 1827, L/MIL/5/398/175

[139] S.C. on the East India Company, PP, 13(1831/32): 195

[140] S.C. on the East India Company, PP, 13(1831/32): 195

[141] Nicolls to Taylor, 10 Nov 1827, *Dispatches*, IV, 147

[142] S.C. on the East India Company, PP, 13(1831/32)

[143] OIOC, General Order of the Governor-General in Council, 24 Feb 1835, L/MIL/5/417(341). Whittingham was a strong advocate of abolition. See Whittingham to Bentinck, 24 June 1834, *Correspondence*, II, 1310

[144] Most of the replies to Bentinck's circular survive in the Bentinck papers in

Nottingham and typescript copies are available in the OIOC. Examples of those who argued that prohibition would not have much of an impact on the army, though some did fear the consequences among the broader society or doubted its efficacy, include Young to Benson, 15 Dec 1828, MSS Eur E/424/2; Lieut Col Waters to Benson, 12 Dec 1828, MSS Eur E/424/2; Lieut Col Paul to Benson, 29 Nov 1828, MSS Eur E/424/2; Major Dickson to Benson, 30 Nov 1828, MSS Eur E/424/2; Lieut Col Skinner to Benson, 3 Dec 1828, MSS Eur E/424/2 and Major Palmer to Benson, 18 Dec 1828, MSS Eur E/424/2

[145] Bentinck, Minute on Army Corporal Punishment, 16 Feb 1835, *Correspondence*, II, 1426; Evidence of William Bentinck, Report from H.M. Commissioners for Enquiring into the System of Military Punishment in the Army, PP, 22(1836): xvi and 279

[146] OIOC, General Order of the Commander-in-Chief, L/MIL/5/418(353)

[147] See for example the article 'Present Discipline of the Army,' *East India United Service Journal* 13(1835): 355-58

[148] See the minutes and memos (1835-1845) in support of its reintroduction, OIOC, L/MIL/5/417(341)

[149] [Anon], 'The Bengal Army,' *East India United Services Journal*, 5(1833): 492

[150] Jacob, *Tracts*, 4

[151] Ellenborough, 4 Dec 1829, *Political Diary*, II, 141

[152] Peter Penner and Richard Dale Maclean, eds., *The Rebel Bureaucrat: Frederick John Shore (1799-1837) as Critic of William Bentinck's India*, Delhi: Chanakya ,1983, 25 and 229-31

[153] This nickname was popular at Kanpur. OIOC, Henry Spry to Edward Spry, 20 Jan 1831, Photo Eur 308

[154] Tucker to Grant, 22 Sept 1834, Kaye, *Tucker*, 480

CONCLUSION:
THE SURVIVAL OF
THE GARRISON STATE

Anglo-Indian militarism is not a master narrative that single-handedly incorporates all the people, institutions, ideas and structures that went into the making of the British empire in India. There were simply too many actors and factors crowding on the stage. Yet it is equally apparent that the imperatives and assumptions of the army were not only paramount (in India though not in Britain), but because of its malleability, this military agenda was also capable of overlapping with other interests when necessary, provided that they were all agreed on Britain's ultimate dependence on the sword for maintaining its Indian empire. Amherst arrived in India with the intention of implementing the Court's economy drive; instead he found himself pushed into war by the strength and unity of an expatriate community of army officers and Company officials who insisted that failure to do so would be potentially fatal to the Raj. The British empire was an 'empire of opinion' in which image counted as much as reality, if not more. It was an opinion that was grounded on Britain's military reputation. Consequently, and in defiance of London's priorities, the political and military elite in India devised a political economy that took as its first priority the maintenance of an army ready to deal with any threat, internal or external or both.

There were exceptions to this privileging of the army's demands to the exclusion of other agendas. Occasionally, as with Bentinck, critics were in a position of some authority. Whig historians, anticipating that reform in India would inevitably follow on from its successful launch in Britain, latched on to William Bentinck with unseeming haste. Many of Bentinck's more spectacular initiatives and most of his rhetoric can easily lend themselves to such a conclusion. We need to bear in mind Eric Stokes' words of warning that 'colonial rule is peculiarly subject to the distortion of bureaucratic structures, which mistake the report for the bullet, the plan for action, and what one clerk says to another for history'.[1] Bentinck's experiences testify that military influences were so deeply embedded in Anglo-Indian society that dislodging them was not an easy task. There were simply too many individuals in India who were committed to the army's cause, sometimes for private reasons, sometimes because they saw no alternative. Even Bentinck was forced to concede to the strength of some of these arguments for the turbulent conditions that prevailed in early nineteenth-century India did not give grounds for complacency nor for optimism. Unlike Britain, where the fiscal-military state that had developed in response to years of continental and imperial warfare had succumbed to public demands for retrenchments, the only public opinion that counted as far as officials in India were concerned — the tiny expatriate European community — was resolutely opposed to retrenchments.[2] Any assault on expenditures threatened their income; any attack on the army's prerogatives imperilled their existence.

The persistence of a militarized state in India was assured for as long as there was a consensus that British rule could never depend for its survival upon the willing cooperation or passive acquiescence of the Indian people. It was all too apparent that while British rule was very extensive in its breadth, it lacked depth. As a result it had to be always on guard against any potential challenge.

In this vast empire, let your political economists say what they will, our power rests exclusively on the fidelity of this native army and must do so for several years to come, for the prejudices of Muhommedans and Hindoos are very strong and hitherto we have made very little impression.[3]

Pessimistic assessments such as the one quoted above were to be commonplace for much of the nineteenth century and more converts were made following the rebellion of 1857. Yet this attachment to a militarized form of rule did not necessarily preclude the possibility of the British seeking a more progressive role in India. In fact the flexibility of Anglo-Indian militarism often allowed its proponents to cohabitate quite comfortably with reformers. Only the most extreme social and economic innovators dismissed the importance of the army; others, like Bentinck, Mackenzie, and Shore, recognized that security and stability were needed prior to introducing any sweeping improvements, even though they may not have always been comfortable with this dependency. Even Dalhousie, whose reign has often been depicted as that of a reformer in a hurry (1848-54), was agreeable to having a strong army ready at a moment's notice.

Anglo-Indian militarism maintained its dominant position within colonial society in India because it not only reflected what many saw as the reality of Britain's position in India, but also because it was sufficiently porous to admit new members into its ranks. Conservatives could see in its attachment to order and authority the natural basis of society; orientalists could argue that its emphasis on military values conformed to precolonial political systems; and liberal imperialists could hope that it would ultimately pave the way for the social and economic regeneration of India by guaranteeing the stability necessary to implant new ideas and institutions. Occasionally this meant that there were profound disagreements within the administration, such as differences over what weights should be assigned to internal and external threats. Even then the question was less whether the army was necessary and more what type of army should be pursued and where it ought to be aimed. Ultimately their differences were smoothed over by the emphasis that they all placed on the army in guaranteeing the security that they all demanded to pursue their further goals. Militarism was not the sole ideological prop on which the empire depended, but it was the one that most easily and completely tied together the rest. Even 'Half Batta Ben' became a reluctant subscriber.

[1] Eric Stokes, *The Peasant and the Raj: Studies in Agrarian Society and Peasant Rebellion in Colonial India*, Cambridge: Cambridge University Press, 30
[2] Philip Harling and Peter Mandler, 'From 'Fiscal-Military State to Laissez-Faire State, 1760–1850,' *Journal of British Studies*, 32(1993): 44–70
[3] Hardinge to Walter, 17 Aug 1844, *Letters*, 30

APPENDICES

MAP 1 - Military Divisions and Garrisons in India: 1815-1835

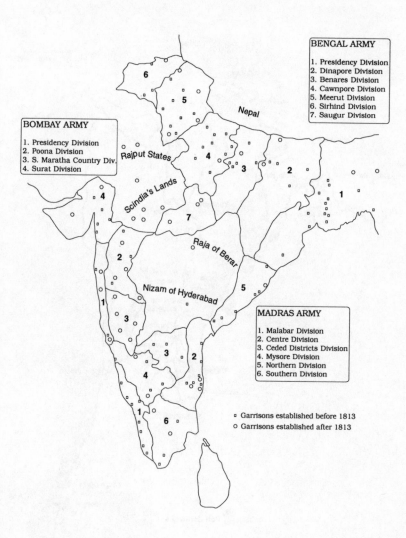

BENGAL ARMY
1. Presidency Division
2. Dinapore Division
3. Benares Division
4. Cawnpore Division
5. Meerut Division
6. Sirhind Division
7. Saugur Division

BOMBAY ARMY
1. Presidency Division
2. Poona Division
3. S. Maratha Country Div.
4. Surat Division

MADRAS ARMY
1. Malabar Division
2. Centre Division
3. Ceded Districts Division
4. Mysore Division
5. Northern Division
6. Southern Division

□ Garrisons established before 1813
○ Garrisons established after 1813

MAP 2 - The Burma War: 1824–1826

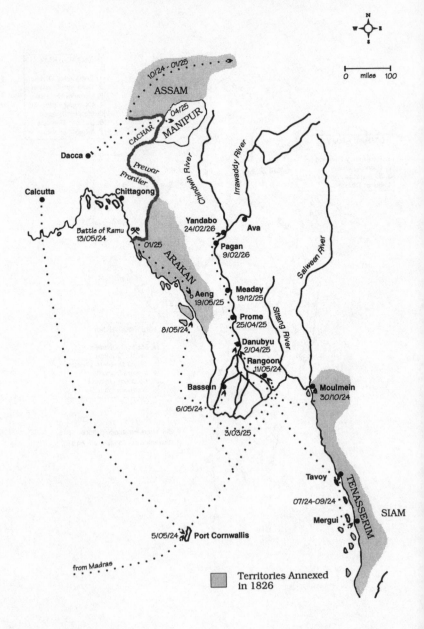

MAP 3 – The Siege of Bharatpur: December 1825 – January 1826

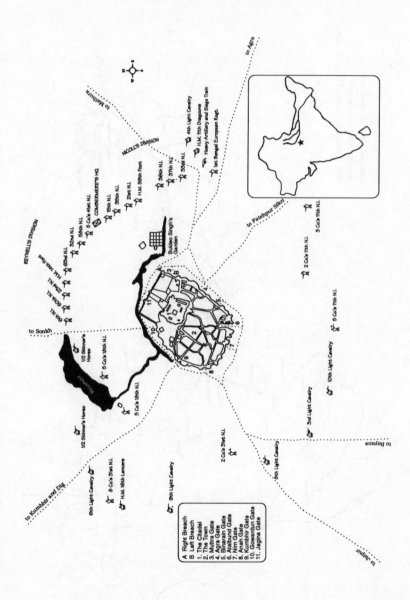

A. Right Breach
B. Left Breach
1. The Citadel
2. The Town
3. Mutra Gate
4. Agra Gate
5. Binarain Gate
6. Atalbund Gate
7. Nim Gate
8. Anah Gate
9. Kumbhir Gate
10. Gowardun Gate
11. Jagina Gate

MAP 4 - North India's Cantonments: 1815-1835

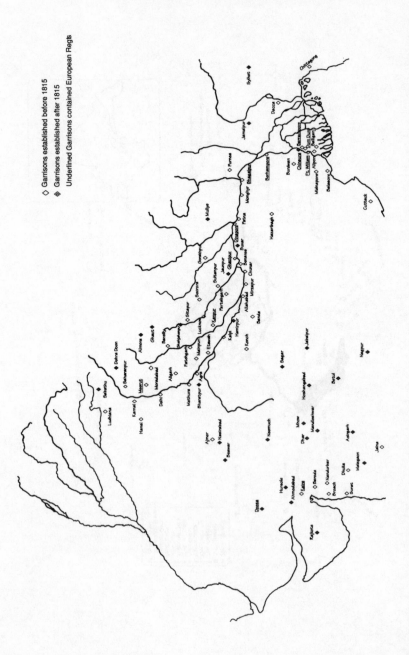

Appendix A
Convictions following Military Courts Martial:
Bengal Army, 1834-35.[1]

Crime	Europeans	Sepoys	Camp Followers
AWOL	9	0	0
Arson	1	0	0
Assault	1	0	0
Indecent Assault	1	0	0
Burglary	1	1	3
Cheating	1	0	0
Child Stealing	0	0	2
Desertion	23	2	0
Embezzlement	0	1	0
Disobedience	1	0	0
Disgraceful Conduct	0	2	0
Disorderly Conduct	2	0	0
Drunkenness	1	0	0
Fraud	0	1	0
Highway Robbery	1	0	0
Insubordination	3	0	0
Malingering	1	0	0
Manslaughter	1	0	0
Murder	1	9	2
Accessory to Murder	0	7	0
Mutinous Conduct	27	1	0
Mutiny	21	0	0
Leaving Post	4	0	0
Sleeping on Post	5	0	0
Riotous Conduct	1	0	0
Slave Dealing	0	2	0
Robbery	10	0	0
Striking an NCO	33	0	0
Theft	8	6	0
Striking an Officer	1	0	0
Shooting an NCO	1	0	0
Wounding	2	0	1
Stabbing	1	0	0
Total	**162**	**32**	**8**

[1] These figures are only for general courts martial which were the most senior military court of law. Only the most heinous crimes, namely those that could be punished with the death penalty, were tried at a general court martial. Soldiers and sepoys charged with lesser offences were tried at regimental or district courts martial; unfortunately these records do not seem to have survived anywhere. Note that these figures are for the whole of the Bengal army, or about 15,000 Europeans and approximately 100,000 sepoys. Figures are taken from William Hough, *Military Law Authorities*

Appendix B

Castes and Origins of Recruits
in the 60th Bengal Native Infantry: 1828.[2]

Company	Lands	Awadh	Other
Brahmin	143	152	0
Rajput	213	87	1
Kats	14	7	0
Guallas	29	25	0
Gosains	4	2	0
Bhats	5	3	1
Challers	10	16	0
Kurmi	19	10	0
Hulwy	2	2	0
Coysee	3	3	0
Rajbhur	2	0	0
Bunneahs	1	1	0
Burrae	1	2	0
Burragee	2	2	0
Bunce	2	2	0
Moorace	2	4	0
Mallee	2	1	0
Lohar	2	1	0
Timbalee	2	2	0
Balun	1	1	0
Soonace	1	1	0
Dheer	1	1	0
Dhanwok	3	1	0
Nawoo	1	1	0
Kahar	1	1	0
Pataw	27	20	1
Sheikhs	54	16	0
Syaids	7	5	0
Moguls	2	2	0
Christians*	10	0	0
Total	**558**	**365**	**3**

[2]OIOC, Nicolls' Diary, Jan 1831, MSS Eur F175/35.

Owing to the wide variations in spellings, as well as substantial shifts in classificatory schemes, not all the names above could be identified. The great number of clan identifications also poses a problem for analysis; Elliot noted 175 different Rajput clans in North India (Elliot, *Caste, Customs, Rites and Superstitions*, 169). However, those that are still undetermined (*challers, coysee, rajbhur, soonace, nawoo, pataw* and *chuttrar*) formed a small portion of the overall army, and were likely to have been middle or lower ranking castes. As for the rest, *Kats* likely stands for *kayasthas*, a North Indian scribal caste. *Gosains* were an ascetic community of North India and were thus viewed as relatively highly placed on the ritual hierarchy as were the less numerous *Burragee* (*bairaji*). *Bhats* were

Rajput minstrels and genealogists, Although further down the ritual hierarchy, *bunneahs* (*banias* - shopkeepers), *Hulwy* (*Halwis* - sweetmeat sellers), *Lohars* (blacksmiths), *Burrae* (*Barui* - paan growers), *tambuli* (*timbalee* - betel sellers), *dhanuk* (*dhanwok* - domestic servants), *kahar* (palanquin carriers), *bunce* (*buncus* - cheroots, hence tobaccanist), and *moorace* (same as *kachhi* - market gardeners) and *Kurmis* and *Mallee* (*Mali* - both cultivators) were viewed as clean castes. Only the *Guallas* (*Goalas*), traditionally cowherds, and the *Dheers* (*dhers* - a depressed caste from Rajasthan) were viewed as unclean. Sheiks, Syaids and Moguls were Muslim groups. Definitions of caste groupings taken from *Hobson-Jobson*; Jagindra Nath Bhattacharya, *Hindu Castes and Sects*, Calcutta: Editions India, 1896; W. Crooke, *The Tribes and Castes of North Western India*, 4 vols., reprint, Delhi: Cosmo Publications, 1974; Elliot, *Caste, Customs, Rites and Superstitions*; and H.H. Wilson, *A Glossary of Judicial and Revenue Terms*, London: W.H. Allen, 1855. I am indebted to Michael Fisher for making some suggestions as to how certain British spellings might be transliterated.

Castes and Origins of Recruits
in the 35th Bengal Native Infantry: 1820-1830.[3]

	Company Lands	Awadh	Total
Brahmins	314	516	830
Rajputs	292	480	772
Muslims	174	231	405
Gwalla (Goalas)	32	90	122
Koomee (Kurmi)	53	24	77
Kyts (kayasthas)	29	31	60
Bhat	6	10	16
Buneeal (bhuinhar)	11	6	17
Chuttrar (khattri?)	5	12	17
Other	50	62	112
Total	966	1462	2428

[3] * Only used as drummers.

Appendix C
Incidence of Corporal Punishment
in the Three Presidency Armies.[4]

	Per Regt of Bengal Cavalry	Per Regt of Bengal Infantry	Per Regt of Madras Cavalry	Per Regt of Madras Infantry	Per Regt of Bombay Cavalry	Per Regt of Bombay Infantry
Number Sentenced	6.1	7.6	15.1	23.8	61.7	36.54
Lashes Awarded	1054.5	1521.8	2984.4	5187.3	12601.7	8104.2
Sentences Carried Out	1.4	3.4	10.5	18.5	20.6	29.1
Lashes Inflicted	209.1	516.5	18.5	3588.7	7656.7	5415.2
Lashes Per Sentence	149.4	151.0	176.4	194.2	372.4	186.2
Number Discharged	43.9	96.9	64.9	84.4	93.0	109.1

Data are taken from 10 regiments of Bengal Cavalry, 72 regiments of Bengal
Infantry, 8 regiments of Madras Cavalry, 52 regiments of Madras Infantry,
3 regiments of Bombay Cavalry and 26 regiments of Bombay Infantry.

Appendix D
**Sepoy Backgrounds
for Selected Madras
Regiments, c 1825[5]**

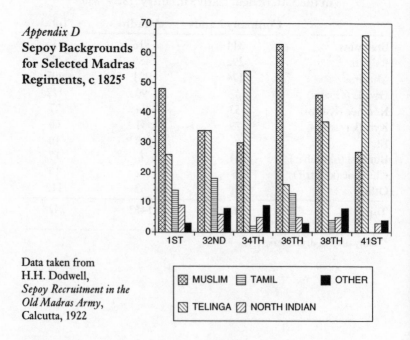

Data taken from
H.H. Dodwell,
*Sepoy Recruitment in the
Old Madras Army*,
Calcutta, 1922

⊠ MUSLIM ▤ TAMIL ■ OTHER

◨ TELINGA ▨ NORTH INDIAN

---

[4] OIOC, Nicolls' Diary, Jan 1831, MSS Eur F175/35
[5] 'Report from H.M. Commissioners for Enquiring into the State of Military
Punishments in the Army', *Parliamentary Papers*, 22(1836): 285

Appendix E

**Sepoy Backgrounds by Caste and by Region
in the Bombay Army, c 1828.[6]**

Caste	Number	Region	Number
Brahmin	190	Arabia	7
Hindus	22171	Mysore	29
Muslims	3245	Goa	26
Christians	276	Bombay	129
Parwari (dhers)[a]	4666	Konkan	11939
Jews	278	Deccan	2453
Moochees	399	Gujerat	665
Rajputs	83	Cutch	4
Soorhy	1	Kathiawar	3
Seedee (Abbysinians)	3	Malwa	57
		Malabar	780
		Hindustan	10630
		Madras	225
		Bengal	3905
		Carnatic	460
Total	**31312**	**Total**	**31312**

Appendix F
**Bengal Revenues:
1814 - 1831[7]**

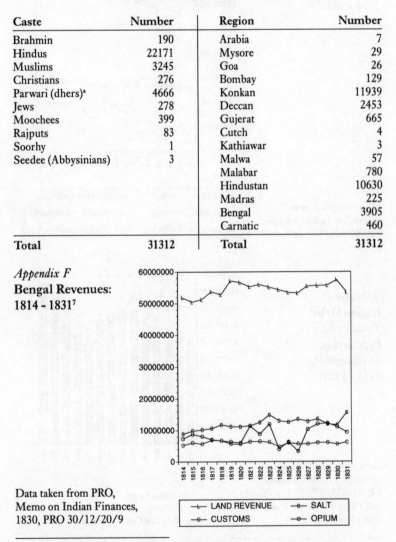

LAND REVENUE   SALT
CUSTOMS   OPIUM

Data taken from PRO,
Memo on Indian Finances,
1830, PRO 30/12/20/9

[6] OIOC, Colonel Frederick, Memo on Bombay Recruits, MSS Eur D 765/3
[a] James Grant Duff equates parwaris with dhers, Evidence of James Grant Duff,
S.C. on the East India Company, PP, 13(1831/32): 484
[7] PRO, Ellenborough Papers, Memo on Indian Finances, 1830, PRO 30/12/20/9

Appendix G
**Indian Revenues
and Expenditures:
1815 - 1829[8]**

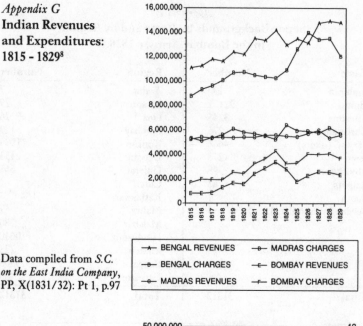

Data compiled from *S.C.
on the East India Company*,
PP, X(1831/32): Pt 1, p.97

Appendix H
**Indian Debt:
Totals and as a
Percentage
of Revenues:
1815 - 1829[9]**

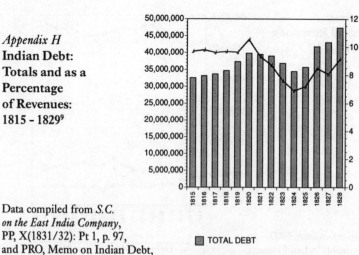

Data compiled from *S.C.
on the East India Company*,
PP, X(1831/32): Pt 1, p. 97,
and PRO, Memo on Indian Debt,
1830, PRO 30/12/31/1

▨ TOTAL DEBT

╼ INTEREST AS A % OF GROSS REVENUES

---

[8]S.C. on the East India Company, PP, 10(1831/32): Pt. 1, 96-7
[9]Data compiled from: PRO, Ellenborough Papers, Memo on Indian Debt,
(?1830), Pro 30/12/31/1 and S.C. on the East India Company, PP, 10(1831/32):
Pt. 1, 97

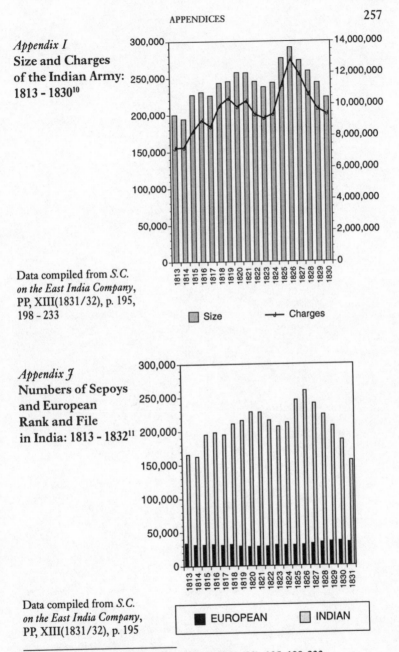

Appendix I
Size and Charges of the Indian Army: 1813 - 1830[10]

Data compiled from *S.C. on the East India Company*, PP, XIII(1831/32), p. 195, 198 - 233

☐ Size   —+— Charges

Appendix J
Numbers of Sepoys and European Rank and File in India: 1813 - 1832[11]

Data compiled from *S.C. on the East India Company*, PP, XIII(1831/32), p. 195

■ EUROPEAN   ☐ INDIAN

---

[10] S.C. on the East Indian Company, PP, 13(1831/32): 195, 198-233
[11] S.C. on the East Indian Company, PP, 13(1831/32): 95

BIBLIOGRAPHY

PRIVATE PAPERS

BRITISH LIBRARY
   Lt. Col. Blackwell, Add MS 39811–39812
   William Huskisson, Add MS 38734–38770
   Robert Banks Jenkinson, Earl of Liverpool, Add MS 38110–38489
   John Parker, Earl of Morley, Add MS 48218–48252
   Robert Peel, Add MS 40181–40267
   George Frederick Robinson, Viscount Goderich, Add MS 40862–
      40880
   Reverend Thomas Streatfield, Add MS 33929, 34103
   Henry Temple, Viscount Palmerston, Add MS 48419–48420
   Richard Wellesley, Marquess Wellesley, Add MS 12564–13915,
      37274–37318, 37414–37416
   Charles Watkin Williams Wynn, Loan 72
   Colonel Young, Add MS 38518
CHESTER CITY RECORD OFFICE
   Stapleton Cotton, Viscount Combermere
ORIENTAL AND INDIA OFFICE COLLECTIONS
[BRITISH LIBRARY]
   John Adam, MSS Eur F109
   William Pitt Amherst, Earl Amherst, MSS Eur F140
   William Bentinck, MSS Eur E424
   Sergeant George Carter, MSS Eur E262
   Francis Henry Dawkins, MSS Eur D290
   Mountstuart Elphinstone, MSS Eur F89
   William Fullerton Elphinstone, MSS Eur F88
   Gunner Luck, MSS Eur E339

259

Macnab Family, MSS Eur F206
Major General Thomas Munro, MSS Eur F151
Thomas Murray, MSS Eur B409
Major General Jasper Nicolls, MSS Eur F175
General Edward Paget, MSS Eur C385
Prinsep Family, MSS Eur C97
William Prinsep, MSS Eur D1160
George Abercromby Robinson, MSS Eur F142
Frederick John Shore, MSS Eur E307

NATIONAL ARMY MUSEUM
Stapleton Cotton, Viscount Combermere, Acc 7203-7225
Lieut. Col. Pennycuik, Acc 7604-7609
Notebook on Burma War, author unknown, Acc 6807/337

NATIONAL LIBRARY OF SCOTLAND
Arbuthnot and Co., Acc 2839
Gilbert Elliot, Earl of Minto, NLS 11721
General Thomas Hislop, NLS 13111-13128
Kelso Manuscripts, NLS 489
Henry Mackenzie, NLS 6362-6402

NATIONAL LIBRARY OF WALES
Charles Watkin Williams Wynn, Coed-y-maen, Aston Hall,
NLW 10798-10806, 4812-4818

NORTH YORKSHIRE RECORD OFFICE
Henry Havelock

NOTTINGHAM UNIVERSITY ARCHIVES
Henry Pelham-Clinton, Duke of Newcastle, NeC
Portland Papers, PwJf

PUBLIC RECORD OFFICE
Charles Abbot, Baron Colchester, PRO 30/9
Edward Law, Earl of Ellenborough, PRO 30/12

SCOTTISH RECORD OFFICE
Bell of Hunthill, GD 1/420/47
Henry Dundas and Robert Dundas, Viscount Melville, GD 51

SCOTTISH UNITED SERVICE INSTITUTE
General Archibald Campbell

SOMERSET RECORD OFFICE
Doveton Family

SOUTHAMPTON UNIVERSITY ARCHIVES
Aurthur Wellesley, Duke of Wellington, WP

UNPUBLISHED CORRESPONDENCE, MINUTES AND CONSULTATIONS

ORIENTAL AND INDIA OFFICE COLLECTIONS [BRITISH LIBRARY]

Court of Directors Minutes	B
Correspondence between London and India	E/4
Board of Control	F
Home Miscellaneous	H/MISC
Accountant General	L/AG
Economic	L/E
Financial	L/F
Military	L/MIL
Parliamentary	L/Parl
Political and Secret	L/PS
Proceedings of Presidency Councils	P

PUBLIC RECORD OFFICE

Admiralty	Adm
Colonial Office	CO
War Office	WO

BIBLIOGRAPHICAL ESSAY

Listed below is a selection of works on the institutions and workings of British imperialism in early nineteenth-century India, organized roughly so as to parallel the chapters in this book. Most of these are recent monographs and surveys; some articles have been included, as have the more helpful contemporary published works. Further references can be found in the footnotes.

I India and British Imperialism

The debates over what prompted British activities in India and the extent to which such activities affected Indian society show no sign of letting up. The classic work on this topic and still useful after many years of service is Holden Furber, *John Company at Work*, Cambridge, Mass.: Harvard University Press, 1951. The late Holden Furber broke free from a tradition of seeking an explanation for imperialism in the high politics of the era, including strategic, constitutional and administrative details, and looked instead at the role of capital in pushing and configuring eighteenth-century imperialism. Furber's position, which avoided the excesses of crude economic determinism, was to prompt further studies of this relationship between metropolitan and peripheral economies and societies. Debates since then have tended to cluster along two axes: whether the driving force for imperial expansion was located in India or in Britain, and the extent to which the British were able to reshape consciously or unconsciously the social, economic and political structures and values of India. With respect to locating the source of imperialism, the case for a peripheral explanation is put forth in C.A. Bayly, *Indian Society and the Making of the British Empire, 1770-1870: The New Cambridge History of India; II.1*, Cambridge: Cambridge University Press, 1988, P.J. Marshall, 'British Expansion in India in the Eighteenth-century: A Historical Revision,' *History*, 60(1975): 28-43, and P.J. Marshall, *Bengal: the British Bridgehead, Eastern India 1740-1828: The New Cambridge History of India; II.2*, Cambridge: Cambridge University Press, 1988. While these works do not entirely dismiss metropolitan pressures, they propose that the timing, direction and framework of colonial rule was dictated more by what was actually happening in India, and stress the important roles played by India's political, military, commercial and financial entrepreneurs in constraining British agents in India. Similar arguments have been advanced by David Washbrook in recent articles, though Washbrook plants his analysis within a more explicitly economic context. David Washbrook, 'Progress and Problems: South Asian Social and Economic History, c.1720-1860,' *Modern Asian Studies*, 12(1988): 57-96. Washbrook takes an even broader theoretical position in his 'South Asia, the World System, and World Capitalism,' *Journal of Asian Studies*, 49(1990): 479-508; here it is Immanuel Wallerstein's explanation of world capitalism (the domination by the core over the periphery and semi-periphery, including India) that is challenged.

The case for the metropolitan origins of British imperialism in India as well as elsewhere has been made most recently by P.J. Cain and A.G. Hopkins, *British Imperialism; Innovation and Expansion, 1688-1914*, Harlow: Longman, 1993. Grounding themselves in what they earlier identified as 'gentlemanly capitalism' (an alliance of Britain's political, financial and service elites), Cain and Hopkins insist that while what happened on the periphery had an important influence on the forms and institutions that imperial rule took, the ultimate source of imperialism lay at home in Britain, and more particularly London and the home counties. They also challenge traditional economic arguments that rest on industrial capitalism or a simple definition of mercantilism. Vigorous retorts to 'gentlemanly capitalism' can be found in Andrew Porter, 'Gentlemanly Capitalism' and Empire: the British Experiences since 1750?' *Journal of Imperial and Commonwealth*

History, 18(1990): 265-95, and M.J. Daunton, 'Gentlemanly Capitalism' and British Industry, 1820-1914,' *Past and Present*, 122(1989): 119-58. Porter questions both the emphasis on the metropole and the focus on economic forces while Daunton queries the membership rolls of the 'gentlemanly capitalists'. Such reservations notwithstanding, this re-assertion of the capacity of metropolitan interests to press successfully on the periphery has lately gained some converts. Bayly, in his *Imperial Meridian; the British Empire and the World, 1780-1930*, Harlow: Longman, 1989, has sought to reconcile metropole and periphery by demonstrating how the events of the late eighteenth century encouraged the convergence of the two streams. Meanwhile, voices can still be heard pushing the claims of aggressive mercantilism, see for example, Mark T. Berger, 'Review Essay: from Commerce to Conquest: the Dynamics of British Mercantile Imperialism in Eighteenth-century Bengal, and the Foundation of the British Indian Empire,' *Bulletin of Concerned Asian Scholars*, 22(1990): 44-62. Claims that the metropole exerted a powerful if sometimes indirect influence have been bolstered by recent works in British history. Linda Colley, *Britons; Forging the Nation, 1707-1837*, New Haven: Yale University Press, 1992, shows how British political culture became more assertive, expansive and militaristic as a consequence of eighteenth-century struggles in Europe. John Brewer's detailed study of the British state through the long eighteenth century has indicated clearly that the consequence of such a political culture was a state that was not only more willing to turn to war when necessary, but was also much better equipped to carry it through, largely because Britain had become in his words a 'fiscal military state'. John Brewer, *The Sinews of Power: War, Money and the English State, 1688-1783*, London: Allen and Unwin, 1989. See also P.K. O'Brien, 'Public Finance in the Wars with France, 1793-1815,' in H.T. Dickinson, ed., *Britain and the French Revolution*, London: Macmillan, 1989. The contributors to Lawrence Stone, ed., *An Imperial State at War; Britain from 1689-1815*, London: Routledge, 1993 have affirmed and elaborated on the themes identified by Colley, Brewer and O'Brien. It is clear that domestic values and institutions were ideally suited to a growing empire. Yet it has been suggested that a state that was so tightly fixed on war and preparing for war could not remain so for long given the transformations that were occurring in Britain's political and economic life. See Philip Harling and Peter Mandler, 'From 'Fiscal Military' State to Laissez-Faire State, 1760-1850,' *Journal of British Studies*, 32(1993): 44-70. But whether the British state in India was confronted with similar pressures is questionable. In talking of fiscal-militarism, there is a peripheralist perspective that also needs to be considered; it need not have been imported from Britain. Its roots can also be traced to India; see Burton Stein, 'State Formation and Economy Reconsidered,' *Modern Asian Studies,* 19(1985): 387–413.

As to Britain's impact on India, the now outdated imperialist and nationalist arguments of the pre-independence area, that emphasized Britain's disruptive impact (for good or bad), yielded in the sixties and seventies to a near consensus over the limitations to colonial rule. These minimalists, taking their cue from such now standard works as Robert E. Frykenberg, *Guntur District, 1788-1848*, Oxford: Clarendon, 1965 and the essays of the late Eric Stokes collected in his *The Peasant and the Raj,* Cambridge: Cambridge University Press, 1979, have like Bayly and Marshall (cited above) stressed the limits to rather than the strengths of British rule. The limitations on colonial initiatives have also emerged as a central theme in volume two of the *Cambridge Economic History of India, c.1757-1970,* Dharma Kumar, ed., Cambridge: Cambridge University Press, 1983. Of late the minimalists have been challenged by those who see Indian society as vulnerable to British penetration, though not necessarily in a simple economic form. In their work on resistance to colonial rule the historians who have collectively formed the Subaltern school have re-emphasized British social, political and economic hegemony so as to account for the depth of resistance that they have uncovered. Their perspective and methodology is clearly set out in Ranajit Guha, *Elementary Aspects of Peasant Insurgency in Colonial India,* New Delhi: Oxford University Press, 1983, and their findings can be found in Ranajit Guha, ed., *Subaltern Studies: Writings on South Asian History and Society,* vols. 1-7, New Delhi: Oxford University Press, 1982-1992. Post-orientalist scholarship has also entered the fray. By looking at the ways in which India was understood and thereafter controlled, a form of intellectual hegemony ('orientalism') has been identified that penetrated Indian society down to its roots and was to have far-reaching consequences in such areas as 'caste' and 'communalism'. Ronald Inden in his *Imagining India,* Oxford: Blackwell, 1990, is one of the chief exponents of this school. An abridged version of his analysis is presented in 'Orientalist Constructions of India,' *Modern Asian Studies,* 20(1986): 401–46. Yet not all are convinced that orientalism was simply the consequence of a European mastery of and monopoly over information about India, and that consequently Indians were powerless in the face of this intellectual juggernaut. See for example David Washbrook's illustration of the degree to which the categorization and classification of South Indian society was partly determined by local struggles for power and influence, 'Economic Depression and the Making of 'Traditional' Society in Colonial India, 1820-1855,' *Transactions of the Royal Historical Society,* 6th ser., 3(1993): 237-64.

II The structure of the Company Raj

With the decline in the 1950s and early 60s of traditional politically or constitutionally centred history, studies of the organization and administration of the East India Company became unfashionable. This decade did, however, see the publication of C.H. Philips' magisterial study of the East India Company and domestic British politics: *The East India Company, 1784-1834*, Manchester University Press, 1961. For the earlier and more rambunctious period of Company–State relations, H. Bowen, *Revenue and Reform: the Indian Problem in British Politics, 1757-1773*, Cambridge: Cambridge University Press, 1991, is essential reading. Philips' work on the Company in Britain is complemented by B.B. Misra's investigations of the Company's administrative development in India: *The Central Administration of the East India Company, 1773-1834*, Manchester: Manchester University Press, 1959. Just recently a return to Company politics has been signalled by Philip Lawson's *The East India Company, a History*, Harlow: Longman, 1993. Lawson's study surveys the entire scope of Company activities, though it is more sharply aimed at the Company's activities in London. The importance and function of patronage within the Company's operations is considered in J.M. Bourne, *Patronage and Society in Nineteenth Century England*, London: Arnold, 1986.

Given this paucity of political and administrative histories for the period, primary sources have to be consulted. For sheer amount of readily-accessible statistics and documents, nothing can beat the reports of the Select Committee of the House of Commons on the Affairs of the East India Company, *Parliamentary Papers*, (1831-32), 6 vols. The then secretary of the East India Company, Peter Auber, also published a series of useful guides to the Company's administrative machinery: *An Analysis of the Constitution of the East India Company*, London: Kingsbury, Parbury and Allen, 1826, *Rise and Progress of the British Power in India*, 2 vols. London: W.H. Allen, 1837, and *Supplement to an Analysis of the Constitution of the East India Company*, London: Parbury and Allen, 1828. Equally important are the memoirs of Henry St. George Tucker, an important member of the Court of Directors through the 1820s and 1830s. In addition to Tucker's *Memorials of Indian Government*, J.W. Kaye, ed., London: Bentley, 1853, his letters and correspondence were later collected and edited by J.W. Kaye, *The Life and Correspondence of Henry St. George Tucker*, London: Bentley, 1854. And finally Kaye, who was himself later to become secretary in the political department in London, wrote the useful if triumphalist, *The Administration of the East India Company; a History of Human Progress*, 2nd ed., London:

Bentley, 1853.

III Ideologies of the Company Raj

The traditional perspective on British attitudes towards India took its cue from the many pamphlets, tracts and speeches published or uttered by British statesmen, missionaries and publicists. The alleged transformation of British attitudes towards India in the aftermath of the Napoleonic Wars has been variously attributed to a new spirit of liberalism, the presence of missionaries, or the increasing arrogance of the British. An example of such studies, and one that plays up the growth of a liberal humanitarian perspective, is George D. Bearce, *British Attitudes towards India, 1784-1858,* Oxford: Oxford University Press, 1961. The compatibility of such attitudes with authoritarian forms of rule has been explained in Eric Stokes, *The English Utilitarians and India,* Oxford: Oxford University Press, 1959. Criticisms from many vantage points have long been levelled against this tradition of analysis, principally on the grounds that the comments and writings that are used as examples are neither examined critically, nor are they representative, nor do the values contained within them square up to Indian realities. A critical rereading of the texts upon which such studies were based, and which insists on drawing out their 'orientalist' proclivities, has been set in motion by scholars such as Ronald Inden (cited above) and Gyan Prakash, 'Writing Post-Orientalist Histories of the Third World: Perspectives from Indian Historiography,' *Comparative Studies in Society and History,* 32(1990): 383-409. The role of the missionaries, while certainly important in forming domestic opinions of India, has recently been shown to have had far less immediate and direct impact on policy in India. See Penelope Carson. 'An Imperial Dilemma: the Propagation of Christianity in Early Colonial India,' *Journal of Imperial and Commonwealth History,* 18(1990): 169-90. The positive and progressive values that were often implied to have been at the heart of Britain's imperial mission have also had to contend with growing evidence of the extent to which Indian society actively resisted colonial rule, and the degree to which the British depended on coercion to subdue such challenges. The Subaltern school has been at the forefront of this revision, but there were some who preceded them. Forty years ago S.B. Chaudhuri wrote *Civil Disturbances during British Rule in India, 1765-1857,* Calcutta: World Press, 1955, in which he provided solid evidence of the long history of resistance. How the British attempted to delude themselves that things were actually different is the topic of Francis Hutchins' short but incisive study, *The Illusion of Permanence; British*

Imperialism in India, Princeton: Princeton University Press, 1967. A useful survey of recent conclusions as to the extent to which Indians actively and passively sought to subvert imperial rule can be found in Sandria B. Freitag, 'Crime in the Social Order of Colonial North India,' *Modern Asian Studies,* 25(1991): 227-61.

By cutting themselves off from Indian society, the Anglo-Indian community became more susceptible to the patriotic and chauvinistic cultural currents then becoming more common in Britain. P.J. Marshall has shown that the British in India effectively isolated themselves from their Indian surroundings in 'British Immigration into India in the Nineteenth Century,' *European Expansion and Migration,* P. Emmer and M. Mörner, eds. Leiden: Brill, 1992; see also his 'Cornwallis Triumphant': War in India and the British Public in the Late Eighteenth-century,' *War, Strategy, and International Politics; Essays in Honour of Sir Michael Howard,* Lawrence Freedman, Paul Hayes and Robert O'Neill, eds., Oxford: Clarendon, 1992. The prime exemplar of this vigorous assertion of a conservative British patriotism in the aftermath of the Napoleonic Wars was the Marquess of Hastings. Unfortunately there is no recent biography of Hastings nor have his private papers survived intact and in one place. However, Richard Bingle wrote an unpublished doctoral dissertation on Hastings and has since published several articles on Hastings' style of leadership and the consequences for India. See his 'The Governor-generalship of the Marquess of Hastings, 1813-1823, with special reference to the Secret Committee and Secretariat, the Residents with Native States, Military Policy and the Transactions of the Palmer Company.' (D.Phil diss., Oxford University, 1964), and his essays: 'The Decline of the Marquess of Hastings,' *Essays in Indian History in Honour of Cuthbert Collin Davies,* Donovan Williams and E. Daniel Potts, eds., New York: Asia Publishing House, 1973, and 'The Governor-General, the Bengal Council and the Civil Service, 1800-1835,' *Rule, Protest, Identity: Aspects of Modern South Asia,* Peter Robb and David Taylor, eds., London: Curzon Press, 1978. There are also several important nineteenth-century collections of material on Hastings: Francis Rawdon, Marquess of Hastings, *The Private Journal of the Marquess of Hastings,* Marchioness of Bute, ed., 2nd ed., 2 vols., London: Saunders and Otley, 1858. Henry Thoby Prinsep, *History of the Political and Military Transactions in India during the Administration of the Marquess of Hastings, 1813-1823,* 2 vols. 1825. Reprint. Dublin: Irish University Press, 1972. Henry Toby Prinsep, *A Narrative of the Political and Military Transactions of British India, under the Administration of the Marquess of Hastings, 1813-1818,* London: John Murray, 1820.

Further examples of the prevailing ideologies together with the assumptions that bolstered them can be found in the writings and biographies of those members of the 'Wellesley Kindergarten' who rose to positions of authority in this period. Thomas Munro has had a considerable degree of attention with two recent biographies as well as two nineteenth century hagiographies. The most recent is Burton Stein, *Thomas Munro: the Origins of the Colonial State and his Vision of Empire*, New Delhi: Oxford University Press, 1990. Stein's reading of Munro is at odds with that produced by an earlier biographer, Thomas H. Beaglehole, who stressed the romantic and conservative well-springs of Munro's imperial style, *Thomas Munro and the Development of Administrative Policy in Madras, 1792-1818*, Cambridge: Cambridge University Press, 1960. Nineteenth-century studies include Alexander J. Arbuthnot, *Major General Sir Thomas Munro*, 2 vols., London: Kegan Paul, 1881, and George R. Gleig, *The Life of Major General Sir Thomas Munro*, 3 vols., London: Colburn and Bentley, 1830. John Malcolm has yet to find his modern biographer, but there is a nineteenth-century life available as well as Malcolm's own prolific writings: John William Kaye, *The Life and Correspondence of Major General Sir John Malcolm*, 2 vols., London: Smith, Elder and Co., 1856, Major General Sir John Malcolm, *The Government of India*, London: John Murray, 1833, *A Memoir of Central India*, 2 vols., 1823. Reprint. New Delhi: Sagar Publications, 1970, and *The Political History of India from 1784 to 1823*, 2 vols., London: John Murray, 1826. For Metcalfe, biographies by Panigrahi and Thompson are accompanied by two nineteenth-century studies. D.N. Panigrahi, *Charles Metcalfe in India; Ideas and Administration, 1806-1835*, New Delhi: Munshiram Manoharlal, 1968. Edward Thompson, *The Life of Charles, Lord Metcalfe*, London: Faber and Faber, 1937. John William Kaye, *The Life and Correspondence of Lord Metcalfe*, 2 vols., London: Smith, Elder and Co., 1858, and *Selections from the Papers of Lord Metcalfe*, London: Smith, Elder and Co., 1855.

Mountstuart Elphinstone has also been noticed in the nineteenth and twentieth centuries: R.D. Chokesey, *Mountstuart Elphinstone*, Bombay: Popular Prakashan, 1971 and T.E. Colebrooke, ed., *Life of the Honourable Mountstuart Elphinstone*, 2 vols., London: John Murray, 1884. For John Adam, there is nothing beyond Charles Lushington's *A Short Notice of the Official Career and Private Character of the Late John Adam*, Calcutta: privately printed, 1825. The impact of Munro's, Metcalfe's, Elphinstone's and Malcolm's views on India on policy-making in London has been reevaluated by Lynn Zastoupil in his study of John Stuart Mill (*John Stuart Mill and India*, Stanford: Stanford University Press, 1994). An alternative reading of these individuals is offered by Martha McLaren, 'From Analysis to Prescription: Scottish Concepts of Asian Despotism in Early-Nineteenth-century British India,' *International History Review*, 15(1993): 469-501. McLaren argues that the views propounded by Munro, Malcolm and Elphinstone were ultimately derived from the sociological positions taken by the Scottish Enlightenment and not because of any pragmatic response to Indian conditions. I have considered McLaren's positions more thoroughly in 'Soldiers, Scholars, and the Scottish Enlightenment: Militarism in Early Nineteenth-Century India,' *International History Review*, 16(1994): 441-65.

The role played by political agents and residents in Britain's relations with neighbouring states has been dealt with by Michael Fisher: 'British Expansion in North India: the Role of the Resident in Awadh,' *Indian Economic and Social History Review*, 18(1981): 69-82, and *Indirect Rule in India; Residents and the Residency System, 1764-1857*, New Delhi: Oxford University Press, 1991. Contemporary collections that are particularly useful in examining these relationships include B.S. Jones, *Papers Relative to the Progress of British Power in India*, London: np, 1832, and John Sutherland, *Sketch of the Relations subsisting between the British Government and the Different Native States*, Calcutta: np, 1837.

IV The military and British imperialism in India

Until recently the military and strategic history of British India has been largely presented in terms of India's strategic position or as self-contained narratives of the major military campaigns in which Indian and British-Indian armies served. Regarding the former, it is the origins of the 'great game' that have loomed largest. Edward Ingram's recently-completed trilogy on this topic emphasizes the inseparability of India from Britain's continental strategies, and explores in great depth the complex interplay between them: *Britain's Persian Connection, 1798-1828: Prelude to the Great Game in Asia*, Oxford: Clarendon, 1993, *The Beginnings of the Great Game in Asia, 1828-1834*, Oxford: Clarendon Press, 1979, *Commitment to Empire; Prophecies of the Great Game in Asia, 1797-1800*, Oxford: Clarendon Press, 1981. Some of his essays on related topics can be found in his *In Defence of British India: Great Britain in the Middle East, 1775-1842*, London: Cass, 1984. In contrast to Ingram's exposure of the interconnectedness of European and Imperial politics, Malcolm Yapp's work on the great game has laid special stress on the 'man on the spot', arguing that the 'great game' was largely played out to satisfy the professional and personal agendas of officials astride the frontier: *Strategies of British India; Britain, Iran and Afghanistan, 1798-1850,* Oxford: Clarendon Press, 1980. Yapp also places greater weight than Ingram does on fears for India's internal security in great gamesmanship — an abridged version of this argument can be found in his 'British Perceptions of the Russian Threat to India,' *Modern Asian Studies,* 21(1987): 647-75. Maritime aspects of Britain's empire in Asia have been left largely untouched, though there is a wealth of material contained in Gerald S. Graham, *Great Britain in the Indian Ocean: a Study of Maritime Enterprise, 1810-1850,* Oxford: Clarendon Press, 1967.

With only a few exceptions, the history of military operations in India has not proceeded very far in the last century. Fortescue's useful if dated and polemical history of the British Army contains fairly reliable narratives of the major campaigns, though his assessments of the causes as well as judgments of Britain's opponents must be read with caution; J.W. Fortescue, *A History of the British Army; Vol. XI, 1815-1838,* London: Macmillan, 1923. One of the best recent campaign studies, and one that is built on the systematic use of primary sources, is John Pemble, *The Invasion of Nepal; John Company at Work,* Oxford: Clarendon Press, 1971. Pemble's forays into the earlier campaigns against the Marathas has suggested to him that Indian armies were weakened in some cases by the adoption of western techniques; John Pemble, 'Resources and Techniques in the Second Maratha War,' *Historical Journal,* 19(1976): 375-404. There have been some detractors to his arguments though, see for example Randolph Cooper, 'Wellington and the Marathas in 1803,' *International History Review,* 11(1989): 31-8.

A great deal of factual and anecdotal information on the Indian army can be found in Roger Beaumont, *Sword of the Raj; the British Army in India, 1747-1947,* Indianapolis: Bobbs-Merrill, 1977, and T.A. Heathcote, *The Indian Army; the Garrison of British Imperial India, 1822-1922,* Newton Abbot: David & Charles, 1974. Neither of these studies provides much in the way of analysis. A more complete picture of the Indian army over the centuries emerges from Philip Mason, *A Matter of Honour; an Account of the Indian Army, its Officers and Men,* London: Penguin, 1974, but Mason's work is not based on primary research, nor has it managed to break free from liberal paternalism. There is not yet anything to compare with Edward Spiers' study of the British army in this period: *The Army and Society, 1815-1914,* London: Longman, 1980. Yet there are several important more specialized studies. Eighteenth-century tensions between army officers and their nominal superiors in London have been detailed in Raymond A. Callahan, *The East India Company and Army Reform, 1783-1795,* Cambridge,

Mass.: Harvard University Press, 1972, and in Gerald Bryant, 'Officers of the East India Company's Army in the Days of Clive and Hastings,' *Journal of Imperial and Commonwealth History*, 6(1977-78): 203-27; while Douglas M. Peers has examined the continuation of this conflict into the early nineteenth century in 'Between Mars and Mammon: the East India Company and Efforts to Reform its Army, 1796-1832,' *Historical Journal*, 33(1990): 385-401. The backgrounds of officers serving in India in the nineteenth-century have been analysed in P.E. Razzell, 'Social Origins of Officers in the Indian and British Home Armies, 1758-1960,' *British Journal of Sociology*, 14(1963): 102-39, while the early history of the Company's European rank and file has been looked at by Arthur Gilbert in 'Recruitment and Reform in the East India Company Army, 1760-1800,' *Journal of British Studies*, 15(1975): 89-111. Lorenzo Crowell has recently published two articles that deal with the question of measuring professionalisation and the all-important but too often overlooked issue of logistics: 'Military Professionalism in a Colonial Context: the Madras Army, circa 1832.' *Modern Asian Studies*, 24(1990): 249-273, and 'Logistics in the Madras Army circa 1830,' *War & Society*, 10(1992): 1-33

Sepoy recruitment, at least for the period prior to 1857, is still largely *terra incognito*. Prior to 1857 there is very little to work from. J.A. De Moor, 'Contrasting Communities: Asian Soldiers of the Dutch and British Armies in the Nineteenth-century,' *India and Indonesia from the 1830s to 1914*, Mushiral Hasan and D.H. Evans, eds., Leiden: Brill, 1987 is a useful introduction to research work in this area that has the added advantage of situating the sepoys within a broader comparative study of colonial armies, but it is more of an overview than a detailed enquiry. For the period after 1860, David Omissi's *The Sepoy and the Raj*, London: Macmillan, 1994 provides a great deal of information and analysis on just who were the martial races to which the British were increasingly attracted. In *Lions of the Punjab; Culture in the Making*, Berkeley: University of California Press, 1985, Richard Fox has demonstrated that 'martial races', in this case the Sikhs, came about when a society conformed to British racialist beliefs in an attempt to extract social, economic and political benefits from the colonial relationship. Lionel Caplan, "Bravest of the Brave': Representations of 'The Gurkha' in British Military Writings,' *Modern Asian Studies*, 25(1991): 571-598, will hopefully encourage more historians to re-examine the essentially nineteenth-century terms through which we still describe Indian soldiers. A more narrowly focused appreciation of the 'essentializing' nature of military discourse can be found in my treatment of relations between Bengal sepoys and their European offices in the 1820s, Douglas M. Peers, 'The

Habitual Nobility of Being': British Officers and the Social Construction of the Bengal Army in the Early Nineteenth-century,' *Modern Asian Studies*, 25(1991): 545-70. Aside from a shortage of sources on the sepoys themselves, historians working on the sepoys cannot evade the conundrums posed by the ambiguous nature of caste. For a discussion on how 'caste' came to contain a wide range of assumptions, including some contradictory ones, see Rashmi Pant, 'The Cognitive Status of Caste in Colonial Ethnography: a Review of Some Literature on the NorthWest Provinces and Oudh,' *Indian Economic and Social History Review*, 24(1987): 145-162. Amiya Barat, *The Bengal Native Infantry: its Organization and Discipline, 1796-1852*, Calcutta: Mukhopadhyay, 1962, is very useful on the internal order and organization of sepoy regiments in Bengal, but does not provide a clear picture as to the origins of their recruits. Nor is there much on this question in the standard nineteenth-century history of the Bengal army, Arthur Broome, *History of the Rise and Progress of the Bengal Army*, Calcutta: W. Thacker, 1851. Although D.H.A. Kolff's study, *Naukar, Rajput and Sepoy; the Ethnohistory of the Military Labour Market in Hindustan, 1450-1850*, Cambridge: Cambridge University Press, 1990, does not really deal as completely with the colonial period as the title might otherwise suggest, he does nevertheless suggest that in talking of high caste recruits, we must first look at how martial communities were set up prior to the British arrival. More information is available on recruits to the Madras army thanks to Henry Dodwell's labours earlier in this century; H.H. Dodwell, *Sepoy Recruitment in the Old Madras Army*. Calcutta: Government Printer, 1922.

The social, economic and cultural aspects of the military presence in India have also only been briefly touched upon, but there are some very encouraging signs of late. Seema Alavi has written on the relationship between sepoys and rural society during the early period of Company rule in 'The Company Army and Rural Society: the Invalid Thanah, 1780-1830,' *Modern Asian Studies*, 27(1993): 147-78. Rudrangshu Mukherjee in *Awadh in Revolt, 1857-1858; a Study of Popular Resistance*, New Delhi: Oxford University Press, 1984, has persuasively argued that sepoys maintained their links with the peasant societies from which they were drawn. This point is further affirmed in Eric Stokes, *The Peasant Armed: the Indian Rebellion of 1857*, C.A. Bayly, ed., Oxford: Clarendon, 1986. The influence of disease and deaths on the deployment of European troops in India is developed in Philip Curtin, *Death by Migration*, Cambridge: Cambridge University Press, 1989. A useful contemporary compendium of information on this topic that also covers the sepoys is provided in Joseph Ewart, *A Digest of the Vital Statistics of the European and Native Armies in India*, London: Smith, Elder,

1859. There is also a wealth of statistical data and tables on the army to be found in *Quarterly Journal of the Statistical Society of London*.

Amongst the vast number of contemporary polemics on the Indian army, Walter Badenach, *Inquiry into the State of the Indian Army*, London: John Murray, 1826, stands out as one of the most detailed and sophisticated enquiries for Badenach does not succumb to sweeping generalizations as were all too common with many of his contemporaries. Military law treatises and manuals are another useful source of information, covering such topics as morale and the level of coercion needed to maintain discipline. William Hough produced a great number of these, including: *Military Law Authorities*, Calcutta: Thacker and Co., 1839, *The Practice of Courts-Martial*, 2nd ed., London: Kingsbury, Parbury, and Allen, 1825, *Precedents in Military Law: including the Practice of Courts Martial*, London: W.H. Allen, 1855, and *Simplification of His Majesty's and Hon'ble E.I Company's Mutiny Acts and Articles of War*, Calcutta: G.H. Huttmann, 1836.

Another fertile source of material is offered by the contemporary press. In addition to the obvious literary monthlies and quarterlies that occasionally treated Indian topics, there were several specialist publications on military affairs that were increasingly dedicating their columns to news and opinions from India. See in particular, *The Naval and Military Magazine*, *Colburn's United Service Journal*, and *East India United Service Journal*.

V The economy and finances of early 19th century India

The standard reference work on the Indian economy during this period is and will likely remain for some time to be Dharma Kumar, ed., *The Cambridge Economic History of India: Vol. II*. Cambridge: Cambridge University Press, 1983. The essays in this volume are of a uniformly high quality, though there are some major omissions in what is covered, and some may cavil at the tendencies of its contributors to downplay the influence, for good or bad, of British initiatives. A useful counterbalance to its minimalist perspective is provided in the review essay by Irfan Habib, 'On Writing Colonial History without Perceiving Colonialism,' *Modern Asian Studies*, 19(1985). Interest in the public finances of British India has long been a dormant area and readers will have to consult the dated but still serviceable works by Thomas and Banerjea: P.J. Thomas, *The Growth of Federal Finance in India*, Madras: Oxford University Press, 1939 and P. Banerjea, *Indian Finance in the Days of the Company*, London: Macmillan, 1928. A more recent study, though one that is aimed more at the later periods of Company rule, is S. Bhattacharyya, *Financial Foundations of the British Raj*,

Simla: Indian Institute of Advanced Study, 1971. The history of banking activities is better served. A useful introduction can be found in Amiya Kumar Bagchi, 'Transition from Indian to British-Indian Systems of Money and Banking.' *Modern Asian Studies*, 19(1985): 501-19. Lakshmi Subramanian, 'Banias and the British: the Role of Indigenous Credit in the Process of Imperial Expansion in Western India in the Second Half of the Eighteenth-century,' *Modern Asian Studies*, 21(1987): 473-510 demonstrates the extent to which the British were dependent upon Indian bankers and moneylenders for capital and for the means to move capital. There are also many contemporary published sources. Some of the more useful ones were written by Henry St. George Tucker, a Company director who had served in Bengal as military auditor general. These include: *Remarks on the Plan of Finance Lately Promulgated by the Honourable Court of Directors and by the Supreme Government of India*, London: np, 1821, and, *A Review of the Financial Situation of the East India Company*, London: np, 1825. Aside from my 'War and Public Finance in Early Nineteenth-century British India: the First Burma War,' *International History Review*, 11(1989): 628-47, there has been little recent work on wartime financing in India. Readers will have to turn to contemporary published sources. See in particular Colonel Edward Frederick, *Remarks on the Government of India, especially in its Military Organization*, London: Levey, Robson and Franklin, 1839 and his *Report on the Military Expenditure of the Honourable East India Company*, London: privately printed, 1831.

If the financial workings of the East India Company have been thinly covered, readers will find rich pickings in the many studies of India's regional economies, agrarian systems, and commercial organizations. Many studies of the commercial world of the early nineteenth century focus primarily on Bengal. Amales Tripathi has written a thorough study of the relationship between trade and the government's finances, but he tends to play up war expenditures as the principal burden under which the economy functioned: Amales Tripathi, *Trade and Finance in the Bengal Presidency, 1793-1833*, 2nd ed., Calcutta: Oxford University Press, 1979. A broader perspective and one that incorporates agrarian, commercial and political developments between 1750 and 1830 is offered by Marshall, *Bengal, the British Bridgehead*. Sugata Bose, *Peasant Labour and Colonial Capital: Rural Bengal since 1770; The New Cambridge History of India, III.2*, Cambridge: Cambridge University Press, 1993, looks more closely at agricultural production and the land revenue systems in use in Bengal. Within India, the chief agents of western capitalism, aside from the Company, were the Agency Houses. A short and succinct analysis of their character and operations is to be found in S.D. Chapman. 'The Agency Houses; British Mercantile Enterprise in the Far East, c.1780-1920,' *Textile History*, 19(1988): 239-54. Readers who wish a more detailed account of Agency Houses in the early nineteenth-century should consult the more descriptive S.B. Singh, *European Agency Houses in Bengal, 1783-1833*, Calcutta: Mukhopadhyay, 1966. A sample of the diaries and letters of one Agency House partner have recently been published by A.C. Staples, 'Memoirs of William Prinsep: Calcutta Years, 1817-1842,' *Indian Economic and Social History Review*, 26(1989): 61-79. Contemporary sources for commercial activities in India can be found in *The Economic Development of India under the East India Company; 1814-1858*, K.N. Chaudhuri, ed., Cambridge: Cambridge University Press, 1971. See also G.A. Prinsep, *Remarks on the External Commerce and Exchanges of Bengal*, London: Kingsbury, Parbury and Allen, 1823, and Horace Hayman Wilson, *A Review of the External Commerce of Bengal from 1813/14 to 1827/28*, Calcutta: Baptist Mission Press, 1830.

Although there has been a great number of studies of land revenue policies under the British, with many of them published in the nineteenth-century, the majority of these are more than the average mortal can cope with. Bose makes the task less daunting for those interested in Bengal. A more general perspective on the policies in use across India can be culled from the essays in Robert E. Frykenberg, ed., *Land Control and Social Structure in Indian History*, Madison: University of Wisconsin Press, 1969. The standard work on the regional economy of North India is C.A. Bayly, *Rulers, Townsmen and Bazaars; North India Society in the Age of British Expansion, 1770-1870*, Cambridge: Cambridge University Press, 1983. Bayly's detailed study convincingly demonstrates the extent to which local economies continued to possess their own dynamics even after the British conquest and it also props up those who locate the impetus to imperialism on the periphery. The tentative nature of Britain's impact in North India is also urged in the essays in Eric Stokes, *The Peasant and the Raj: Studies in Agrarian Society and Peasant Rebellion in Colonial India*, Cambridge: Cambridge University Press, 1979. These should be read in conjunction with Richard B. Barnett's *North India between Empires: Awadh, the Mughals and the British, 1720-1801*, Berkeley: University of California Press, 1980, which looks more closely at Awadh and details the political interplay between the Mughals, the Nawab's court and the British. Rural power politics in Awadh are covered in Thomas R. Metcalf, *Land, Landlords and the British Raj: Northern India in the Nineteenth-century*, Berkeley: University of California Press, 1979, while agrarian production has been dissected by Asiya

Siddiqi: *Agrarian Change in a North Indian State; United Provinces, 1819-1833,* Oxford: Clarendon Press, 1973, and in his 'Money and Prices in the Earlier Stages of Empire: India and Britain 1760-1840,' *Indian Economic and Social History Review,* 18(1981): 231-62.

For western India, see Kenneth Ballhatchet, *Social Policy and Social Change in Western India, 1817-1830,* Oxford: Oxford University Press, 1957 and Neil Charlesworth, *Peasants and Imperial Rule,* Cambridge: Cambridge University Press, 1984. Another evaluation of the impact of British rule can be found in Sumit Guha, 'Society and Economy in the Deccan, 1818-1850,' *Indian Economic and Social History Review,* 20(1983): 389-413, and the same author's, *The Agrarian Economy of the Bombay Deccan, 1818-1941,* New Delhi: Oxford University Press, 1985. The extent to which South Indian peasants accommodated themselves to British rule, and the tactics they employed, are just some of the topics addressed in Annales-like fashion by David Ludden in *Peasant History in South India,* Princeton: Princeton University Press, 1985. Stein, *Thomas Munro,* is also very useful on Madras revenue policies.

Walter Hamilton, *A Geographical. Statistical and Historical Description of Hindostan and the Adjacent Countries,* 2 vols. London: J. Murray, 1820 is a widely available and useful source for contemporary impressions of India, while Reginald Heber, Bishop. *Narrative of a Journey through the Upper Provinces of India,* 2 vols. London: John Murray, 1846 is very good for northern India.

VI The Burma War and siege of Bharatpur

The most recent account of the Burma War is to be found in George Bruce, *The Burma Wars, 1824-1886,* London: Hart-Davis MacGibbon, 1973. Bruce provides a very brief sketch of all three wars, based mainly on secondary sources, and with little analysis to accompany the narrative. A.C. Banerjee, *The Eastern Frontier of British India, 1784-1826,* Calcutta: Mukerjee, 1966, is a valuable chronology of relations between Burma and Britain. D.G.E. Hall, *Europe and Burma: a Study of European Relations with Burma to the Annexation of Thibaw's Kingdom,* Oxford: Oxford University Press, 1945, is also useful, though his timeframe is considerably longer than that of Banerjee, and he casts the Burmese Court in the role of the villain. Others have recently pinned the blame on British aggressiveness and greed, see for example, G.P. Ramachandra, 'Anglo-Burmese Diplomacy; September 1823 to July 1824,' *Journal of Indian History,* Diamond Jubilee Volume (1982): 71-107, and also his 'The Canning Mission to Burma of 1809-1810,' *Journal of Southeast Asian Studies*, 10(1979): 119-39. Oliver Pollak, in his *Empires in Collision; Anglo-Burmese Relations in the Mid-Nineteenth-century*, Westport, Conn.: Greenwood Press, 1979, situates the diplomatic conflicts within a larger picture of two expansionary empires and he applies with mixed results the 'turbulent frontier' thesis, long a standby of North American and South African historians, to India. Laurence Kitzan has written two articles that describe Amherst's role in the origin of the war and the terms demanded of the Burmese: 'Lord Amherst and Declaration of War in Burma, 1824,' *Journal of Asian History*, 9(1975): 101-27, and 'Lord Amherst and Pegu: the Annexation Issue, 1824-1826,' *Journal of Southeast Asian Studies*, 8(1977): 176-94. Contemporary documents that outline British relations with Burma can be found in G.T. Bayfield, ed., *Historical Review of the Relations between the British Government in India and the Empire of Ava*, Calcutta: Supreme Government of India, 1835, *Discussions with the Burmese Government, 1812-1824*, London: East India Company, 1825, and W.F.B. Laurie, *Our Burmese Wars and Relations with Burma*, London: W.H. Allen, 1880.

Conditions in Burma at the time of the British invasion are discussed in Michael Adas, *The Burma Delta; Economic Development and Social Change on an Asian Rice Frontier, 1852-1941*, Madison: University of Wisconsin Press, 1974, and in Victor Lieberman, 'Ethnic Politics in Eighteenth-Century Burma,' *Modern Asian Studies*, 12(1978): 455-82, and Victor Lieberman, 'Reinterpreting Burmese History,' *Comparative Studies in Society and History*, 29(1987): 162-94. Adas's 'Imperialist Rhetoric and Modern Historiography: the Case of Lower Burma before and after the Conquest,' *Journal of Southeast Asian Studies*, 3(1972): 175-92, provides a welcome corrective to long-standing myths of Burma that the British employed to justify their conquest.

If recent scholars have been reluctant to write of the Burma War, contemporaries showed no such reservations. A large number of accounts of the war were published in Britain. One of the important memoirs of the war is J.J. Snodgrass. *Narrative of the Burmese War*, London: John Murray, 1827. Snodgrass was Campbell's military secretary (and son-in-law) and provides here what was obviously intended to refute some of the criticisms that were being levelled against Campbell for the manner in which he conducted the campaign. Also of use are: J. Butler, *Sketches of the Services of the Madras European Regiment during the Burmese War*, London: Smith, Elder and Co., 1839, Frederick B. Doveton, *Reminiscences of the Burma War in 1824-5-6*, London: Allen and Co., 1852, Henry Havelock, *Memoir of the Three Campaigns of Major General Sir Archibald Campbell's Army in Ava*,

Serampore: Baptist Mission Press, 1828, H. Lister Maw, *Memoir of the Early Operations in Ava during the Burma War*, London: Smith, Elder and Co., 1832, and John Marshall, *Narrative of the Naval Operations in Ava during the Burma War*, London: Longman, Orme and Rees, 1830. Aside from military and naval personnel who left accounts of the Burma War, there are a few accounts by civilians. Thomas Campbell Robertson's *Political Incidents of the First Burmese War*, London: Bentley, 1853, was written from his vantage point as the political agent assigned to accompany Morrison's column which invaded the Arakan peninsula. Henry Gouger, *A Personal Narrative of Two Years Imprisonment in Burmah, 1824-1826*, London: John Murray, 1860, gives some idea of conditions within the Burmese Court during the invasion.

There has been no recent biography of General Sir Edward Paget, but a heavily edited collection of his letters was pieced together by his daughter: *Letters and Memorials of General the Honourable Sir Edward Paget*, collected and arranged by Harriet May Paget. London: privately printed, 1898. Nor does Combermere have a recent biography, but again a Victorian life and letters is available: Mary Cotton, Viscountess Combermere, *Memoirs and Correspondence of Field Marshall Viscount Combermere*, 2 vols., London: Hurst and Blackett, 1866. Combermere's victory at Bharatpur has been described in some detail in Fortescue, *History of the British Army*, cited above, as well as in accounts published in British military periodicals. The diplomatic breakdown that led to the siege can be followed in the edited collection of Ochterlony's official correspondence: *Selections from the Ochterlony Papers (1818-1825) in the National Archives of India*, N.K. Sinha and A.K. Dasgupta, eds., Calcutta: University of Calcutta, 1964.

VII Bentinck and the Age of Reform

Bentinck and his alleged Age of Reform have long proved fascinating to historians. The intentions of the reformers are considered in Stokes, *English Utilitarians*, Bearce, *British Attitudes*, and Ballhatchet, *Social Policy and Social Change*. The most complete biography of him is to be found in John Rosselli, *Lord William Bentinck; the Making of a Liberal Imperialist, 1774-1839*, Berkeley: University of California Press, 1974, which, as its title implies, revises the earlier impression and presents Bentinck as an imperialist tinged with liberalism and with an authoritarian streak. Readers can reach their own conclusions as a two volume collection of Bentinck's correspondence and memoranda is available: *The Correspondence of Lord William Cavendish Bentinck*, C.H. Philips, ed., 2 vols., Oxford: Oxford University

Press, 1977. A useful but tentative discussion of whether this really was an age of reform lies in C.H. Philips and M.D. Wainwright, eds., *Indian Society and the Beginnings of Modernization*, London: Curzon Press, 1976. A note of caution about employing the term 'reform' to this era is raised in Bayly, *Indian Society*. Indian participation in reform has normally been presented in the person of Raja Rammohan Roy and his founding of the Brahmo Samaj; see David Kopf, *Brahmo Samaj and the Shaping of the Modern Indian Mind*, Princeton: Princeton University Press, 1979, though reservations have also been aimed at this component of the 'Age of Reform' paradigm. Sharp criticisms of Bentinck dominate Frederick John Shore's *Notes on Indian Affairs*, 2 vols. London: J.W. Parker, 1837. Shore, an official also committed to reform, has lately been subjected to scrutiny in Peter Penner and Richard Dale Maclean, eds., *The Rebel Bureaucrat: Frederick John Shore, 1799-1837, as Critic of William Bentinck's India*, New Delhi: Chanakya, 1983. Lord Ellenborough, Bentinck's sparring partner and future governor-general, desperately needs a new examination. In the meantime, Albert H. Imlah, *Lord Ellenborough*, Cambridge, Mass.: Harvard University Press, 1939, provides an overview of his life and ideas. Fortunately Ellenborough's published diary can be consulted: Edward Law, Lord Ellenborough, *A Political Diary*, 2 vols. London: R. Bentley and Son, 1881.

The strategic position of British India at this time has not been dealt with to any great length, except as regards the 'great game' in which case Yapp's and Ingram's studies provide plenty of food for thought. Otherwise, there is the unpublished thesis of David John Howlett, 'An End to Expansionary Influences on British Policy in India, circa 1830 to 1860.' Ph.D. diss., Cambridge University, 1981, which ties the reform debates to deliberations over imperial expansion and security questions. The persistence of the internal enemy argument during Bentinck's reign can be gauged in Thomas Campbell Robertson, *Remarks on Several Recent Publications Regarding the Civil Government and Foreign Policy of British India*, London: John Murray, 1829. Otherwise, Bentinck's military policy is touched upon briefly in Rosselli's biography and much of his correspondence on army affairs is contained in Philips' edited collection of the Bentinck papers. Bentinck's decision to abolish corporal punishment for Indian soldiers is debated at length in 'Report from H.M. Commissioners for Enquiring into the System of Military Punishments in the Army,' *Parliamentary Papers*, (1836), 1 vol. I have looked more closely at military punishments in India in 'Sepoys, Soldiers and the Lash: Race, Caste and Army Discipline in India, 1820-1850', *Journal of Imperial and Commonwealth History*, forthcoming.

INDEX